LOCAL
HEROES

LOCAL HEROES

by

BILL BERKOWITZ

Lexington Books

D.C. Heath and Company • Lexington, Massachusetts • Toronto

Library of Congress Cataloging-in-Publication Data

Berkowitz, William R.
Local heroes.

1. Volunteers in community development—United States—Interviews.   2. Volunteers in social service—United States—Interviews.   3. Social reformers—United States—Interviews.   4. Community development—United States.   5. Community organization—United States.   I. Title.
HN90.C6B48   1987   361.3'7   86-46364
ISBN-0-669-15829-1 (alk. paper)

Published simultaneously in Canada
Printed in the United States of America
International Standard Book Number: 0-669-15829-1
Library of Congress Catalog Card Number: 86-46364

The paper used in this publication meets the minimum requirements of American National Standard for Information Sciences—Permanence of Paper for Printed Library Materials, ANSI Z39.48-1984.

∞™

ISBN 0-669-15829-1

87 88 89 90 8 7 6 5 4 3 2 1

When your luck is battin' zero
Get your chin up off the floor;
Mister you can be a hero
You can open any door,
There's nothin' to it, but to do it.

—From "Heart,"
in *Damn Yankees*

Contents

Preface

THIS is a book about community, and about heroism, and about where the two join together. It's a series of interviews with ordinary people of extraordinary community accomplishment. Its purposes are to suggest why they succeeded, and, if done right, to inspire.

The word "hero" today is in disrepair. Some say heroes no longer exist. Others claim we are all heroes, for traversing daily life is heroic in itself. Still others cite specific hero figures, and frequently these are celebrities. In one recent poll, Clint Eastwood heads the list.

Historically, the hero reflects the values and, in particular, the aspirations of a society. Celebrity heroes, we'll argue later, don't do the job. But we can't simply decree who shall be called a hero and who falls short. What we can do is propose a new heroic model for our time.

That model is the local hero, working at a community level. There might be one close to you. The local hero aims to make community life stronger, tighter, happier, richer. The heroism here comes partly from the magnitude of the achievement, but also from the humbleness of the beginnings, and particularly from the mismatch between the two—the surprise and the wonder that something so consequential could have come from origins so plain.

In other words, there may be an inner dimension to social change, some personal qualities not yet elaborated. There should be something going on inside the person to make things happen, and we hope to discover what it is.

Why the local hero, of all hero-types that could be summoned? Because the local hero does embody community values. Because the local hero aspires and dreams. Because the local hero is true to tradition—someone who has journeyed, sacrificed, taken risks, and conquered adversity. Because the local hero's achievements are within our own reach. And especially because the local hero builds community, which may be the most neglected need on the domestic scene today.

So this is a book of stories about building community, told by the builders themselves. To me they are inspirational in both spirit and deed, heroic in the untrivialized sense of the word, but definitely not beyond this world. Quite the opposite: the tellers are human beings of dimension and flaw, who have tried very hard, who have reaped some rewards, and accepted some costs. Their work deserves analysis—and imitation—but it can't get either unless brought into the open, onto center stage, and that's our intent here.

We begin by setting that stage. If community building is "the most neglected need," what do we mean, why is this so, and what can be done about it?

INTRODUCTION

How to Build Community Life

Five Vignettes

LOOKING out my window onto the street, what I see is boxes. Other houses like mine, the humans tucked away. It is winter; light snow is on the ground; but in summer the scene's little changed. The streets are virtually empty. More trucks go by than people. Community life, if it exists, is not visible to the eye.

From a recent Roper poll:[1]

> Would you read down this list of activities and call off the ones, if any, that you usually enjoy or look forward to during the day?

The top eight responses, in order:

Watching television
Checking the mail
Going to sleep at night
Taking a shower or bath
Spending time on an interest or hobby
Getting in the house once the day is over
Listening to the radio
Being by yourself

A similar theme, another vantage point. The Gallup Poll asks: "Do you, yourself, happen to be involved in any charity or social service activities, such as helping the poor, the sick, or the elderly?" In 1986, 36% of a national sample said "Yes"; 64% answered "No."[2] Gallup again, in 1982: "How many voluntary organizations in your community, other than a church or religious group, do you belong to?" According to 65%, "None."[3]

In my own community, a statistically average metropolitan suburb, which seems at least medium-friendly and is often described as "highly political," about twenty-five percent of registered voters vote in town elections in a good year. Three-quarters go into hiding. We have a representative town meeting government, with elected town meeting members. In a recent election, about half the precincts couldn't field enough candidates for the available seats. Write-in candidates can and do get elected with one or two votes.

Think of your own neighborhood. Draw an imaginary circle around your own home, with a half-mile radius. How many people do you know inside the circle? How many will you ever know? How many do you want to know? What is your reaction to your answers? What do your answers say about community for you, and its relationship to your life?

Privacy and Community

Those wanting to make community change, to make community life better, to get others to take up their cause, and I am one of them, must eventually come to terms with the desire and probably the basic human need that each of us has to be alone. The need for solitude, as distinct from loneliness, and even from privacy, is pervasive and enticing, affecting volunteers and activists (perhaps especially activists) as much as anyone else.

We remain unmoved and unblinking, not only out of alienation or powerlessness or pure combat fatigue, though many of us feel all three, but also because we simply prefer to be by ourselves, boxed in, wrapped up. There is Greta Garbo in all of us, and the tougher the day, or the heavier the demands, the greater the need to put on dark glasses. Those who seek community change must understand and accept that need in others. Better yet, they must honor it, work with it, and not confront it directly, for to do otherwise risks resistance from the community and burnout for themselves.

It is not that we are hermetically sealed in darkened apartments. If someone is in perceptible trouble, we may help; if a solicitor comes to the door, we might give. And it's not that we don't care about our own communities; most of us do care, at least a little. But that caring is fleeting, unfocused, as for background music. There are only so many things in life we can care tangibly about, only so much emotional storage space. There's work, there's family, and there's personal pleasure, and in the absence of powerful reasons to the contrary, neighborhood and community concerns can easily get stuffed in the closet.

We cherish privacy, and yet it's abundantly clear that we need close community in our lives, perhaps more now than at any time in recent history. There are two main reasons:

We need community, first of all, because government is retreating. As government pulls back, the neighborhood and the home community get pushed forward. If government no longer provides the social services we want, we'll have to provide them ourselves. The merits of this approach are not the point here: this is reality we must deal with. With less government involvement, all of us will be obliged to take more personal responsibility for our own neighborhoods and communities, joining together to make the community changes we desire. No real alternative exists.

And we need community, in the second place, because we all need social support. That's common sense, but in the past decade there's been compelling research to bolster that view and enlarge it.[4] The gist of that research is that people in your life space—family and friends, but also neighbors and colleagues—strongly influence personal well-being. When we need help, we look there first. When natural supports are strong, we simply feel happier and more at ease. When they are weakened, we feel a sense of loss. When they are chronically weak or absent altogether, emotional illness can result; physical illness, too, for people do get heart sick. Our need for community is rooted in evolution; our ancestors did travel in clans.

But many supports in modern life are institutional, and because of their institutionality they are vulnerable to policy shifts and to economic hard times. Services we get from agencies may depend on government funding; so might supports we find at school; while supports from our job may depend on an economy healthy enough to make that job possible.

When there's pullback or hardship, institutional support layers, governmental or corporate, get stripped away. Our outside involvements diminish as well, for there's less money to support them. To maintain social equilibrium, remaining sources of support must be strengthened. And so we look more closely for what we need in our own territory, close to home. We come to depend on each other more, for there's no place else to go.

It's not just that people need close community—they want it too. For more than a decade, the polling firm of Yankelovich, Skelly and

White has been measuring a "search for community" social trend. Thirty-two percent of a national sample reported experiencing a "hungering for community" in 1973. (Not a "desire," but a "hunger.") By 1980, that figure was up to forty-seven percent. Since then, and through 1985, the percentage has continued to climb.[5]

A provocative finding, if a little vague; we're not fully sure what that hunger means. It probably doesn't mean a need for intimacy with everyone on the block, nor total absorption into neighborhood life. It probably does mean a wishing for more community than one has now. And it possibly could mean a yearning for a community where people are affirmed and respected, where they feel safe and protected, where they know their neighbors and are known by them, where they can count on others for help and be counted on in return, where their half-mile radius is filled with friends, where their creative energies can be released, where they feel embraced by their surroundings, and where they will smile when they walk down the street.

I am projecting, for this is a community I want to live in myself. This vision is idealistic and romanticized, and unapologetically so; these qualities are virtues if they reflect what we want. I believe most of us do want a community like this, and that most of us can find it. I believe too that this kind of community is achievable through the individual actions of plain citizens acting in their community's behalf, and that is what this book is about.

Creating the Ideal Community

The question is how to create this ideal community. More precisely, how do you influence people whose hunger for community, however felt, usually goes unsatisfied? What do you do with or for or about a person, or that part of ourselves, who comes home from work, locks the door, checks the mail, and wants only to nap? How do you rouse that peacefully dozing person and spur him or her to wash up and charge into the night? What can one person do to create local change or to get others to do the same? The general answers, I think, are that it is hard, it is slow, it is possible, and there are multiple ways.

You can work at changing institutions. You can get involved yourself. But for the advocate at a distance—the writer, researcher, or teacher—I can identify three distinct strategies for building community life, each of which is necessary and useful:

1. You can give people community-building skills. You can teach them how to assess community needs, make plans, execute, and

evaluate their work. You can provide them with textbook principles of community organization. On a more day-to-day level, you can show them how to produce a flyer, how to run a meeting, how to raise some money, and how to hold their group together. These skills come in handy and are sometimes absolutely essential, no doubt about that.

2. Or you can give people ideas. You can tell them of dreams that could be realized, ideas others have implemented somewhere else. Just about every community in America has at least one or two little community-building ideas that have worked well for it—clever ideas, offbeat, practical, and, typically, unknown. So here it's a matter of digging them up, dusting them off, and setting them out for review. Someone has to supply the vision, do the consciousness-stretching, get others to think about what could be. Their skills might as well be aimed at utopia as at another turkey raffle.

3. Or you can give them personal examples. The premise here is that barriers to action are mostly internal; the flesh is able, but the spirit is weak. In this view, what people need at least as much as technique and ideas, are the motivation, the confidence, the desire, the will, to go out and get entangled. And you can fortify civic will by providing examples, stories, personal accounts of similar people who have done just that, and who not only have been successful, but also have emerged as more fully realized human beings. This is the approach taken here.

It's a venerable genre, dating back to the dawn. It's easy to argue that one purpose of literature, of art, of formal or informal education is to influence through moral illustration. We can go as far back as the Bible or the Greek epics, or as far forward as best-seller biographies, "most unforgettable character" stories, and fan magazines. In all of these, others are held up as examples to be admired and imitated, and they are.

And it's a genre that works, that won't wear out. It's based on the core learning principle of identification: we're shown models of what can be done, those models are like ourselves, the models are rewarded, our model-valuation increases, our tendency to imitate increases as well—if not dramatically, then incrementally will do. This learning process may be wired into our circuitry. On another level entirely, though, it is fun and it is deepening and it can be ennobling simply to read success stories about people who could be us, for we're always looking for inspiration, and we want to do the right thing.

So if community involvement is our goal, there may be merit in offering examples of people who have gone out and done the job where they live. People whose community achievements are superlative, at the top of the list, but who themselves were not especially privileged or credentialed or blessed or without sin. People who began pretty much from square one, who acted largely by themselves, but who made something important out of nothing. In other words, people starting out like us, or so it would seem.

If we can find such people, they could enrich our lives. If we can learn more about what they did, it could help spark the community-building potential within us. And if we can learn more about how they did it, why they succeeded, what they had in common, we might acquire a new technique or two, as well as new appreciation for what we already know.

Here, then, is a book of first-person accounts of ordinary people who have made extraordinary accomplishments in local community service. In their way, they are local heroes.

Ordinary People of Extraordinary Accomplishment

Most social change work is done by ordinary people in any event. On a local level, who else is around? Municipal government is safety, schools, water, trash. There's no office of community spirit, or department of neighborhood life. Social agencies give help mostly to individuals one-on-one, and usually have no mandate for or interest in changing the broader society, even if they could. If social change professionals exist at all, they are likely to be college professors or institute researchers, bound up with classroom or bureaucratic obligations. Our society employs few practicing change professionals, and offers them little incentive for doing social change on location. Rarely has any society done so.

We're left with ordinary people, if only by default. But ordinary people are capable of astonishing community achievements, or whatever adjectives you'd care to use. I've been lucky enough to see some with my own eyes, before this study began. I had a student once, a twenty-two-year-old woman, who came uninvited into a poor and indifferent urban community as a complete stranger, and who set up a free adult learning center—a full-fledged, multi-site, incorporated, and self-perpetuating social agency—from absolute zero to grand opening in three and a half months. And I knew a fellow living just above me in my own house, the shyest of the shy so he appeared, a part-time computer programmer then, who wound up starting a men's organization to prevent domestic violence, one of the very first of its kind, now a regional leader in its field. These two seemed ordinary, at least on the surface. They didn't glow in the dark, not right away.

You probably know some people like this from your own experience. If you don't, read the paper often enough, or watch the news, and examples will come your way. Local achievers make headlines and they capture our imagination. Their stories are reassuring, even if we distance ourselves personally: "That's wonderful. Well, I'm glad something's going right in the world."

But for this book we'd like to know why these achievements happen. Under what conditions do they occur? How much is situational, and how much is beneath the skin? What is the essence of community work? What does it take inside the person to make community change? Maybe these ordinary people are not so ordinary after all. And if that is so, maybe we can pinpoint what is extraordinary, distill that special quality, bottle the essence, and put it on the market. But maybe they really *are* ordinary, just like us. And if *that* is so. . .

As it happens, "ordinary people of extraordinary accomplishment" come in sizes and shapes. So the first step toward answering these questions is to specify the type of person and the type of achievement we are looking for.

To begin with, by "ordinary people" we mean nonprofessionals, people not specifically trained or employed in the area they ended up in. We're looking for people who began with little in the way of money, resources, expertise, outside backing, or formal power. Three-dimensional people, not living saints, yet who were motivated by service rather than profit. People, in other words, who started with nothing and came out of nowhere, but who simply saw a need in their community, went after it, and met it.

And since this is a book about community, we are looking for accomplishments that directly served the community in some way, that brought people closer together, but more particularly that put something tangible in the community where nothing existed before. We seek accomplishments that are local, specific, focused, empowering, measurable, distinctive, unique, and enduring. Combining our criteria, then, we bypass situations where actual results cannot be pointed to, as well as people whose initial efforts were national in scope, or who held to a beaten path, or whose work first came from their regular job. And for these same reasons, we generally exclude scientists and philanthropists, office holders and business persons, as well as multi-issue organizers and all-around volunteers. We're looking instead for cases where citizens placed a new mark on the community map, where outcomes surpassed most reasonable starting expectations, and where there was surprise, amazement, and perhaps a tinge of awe.

Take Trevor Ferrell, for instance, who's not in this book. He's someone who happened to be watching a television report on the homeless, just as you or I might, except his conscience got caught. He went downtown with a blanket and pillow, then again with more blankets, and with food, and then he couldn't stop. He kept going back night after night. He began to round up supplies from others. Donations started to trickle in. Momentum built quickly: volunteers began to cook meals; someone else donated a thirty-three-bedroom rooming house. The Ferrells closed their family electronics business. Very soon after, homeless people began to move into the rooming house, "Trevor's Place." Contributions topped $100,000. There were awards, book projects, movie contracts, newsletters, chapters in other cities and abroad . . .[6]

His story raises issues, as will the others. In the first place, since Trevor Ferrell was eleven years old at the time, one wonders about the potential for children not just to be helpful and kind, but to perform acts of dramatic impact and true social magnificence. Then there is the matter of individual versus corporate versus governmental responsibility for the poor. Then there are issues of personal and family costs (Trevor losing a year of school, his family losing much of its income, sacks full of mail), issues of the desirability and the effects of national media attention, and so on.

But stripping away the media glitz, considering only the actor and his action, here is a schoolboy who helped create a shelter for the homeless and prompted a national campaign in their behalf. And stripping away sentimentality, here is someone whose spirit and actions deserve imitation, and who is an excellent example of a local hero.

The Interviews

Having targeted the species, the next steps in this project were conceptually simple: find the best possible living examples, bring out their stories, and see what they reveal.

I had begun with some names from an earlier book on community life, but knew more names were needed. Almost by definition, the people I was seeking would be scattered across the country. A multipronged search was called for, and that's what was attempted.

The search included writing recruitment letters to national community organizations, writing similar letters to my own friends and acquaintances, contacting federal agencies (e.g., ACTION), submitting queries to national magazines and the *New York Times Book Review*, as well as researching past lists of volunteer award winners (particularly citationists and winners of the President's Volunteer Action Awards, and those cited in *Voluntary Action Leadership* magazine). These steps were accompanied by reading and note-taking from current books and reports on community activism, from recent years' issues of specialized community journals and newsletters, from daily newspapers, and from popular magazines.

The combined search methods yielded about four hundred candidates over a year's time. Written or telephone contacts, requesting further information, were made to more than one hundred of the most promising leads.

In selecting people to interview, I tried to follow the criteria outlined previously, paying particular attention to the creation of a specific community service or program; a local focus, at least at first; lack of starting resources; lack of relevant expertise, in the beginning; magnitude and duration of accomplishment; uniqueness; and potential replicability elsewhere. I knew I also wanted people working in different content areas, minimally overlapping, and in a variety of physical settings.

Beyond this, I tried to choose people whose stories might be especially evocative or revealing, though I'm sure personal biases played a role here. Some arbitrariness is built into the process, for there are no agreed-on prior means of authenticating a given selection.

I contacted thirty-six people and interviewed thirty-three; twenty interview accounts appear here. Of the twenty subjects, ten are women, eight are men, two are couples. Some have national visibility by now, but most do not. Their ages at time of interview (1984) ranged from twenty-seven to eighty-two. They made their livings as bus drivers, realtors, folksingers, fabric designers, tutors; some lived on retirement income, a few were now salaried by the program they started, and a few had no personal income at all. As for their community work, most had begun around ten years ago, typically in the mid- to late 1970s. Their areas of service included crime prevention, job training, housing, community theater, food collection, beautification, skills exchanges, festivals, poor people's advocacy, toxic waste, neighborhood mediation, and parent support.

Each participant was initially contacted by phone, then briefed later by phone and twice by letter. The first mailing packet described the purpose of the project, while the second contained interview guidelines and a set of sample questions, along with a request for additional background material. Participants were interviewed in person at their home or office. All interviews were tape-recorded.

The interview format was semistructured; all participants were asked some questions in common (origin; obstacles; feelings; techniques; outcomes; costs; plans; lessons), but also given free rein to speak to their own concerns. Average length of interview (actual time on tape) was between two and three hours.

The accounts in this book are interview transcripts, edited down. Some material has been reordered, mostly for continuity. All the interview text is verbatim, excepting the occasional correction of syntax for clarity, and the occasional insertion of transitional conjunctions, articles, or prepositions. The interviews are generally punctuated as spoken, even when this conflicts with conventional punctuation rules. The goal was to let the subjects speak for themselves, keeping content, style, and speech rhythm essentially intact.[7]

Each interview raises its own set of concerns. In another kind of book, there might be study questions, textual analysis, perhaps even a running commentary. But the choice here has been to let each story stand largely by itself. There are background lead-ins to each account, which do aim at integration. There's an interlude in the middle of the book, on the nature of modern heroism. Toward the end, all subjects return to respond to a summary question, in a chapter called "The State of the Art." The final chapter offers some general conclusions and implications, with some rethinking about community involvement in modern American society. Still and all, the reader will be called on to do a lot of reading between the lines.

The interviews themselves could logically be ordered in several different ways. It's hard to choose among them. But one way to settle the issue is to begin with a story that was particularly instructive for me.

Interviews

PART ONE

Vern Homer

I will hook people. I'll talk them into it. I can beat them down, with sheer enthusiasm.

Marti Stevens

THE CORNVILLE PLAYERS

J UST after I began this project, a letter arrived from a friend of a
friend, just returned from rural Maine. Look up a woman named
Marti Stevens, she wrote. "With the budget of a beggar, she has produced and directed scores of plays in the Cornville Town Hall . . . and
has done more to promote sensitivity, understanding, and good times
than anyone I can think of."
   So I called.

Some people do stand out in a crowd—do we really know why? Marti
Stevens had asked me to meet her at an art show on a church lawn on
a summer evening outside of Skowhegan, Maine. I'd never seen her,
and she blended right into her setting, but there she was, as if wearing
a light bulb. I don't especially believe in auras or in personal energy
fields, but am stuck for better explanations.
   Marti is founder and director of the Cornville Players, a theater
company in a village of 670. They've built a statewide reputation, and
they've toured through Maine. But the point here is that this village
theater has become a social center, a clearinghouse, a resource exchange, a community-reviving force. The grange once served likewise
in rural America, but granges are dying and dead.
   Why her as founder? It wasn't planned to be. Possibly childhood
history: "Born and raised in Chicago. City girl all the way. My parents
were musicians. I stayed home as a young kid 'cause I was ill a lot.
Radio was a big part of my life."
   Possibly prior experience: a journalism major at the University of
Missouri, hated it, came to seek fortune in New York City in the avant-

garde theater of the 1960s. Possibly something else—something inside; this might get clearer as we go along.

She reached the end of her line in New York, broke for Maine in 1969, lined up a teaching job, had no intention of doing anything else. Her sixth day there, she got into a serious auto accident, was hospitalized, couldn't drive, lost her job, no others around.

"I was desperate." Lived on zucchini, went on welfare, but wanted to work. Her caseworker set her up tutoring other clients needing job retraining. And so the Cornville Academy was born—a one-woman schoolhouse.

The Cornville Academy lives still, based around kitchen tables. Marti has also been teaching these days at the state college, coordinating the state's literacy program in her area, tutoring privately, and running a separate local theater group for teens. She's also the former town plumbing inspector. Rural life encourages versatility.

Marti Stevens lives alone in a farmhouse full of plants, curios, fabric hangings, and exotic face masks. In the barn nearby, her dairy cows are listening to classical music, which keeps away bears. Inside, her boisterous dogs knock over my tape recorder. She speaks with great concentration, animation, vocal swoop, and many hacking coughs.

Her first words into the recorder are, "The coffee's handy, and there's plenty more to go." Somewhere well past midnight, before tape side six, she says, "You must be getting weary." The next morning she's gone by dawn on a long drive to Augusta, where Ivan Illich is teaching.

✱

I had come up here thinking I had left theater at Kittery, when I crossed the bridge.* It was a conscious choice. I didn't have the mentality to go peddle myself, the way you had to in New York, and I'm not deriding those who can.

I worked a lot in theater. I mean I directed, I was reviewed—a little squib, a teeny little squib. But it wasn't enough. I tried acting, but I didn't have that kind of drive to go up to casting agents day after day. In retrospect I was probably pretty naive, even ten years into it. It finally began to dawn on me that maybe I wasn't as good as whatever the competition might be. I didn't have that push. . . .

So I said, it was a wonderful part of my life, I learned a lot, but now I'm on to something else. I was ready to live here; I had endowed myself with a

---

*Kittery is located at the southern tip of Maine, where the highway bridge crosses over from Portsmouth, New Hampshire.

new training and a new skill, which was teaching, something I had not planned ever to do. So I talked tomatoes, I talked houseshit, I talked how you find the best calf and how you tell from the pinbone whether it's a good milker, by two hands between the ribs. I mean, I actively sought that information. It was a new life for me. And really, I didn't mourn the loss of the theater, 'cause I felt it had served me well and I had done my best to serve it.

But two years into trying this, I felt a dissatisfaction that I couldn't identify. I wasn't sure where I was going. I was teaching here, in the kitchen, and very happy with that, but there was still part of my life that was empty. I could have attributed that to lack of a partner, I could have attributed it to a number of things, but there was an emptiness.

The local grade school principal wrote me a letter and said he had heard I had some theater background, would I please consider directing the fifth grade in the play. And I loathe kids. I do not like children at all. And my first reaction was no.

But then I thought, hey, you're in a community, you want to be accepted, you owe them something, they've been okay to you. They haven't hustled you out, which would have happened in the Midwest. A woman living alone is a peculiarity, at best. But I was treated very well; suspiciously, but well. You owe something.

So I said okay. I answered the letter and said as long as they were willing to do a straight play, some seriousness of purpose, some quality to it—I wasn't going to do *Miss Tillie's Toys,* or something. I went over and said, "Okay, if you can do something honest, I'll be happy to."

We had agreed to do the show in the school. I looked at the school. It was a dismal, you know, concrete box, no stage, and I asked if there was any other building in town that had a stage. "There's something in Town Hall, but we don't go there anymore. We have the town meeting at the school." And I said, "Well, can I look at the Town Hall?" And it was a wonderful building. One hundred years ago it was a church, and they altered it for grange hall and Town Hall. . . . It was in pretty desperate shape. They said, "Nobody wants it, the grange has abandoned it, the town doesn't use it. It's up for grabs." So I said, "Could we spiff it up, perhaps, and build some scenery out of sheets or something that would look presentable and do the show there?" They said, "Oh, well, sure, why not?"

So the kids performed *Peter Pan,* and those people came into that Town Hall for the first time in fifteen years, and of course these are the parents of all the children in Cornville. And they came with such love for the place, it was like coming *home,* and I listened in the audience: "Oh, yes, we had the bean supper up there"; (in Maine accent) "Oh, God, remember when Flora did that little vaudeville act she used to do?" Because the grange was a theater for these people, the grange was theater. It was before TV, it was their entertainment.

Fortunately the kids were very good, even by my standards they were good. So the parents at that time said, "Gee, maybe we could have something like this." "Yeah, I'd kind of like to do a play." And I said, "Well, I'm not doin' it. I'm tired of organizing and getting all this together. I did it for the kids, but that was just kind of my payback to Cornville. But that's the end of it."

The next year, Mac—by then he was Mac, not the principal—called me again, and said, "How about it this year?" I said, "Wellll, okay." And again we went to the Town Hall.

By that time, town meeting had occurred—this is an old-fashioned town meeting system here, they have articles that are presented in the warrant— and the Selectmen had presented for the town's consideration an article to sell or destroy the Town Hall. And the vote was against it, against destroying it, because they had been in it for the first time in all this time. In fact that was when revenue-sharing funds became available, and somebody said at that meeting, "Why don't you investigate the use of revenue-sharing funds to rehabilitate the hall?" So the following year the Selectmen did.

That summer right after the second year we did the show, some of the adults again—the parents of these kids—said "Well, we talked about doing a theater group, how about it?" I said, "Well, okay, I'm willing. I'll send out a letter. If anybody shows up, we have a theater group, and if nobody shows up, that's the answer."

So I sent out a letter, on July 11 [1974]. I can't remember how many. It just said, "Some of you have shown some interest in putting a group together. If you're interested, show up, invite your friends." We had a meeting, and they did. Forty people showed up. Parents of the kids in the school, basically, or people I had known through tomato talk who were also getting to the point where they had to have something else in their head.

Other groups have started, and have been entirely out-of-staters*, who didn't include the local people. It was almost—"We are bringing our art to you . . . we have something so special that we're bringing it to you as a favor." It's very patronizing. But this, on the other hand, was "You want it? You want to try it with us?" It was a mutual effort, and because it was mutual, it survived.

Okay, we'll do a show. We'll do a show. It seemed like we all wanted to. It was an age range between sixty and fourteen; some of the teenies wanted

---

*That is, people born out of state, though they might have lived in Maine for some time. The Cornville Players are a mixture of locals and out-of-staters, in that sense.

to be in it too. One of the shows that I had sort of had my heart set on doing, somewhere, sometime, and never got to, was *Little Mary Sunshine*. Do you know it?

Oh, it's a potboiler. It's wonderful, it's simply wonderful. It has everything. It has Indians, and rangers, and little misses, and dimples, and schoolgirls, and it's a wonderful show. I wanted to do it, 'cause I'm an operetta buff, personally. It didn't require much. In this community, it seemed doable, and something people would enjoy seeing.

So we just got started. The first thing we did was hold a cookie sale (laughs). It was so kitschy it's embarrassing. But we held a cookie sale at the Town Hall. And then we held a rummage sale to get the money to make the costumes, to pay the rights, to pay the royalties.

Anyhow, after we had raised the money, then we set about casting the show. And, God, the cast was insane. We had a very good, untrained, but very good singer who did Mary, a very tall, gorgeous redhead. She dimpled properly, and she was absolutely wonderful. And we had a Captain Jim who was even taller, and he was properly ranger-like. And we had a proper tenor. We had everything. It was really fun—the women were playing schoolgirls in a finishing school, and those women ranged literally between fourteen and sixty. And we had to like plunk wigs on their heads to cover the gray (laughs). Heavy makeup to cover the wrinkles.

But who cared? This was the very first show, and this, for many of them, was the grange again. It was that kind of thing they used to do, and they plunged in. The local women plunged in a little more than the men. They needed something—it's hard being a farmer's wife. Boring too, sometimes, when all the money gets tucked into the barn or into the house . . .

So these women, they helped us clean the hall. We scrubbed it down. The only thing we had to make scenery out of was cardboard boxes, so we raided the Sears and the whatever for the biggest cardboard boxes we could find, painted the sets with these things. People's woodpiles supplied the lumber. There was no heat in Town Hall at that time, just woodstoves, so the price of membership in the Cornville Players was for each rehearsal everybody had to bring three sticks of wood at least to keep the fires going. And that went on for quite some time.

And that was it. That was the first show. And people came—stunned, you know, just because it could be done. This show passed Hilda's test, Hilda being a Maine lady with a rather salty humor, though she's sort of straight. She was in the first show, and she had to swing on the swing—we made these incredible swings—and here she was, fifty-five, sixty, with this blond wig, bow tie, and hat, this teenager, you know, Victorian, 1910 dress, swinging on this swing with all her heart (laughs). She looked pretty good, as a matter of fact. I don't know why she abandoned herself that totally to it.

When I think what chances they took, what personal chances they took, you know, from some nutty out-of-stater who comes breezing in and says, "YEAH, you can be an actor!! Why not?!" Why did they believe me? I mean, why do I believe me? I don't know. It was an incredible chance on all our parts. But they wouldn't be laughed at.

It was a magic moment. I had joined. I had joined something very special, a community. They had joined with me. We were all doing something that . . . it was totally impossible.

I mean, it wasn't any big thing. But I came here as a real interloper, with no business being here. I wasn't sure quite why I was here either, except as a way of finding a new part of me. All of a sudden, theater had a new sense. I mean, this was my contribution perhaps. This is how I could join, without being patronizing. I could say, this is part of me, but it's part of you too.

Everything feeds into it. I was thinking, half the people in that room tonight [at the art show] have been either in the audience or on stage. And I realize how much I connect, now—it isn't just I go to the theater and do the plays. I recruit them from my class, I still do. You start saying, "Hey, Tony, I got this great part for you!" And they would do it. I mean, that's a sense of community, isn't it? It just doesn't happen on Fridays and Sundays, at the Town Hall, from seven to ten. It happens all week.

In fact the word is if you have anything to do with Marti, you're going to be in the theater one way or another. And they are. And that's what they want. I mean, it's part of their life too.

I had a student who was in jail, I was tutoring him in jail, very nice guy. I sort of felt that if there was something beyond his life of crime, some other goal he had in mind, something else he felt proud about, maybe larceny wouldn't be quite so attractive. So the sheriff and I knew each other well, and I said, "Would you mind if I sprung him on Friday and Sunday nights and took him to rehearsal?" And he said, "Why not?"

So I would go and pick him up at the jail, and take him to rehearsals, and bring him back. And that worked fine, except . . . two days before the show, as I recall, he skipped. Not on me, but he left jail. So there I was, without my actor, and without my student. That's the way it goes. And I was really in trouble, 'cause it was a very key part. You had to be a rather attractive young man with some muscles, and we didn't have anybody around that matched that.

I was sitting here in the kitchen—I had a class that just left, didn't see any muscles in that bunch. And a poor kid got off this gas truck to deliver this tank of gas, and I happened to look out; he was gorgeous, he was a gorgeous guy.

So I said, "You're new, aren't you?"

"Oh, yeah, I don't know anybody in town."

"Would you like to meet more people?"

"Sure would."

"What are you doing tonight?" And he came down, and he was absolutely wonderful, he learned the lines in two nights, and he went on—wonderful, great.

But that's the delight of it. That's a real delight. 'Cause it is a community theater, it does draw from every possible source.

After the first play, we had to take ourselves seriously. Somehow we had done something, and now you have to do it again. And that was very fear-inspiring, because it was kind of like, well, we pulled it off once, that's kind of lucky, maybe we should stop right there.

I know we did a string of musicals. *Little Mary Sunshine* was followed by *Li'l Abner,* and again I was purposely picking things that I thought would attract. For the first couple of years we did nothing but musicals, because people here enjoy them; they're fairly simple to do, the plots are not too complicated. I'm not belittling the community, but I wasn't sure what the community would accept at all.

But at some point, we tried *Picnic,* which is small-town and deals with issues they can understand—the need to leave—and they bought it. They absolutely bought it. That was kind of like, whoooo! Well, we can do something of—I won't say real merit, 'cause musicals have merit too—but with a little more strength, with a little more sensibility. And they did buy it.

And so then we went into a pattern of at least one musical a year and at least one straight. We did *Look Homeward, Angel, Of Mice and Men. . . .* The straight play was really kind of my reward, for having done the other stuff. We were doing pretty steadily three shows a year, two or three nights a week, shows and rehearsal. And we'd go into rehearsal for eight to ten weeks.

I will never turn anybody down for a part. I mean, if somebody has the guts to walk into the building and say I want to be in a show, a musical, anyway, I'll find a part for him. But we have grown to the point where we're not going to do something just to satisfy my ego or the actors' egos. We're on the stage to have fun, but now our audience has come to expect more and more of us, 'cause we've grown and they've grown. I think we have to offer something first, initial sociability, or something to do on Friday nights. But then there has to be a need to be good.

For the audience up here, I'm thinking that perhaps theater may be more important to them than theater would be—

In New York. Oh God, yes. Oh God, yes! It's theirs! I mean they have real ownership in this theater. I mean, not only is it their friends up there, they've watched us grow. They've watched me grow, I hope. They've watched us grow older, trying new things, a little more daring things, not always successfully, but trying to . . .

So theater as a community-building device . . .

Yeah! Oh, yeah! The Town Hall was saved, I keep going back to that, but we plan, as part of our budget, every year to do something for the Town Hall, whether it's put curtains up or polish the floor, or put urethane down, or put a rug down—'cause that's part of us. The town has given us, we give back.

But jobs have been created. People have found work, because it's a grouping; it becomes a clearinghouse of information, of skills. Somebody did some seamstress work on a costume—"You sew that well, could you do a Christmas dress for my. . ." It becomes a clearinghouse in the community, not the only one, but it has become that, for me anyway. I love the fact that no matter where I go in this little fairly closed community, there's another piece that somehow all ties back. And maybe that's what theater should be. Theater, tribally, was part of life. I guess that's it.

About three years ago we hit a midlife crisis. I had more energy—the phases of the moon or whatever—I became dissatisfied doing easy stuff. I wanted more of a challenge. I felt the need of doing some heavier drama, something with a little more substance, a little weightier.

And I had some actors who were crazy—crazy to work. I then did three or four plays a year, they were still ready for more. Most of our actors will do a show a year, and that's about as much time as they're willing to commit. Most of them are family people. But this particular group were either singles, or recently divorced, or in the throes of some sort of change.

And I have been accused, and rightfully so, of looking for people who are in trouble. Because good actors, good amateur actors, often come from conflict, and it's a good place to work that out. They admit it, and I admit it, which is one of the reasons we've got a rep in town for being the divorce-makers in the area. But since I don't have time to teach ten years' worth of acting skills to somebody who's just walked in the door, then if I can find someone in a crisis I can use it. Not always very kindly, I'm afraid, but that's my secret.

So I picked three one-acts, and gave everybody who had come out to auditions a part. They were *wonderful*. It was a wonderful time for all of us. We did a bill of one-acts, put it on in the spring, and wow, we hadn't done that kind of stuff in Cornville. Well, let's do more. So we started reading the literature, came up with three more one-act plays, did them in six weeks, and then people started hearing about it. One weekend we went down the state, and we went to Portland, and all of a sudden we were on the road with this crazy company, the Cornville Touring Players. We were paid—we were making expenses. We were reviewed. And very favorably. And that summer, we did radio shows; and the [original] Cornville Players had a play going at the same time.

And all of a sudden it was like Boston, New York, and I started thinking, oh, wait a minute. You're crossing back over those borders. You said you weren't going to go south again. But it was very tempting professionally, because I was starting to get the kind of recognition that I had tasted in New York, and it was getting very heady for me. It was like, you better stop and evaluate what you're doing here, lady.

And finally I did realize that I was going to lose more than I was going to gain. I could have kept going—I mean, I could have balanced it because I don't have a family, because I can do what we do on two or three hours sleep generally. But I was going to lose my actors pretty soon. One of the real crazies was the Assistant D.A. His court cases were suffering, rather dramatically. He responded with lines from *Zoo Story* automatically (laughs).

But we kept it up for about a year and a half. It caused some ill will in the Cornville Players, because this had become an elitist group. And it was intentionally elitist. I had made no bones about it.

It was a great time; I don't know that I could do it forever. I sort of miss it. And I'm kind of willing to try it again. We worked last January, in Waterville, we toured as far as Waterville . . .

What makes you a strong director?

(Sighs) . . . That's a good question. . . . I think maybe the ability to . . . excite other people. The minute that I get bored, or I lose interest. . . . It's not confidence as such, I'm never confident about going into a show. I all of a sudden realize, oh my God, why did I pick this? I'm not sure I know anything about this play at all. But I'm excited about it. And I think it's maybe that ability to communicate excitement. I think it can be shown by example. I don't think it can be taught—not at all.

I will hook people. I'll talk them into it. I'll con them into doing something that they don't really . . . 'cause I can beat them down, with sheer enthusiasm. Back in the privacy of their room, they're not sure they want to do it at all. And I've overdone it a couple of times, on that basis. You know what I mean, I've carried them along or swept them along with my enthusiasm, or excitement about doing something.

There's a wonderful line in *Cat on a Hot Tin Roof,* when Maggie says to Brick, "You've drunk so much tonight. When are you going to stop drinking?" And he says (whispers), "I drink so I can hear that magic click." And for me, that's what I wait for, in every performance, is that magic click. And if I don't get it, I've been cheated, and I tell my class that. Something has got to move me incredibly.

A recognition of that . . . has made me a better teacher. I look for that in a classroom situation, whether it's one-on-one or a group of twenty. "Have you got it yet? Have I moved you yet as a teacher?" Or as a director, "Have I gotten you yet on this? Are we talking?" Maybe I miss that anonymity of New York once in a while, but this is life blood now. I go on the streets and I try to get people in the eyeballs to see if they're really paying attention.

Every year we have an annual meeting and we say, "Well, the best thing we could do is to plan our schedule right now. And let's decide what shows we're going to do, and set the dates, and then we can advertise ahead, and we can sell season tickets, and . . ." We always say this and we never do it, and I think it's just as well. I don't know that I want to make plans for anything. Because that's locking it into a day job kind of attitude. And then you start thinking in terms of salary. You start thinking, you know, why aren't I getting more? But to go for federal funding would mean we'd have to pay salaries, and who would we pay?

Actually our biggest seller is the cookie table. We have not graduated past the cookies, that was such a big success. In order to be a member of the cast, you have to pay a dollar membership fee, which pays for postage; you have to agree to bake at least three dozen cookies, and help provide your own costumes. Those are the requirements. We have to pay our share of the insurance on the Town Hall, the lights and the heat as we use it. So we're broke. We've got some money in the bank, but . . .

So five years down the road from here, do you see yourself as doing the same sorts of things with the Players?

Yeah! I'm afraid so. I mean, I always think that's not like moving, you know, somehow that's not moving anywhere. And that would have worried me some years ago, that I couldn't promise to be doing more. I'm smug to say, "Yep, I want to be doing the same thing," but I think I do.

I want to do three major shows a year and some little tasty tidbits on the side, that please me in a little more personal way to do. And so far there seems to be the energy basically for doing that. Only I'm not doing it for the betterment of Cornville. I'm getting those magic clicks.

I'm here alone. I support myself by means that are not clear to them (laughs). My income doesn't seem to come from anyplace they can perceive directly. I keep weird hours. Strangers will come to my house. All sorts of people have lived here, and that is true. If there's any undelivered mail in town, it comes here. It does. I mean, it really does. But that's okay. And the gossip has been wild, but never malicious. It's just because they kind of like it. It's kind of neat to have somebody to tell a story about. Once in a while I've felt kind of hurt because sometimes it got kind of heavy. But I feel

Maine kind of honors that, you know, and theatricality is okay, in a funny kind of way.

I've got to say that if it wasn't fun I don't think I would have done it. I'm not quite that masochistic. . . . No, I've often thought the Town Hall is my second home, kind of. I feel very comfy there. It's a dark, gloomy little hole, and I love it to pieces—it's my home. It's a very . . . God, it's a very vast part of my life.

I like to be God (softly). And I tell them—and I do mean this, and they know I mean it—I like to direct. I love watching pieces fall into place. I like playing out my fantasies and moving people around, and I built that network, very selfishly, so I could survive. I mean, I've gotten jobs out of this, because I've given somebody a part in a play.

My enthusiasms aren't just theater, and my excitements aren't just theater, 'cause that's narrowing. But I justify it all, the cows, or the plants, or my collections. I have dragged calves and sheep on stage, and I have justified my buying the sheep so I could use them in a play. That's my whole justification. Everything's going to be a prop in a play sometime. . . .

I have this vision of little green men coming down to this planet, and seeing people not doing a damn thing because nobody's paying them a dollar.

Henry Ware

THE USEFUL SERVICES EXCHANGE

NOT all of us have cows or sheep to drag on stage, or even stages to drag them onto. We want to help, but our goals seem a lot more modest, our talents more commonplace. Where to begin? Here's one example:

Consider your own talents and skills, then multiply them by all the people living around you. Every community, every neighborhood, has enough abilities to fill a small yellow pages. But many, or most, are locked up, like good china, for an occasion that never comes. Communities are skilled, but their skills lie fallow.

Yet if local talents could be better publicized and exchanged, collective self-esteem would rise; strangers could become acquaintances, acquaintances friends; money would be saved; trust, cooperation, self-reliance would all grow; the community fabric would be strengthened. If nothing else, there'd be social insurance against a rainy day, or storm.

All it takes is someone to log the talent, spread the word, and set the wheels in motion. The concept seems so simple, the gains so tangible, you wonder why it's not been done before, or is not done more now. Barter, defined as goods exchange, is thousands of years old. But barter, defined as structured exchange of services, is something else again. By one reckoning, the first formalized skills exchange in the United States was not established until 1975. It was launched in Reston, Virginia, by a retired economist named Henry Ware.

Reston is a new town, founded in the 1960s, about fifteen miles from Washington, D.C. Its physical layout encourages social interaction; you can feel that while browsing in the outdoor shopping area, or wandering along the walkways threading the houses, or noticing the

placement of the homes themselves. Its residents as a group are reason-
ably well-off, and self-selected, so in that sense Reston is special.

Henry Ware, at first meeting, is not so obviously special. He is
unassuming, deflects credit elsewhere; he's not primed to talk of inner
feelings. He speaks slowly, gently, with dignity and reserve, without
high emotion. What he projects is a gritty persistence, a quiet, me-
thodical quality which says, I took this work on freely, and I'll see it
through until it's done. More than one style can lead to substance. If
Marti Stevens is theatrical, Henry Ware is straight-ahead. She moved
to Maine; he left it as a child.

The Useful Services Exchange was his second retirement job; he'd
previously set up a transportation program in a nearby town. When
USE reached a peak, he stepped down from there as well, turning leadership over to others in the community, though he's stayed highly involved, as member, and as consultant to many of the hundreds of skills
exchanges now active nationwide.

There's a time to exit, thoughtfully and gracefully. A program
should last beyond one person's push. The training wheels have to
come off, and if there's wobble or fall, that has to be accepted. There's
a lifetime full of civic jobs, in retirement and before; and much wisdom
in community work lies in knowing when to move on.

✳

I knew we had neighbors who had very much in common with us, and once
in a while just in talking with a neighbor, you'd find they had a very valuable
talent. And you'd say, "Well, what are you doing with it?" They'd say, "Well,
um, I'm not doing anything with it." People say, "Well, I'm good at
wallpapering, but I don't need to do any more wallpapering. I just finished
wallpapering, and that's all I need to do."

I'd say, "Well, if you had a neighbor who wanted wallpapering, would
you be willing to help that neighbor?" And that person would say, "Well,
sure, I'd be glad to help the neighbor wallpaper." And then you'd say, "Well,
is there anything that *you* need?" And the person would say, "Well, yes, I
have some plastering that should be done, and I don't know how to do
that." So we'd say, "We have people who can help you with plastering too."

People had all kinds of talents and interests, and it just didn't make
sense to me that you'd have to wait until somebody offered you a salary
before you could do something worthwhile.

So I talked with a few people, they said yes, it sounded like an
interesting idea, they'd like to exchange services. It just made sense that if
people are neighbors and they can help each other, and they'd like to help

each other if they knew who needed help, and they liked to find exposure for their talents in the community, and they liked to meet neighbors, that given the opportunity they would do it. And that's the basis upon which it was built up, gradually.

I took it just as a challenge, almost like working on a puzzle. I was convinced from my analysis that it just had to work. And since we had no model, we had to figure one out as we went along. It was just something that was due for its time.

We started from scratch. I got someone who had an office with a room they weren't using, and they let me use the room. I didn't want to charge for people to belong to the system, because I figured they don't know whether it's going to be of advantage to them or not, so I just put my time in on it. For three years I put in five hours a day running the thing, running the exchange.

I built up a list of about twenty-five or thirty people who would be willing to come in and help if and when needed, in the office. We did everything from the office, including publicity. I wrote an article for the local newspaper once a week on what exchanges had taken place and what interesting things came out of it. We did have to have money to pay for the telephone, postage, and that sort of thing, but we found that for about fifty dollars a month, we could run the whole operation. The people who worked in the office got hours of credit for the work they did. And that's the way we got it going.

You make it sound all so simple.

Yeah. Well, that's right, but as I say, this was a pilot project. You had to try things in an experimental way—some things worked, some things didn't work.

Because there was no real commitment to start with, people figured well, sure, I'd be glad to help somebody with remedial reading, or I'd be glad to give somebody a ride. And they were rather intrigued with the idea that they could get something in exchange for it. So that wasn't the problem.

And by keeping the organization simple, of not having requirements that people send in written responses and signed receipts and all that—well, they liked that idea, 'cause nobody wants to be organized in any way other than necessary. So we kept it as loose as we could.

Well, we asked them what services they had to offer and we listed those services, and then gradually I guess after the first year we had fifty, seventy-five people in the system. And we kept growing, more people came into it, and as they came to it they registered more and more services, and then we had to figure out how to categorize them.

For instance you'd have repair—that would be one category—teaching or advising would be another category. Sitting would be a category, sitting for dogs, houses, plants, or whatever. And giving a ride would be another category. Then we got into the question of how about things like lending and sharing? A lot of people had tools and equipment in the house that they didn't use all the time, like a big roaster or a wheelbarrow, or freezer space you don't use in your home freezer.

The idea would be that an hour's worth an hour, basically, regardless of your skills. But we decided then that obviously if somebody takes care of your dog for a weekend, you're not going to give them an hour for an hour for all the time the dog was there—you figure, well, you'd have to walk the dog, and you'd have to feed the dog, and that would be the amount of time.

But there was one time a lady called in after a dog had been in her house for a weekend, she asked for about twice as much time as we thought it was worth. So I asked her, "How come you're asking so much? You couldn't have spent that much time on the dog." She said, "Well, the dog was shedding, and I had to vacuum the rug every two days, and that was extra time." So the person who owned the dog figured that was reasonable, and she got the time that she wanted.

The interesting thing is that it's quite different from the competitive system. When a person offers to do a service for a neighbor through this program, generally they do not try to get as much credit as they can get—it works just the other way around. The person who does the job says, "I was glad to do it, you're a neighbor. I'm glad to help you, no sweat, and I don't require that you give me a lot of hours credit for it." And the person who gets the service says, "Well, this service was worth a lot to me; I'd be glad to give you more credit-hours than you're asking." So it changes the whole motivation, you see, from a competitive type of approach.

I think it's basically the motivation of a neighbor to a neighbor. It puts people in touch with each other. It's in your own community, and you like to do your neighbor a favor, if it's not at your expense. As a matter of fact, it's worth something to you to have your neighbor appreciate your talent. If you're good at something, you can help a neighbor, and the word will get around, and you get satisfaction out of the fact that you are accepted in your community as a person who can do something creative and worthwhile.

We tried to keep things as simple as possible, so we decided that the people who wanted a service would talk to the person offering the service, and find out among themselves whether they felt that person was capable of performing the service.

And another thing—in many exchange groups that have developed since, they had to write out receipts for the time given, and send the receipt into the office, and the office would record it. Well, we decided we didn't need that—this was a community, and the people were all doing it on a friendly basis. We stressed here that this is not a business responsibility; that your relationships to the other members are merely a moral responsibility.

Another thing—some people were so conscientious that they wouldn't ask for a service until they had earned the credit. In other words, I wouldn't ask for three hours of help and consultation with you, because I haven't earned three hours. So we told them, well, look, that's going to interfere with the system; we *want* people to go into debt, we *want* them to get the service, and let them pay back later. And so people would agree to do that.

Getting funding—I had very little experience in that. I found it easier to do our own funding through this idea of having a banquet or having a bake sale or something like that once in a while. We would charge, say, five or six dollars for the dinner. And that money would go into the till, to pay the phone bill, and to pay the postage and the duplicating expenditure. Everybody who produced food for the banquet would receive credit for the work they did, so that helped.

And then of course the people at the banquet would talk about the experiences they'd had, and aside from what we arranged through the program, there'd be a whole lot of other additional exchanges taking place. Just people informally talking with one another.

When I first started to get this program going, I had a couple of eye-openers. I presented it at a meeting of people who were working with the senior citizens, and I was surprised to find out that some people didn't like the idea at all, because apparently they wanted the senior citizens to be dependent upon them—they were helping the senior citizens, they were dispensing charity. There're still a lot of people who look at their services to people, quote, "less fortunate," you know, as something which they give of themselves, but in order to do that, they want to keep the people in the position of having to take.

And that's one of the things which this whole barter program overcomes, because in the charity game there are the givers and the takers, but in the barter arrangement those people who give are also those people who take. And you don't take anything unless you give, and you don't give anything unless you take. So it puts people on an equal footing.

So many elderly people would rather go without something—even if they're sick in bed and they need food, they wouldn't ask a neighbor to bring it to them because they don't want to be beholden to somebody, they don't want to feel that somebody's doing something for them, they can't return it. Some people just have a terrible feeling that if you accept charity you're somehow humiliating yourself. But if they joined the exchange, then they don't have to feel that way at all, because they can reciprocate.

Basically, I ran the program those first three years. And I made the decisions; when something that was innovative perhaps didn't work, it would be up to me to abandon that and try something else. I gave myself a year, and then I kept on with it to a third year, and then I figured, well, I'd been with that long enough. I figured that it was a community endeavor; if it's going to be of value to the community, the community has to take it over. It should run on its own momentum if it's viable, which is what it's done.

Since then, we've had several people who have been in charge of the office for a year at a time or even two years. And we ran into the problem, after I left, that there was no one willing to put that much time in on it. I was there, as I say, five hours a day. But I had no salary, you see. And you're not going to get anybody to put in that work without a salary.

The actual amount of service—the number of service exchanges—in the last few years has gone down. Once they get into it, a lot of people really enjoy it and say it's the greatest thing they've ever seen. It's fantastic; they enjoy it. But there's the inconvenience of taking responsibility, which you don't have to take when you're buying with money. You see, if you have a dollar in your pocket, in a sense that frees you from having to deal with your neighbor.

It's much easier to go out and buy something and pay money for it than it is to arrange mutual convenience with a person who's going to do something for you. And a lot of people don't want to go to all that trouble. They don't like the hassle. They say, well, I've called up five or six people and I haven't gotten anybody yet who will do what I want when I want it. There's nobody waiting around to serve you hand and foot and say that the customer's always right. Everybody says, I'll do the job if and when I'm available, and you have to recognize that.

So if you have a dollar and you can afford service and you can get it commercially, in many cases you would prefer to do it that way. The thing that's unique, the thing that's unusual is not something necessarily that appeals to everybody.

The people who need the Useful Services Exchange the most are the people who will not join it. It's the people in the lower income bracket, the people who feel themselves behind the eight ball—they're not going to take a chance on something they don't understand. Apparently they're used to the idea that either something is given to you as charity, or else you have to pay for it; you don't get anything for nothing. At least we haven't been able to get them to participate in this project. It's only the middle-income people who have been participating.

Still, I'm really interested in why a concept like USE isn't seen more widely. Because what you describe seems so simple, and so risk-free—you can get out at any time, you can come and go pretty much as you please. It seems ideal.

But who's going to run the organization? That's the chief problem. I think it has to be someone who's paid to do this. I think you have to have somebody who's financing an organization, because it's very unlikely that you have anybody who is as eager as I was to try it, and to put the time in that's necessary to do it.

But in some other communities, somewhere, maybe there are people of your age, or people who for one reason or another don't have to earn a salary, who are also eager—

Yes. Well, there are. Yes, it could be done, and it should be, probably. There certainly are plenty of people who are innovative and people who are interested in the concept, and there are plenty of retired people who have time and would like to do something constructive like that. It's just a matter of getting the thing going, I suppose.

The real problem here is not to attract people to follow, but to attract people to take the initiative, to be the leaders themselves, and to give them the confidence of knowing that they can do it. . . . Isn't that the problem?

Then how do you go about giving people the confidence that they can be leaders?

Well, that's where you come in (laughs).

I think Iris and the other people who have come after me on this have a certain amount of charisma and an ability to inspire other people.* Iris is moving out now, and some younger lady is doing it who likes the idea, the challenge of organizing. She wants to try her organizational ability; maybe she'll succeed, and maybe she won't.

But on the other hand, I realize that you can't quantify this thing, really. For the people who are participating in it, it has real value, and many people who have participated have made friends and friendships which have continued outside of the system. Many people who were introduced to their neighbors through the system have found that they can continue without the system. We do know that many new neighbors have become friends.

I've shown that it could be done. I felt confident that it could be done, and I felt I couldn't rest until I could show myself that it could be done. That I could do it.

---

*Iris Lloyd, one of Henry's successors as president of USE.

Probably in a couple of years now my wife and I will be moving into a condominium for elder people, and almost certainly I'll be starting something there, to improve the quality of life. It will make life much more interesting for me, and for my wife, and for everybody else.

I'm interested in gardening—we have a garden plot area, some fifty garden plots, and so I've organized something up there for the exchange of vegetables, the exchange of know-how. The gardeners get together, we have a chart and people have phone numbers, and we have a telephone pyramid so we can get in touch with each other. Well, somebody had to do it—so I figured it's a good thing to communicate with your neighbors and exchange things, and it makes it more fun, more interesting, so I've started that, you see.

I have this vision of little green men coming down to this planet, and visiting us and looking around. Seeing these people—perfectly able-bodied people, all their hands and all their facilities about them; eager, capable, intelligent, skilled—sitting around and not doing a damn thing because nobody's paying them a dollar. It doesn't make sense. And you take it from there, you know. There's got to be some way. You can't be hypnotized by the green stuff. . . .

Vin Quayle (right) discussing housing issues with colleagues at St. Ambrose.

The only important thing worth doing in life is being a saint. But how can you say that without embarrassing me?

Vin Quayle

ST. AMBROSE HOUSING AID CENTER

S TARTING a community program is one achievement; but as Henry Ware points out, sustaining one is quite another. Community programs are living things, and like all living things they are energy-dependent, even when grown up. You can back off for a while; but neglect them too long and you are in trouble.

It's possible that the qualities needed to sustain are in fact different from those needed to initiate. On the other hand, most people interviewed here were both starters and sustainers, having stayed with their creations for five to ten years or more. Either our program starters are doubly blessed, or there's something linking the two. I accept both views, but would emphasize the latter.

One link may have to do with religious faith. The fact is that regular churchgoers report more community service involvement. People in religious vocations are still more likely to serve, if only because they have more time and need less money. Maybe there's much more to it. Yet it's not too surprising that a priest and three nuns are in this book, though three are ex- and one's now married.

Vin Quayle is a married ex-priest who started the St. Ambrose Housing Aid Center and has sustained it since 1974. St. Ambrose's purpose is to ensure affordable housing for low-income people in inner-city Baltimore. Vin began with nothing; his staffers now do prepurchase counseling, inspect homes, repair homes, negotiate sales, draw up contracts, underwrite mortgages, prevent foreclosures, teach rehab, do rehab, generate housing conversions, and make syndication deals. St. Ambrose is considered a model housing program in the United States.

Was it something in his childhood? His father was a stockbroker with his own seat on the American Stock Exchange. His sister brokers for Salomon Brothers, and his brother works for Merrill Lynch. He grew up in a middle-class Irish-Jewish neighborhood in Queens, where the church was always a major part of his life: altar boy, CYO, Catholic high school. His childhood hero was Jackie Robinson.

In high school, his English teacher was Daniel Berrigan, the activist priest, later war resister and inmate. "But he also ran the sodality—you had to go out and do something in the community. And my job was to go play pool with Puerto Ricans in Spanish Harlem, once a week. I was a little high school kid, I was scared stiff, and I used to purposely lose. I was a good pool player (laughs)."

A family of financial success, a religious background, and a teacher of social conscience. Whether these summaries are more than superficial is hard to say. The links between childhood variables and social activism are not fully clear. We may not be able to clarify them much; biography is not our major concern.

Vin Quayle became a Jesuit priest—might have, he thinks, wound up teaching Jesuit school. Chance or fate led him from the seminary to Chicago in the summer of 1968. A triggering event? Perhaps. When he came back he a got a real estate license and started selling houses and picketing banks. Things moved from there.

When we meet, on a rainy Saturday afternoon, he's locked out of his own office. He's had to fire a staff member for stealing; the locks have been changed; he has no key. We head home, Vin stopping along the way to buy a case of Budweiser, which he sips as we talk in his basement while young children scamper overhead and call his name.

The story picks up when Vin has returned to seminary in the U.S. from missionary work in Africa. He'd gotten caught in the Nigerian civil war in 1967, and had narrowly missed being shot . . .

✳

I got back, and I hadn't been in touch with the outside world in six months. One thing when you leave the country, you're out of it when you come back. I had a terrible inferiority complex, because I hadn't been thinking the thoughts my peers had been thinking, or reading the books, or conversing with them. And nice as they were, when you come back from another culture people say, "What was it like over there?" and after your first sentence, you know they're not listening.

So the conversation when I came back was Vietnam, the peace movement. Phil Berrigan used to come out every week to get us involved.*

---

*Phil Berrigan, the peace activist, brother of Daniel, was arrested many times during the Vietnam period and afterward for antiwar protest activities.

Fellow seminarians were burning their draft cards and marching and all that; I hadn't been prepared for this at all. So I meticulously did my studies for the year. I went and sat with Phil Berrigan, I listened to him. He was trying to recruit me, I knew that. I was scared.

Finally I heard about a program in Chicago, for priests and seminarians who were going to work in the inner city. This was going to give me an introduction to city work. It was run by an Episcopalian guy [Tom Gaudette], and I got exposed to a Jewish guy out there, Saul Alinsky.

I went to Chicago that summer, the summer of '68, yeah. And that really was the event that changed me, that gave me a sense of direction.

As part of the training center, you went out and worked in a community organization. And I was sent out to this one built on Alinsky's philosophy of organizing, that whole business. At the same time I got immersed in an issue. Housing. Racially changing neighborhoods. And it gave me some skills and some confidence in myself out there, for six weeks.

When I came back from Nigeria, I wanted to do something about Biafra, because the Americans hadn't taken a position. But what Alinsky and Tom Gaudette told me was that if you deal with the problems on that level, you're never going to do anything worthwhile in life. You got to pick off a little piece of reality no matter what it is, and immerse yourself in that, and everything will flow from there. You'll find out that your life takes on a whole new meaning. Just pick out a little, bite off a little chip of reality. And that probably was the best advice I was given as I look back over my life, aside from the Jesuit spirituality.

I came back [to the Baltimore area] and a diocesan priest called me, a priest from one of the parishes, and said, "Listen, we hear you have some training in inner-city stuff. We just had a racial incident in our parish; there's a little black church and a group of whites went in and stoned the church, and painted it and did all sorts of things." This is the fall of '68.

So we come on down on Saturdays, and I organized the white folks to go out and have a cleanup at the church. I just used a little of the skills I had learned. Organized the folks, and we had a good media experience, the press came out and [said] aren't these white people nice for cleaning up this church.

I thought of myself as an organizer then. And I thought, gee, this is something I'd like to do. And I spoke to my superiors there, and they said as long as it doesn't interfere with your studies, fine. The Jesuits from on top were getting the young guys involved in the civil rights movement.

I swear there was something really strange going on with real estate, and the same thing happened in Chicago. It was the racially changing neighborhood, with the "for sale" signs all over the place. The whites were all afraid and they were fleeing the neighborhood, and the blacks were coming in. A handful of big speculators controlled the market; they were buying all these row houses up. They would buy them for $5000 and sell them, often on the same day or within the same month to a black family for $15,000, which was a lot of money in those days, back in the sixties in Baltimore.

So I started organizing with another seminary fellow. He was good, he was a lawyer and could do the research. I was terrible on research, but I was good on the street—I was outgoing, and had a lot of those skills. I didn't know what a mortgage was, in those days, 'cause I was in a seminary; what did we learn about mortgages? We did learn things from the grass-roots level, but that's what we were trained to do. That's a liberal arts education. That's the beauty of liberal arts, right? 'Cause you take what you learn, and you can apply it to anything! Anything.

We decided to research this damn "for sale" sign—what was going on. And we were very lucky in Baltimore because we had a tool the real estate industry used, a simple periodical that came out for the benefit of the banks and the real estate people on every sale in the neighborhood, the Lusk real estate reports. So we were able to get copies and know exactly what was happening on every street, who was buying the houses.

And we just started raising hell. I mean, that was the approach I learned in Chicago, to raise hell. I think the issue we took on was too big at the time, that's what Alinsky would have said: "Geez, why did you take such a big issue on?" But it was the issue, the immediate issue in the neighborhood, and we got the media involved, television especially, and somebody did a week series on the problem, and we're just kind of raising hell in the city.

I was trying to figure out how the real estate market works. I said to myself, okay, what should I do next? So the only way, the best way I thought of learning it was to get my real estate license. First of all, I could pay my own way that way. I would have income coming in to support me, and see where we go from there.

So I went to my superior and I said, "I've got an idea" (laughs). He said, "Well, you're going to have to get the pope's permission for that, because there's a law that says no cleric is allowed to go into business"; they can't do business without Rome. He suggested that when I write, stress the civil rights aspect of why are you doing it—for poor folks—and I had no trouble.

My goal was to go to the old white people before they sold their houses and say to them, "Don't sell. Let me find a family, a black family for you, and they will buy it for $10,000, which is the fair price." Well, if I could get them to buy it for $10,000, the white family would feel better, even though they were going to move. The black family would be getting it at a better price, and we'd have a homeowner in the neighborhood. It wasn't that sophisticated at the time. I just said to myself, this will be a healthier neighborhood if the black people own their homes.

Word came back [from the Vatican], fine, go ahead. We're up to '70, '71 now. So I got my license and I sold for about a year and a half, about thirty homes. And I said to myself good, that's nice, you know what's going on now. So what are you going to do about it? You're not going to sell houses the rest of your life. Someone told me about a group in London, run by a priest. It was called SHAC, Sheltered Aid Housing Center, and I got permission to go over to England.

When I visited in '71, they had become the model housing center. Every minority in London was coming to them to get a house, ten thousand families a year. And not only were they serving these families, but they were a recognized voice in the London community on housing, on housing policy, housing issues. So that was the model that I tried to bring back. I said, I'm going to take this model and start it in Baltimore.

So I came back, and there was another young Jesuit, who was just ordained, George Byr. He said, "I could get interested in this." So I said, "Well, let's go do it." So the Jesuits put up maybe six or seven thousand, they said we'll cover you for a year, and we went to Catholic Charities—and that's really how it got started.

So George joined me and we opened St. Ambrose, June '72. There was a lot of turmoil between the whites and the blacks at this time. It was very hostile out there. And we were all whites, so we knew we had to do something. Let's take the name that the black community will have confidence in, and we took the name of St. Ambrose, which was a big black Catholic church, even though George and I weren't working on that side of town.

So the question then became, well, how do you set up a mechanism that can deal with a much larger number of families, all right? And what we decided to do was instead of going out and selling houses, we would teach; we would get the black family into the office, teach them the process.

That's one thing about the Jesuits, we're all trained to be teachers. Maybe we'd all be doing much better things for society if we were back in the classroom, but we took our teaching skills and brought them to the housing, that's what we did. We learned the language; instead of French, we learned housing. And now we started to teach.

And our goal was always not merely to be teaching these individual families. That was important, but really our goal was to shake things up, to see some structural changes out there, you know what I mean? We wanted to get rid of the speculators. We blamed the speculators for what was going on, the landlords. It wasn't till another year that we said, hey, wait a second, there's another level going on out here. The speculators are out on the streets, but where do the banks fit into this whole operation? And it was only then that we began to realize that your banking industry wasn't lending to the black families—they weren't welcome.

I was a priest, so that gave us a lot of power, putting on the collar, using our church connection to do this. And we used our services as credibility; if we were housing people, then the banks had to listen to us. I used to list every address of the families we helped to buy, so that the business community could say, geez, they're doing something; maybe they know what they're talking about. But in our own mind, the service, while important and of value, wasn't the principal thing we were about.

The banks were the problem. We picketed banks with six people, or five people. But that's all you needed (laughs). We had a core of black guys who were terrific. We had these two old-time civil rights guys, and we put them on our board of directors. And then we had a young black guy who really looked tough, he ran the picket lines, and he was the gentlest guy the world had known, but they thought he was this big radical.

We always tried to get nuns in the picket lines too. Anything that would get the attention—I mean, the whole purpose of picketing is to bring the media into it. Get the word out. And Baltimore's a small town, so it wasn't hard.

There were five savings and loans who were calling the shots in Baltimore. The savings and loan industry is primarily Catholic. That was a lot easier; we felt more comfortable out there picketing the Catholics. We were picketing Loyola Federal, Loyola was the biggest, and sometimes businessmen would come up to us and scream at us, "You should be ashamed of yourself, Father!" And every time they did I'd say (shouts), "Here's another man who just took his savings out of Loyola Federal Savings and Loan! (laughs). Take your savings out of this bank; it's anticity."

The head of Loyola, we called him up, and said, "We want to come down to you; you haven't made any loans in the city of Baltimore in the last couple of years." He said, "Don't bother." We went out on the picket line and the chairman of the board was on the phone in five minutes. And he said, "Come on in, we want to talk to you." And I said, "No, we've gone through a lot of work to put these picket signs together (laughs). You call us next week; we're going to spend a week out here, let the world know what you've been doing."

So we got them to the negotiating table, five presidents of the savings and loans came out. That was one of the best things we ever did, picket the banks. And that led to some of the changes.

The thing to do then was get the word out. People started coming; the banks started sending us people. Churches—we sent the word out to all the Catholic and Protestant churches around: any family's thinking of buying a house, have them check with us first; we'll make sure they don't get taken, and all that stuff. And we put up signs on all the buses in the city, we got free advertising. We put together spots for all the radio stations: "Thinking of buying a house? Go to St. Ambrose. Have a talk."

Then it just grew. That service just grew from year to year.
Our overhead was low enough. George and I worked out of our home
for a while, and then we opened a little office up by the Oak Road. Each
year I went back to Catholic Charities to get some more money. Then we
had a creative guy go in to run the housing department for the City of
Baltimore, and he got us some money from the city. I was usually going out
to get money for a salary to hire another person. But the services kept
expanding, and we kept bringing more people in. . . .

*

Their basic service is teaching poor families to buy houses. Their basic
role is advisor and coach. Three thousand families have bought through
St. Ambrose. Average sale price: $15,000, believe it or not.

St. Ambrose also helps families who are facing foreclosure. They
repair several dozen houses yearly, so elderly homeowners can keep
living in them. They finance tenant conversions with their own mortgages. They've bought their own lead paint analyzer, and do their own
testing.

They buy up vacant and deteriorating houses, fix them, and sell
them or rent them. They buy up good houses, after older homeowners
die, and keep them from speculators. They own and manage 130 rental
housing units. There is more. Millions of dollars are being leveraged
here.

The basic idea is that everyone should have a decent place to live.

*

The pacing and the humor. The fun. I would say they're the critical elements.
In the early days we used to go to the horse races. We'd just close down St.
Ambrose on Wednesdays. We'd say, "Oh, shit, let's go to the track
tomorrow. Put the phone on hold, Anna, we're not coming in tomorrow.
We're all going to the track."

Or we'd have great picnics. We'd just close the office for a day and have
picnics. Friday afternoons, four o'clock Friday afternoon, we'd go out and
get a few six-packs of beer and wind up the week just sitting around
drinking beer. You know, just for an hour and a half Fridays, you unwind,
and that's important.

A lot of us who work at St. Ambrose also share our social life together.
Our families are very close. And some of my best friends are the St. Ambrose
crowd, or they used to work at St. Ambrose, so we socialize as well. Not all,
but a lot.

There are beautiful things about the nonprofit world. There's the informality of it you can't have in the business world. We have people come, St. Ambrose is the best place they ever worked. They were just treated differently. It was fun, we can wear these clothes to work, [Vin is wearing plaid Bermuda shorts] everybody works hard.

It hurts . . . it's harmful as you get bigger because you begin to employ people who see St. Ambrose as a place of employment, all right, and those people do not work out well. For example, this woman who, uh, who we just fired, she was taking time off, sick time, almost a day a week, or a day every two weeks. We never had that experience before. We had never had anyone take time off because of sickness unless they were really, really sick, okay? We never had to have people sign in, keep track of who was here today or anything like that. So we've had some experiences like that, and I can see how an organization has to go, has to become like Baltimore Federal and Loan, that has all those strict requirements.

But there's a core group here, and it just makes all the difference in the world. I don't have to worry about standards, because they would do anything in the world to stay on board with the services. I go into St. Ambrose in the morning, and I say, "Well, what shall I do today?" Okay? And I'm able now to do whatever I want.

Now the one thing I have to do—I'm responsible for money. No one in the organization is allowed to worry about money. They do the job, they get the work done, I take on the headaches about money, all right? Because most . . . many nonprofit organizations that I see out there—and I'm on the board of a number of them—the staff has to worry about money. And by necessity they're not doing a good job. They're not doing the best they can do because they're nervous about the money. But they have to do that, I guess. Maybe not, maybe not.

Do you worry about money?

Not as much as I used to. But an organization like ours, as we go into a fiscal year, I don't know where $200,000 is coming from. . . . You're damn right I worry about that.

You mean lie-in-bed type worrying?

There are nights when I wake up, five o'clock in the morning, and I can't get back to sleep. There have been those nights. Now, do I do it every night? No. And am I doing all right now? You caught me at a good time, we're doing well financially right now.

But, well, that for me is my primary responsibility, freeing the staff up from any monetary worries. And then the second is trying to make sure everyone's having a good time. That's my second one.

Two concerns that have been with us from the very beginning—[one is] the distinction between service and advocacy. One of the criticisms of some of our staff, and of people outside the organization, has been that St. Ambrose now is so involved in service that it's lost its advocacy role, all right? What are you doing about the big picture? Even one of our board members said, "Why aren't you down picketing Ronald Reagan? There's the issue; look what he's done." And that is a constant tension.

But the other one, and this is my worry, is the money versus your, um, integrity. How do you run an organization with a $600,000 budget that you have to raise each year and still keep your original vision of raising hell on the issues? That's a constant tension. And what do you do? You compromise (laughs). I mean, in the real world, what do you do? You compromise. And when have you compromised too much, you know, so much that you know you're not being honest?

You *always* have to compromise. I have a black guy, Ron Morris, [not his real name] who is always raising hell, attacking the mayor every opportunity he gets. And I'm churning inside here; I have to go to the mayor to get money to run the organization. And when the fund requests come in, the mayor will say, "Damn it, he wants me to pay Ron Morris's salary" (laughs). Funny. I can work it out. But I have to do things with the mayor so that the organization doesn't get hurt, and the question is do I shut Ron up or do I support him?

So what do you do?

I support him.

But that's not a compromise, in this case.

Well, I compromise by saying to Ron, "Go ahead. You believe in it, go do it." Still I have to get to the mayor somehow and say, "Mr. Mayor, oh, don't worry about Ron, you know. He's workin' really hard, and he's overpressured. He didn't mean anything personal." All that stuff. That in a sense is compromise.

It hurts to do that?

I have to do it.

But it hurts inside to do that?

There are times I have not walked the picket . . . there are many times I have not walked the picket line with Ron, when I should be there . . . because if I'm there, it's going to be a harder job for me to pay Ron's salary.

And that feels okay?

In the world as it should be, it feels awful. In my world, I live in the world as it is. (Whispers) I have no problem with it. . . . I did, I have at times, but no, that's what I have to deal with.

So it's better to have a $600,000 budget and to bend a little bit to what the real world is, than to have a $50,000 budget and be completely ideologically pure?

It's better for us at this time in our history to do that.

You wouldn't generalize beyond your situation?

No. I think we need groups out there with the $5000 budgets who can raise hell. The problem is there aren't a lot out there anymore. But personally, I don't have the energy to do all that, a whole lot of that anymore.

Once I turned forty I don't go to any night meetings. I work nine to five, all right? But no more night meetings. Because I need my nights, with my family, my marriage, my kids, myself personally. I don't bring any work home. And I don't have to do it now, because I've such a tremendous staff. The young kids can go at night. I don't want it.

From twenty to forty, I went to three or four night meetings a week. And then when I was a priest, I was working five days at the housing, three or four night meetings, Saturday I had to prepare my sermon for Sunday, and you're nervous when you're preparing. You preach two masses on Sunday, you might have a baptism afterward—you're wiped out. I used to come home at four o'clock on a Sunday afternoon, flop down with a couple of beers in front of the television set, and watch a ball game. Monday morning, you get up, go back at housing.

You just have to learn. Somewhere along the way I said, there's got to be more to life than this.

It's very hard to duplicate St. Ambrose as an organization. We have people coming in from all over the country who want to go back and start a St. Ambrose and I know how hard it's going to be.

We have hidden strengths, like the church. We have the church connection, which means that much of the outside world looks upon St. Ambrose as the Catholic church's housing effort in Baltimore, at least a significant part of it, which is a real strength. We use that; we go to the state of Maryland and get financing to do a building, because they know we're part of the Catholic church. That's a terrific strength. Most community organizations don't have that.

And then there's the ultimate strength of what keeps the core of people going at St. Ambrose, all right? That's what you're trying to get at in this. And that's the intangible. It's . . . I can talk about it, but we never do talk about it. We never share at that level, because it's implicitly understood, and we're embarrassed to talk about it. . . . (sighs) Why are we embarrassed to talk about it? . . . Because the words don't . . . I can only talk about it in religious terms. And we're not into religious terms. I mean, we're a Catholic organization, and all this . . . um—we're embarrassed by religious talk. Because most of it is such crap. Whatever it is, we don't feel comfortable with it.

I was going through your questions and I kept getting back to the Jesuit spirituality. What is it really in life that you're looking for? (Softly) The only important thing worth doing in life is being a saint. (With passion) That's the only thing worth living for. I can't go out and say that. I mean, I can say it, but you can't say to people, (whispers) "What is it really that makes you tick, Quayle?" "I want to be a saint." Because it's the only thing to be; *nothing* else matters.

That's our value system. And we don't talk about it. We especially don't share it with each other, 'cause we laugh at each other (laughs). And then, in the language of the world, they don't know what we're talking about. By the world's values, all the superficial values of success and money, self-respect, all this garbage that people live—(very softly) we've rejected all of that. And we forget about it, and it's so unconscious in my core staff. They would be embarrassed if they heard me telling you this. But I *know* it.

And they may not even believe in God (laughs wryly). So what it is, it is the Jesuit spirituality. . . . Now, how do you duplicate that?

What are St. Ambrose's weaknesses? I would say we're not as well organized as we should be. We're not totally efficient; we don't have a secretary in the office. Thirty-three staff without a secretary. We have a receptionist, but everybody types his own, or her own. Managerially we have weaknesses that could be improved on. And partly that's me, I'm not a very well organized person myself.

We have had troubles with local politicians in the city. They don't like us. And some of them, the black politicians, they have tried to destroy projects of ours. Because they don't control us. I wouldn't have that problem if we were part of a larger parish. I'd have a lot more power to confront them with, and confront the mayor with.

We have not done well in training our black staff to go on to bigger positions. One of our goals was to take these young black guys and expose them to this stuff and then try to bump them into the corporations, the banks, the savings and loans; we've had a couple of successes, but we haven't done too well on that.

Where are our weaknesses? We have lots of weaknesses. And after fifteen years, I think some people would say that we should be doing much better. We should have a lot more money. I would say I'm pleased with our growth. But bigger isn't necessarily better. That's the tension, that's one of those tensions I mentioned before. Have we become too service-oriented? Have we lost our standard of community? We don't raise hell a lot anymore. We do on a particular bank that's screwing someone or the FHA or somebody, but we are not out there on a big issue right now.

But we don't know what the issue is right now. It's more complicated now out there. How do you deal with interest rates? You know, it's easy to deal with the bank who wasn't lending money, or with the speculator. The lending problem isn't there anymore. The banks that weren't lending fifteen years ago, now they're lending, all right.

The major problems now are the national problems: inflation, the cost of repairs, they're the problems that all of the organizations are struggling with. How do you get a family that earns $15,000 into this house that's gonna cost $50,000 to renovate? I don't know the answer to that—big subsidies. The mood of the country is against big subsidies.

Maybe we should be down in Washington screaming and hollering, but one of the things that Alinsky taught me was that you gotta deal with an issue that's specific, immediate, and realizable, and that's what I believe in. The inflation is specific and immediate, but a solution is not realizable. I don't know how to deal with it. For myself I need to see the results of my actions. I am not going to go down and picket in front of the White House, because I don't think it will do any good. A waste of my time.

Oh, if I thought we could win something I would do it.

But we're busy. We're busy with the services. So are we looking for an issue? We may not be looking for an issue, right now. We may be very happy with the services and surviving. I don't know.

And our independence is important, it's always important. When we were a little organization, money wasn't an issue. We could do whatever the hell we wanted as a little organization. And there's a part of us that would like to go back to those days and have that freedom. But I was a priest in those days, I could live off a few grand a year. Now I have a third kid on the way, can't do it.

I suspect I'm going to die with St. Ambrose. I would leave St. Ambrose tomorrow if I knew what to do. If I felt I could do something on the peace issue and still have my family life and all, I would . . . I'd try . . . I would leave St. Ambrose to do that. I don't know how to get a handle on it. So I don't do a whole lot on it. I feel guilty that I don't, that's one of those things. But I get back to specific, immediate, and realizable.

The thing I want to do is get at least the Catholic community more involved in the social issues. That's the thing I want to do most. It's more motivating people, attracting people, and inspiring people, getting them involved. I mean, I could talk to you about managerial skills and all this garbage, and how to raise money. Everyone thinks I can raise money. I don't know how to write a foundation grant or anything like that. And we never did. Ford Foundation—I never got any money from any of those groups. I don't know how to do it. So I guess, yeah, I'd like to know how to raise monies so that I don't have to worry about it as much, but, that doesn't really concern me. It's more how do I get the church in Baltimore, the Catholic church first, but then any church group, to get involved?

When I look at my life, so much has been given to me, I can *never* repay society, I can *never* give back for everything I have received, I can *never* give it back. Now, in the Jesuit spirituality, it takes on a theological context; that God so loves you, if you realize how much God loves you, then you become inspired to go out and love God, okay?

But every Catholic I meet, I've got to convince them of that, and one of the problems is, they don't see it. We have Catholics coming out of Catholic colleges today—these are college graduates, fairly intelligent people—not only don't they go to church and give to the church anymore, but they don't do a damn thing in their life except watch the dumb ballgame. How do you deal with someone like that? That's my driving force. That's what I spend most of my time thinking about. It pisses me off no end.

Guilt doesn't work anymore. In the old days, we had the guilt, we could get up in the pulpit and say, damnit, you're going to hell if you don't do something with your life. It doesn't seem to work anymore, 'cause you damn psychologists are telling people they don't have to [feel guilty].

I mean, that's part of the problem. How do you motivate people, whether they're clods or whether they're good people who just don't have confidence in themselves or whatever? How do you motivate them? Slowly.

Everybody is called to strive for sainthood. Everybody. A lot of people don't realize that, they don't even want to talk on that level or think on that level. Everybody is called to that.

But how can you say it without . . . without embarrassing me? Just say it in a way people will know, will understand. That's what you got to know. I mean, most people hear the word "saint," they say, "Ah, a bunch of shit." Our world today doesn't want to deal with that; they don't want to think about saints. They think saints are all these crazies or something like that.

But it's the people who understand this and are struggling with this, who are doing some things out in life. That's one of the great principles, it's one of the hardest ones to do. I mean just on a normal day-to-day level. . . .

The Keene (N.H.) Sentinel

It seemed to be a nice idea to celebrate the wackiness of it and have a good time.

Chick Colony

THE INTERNATIONAL ZUCCHINI FESTIVAL

E VEN saints must raise money sometimes. The nature of American community life is that people belong to voluntary groups, and more often than not these groups must spend cash.

Traditional fund-raisers are very much alive. At any moment of the year, you can bet safely that someone is holding a bake sale, flea market, or quilt raffle, or charting one out. And with good reason, for these methods work—at least well enough that the same groups will be back next year, with nearly the same events.

But it's also possible to think bigger, to do something with a few more ripples and a little more splash. If you can stage an event that kindles a lot of laughter, makes a lot of money, builds a lot of spirit, starts a new tradition, and puts your town on the map in the process, that might be worth paying attention to. Especially if you come from a country village such as Harrisville, New Hampshire (population 901), and if you use homegrown ingredients, in this case zucchini squash.

I first heard about the International Zucchini Festival on the car radio while driving home from vacation. I remember smiling, then later on reflecting why the smile stayed with me. Maybe it has something to do with the need for fun and celebration, for unraveling and release in our lives. If someone took a poll, "Are you having fun right now?", I wonder what the answer would be.

Now, to have an International Zucchini Festival or something of that order, the main ingredients would seem to be some people willing to put it together, a theme, possibly a cause, and not much more. But if that is so, then why aren't events like this taking place all over the countryside? Or in other words, why is so much community life so dry, and what happened here that made the difference?

Many people have shared responsibility for the zucchini festivals in Harrisville, but the starting idea can be traced to Chick and Pat Colony. Chick runs a fabric design and weaving business. Pat was raising three young children. They live directly above the post office in the middle of town. Chick, for his part, studied English literature at college, served in the Coast Guard, dropped out of business school, got involved in local historic preservation; but neither he nor other villagers has acknowledged formal training in fund-raising or festival organizing. So reasons for success must run deeper.

The International Zucchini Festival has been enormously successful by any common standard—new festivals have sprung up as far away as Oregon—but Chick's own manner is notably low-key. This creator seems unattached to his creation, which is one way to approach your work.

It may be that Chick has placed the festival in its proper perspective; or that other life events have taken up space; or that Chick has simply realized that success can seed its own destruction. There's more than one way to have fun, and nothing dictates that any effort should be forever—even though, when in the midst of things, you might let all doubts slide.

✳

I was wondering myself how we fit it together. One thing that's important is that zucchinis themselves are kind of an agricultural joke around here. I mean, anybody who has a garden in New England has this problem of what to do with these things that grow so fast that you fall over them in the morning and they weren't there the night before.

I remember, we used to define loneliness as someone buying zucchinis late in August in a supermarket (laughs). And then we used to say around Labor Day, you'd better lock your car when you go to Keene*, because if you don't people are going to fill it with zucchinis (laughs). Every year these incredible things would grow. And it got to be sort of a joke.

Well, my wife Pat and I sort of came up with the idea—I don't remember how except probably just talking about it—we thought we should have some celebration of this phenomenon. The humor of it seemed to be a natural, and it seemed to be a nice idea to celebrate the wackiness of it and have a good time. So we just started making lists of contests—we sort of fantasized about this festival, without really ever thinking that it could happen.

---

*The market town closest to Harrisville.

It got to be kind of a topic of conversation. So when people would come over for dinner, and even total strangers, after dinner we'd be sitting around and talking and somehow the subject of zucchinis would come up. We didn't actively try to bring it up, but we got to the point where we had this list of events, and we used to keep it in a drawer in our dining room. And many times we'd just reach over, open the drawer, pull this list out, and talk about this festival. And then other people would add to the list, we'd just write them right down.

Everybody seemed to like the idea, you know, things like the zucchini look-alike contest, or the longest-traveled, or the furthest or the roundest or the biggest or the best—I mean just all the obvious things. It was never meant to be anything very serious.

Then as two or three years went by of doing this, we used to talk a little more seriously about whether actually anything like this could ever happen. Pat and I both had quite a good picture in our minds of how the thing might happen—not that it really would happen, but wouldn't it be really nice if it could happen. So I guess it grew from a joke to being something that looked like it might actually be possible to do. We never could figure out a reason for it to happen. It had to be a cause, I think; just to do it for the fun of it I think would be pointless. So it needed a little more focus, or a little more raison d'être.

And then the cause arrived. Antioch-New England [a graduate school specializing in counseling and psychotherapy training] moved from Vermont to Harrisville. And while they were here, one of the projects they started was a preschool, a private preschool, called the Harrisville School. And when they moved to Keene, they left the school behind, because some people in the community had gotten interested in it, and the school became the town's.*

Their fund-raising had been a constant problem for them, in that they could never generate much money at any one time. So they would have a contra dance; they would have a food sale; they had a talent show. Then they had once a year something called the Black Flies Ball, where you would just take something like black flies, which is a given and a nuisance to everybody, and somehow kind of celebrate it, making it a little more bearable than it might otherwise be. So they had a track record of a humorous approach to doing things.

So we knew they were having problems with their fund-raising. And what we did one day is we talked to someone who was quite involved in the school. We said, look, would the school be interested in a major fund-raising

---

*New Hampshire has no statewide public kindergarten, but the town of Harrisville had voted to fund one year's tuition to the Harrisville School for all residents. So while the school was privately owned, in a sense it was a public institution.

event? It would involve a lot of planning by a few people, and a lot of work by a lot of people for one day. She said she thought so. So what she did was ask a number of people at the school to get together, and they came to our house and we had a meeting, in the dead of winter, around our dining room table. And we talked to them about the concept.

I'd say the first meeting was sort of a spiritual meeting, you know—let's talk about the idea, get a lot of laughs. Everybody started throwing things in. Like my wife Pat had seen "zucchini power" and a clenched fist holding a zucchini as an offshoot of the takeoff. And someone said, "Well, why don't we call it 'no cukes'?" We don't have a great bunch of comedians here, but it was that sort of spontaneous creativity that immediately lent itself to the thing. And we started talking about an organizational plan for how we'd do it: what we'd have to do before, what we'd do during, what we would do after. This was just on a note pad. This is an organizational chart, the first one.

Right away, most of the issues became apparent. It's easy to say what the jobs are. It was a little more complex to get them assigned and done. We sort of picked people who would be in charge of each different thing, like promotional materials, publicity, liaison with the town.

And I think Nancy had a very good sense of what talents were available to her.* She had a very interesting way of doing it. She made a big list of people who could be of help, in lots of different ways; she had almost a hundred names on this list. And we went to a party at her house, she had dinner for us, and part of the job was for people to select helpers from this list. In fact, she had each name on a little sticker, you pull off and stick on. And someone would say, "Well, I'm going to be doing T-shirts, so I want this person on my committee." We all just kind of made those judgments ourselves. She was very good; I didn't realize how organized she was.

The core organization became called Zucchini Central. Everything was kind of tongue-in-cheek. We were maybe eight, eight to twelve people I would say. We worked independently; there wasn't that much to do, physically. There was mainly the coordination, and Nancy got a notebook under her arm and went around all the time with it—and she's the one who would call on the phone and say how are you doing with such and so, do you need any help, can we get anybody to do this? We didn't do too much as a group; we probably met four or five times between then and summer. But we knew right away that the real involvement was going to come just

---

*Nancy Hayden, then the key contact person at the Harrisville School, and the person who coordinated much of the original festival planning.

the week before. What we wanted was to hold everybody back and then really concentrate on the day itself.

We actually did do press releases and things. We didn't try to overdo it, although what happened was that the media got kind of excited about it, and so they would tend to embellish it like crazy. They weren't asking us for things, they weren't leading us on, but they sure gave us lots of play. And they enjoyed it. So not only would they just have it in the news, but radio announcers would jawify about it and bat it around. It was one of those things that kind of snowballed on itself. For instance, here's a clipping in early August of '82—right in the front of this little shopper newspaper, there's the Postmaster of Harrisville in his garden looking at zucchinis. Now nobody asked him to do that. I mean, people just started doing things (laughs).

We were selling T-shirts maybe a month before the festival. The shirt was a strike fist that said "International Zucchini Festival," yellow with green printing. We didn't even dare put the date on them, 'cause we didn't know how many we'd sell—you know, we might want to use them next year. So a lot of the front money was provided by the sale of these T-shirts. And we kept running out, printing more, running out, and we sold them in the local store, health food store, fabric store, things like that; that sort of helped get people's spirits up for it.

I mean, everybody did their own thing. I took it on myself to make the buttons. The signs were done by the people who were running the events, and using zucchini as a word in strange ways was part of making the sign, like the zucchini regatta, or the zucchini balance beam, or the zucchini peel-off. We also put out this little brochure in advance, and the tone of the brochure got people all charged up about it, just the way it was put together. And then we had a program for the day itself. These are a couple of pictures of one of the kids jumping zucchinis. . . . People just did things they wanted to.

We charged people money to get in, but we didn't want people having money all over the place. So we thought it would kind of be adding to the festivity to have play money, and we came up with the idea of using what we called zukes and gadzukes, and I think it did work. They were actually poker chips.

That reminds me of a story about the poker chips. . . . I said, "Well, look, I'll worry about getting the play money." So I got out a catalog and I tried to figure out where poker chips come from. And I found this little company down in Rhode Island, Providence, and I called this guy up and I said we need them for a festival and we need green ones, and he said he could have green ones. And I said, "Well, what do I do? I mean, how do I get them?" He was a real Providence kind of a guy, you know, and he said (in mafioso voice), "Well, we make them up. And when we're ready, I call you. And you send some of your boys down to pick them up" (laughs). It was fun. There were a lot of little things like that.

I tried to be realistic about my expectations, and I thought there was a good chance that a couple of dozen people would do crazy things with zucchinis, and a couple of thousand people might watch them. But I first started to get encouraged when my father was really building toward an entry in one of the contests. As it turns out, it was the motorized zucchini contest that he was interested in getting into, and he developed a rocket-powered zucchini. I could tell he was really excited about keeping it a secret from everybody and building this, you know, zucchini on wheels, powered by a rocket that he bought from a local fireworks factory. I mean, seeing someone like that getting interested in participating made me think, gee, maybe this will actually work.

So as the summer built up, there was kind of a crescendo. But as we got closer to the actual date, we got a little bit nervous, because there had been all this media attention. For instance, there was one particular person, a vacation resident, who owns a house in the area where we were going to be. About ten days before the festival, he came to me, and he was really upset. And I said, "Well, I've been talking to you about this for months; how come you're upset now?" "It's because I hear it on the Boston radio stations, I mean, 'Dave Maynard in the Morning' telling me about this incredible festival in my backyard" (laughs).* He said, "This could be something. And you people don't know what you're getting into." Well, we got a little nervous, because we didn't know what was going to happen.

There was a set-up crew that worked a little bit the night before, then the next morning we all got up at six o'clock to pull it together. But seriously, until the thing started, we had no idea what it was going to be like.

We hadn't really thought through the coordination of people arriving, so we got caught off guard. For instance, in my naiveness I had my parking assistants show up at ten. Well, I forgot that the parade starts at ten. And so lots of people started arriving at 9:15. Well, it was total chaos, with people trying to get this parade ready, and cars arriving, and (laughs). . . . It really was a mess. But everybody was good-humored about it. I mean, it didn't seem very good-humored to me, because I was the one getting pounded on by the police and everything else, but it somehow worked.

---

*Boston is about seventy-five miles from Harrisville.

And it was exciting. It was a beautiful day, one of the first cool days of the summer. I would guess that probably three or four thousand people came and went. Mostly local, I'd say. But in parking cars I'd talk to people, and they'd say they'd come from Manchester or from Boston. Some people did come some distance.

And as it turns out, it was incredible. I mean lots of people came wearing zucchini jewelry, dressed up as zucchinis, entered contests, and everybody sort of took part. It wasn't a spectator thing in that sense; anybody who wanted to could do things. Every contest was whatever you wanted it to be. Like we had an itsy-bitsy teeny-weeny zucchini bikini contest—now, some people entered that with a zucchini with a tiny bikini on it, or a tiny bikini made out of zucchinis. I mean, you could sort of interpret every event any way you wanted to.

Take the agricultural hall, for instance. There was a contest there for best zucchini dessert—and how many do you know? There were twenty-five entries that just appeared that morning. People made cakes and puddings and all this kind of stuff. Some of them were jokes, but some of them were for real, and some of the things people did took an awful lot of work.

I'll never forget something at the festival itself that to me sort of summarized the whole thing. I was standing at the Zucchini Central at one point, and this fellow comes up to us—a total stranger, a man of about fifty-five, sixty years old, quite a heavyset man, in a coat, suit, and tie—and he said, and he was dead serious, "I've been to the agricultural hall, and I'm pretty upset there wasn't a category for my zucchini." And George [the master of ceremonies, or Zuke of Earl] said, "Well, you should go back over there, because you can create your own contest and enter your zucchini. What is it, anyway?" And he said, "I'll show you." He reached in his pocket and pulled out a little zucchini about that long, and he held it up to us like that and said, "The nicest" (laughs). It was like a little miniature zucchini. And we both looked at it and we looked at each other and we said, "You know, that *is* the nicest little zucchini we've seen" (laughs). And then he didn't break into a big laugh or make a joke out of it, he just walked away. People did sort of get into it in that sense. It was amazing. And we would look at each other and think, this is really working somehow (laughs); and it was good.

A lot of people came to the event, stayed an hour, got in their cars and went home, and got their friends and came back. I saw a lot of that in the parking lots, so it sort of built on itself. Everybody had a good time. We had to sort of forcefully shut it down, about four o'clock. People would have stayed . . .

This wastebasket just accumulated all the money. Nobody had any idea of whether we were making any money or not, although there seemed to be quite a bit floating around. We grossed about nine thousand, I think. And we made about half of that, which was more money than they'd ever made on all their fund-raising things put together in a year. The funny thing for Pat and me was the way the event came off was almost exactly the way we had visualized it. It worked just as well as we hoped it would work. And that really was amazing.

We didn't do it to pull the community together or anything like that. Harrisville is not a town that cries out for lots of changes. Although one of the things that became obvious was how much fun it was to celebrate something right in the middle of the village. During the festival, many people who live in town came up to us and said, "Isn't it great to be doing something like this right here in town?", because the town no longer has an old home day, it doesn't really have anything that celebrates itself, and it *should* have something like that.

But because of the preservation effort in the town, we've always tried not to raise a lot of attention in people's minds about Harrisville. There is something about the beauty of the setting that makes the festival go. No doubt about it. This is one of the particular problems that I find myself in now: the festival in a sense shines a light on the town that nothing else does, and that may not, in the long run, be good for the town. When we started the preservation project, many of the older people said to us: if you try to save this town, you're going to ruin it. Just by saving it, you will change it. And that will be bad. Well, that was the same risk we had here. And it's something that I worry about even still. You know, are we doing the right thing?

The festival was so much fun and so successful here that the people running it didn't want to change it; they wanted to recreate it exactly the same way the second time. To me that is really dangerous, especially for something as spontaneous as this was, because you're never going to be able to create quite the level of spontaneity you had.

Pat and I wanted to move the festival, because of the potential harm to the town. Our idea was we could do it once and probably get away with it; do it twice, it gets harder. We figured that if we had three thousand people the first year, we should put it in a place where we can *really* promote it and make a lot more money for the school—for instance, a ski area, where they have rock concerts in the summer. Because if three thousand people can have fun, ten thousand people can have fun. But ten thousand people can't have fun in Harrisville, because it's impossible to have ten thousand people here.

Well, the first year, we had to convince everybody to have it here. The second year, we had to convince everybody to move it; nobody wanted to move it. And they kind of wore us down. So the second time, fine, why not? And the third time around . . . the issue hardly even got raised.

Very easy to do it the second time. Nancy came around to all of us afterwards, and asked us if we would each write a one-page statement of what we did and how we did it, so that she could pass on that one page to the person who was going to do your job next year. And then a lot of people came forward and said, this is fantastic, how can I help, I'd like to be part of it. We toned down the publicity—the media was tired of it by then anyway. We sold tickets in advance, because the police and the people who coordinated it in town really wanted to get a handle on this thing—what *if* 10,000 people show up? And I think the potential in the second year was there, if we had wanted it to be.

It was much better run; I mean, we all knew how to do it. We knew where we had made money and where we hadn't made money the first year. And so the second year we maybe grossed twenty thousand dollars and made ten thousand dollars, off almost the same number of people who came. We realized we could charge more than a dollar to get in, nobody would care. We made more money on hot dogs and hamburgers, we made more T-shirts and sold them sooner, we just kind of refined the commercial aspects of it, without overdoing it—it was still a lot of fun. I was very skeptical, especially trying to recreate the same thing the second time. But it was very successful.

Anything that you organize, whether it's a business or an event like this, requires a certain amount of vision about what's going to happen when you get there, and what needs to be done between here and there, and a certain amount of planning. You can apply the same principles almost anywhere; but there has to be some seriousness going along with it. We were fortunate in the way it fell together; but I think in concept almost anybody who sat around and thought about it for a while could do it.

It was easy in that we didn't force it. It was not a great deal of hard work that anybody had to do. There was enough organization so that it delivered, without being overdone. People got something when they came here, even though their expectations were not sky-high—they came here with really no commitment or challenge to us to see something happen, and they were surprised when things did happen. Many of the people had worked together before. The things that were successful were allowed to become more successful; the things that weren't successful were allowed to die gracefully. The weather was terrific, the setting was just right for the number of people. We had a good sound system. It wasn't overly crowded, but it also wasn't spread out—and the humorousness of it made it go.

It was very hard to say what was going to happen (laughs), luckily. So there was a very strong element of surprise in it, which was good. And lack of division between you a spectator and you a participant; the way the festival worked was if we were going to have a zucchini relay, you'd say, "Hey, step back, here comes the zucchini relay!" Everybody was right in amongst it—I mean, the guy standing next to you could be in costume. You'd walk in a gate, and it would be like joining the fantasy of what was happening there. You couldn't get away from it. Now that we're talking about it, this may have had something to do with my own personal conditioning, because I lived in the French Quarter in New Orleans for three years, and I lived through Carnival . . .

I have no idea of what's going to happen this year. I mean, we're going to have it again, the third year. It's the same school group, some of the same people. And some newer people too; one way to keep it going is you change the people. I have some personal doubts about it; last year when we finished, my attitude was let's change it radically and do it a different way.

But success is hard to walk away from. It's hard to say, okay, we're not going to do it again, we're going to do something else instead. I'm a little doubtful about the ability of the thing to sustain itself much longer. But it's all in good fun—it can't be a major disaster.

The fact that it can't sustain itself I don't think is anything negative about the event at all. In fact, I think that may be a good thing, that it can't sustain itself. That's a testament to its originality. You asked me before would it bother me if it didn't continue, and I don't think it would, you know. We've done what we wanted to do with it.

I mean, I'd just as soon do it, but I certainly don't have the enthusiasm I had for it the first time. If you have the enthusiasm then you can project enthusiasm, and then generate it at the event. If you don't—if you're flat, you'll appear flat, and the whole thing will be flat. It can never be as good as it was the first time. The intensity or the spontaneity of it is almost impossible to sustain. Although we did pretty well—I mean, we made twenty thousand dollars in six hours, which isn't bad for a bunch of volunteers.

What I'm really concerned about is the school itself. You know, being able to fill the gap, the financial gap, left in its wake. But I think there are people in the school thinking, well, if we're not going to do the Zucchini Festival, let's do something else, a one-day big-time event. I don't know. I'm not sure. . . . In fact, we have another meeting . . .

I remember someone sitting up there giving a zucchini poem, and I was thinking not how great it was that we gave them a chance to get up there and give it, but look how much fun that person's getting out of delivering this zucchini poem. So I think the originality of the idea was fun, but seeing how people responded to it was the most fun.

And people responded in very personal terms. We didn't take any credit for it at all. I think it's sort of an abstract thing to be taking credit for. We didn't do that much; we didn't feel that we were promoters in that sense. We let it happen, kind of. . . .

*

The Third Annual International Zucchini Festival was held in Harrisville in August 1984, as part of the 1984 Vegetable Olympics—zucchini against all comers. The games began with the arrival of the edible torch. A local pundit, Gourd Orwell, remarked in that year's program, "Some vegetables are more equal than others."

The fourth festival, a year later, did in fact move from Harrisville to the larger town of Keene. The theme was "Zucchini Goes to College!!!! Off the Farm and into the World of Competition—Watch Out World!" Contests that year included Most People Squashed into a Zucchini Crate, Best Zucchini Rock Video (½″ VHS tape), and Zucchini Least Likely to Get a Date to the Prom.

The problem in this society is that we've taken most civic work away from people, so that most people don't know what to volunteer for.

Ray Shonholtz

COMMUNITY BOARDS

W HEN people are decently housed, and maybe having fun, one next step toward an ideal community is helping them love their neighbors as themselves. Failing that, we can at least keep neighbors from each other's throats, and cleanse the air of menace that pervades many urban streets.

Conflict may always be with us. And conflict resolution, current reports say, is a growth industry. But Ray Shonholtz sees conflict as a growth *opportunity*, an opening for making community life better. It's not unlike the way Marti Stevens uses conflict to extract an actor's best performance: emotion must be expressed before the listener can be moved.

For small-scale neighborhood conflicts like barking dogs, curbside litter, or parking of cars, you're not yet ready for a lawyer, and you can't call the police night and day. These are the black flies of urban living, conflicts that seem so small yet can drive you mad. But there's an alternative to despair or rage or doing something you might regret, and that's using the conflict-resolving skills neighbors already have available. When properly motivated, Ray Shonholtz believes, people have an enormous desire to do civic work.

Ray Shonholtz teaches and refines conflict resolution skills and has created a full-dress volunteer neighborhood justice system through a model program he started called Community Boards. Neighborhood residents, trained in listening and communication techniques, sit on panels. Disputants come before panels to work out resolutions, with the panels' help. No judgments are made, and no costs are incurred.

It's 5:00 P.M. on a Friday afternoon, and it is *hot* for San Francisco, eighty-five degrees or so, your average summer high plus fifteen. But in the Community Boards office downtown, papers rustle and copiers hum. No one seems to be going home. I comment on that, and one staffer says, "This isn't like the rest of the world. I thank God every day I work here." Ray must not be your average boss.

Inside his office, there are honors and community tributes on the walls. A Bobby Kennedy quote on the responsibility of citizenship hangs nearby; the sixties live. A card signed by the staff wishes Ray a happy and well-deserved vacation. There's also a placard which says, quoting roughly:

> I hereby pledge all my property and personal possessions to Community Boards. If called upon, I will gladly give my life for Community Boards.
>
> _____
>
>   (signed)

The man himself is visibly tired, and is popping cold capsules when we get back to his apartment. He listens first to messages from woman friends on his answering machine, and calls one back; then we're ready to roll.

In doing these interviews, sometimes I'd need to ask a lot of questions, while other times I'd simply press the "record" button. Ray falls in the latter category; but in no interview before or since have I heard anyone speak in such complex, eloquent, rich, and heartfelt sentences. This is a man who completely believes in the civic responsibility and the civic capacity of the ordinary citizen, and who knows how to draw it out.

I've been involved in community programs since the mid-1970s, but tonight I am a student. I remember driving away after the interview, no car music, and thinking that here is someone who has truly taught me about the philosophy and the strategy as well as the style of community work.

*

I really came about 1974 to feel strongly that the legal system is not reformable. You can ameliorate its worst aspects, but it is an industry. It's an industry, and like most industries it's most likely to be reformed by economics—that's what lawyers are feeling now. That allows for new things to happen, that might be reformist. But basically, it's not a reformable system.

The whole professionalism of social life makes people feel impotent.

Professionalism is a decision by a society to give more resources to fewer people. It is to say that one does better by developing a cadre of people with special skills, instead of dispensing those resources over a broader number, giving everybody a certain modicum of those skills. You end up having a group of people who say that they're so professional no one else can do it. Lawyers have a monopoly on dispute resolution. Doctors have a monopoly on anything to do with medicine.

The effect of that, though, is to make people feel incompetent. If this is a legal or this is a medical matter, who am I? I don't have those skills. And I think that's very dangerous in a democratic society.

What you really want to do is to make people responsible. Because if they're not responsible, then they'll shuck it, and they'll say, "Oh, that's a medical issue, that's not my business"; "Oh, that's a legal issue, call the police." Yet we clearly see, particularly in the area of prevention, the early identification of conflicts and problems, that if citizens don't perform the function, none of these professions drops low enough into the community to perform it. That's why they're all after-the-fact bureaucracies and systems.

The nature of Community Boards is to get conflicts *before* they violate, say, the criminal law—an area that the state in a democratic society can't ever enter. The way we have it set up in our constitutional system, there is no state interest in a conflict unless there's a violation of law. The violation of law is the *lowest* standard of behavior. Neighborhoods need a *much* higher standard of behavior than the lowest denominator articulated by the criminal law.

People need to know they can walk down streets and greet their neighbors, as opposed to being hit or spat upon. We *do* want kids to help old ladies across streets, and take cats down from trees. I mean, we do want all that kind of stuff, it seems to me. But only people can model that; nobody can order them in a democratic society to do anything like that.

When there are disputes in the neighborhood that are at such a point that intervention would be useful to de-scale the tension and hostility, only citizens can do that work in a democratic society, because there's no violation of law that brings a police officer legitimately to intervene. That's a roundabout way of saying that there's tremendous civic work to be performed, but it's all pre-fact, it's before the fact; our entire justice industry is after the fact, just like the health industry. It's all after the fact; primarily because that's where professionals make money.

But a society needs many prevention tools. And only citizens in their *civic* capacity, in their *civil* life, can perform that. Well then, there's a whole range of work for people to perform. The approach of Community Boards was to get the cases before they got to the police.

As I travel around the country, increasingly I'm feeling there's a tremendous hunger by citizens, all races and ethnicities, to engage in civic work. Because it makes them feel more relevant; it makes them feel more connected to people in their community, the things that they hold dear.

The problem in this society is we've taken most civic work away from people, so that most people don't know what to volunteer for. There's the PTA, that has no power within a school; there's people candy-striping for hospitals, who have no power within that setting. That's not what I mean by civic work. I mean realms of work that but for the citizen's participation wouldn't get performed, wouldn't be accomplished. Community Boards is an excellent example of that.

The people themselves, if they're provided an opportunity to work, will do amazing things, as long as they own that work. If it's truly their work, and they can see some legitimate, relatively immediate results from it. And if it improves the quality of their life, their children's lives, the neighborhood, the school life—people will give a tremendous amount of time. There's nothing that these people couldn't do, if they wanted to do it.

The idea for Community Boards comes out of a task force of attorneys I was directing in 1974 and '75 for the [California] Assembly Committee on Criminal Justice. We were charged to redraft the state penal code. In the task force, we were all of like mind, that the earliest exclusion of youth from the justice system would be socially advantageous.

We looked at a couple of models, one in Norway and one in Scotland. The Scottish program had citizens, Scottish citizens, on juvenile panels, appointed by the judge. And then Norway has what they called temperance boards, referring people who are inebriates to panels made up of one's peers. But this was not viewed as a criminal action, it was viewed as a social action, using the idea of peer pressure, versus penal pressure, to [get] somebody to straighten up their drinking habits.

Both these ideas, the idea of the social pressure and the citizen panels, I felt had tremendous merit. I remember constantly being bugged by this notion of panels. I was constantly thinking about it. I thought, "What an intriguing idea. . . ." I myself have a fairly strong trial background; I'm a criminal attorney. And really, I felt like for the vast majority of cases, citizen panels couldn't do any worse than the nothingness that was happening through a very expensive penal system. I mean, there isn't a single urban court in the United States that hears more than five percent of the cases filed. So the bottom line was, even if it was a failure, it couldn't be a complete failure; I mean, there would be a lot of social advantages from it.

Well, when I started Community Boards, I understood that it was . . . an unusual idea. The notion of lay people and citizens in the community being recruited and asked to do conflict resolution work in the community needed a lot of support. Particularly to funders, and to political people.

My first effort was to build some credibility for the idea by associating people with it of some standing in the criminal justice community, which meant people in the bar association, the district attorney's office, et cetera— to at least say it was an interesting idea, worth experimenting with.

I wrote a concept paper in very early '76, made fifty copies of it, distributed them to the legal community, and to some community organizations. And then asked some friends of mine around the city to put me on the agenda for community organization meetings, public defender office meetings. And I started making contacts with all of them, not [for them] to endorse it—I never asked anybody to endorse it—but merely to give it conceptual credence.

The advantage of that is that you avoid anybody critiquing it too early, and kind of have all the benefits of getting what you really want, which is some green light like "This idea interests me," signed, "The Prosecutor." Since I didn't ask for more, I didn't get more, but those kind of support positions grew to be extremely useful with funders.

I also felt that the idea needed as much political support as possible. When I started, the federal government under Carter was interested in dispute resolution. And Community Boards at that time was the only experiment even being conceptualized that actually was a complete community-based model, not annexed to any justice unit. And that was leveraged a lot. So when the federal government came out with a report on different potential neighborhood justice models, Community Boards was one of the six cited, . . . which in turn gave it a possibility to turn around and cite the federal government, as giving credibility to the idea. It feeds on itself.

And I was a credible person: teaching at the law school, being an Associate Professor of Criminal Law, putting it on law school stationery, circulating the idea around. That added to the credibility of it, because stature, name, connections, I think, have a lot to do with whether an idea gets some hearing or is quickly dismissed. I spent a lot of time around the politics of the idea, so that nobody came out opposing it. There were some people who were skeptical, but then I only would ask for conceptual support, for trying it—not in the sense that it was a meritorious idea, but one that ought to be given some chance.

Well, there are very few people who won't give you that, you know. So I had very little if any opposition in the early days. Not that it has any now, but it was very important to build a conceptual constituency within the legal community for it.

Before any services were delivered, I built a board of directors of name people, who expanded on the idea of giving it a chance—some community people, but a nice balance of lawyers and judges, very friendly to the idea.

Then, in the funding proposals, I would cite the support that we had received from different organizations, and leverage that with the funders, to say, "Look at the range of interests in this unique idea." In addition, I became relatively skillful at educating the funding base.

The only public money that was around was from the Law Enforcement Assistance Administration, which had then a terrible track record with community people. And in a city as political as San Francisco, the law enforcement money just wouldn't fly. So in the early days, it took a lot of engineering to get them to not support the project; but not to not support it to such a degree as to ding it, just not to give it money.

I didn't want their money. But the foundations asked, "Why are you coming to us? This is a justice project, where is the government?" My response was, "This idea is too advanced for the government. This is too experimental. The government won't support it." And then what I did was I submitted proposals to the government in a manner that I knew they would turn them down. So when they turned them down, I said, "You see, I showed you that at least I applied. And see, they turned it down. But you, Mr. Foundation, you're far more progressive than the federal government. Your job is to fund innovative risky projects."

Now, I also learned, foundations fund people first and ideas second. The foundation wants to know that the person they're funding isn't a kook. Regardless of what the idea is, they want to know that the person has a reasonable chance of delivering, or at least making a reasonable effort to attempt to deliver it, if it's a very risky idea. So credibility becomes the first and primary issue for most sophisticated foundations. Who you are and who supports you will be the first determining factor of whether a foundation gives you money.

And my process with the funders was always to see the executive director of the foundation, not a program officer. It's to use one funder to network with other funders. So if one person in the funding community felt strongly about it, I would ask her or him who this should go to, could I use their name in the letter; or better yet, would they make a call for me indicating that I was going to call so-and-so. If not that, could I use their name as a reference in the letter. And invariably they'd say yes to one or the other of those openings.

The issue with the foundation is getting through the door. Once you're through the door, you have to be your own salesperson. But you need a door-opener; somebody has to be the bridge, help you over the bridge, that's been my experience. So if I wanted to deal with the Ford Foundation, I'd need somebody who knew the Ford Foundation who would say, "Hey, this program you should look at, and I'll let so-and-so know you're going to call them." And that of course is a time-honored approach; I don't think there's anything unique about that.

But the funding community responds well to that, because they get so many requests, and most of them don't have the staff to screen, so they don't know . . . see, they all operate on the basic principle of people first, ideas second, I think. That might be simplistic, but I think it's generally true. That increases the importance of somebody to take you through the door.

There was a lot of pressure early on, mostly by funders, to say, well, okay, if we give you the money, where are you going to start? What part of San Francisco are you going to do it in? And that became a very important question.

I wanted a community that was sufficiently interested in justice issues, and did not have many competing community interests or organizations, and that was isolated enough. So I was looking for a community where it could succeed, and at the same time where I could cut my losses if it didn't. And I found a community like that, in the southeast section of the city, Visitacion Valley. Very interested in a variety of social, mostly crime issues, didn't have a lot of community leaders, very few community organizations, the local churches weren't terribly strong. So it made for coming with a new program idea seem ideal.

I went to them and explained the idea. In most organizations, there are a few key people that make the difference. I spent time with several of those key people. So when the meetings came, those key people were prepared to stand up and say this thing deserves a chance, or I'm interested, or I'll go through the training; that broke the ice.

I had two organizers also that I had hired at that point. And we put together a planning group, of about twenty people, about ten black and ten white. And we were the first organization in the city that brought facilitation to the neighborhoods; we hired Interaction Associates, and they facilitated a series of planning meetings. People had never seen a facilitator before; what the hell was that all about? But it freed everybody up to work, because the essence of good facilitation is building consensus towards the product, and doing that in a heavily black-white community is a very important strategic piece.

Then we went to the housing projects, leafleted the housing projects, door-knocked on the housing projects, door-knocked in the community, concerning the first training program. We had target areas. We used churches, one or two community organizations. And we attracted a small group of people, maybe twenty, twenty-five, something like that. And we put them through a training program that we had designed, conflict resolution modeling. We contracted with the American Arbitration Association and the Community Relations Service to deliver the training the first time around, because we really didn't know enough about it to do it ourselves.

And then we worked like dogs to get cases. You know, how do we convince the disputants to give us their case? If you're a disputant (laughs), you don't know anything about this thing, you're going to be somewhat reluctant. It took a lot of education. One of the tremendous needs of all these kinds of volunteer programs is education, because everybody is told to call 911, 911, 911. Nobody is told to call Community Boards, call Community Boards, call Community Boards. That was a lot of hard work.

We didn't hear our first case till the very end of '77, something like nine months or so [after we started]. That still holds to be the norm.

We got our first case . . . we leveraged our first case, advertised widely about the first case, heard subsequent cases. And then, I decided it was really important to keep the program moving. There's an advantage to complex social programs to maintain a high degree of momentum, moving down several tracks simultaneously. The merits of the idea could not be decided on Visitacion Valley. We had learned a lot, and jumped over to Bernal Heights, a whole other community.

And it went like wildfire in Bernal Heights, for the first two years. Organizing was very well done, 'cause we'd learned how to do it. We had a lot of potlucks—food is an important issue, in terms of people breaking bread together, and the other camaraderie. So Visitacion Valley and Bernal Heights were very strong communities.

And then, based on that, we raised more money, on the basis of wanting to say, well, it's interesting that it works in a relatively heterogeneous community, but would it work in a Hispanic community; would it work in a straight middle-class white community? Those questions were of sufficient interest to the funders as well.

I continued to raise more money, and as I did I could open more offices, the notion being that . . . this wasn't a poor person's program, it wasn't a low-income person's program. And it wasn't a white person's program, it wasn't a black person's program; this was just a people's program that provided services for everybody. And it would be used by everybody if it was accessible, at the neighborhood level. It was based on using the diversity of neighborhoods by having people coming together for a common purpose. I was able to generate a lot more money. And that's how I did it.

So Community Boards went from about $86,000 in 1977, to $350,000 in 1981, to $600,000 in 1984, so it's grown tremendously financially. It also has a very very large funding portfolio. I would say probably as many as thirty foundations over the history of the program have supported it, and about maybe a dozen and a half actively support it now.

That was a very intentional strategy on my part; it's worked very well. It takes a hell of a lot more work, but no one foundation is into you so much that, (a) if they pulled out they'd remove your possibility of functioning, and (b) none is in it so much that they could dictate what you're to do. So it leaves the impetus constantly on the creator and the organization to move. Even if they give you $100,000, it's still a $600,000 program.

✳

It's more than a $600,000 program now. Community Boards has been branching out, into more than twenty San Francisco neighborhoods, across into Oakland, and into other cities. A local affiliate, the Community Board Center for Policy and Training, does workshops cross-country. The program has sparked interest overseas as well.

Closer to home, a School Initiatives Program started in 1982. Conflict resolution courses and student "conflict manager" programs were launched in San Francisco public schools, the rationale being that if you learn to take more responsibility for conflicts as a child, you will take more responsibility for conflicts as an adult. Community Boards is investing in the next generation.

✳

I loved the idea. I mean, I've loved Community Boards. I've been doing it a while, and I probably don't radiate the same enthusiasm perhaps, but there was nothing in the early days I could read that I didn't translate into relevancy for Community Boards. And I was working fifteen, sixteen hours a day, six, seven days a week, that was my regular tempo. I've been the big drumbeater of Community Boards, for sure, in terms of time, and, you know, kept the staff working at a very heavy pace for several years.

I don't think I'm the only person who could have done it, but I tend to think that a combination of a lot of things was very important: the connections with political people, credibility in the legal community, and enthusiasm. I think probably the greatest ingredient for someone who's starting something new is to be able to articulate and transmit the enthusiasm, so that it's contagious. And my enthusiasm got transmitted to the volunteers, that had a lot to do with it.

I think the enthusiasm is critical. I think that one could have intellectualized this work and not gotten anywhere in the neighborhoods. People engage your sincerity. Since they're not being paid for the work, they have to feel they're part of a bigger picture, they're part of something that's really exciting. And that the person who's talking about it is not only excited about it but prepared to put body and limb on the line and be there, knock on doors, and go to the potlucks, and go to all the hearings. In the early days, I went to all the meetings, all the hearings, everything. I mean, nothing took place in Community Boards in any of the neighborhoods that I didn't attend.

In terms of where the enthusiasm comes from . . . I think for someone like myself it comes from the excitement of making a real contribution, a real change. I think I was a very good trial lawyer, but just never felt it made a difference. That's a big part of it.

I think you have to be committed—if you waffle on that, people will feel it, that you're not one hundred percent committed to it. That's probably critical for more intellectual, professional people who've got training, like myself. Because I don't think community people are necessarily trusting on day one; you have the option as a professional person to be there day one and gone day two.

What motivates people is the feeling that they make the difference. They are the critical principle. And then, as they become enthusiastic, it's the affinity ties—white to white, black to black—of enthusiastic people that bring more people.

An example: Community Boards opens a job position, it'll get anywhere from one hundred to four hundred responses in the city. It doesn't matter what it pays; it's so well known in the city as a good organization to work for. If we open a senior position, my God, we get deluged with résumés, from people who've got great jobs, who'll take salary cuts, because there's something about the élan of it. . . .

So, as Community Boards started to grow, and as my own conception of it began to expand very dramatically, I began to see it as a whole other system.

I mean, it's many things. It's a new justice model. It's a neighborhood stabilization program. It's a volunteer service delivery system. It's training volunteers to assert leadership in their community. It's a new philosophy about conflict, viewing it positively instead of negatively. It's a prevention program. It's like a diamond with many facets to it, so that it depends who you talk to, which facet you emphasize.

When we first started, we were recruiting people just to sit on panels. The breakthrough for the organization and for my own thinking was when some of the community members who had been panelists wanted to be trainers [of panelists]. They'd sat on panels and they wanted to participate. Some of the professional people that had been around the program refused to train them, on the grounds that we couldn't train lay people as trainers.

We struggled a lot around that. Then we found some people who would help us train them. And we upgraded one of our own staff people to learn how to be a trainer—we brought that skill in-house.

But the fact that community people wanted to be trainers was for me one of those lights that dawned; because I said, well, if community people can be trainers, then they could do the casework and the outreach, they could do everything else—and that's where we are now conceptually in the organization.

Now we recruit people to do casework, the outreach work, the follow-up work, the planning, the training, all the governance work; we've opened up enormous civic roles for people, all throughout the program. That's one of the reasons very few people leave Community Boards. 'Cause there's always another job they can get trained to do. There's an infinite range of functions for people when you start opening a volunteer service delivery system; it has tremendous needs. And a neighborhood has all the people in it who can fill all those needs.

And I've gotten to be very hard on people in our community, saying, "Look, if you want it, you have the wherewithal in terms of people to do it." Communities have to hear that they have responsibility and they have to take it. They can't bitch and moan that they don't have any power. The irony of the democratic society is that the citizen is really and truly all-powerful—and should they organize, my God, they are *incredibly* powerful.

But they're left to feel like they're impotent. I think that's done on purpose—so citizens feel like they can't do anything, you know. But you bring some together, and you build around it a reasonable organizational structure, and you have clarity of purpose, then community people can do an incredible amount.

All urban communities for the most part in the United States, particularly larger cities, have tremendous social problems. People say they have housing problems, they have unemployment, they have all those. Those problems generate the problems that kill people.

A person loses his job, he doesn't shoot his wife because he lost his job. It's the tension that situation creates, that after a while he goes berserky. Loss of job is a real important social issue and I'm not discounting that at all. But the terribly negative impacts can be ameliorated for the home life if one has some tools to deal with it, so you don't end up in a fistfight at home. Then you can deal with the fistfight at home. So you're then better able and better equipped to deal with the loss of a job.

And when a plant closes, and thousands of people are thrown out of work, we know that there's going to be social problems, and personal problems. There's no way there's not going to be conflict. Well, if the community was really prepared for that, it would have developed intervention mechanisms. The community would respond, not in a penal way, but in a caring, social way.

The primary issue for a community is to develop a mechanism that can help people assist people in the resolution of conflict—but not to get the disputants to resolve it, as much as to express it. Because if you can get people to express their anger, and really and truly express it, and really get it out, well, they're not going to be angry at the same level. I mean there's just so much anger and emotions that people have. They will get it out of their system.

It doesn't mean they're buddy-buddies with the person they're angry with. But they're not going to be violent with that person. In fact, numerous times in the Community Board cases, people will come in angry at one another, walk out arm in arm, or one disputant will take the other disputant home; and that's true even if they haven't resolved the dispute. Because they've got the anger out, and they've also had a chance to hear the other side.

The flip side is you can walk into a small claims courtroom any day, any part of the country, and the judge is giving resolutions out right and left, but people are often leaving the courtroom angrier, more pissed off, than when they went in.

And that's why I will say to people at the graduation: "Your job is not get people to resolve a dispute. You never have to dream up a resolution for anybody. You never have to think anything up; that's not your job. Your job, when you sit on that panel, is to make certain you're applying all your communication and conciliation skills towards getting the disputants to express their emotions in the conflict.

"Because if they do that, and they do it well, they won't be violent towards each other. So you in the community who are doing this service to reduce tensions and hostility, you have succeeded; that is success, right there. If they go forward and make the world better for themselves tomorrow by resolving it, that's their responsibility. But you don't have any responsibility to come up with—as a judge might—with some resolution. No way. No need to even dream it up."

It's very freeing for the panelists then; the panelists don't have to play judges. The worst panelist is one who says, "I think you should do X." Because the disputants don't want to hear that. They don't want to be told—no American wants to be told what to do, you know—they feel like saying, "Tough." And if nobody says anything to them, well, they'll come up with their own resolution. Because the truth of the matter is, most people are intelligent, and people will tell you what they want out of a conflict, once their emotions have been dealt with.

But we also have numerous instances of community members seeing a dispute, then crossing a street in their neighborhood, walking right over and introducing themselves and saying, "I think I can help." These are handled, and Community Boards never knows about them at all, until somebody comes up and says, "Gee, I did this interesting thing at my work site," or "I did an interesting thing with my two neighbors," or "At my bridge club meeting, I did. . . ." These are stories I hear all the time.

Now if you had those taking place throughout a whole community, or a whole city, on a regular basis—first of all, the mirroring of that form of caring, is desperately needed in an urban society, desperately needed. [It would] certainly affect the issue of alienation and isolation of most urban dwellers' experience; it would itself effectively decrease the level of tension and hostilities we experience.

And if we did that one or two generations, over a twenty-year period— yeah, you'd see marked changes. I don't think these things are terribly mysterious.

After the system is functioning, it's not that you run out of ideas, but you might get bored. Boredom is a very important issue for a founder to be careful about, I think, because that's a sign of burnout. An early warning signal. If it starts becoming repetitive, or you're creating structures just for your own desire not to be bored, that's the time to say, okay, how do I get out of the organization, in a way that leaves it intact? How do I disengage and at the same time strengthen the organization?

That's very hard for most people to do. First of all, emotionally, 'cause you get, "Well, I am Community Boards. What'll I do, if I don't . . ." So there's a psychological dimension to it. And the second part is working very hard, and often bringing in some skilled people, to help you make the transition from a founder-based program to an institutionalized program, so all the founder functions are in the governing unit. It's a difficult process. Or it's an easy one, if the founder's relaxed. It can be a very good process, a growth process.

For about a year and a half or even longer I have been actively trying to turn over Community Boards to an elective body, and institutionalize all the founder functions, so they don't depend on me any longer. The Board of Directors and myself worked very hard last year, and fashioned a very impressive and strong elective representative unit, the San Francisco Governing Board, with a clear manifesto in terms of responsibilities and obligations and powers; gave it money; gave it hiring responsibilities. I mean, we just took the leap of faith. We just said, okay, we're going to do it.

Elections took place in the neighborhoods, and they ran very well; the board is an outstanding board. They went through the process of hiring a director, and it remains a very strong, democratic unit of the program. I sit on that board, as one of two representatives from the Board of Directors, and I'm now one of fourteen people. The institutionalization of the founder's role, that's a critical piece of recognition to community people that we're all grown up—the founder's stage is over. And for the last year and a half I've been anxious for this to happen.

Because I've been running Community Boards and running national programs and starting other things, and I've been very tired; I don't want to say burned out, but . . . tired, very tired. I think it's taken a toll out of me, this last year and a half.

✻

Ray has just moved into a new apartment. The only thing in the refrigerator is apple juice.

✻

Well, my personal life has changed. I was with a lady seven years, and her two kids, and I'm not with them any longer. I think being a workaholic, you know; being committed to making certain this things runs to a safe harbor, trying to be committed to it came first.

Work came first. And then completing this transition was very important. I think that my personal life in that regard has suffered, or I didn't provide enough time to my family life. I'm not too certain I have that many regrets about that, but I know it was a cause. . . . And I think by not taking care of myself I've gotten more tired than I otherwise would have.

Physically and emotionally. This society . . . most groups kill off leaders, you know; leadership is a fragile thing. It doesn't surprise me when someone shoots the pope, and somebody shoots the president. Leadership is constantly endangered in this society; people kill off leaders literally and figuratively. They kill them off.

So that when people say they are burned out, that's an important internalization of working hard. Its broader characterization is that the organization has worked to burn them out. They go together; it's the other side of the coin. As people in the organization become more powerful, they feel that the person they need to struggle with most is the founder, because the perception is the founder has all the power. That's probably not true; by the time people feel powerful, the founder has done a good job of giving up the power. But the imagery and the voice of the founder remains very very strong. It's the old totem thing, killing the king. It's very real in organizational life.

I think I've managed to escape that; it's been costly, but I'm alive and well (laughs). I know I'm alive and well, because I've been very strongly committed to the building of a democratic unit. You have to stay with the task until it's done, you can't waffle on it. And there'll be casualties along the way. But the truth of the matter is that it takes time, like anything else. If crafted well, it'll take more time, but it'll function.

So I think I have escaped being killed off, but, I don't run the organization. My title is President and Executive Director of the corporation, but I don't have directorship responsibilities over staff or training. So there's a trade-off—not getting killed off is to institutionalize the responsibilities in a unit that is reflective of a democratic sense of community.

It feels tremendously wonderful. And so, now, not running Community Boards, but being on the Governing Board, I feel tremendously freed up to do things that I think are so important to the field now.

My interest has been to build a new justice system. Not to replace the existing one, but to be complementary to it, yet a new justice system nonetheless. San Francisco's a place that's been selected to do that. I live here. I think it's a good city to do it in.

But the interest hasn't been to build a new justice system for San Francisco. I'd rather build a new justice system that's modeled by San Francisco, so that it's applicable anywhere. The level I'm actually working on, the practical level, has been a particular city. The application, however, is national. I tend to think quite frankly the work is international. Community Boards is now being looked at in France and Norway, Japan, Australia.

The same problems exist in all industrial countries. There's a hunger for a new model that will deal with local issues. The other side to it is—I know people say this and they kind of brush it aside—but I think it's very difficult to believe you can have peace internationally if you can't have peace at home. People don't know what it means to have peace internationally. I mean, if you can't trust your neighbors next door, can't talk to them, don't know how, you're more likely to feel like you don't know the Russians either, don't trust them and don't know how, and are more likely to be whipsawed around by that in terms of politics.

If everybody in the country had peacekeeping and peacemaking skills, then they'd ask some very basic questions about their government: Well, why aren't they practicing those things at a larger level. If you can do it, if blacks and Hispanics in low-income neighborhoods can get together, and do conflict resolution work together, those people will ask the question; well, why in hell can't the Russians and the United States do it?

They will ask, "What is so complex, really, about resolving this issue?" Is the issue trust? Well, hell, I didn't trust the black person next door six months ago either, but I went to a resolution and now I trust him. I may not like him—but I know he's not going to throw garbage next door, or over my fence any longer; I trust him on that. And when I think there's been a problem, I go over and talk with him. . . . Because I have direct experience in resolving that conflict. I've learned new skills.

So what disturbs me so much about the international stuff is that it's the same issue.

Three things need to take place: Community Boards in the city needs to be institutionalized as a public service, publicly funded, on the same basis that the city supports the prosecutor or a county hospital. Secondly, the state needs to develop these [programs] in neighborhoods throughout the state. Third, there needs to be a national association, which we're now helping develop, which will serve to champion the primary issue of citizen involvement in dispute resolution; and a national structure of organizations, the idea being that the major social structures in our society endorse that notion. Those three things will take place I think over the next twenty-four months.

I think the next thing I'd like to try, I've been playing around with a long time, is a medical prevention program. Train people to do medical prevention in neighborhoods, a volunteer service delivery system. Use the same model as Community Boards organizationally, because I think it's a good model: recruit people; let them do the service work; take some of them, train them as trainers; train the next group of people as service providers; then take the trainers, train them to be trainers of trainers; then develop a vertical and ever-expanding line of service providers.

We know clearly that the United States designed the best barefoot doctors program in the world. We did it in Iran in 1971 and 1972: we trained semi-literate village people in basic preventive health. We haven't ever done it in the United States. Why don't we do it? Because the AMA won't allow us to do it, that's why. It intrigues me. I think the medical field is an open field, a real wide open field for prevention. . . . Increasingly—I want to think, write, and develop a democratic volunteer service delivery system.

The democratic aspects of society are very weak. I think they need to be immediately shored up by real work. Unless people work, they don't understand what it means to be in a democratic society; they view it only as free speech, or getting the vote.

Those are important aspects of it, certainly, but it's much more than that. It's the opportunity to do civic work. If you don't do civic work, you can't be networked, and you're going to be alienated in a democratic society; you'll be treated like an atom. The only thing that brings people together is social work. There isn't anything else. You're not going to get paid to do social work, but it needs to be done; and it's the bonding that unifies the society.

It's now so essential that more people experience democratic volunteer systems. By their nature they're empowering, because they're skill-building and they provide training. So even if it bombed, even if it totally bombed, there's no way that you wouldn't leave people behind feeling infinitely more powerful in their own lives. Certainly more skilled, more informed, more connected. On that level it would be a great success. There's no way it could really fail. . . .

*You just have to say, I'm helpless, I don't know what to do,
before you can reach out.*

Phyllis and David York

TOUGHLOVE

L IKE several, but not all the people in this book, Phyllis and David
York got involved in community work that arose from personal
trauma.

Their youngest of three daughters was arrested for robbing a cocaine dealer, the capping point of a history of troubles. They'd tried
everything they knew to help her, without success. (And they were
family therapists, though not immune from family problems themselves.) A threshold had been crossed: they couldn't bring themselves
to bail their daughter out of jail. When the last straw has been applied,
you've got to get out from under.

Instead they turned to their friends for help. They asked for community support, and they got it. Out of that incident, *TOUGHLOVE*
was born.

TOUGHLOVE is an approach for parents who have trouble raising
their teenage children, or whose teenagers are getting into trouble, and
usually both. The approach typically involves parent self-help groups
which meet regularly to support each other, to change family behavior,
and to set limits, or "bottom lines." More than one thousand such
groups meet nationally.

The "love" part of *TOUGHLOVE* includes setting reasonable and
fair behavioral standards, so that teenagers can grow to be responsible
and caring adults. The "tough" part means enforcing those standards,
calmly but unfailingly, up to and including, if necessary, committing
the teenager to treatment, refusing to appear in court, and evicting the
older teenager from the house. Other *TOUGHLOVE* parents, if
needed, can temporarily take your place. These more extreme and
media-catching, if relatively infrequent actions have not met with uni-

versal approval. *TOUGHLOVE* can really be tough, and may not be for everyone.

What often gets lost in criticisms of *TOUGHLOVE* is the Yorks' belief that the community is accountable for the raising of kids. If kids go wrong, it's partly because community standards have been poorly defined or poorly taught. Parents have primary responsibility, schools have some, but you and I are also responsible for making sure that kids stay essentially in line. The community has to take care of its own; and in that respect *TOUGHLOVE* is an intentional model for community involvement.

The Yorks started *TOUGHLOVE* mainly for themselves and for people around them, not thinking in larger terms until a local magazine story appeared, got spread around, and touched a national nerve. Now they manage what amounts to a cottage industry from their house— you can attend training sessions across the country, or buy books, manuals, T-shirts, cassettes, or posters suitable for framing. As Chick Colony found, success is hard to walk away from.

Phyllis: "You have to laugh at yourself. It's funny. It's funny. Yesterday I didn't know anything, today I got brilliant (laughs). It's very funny, really."

The interview takes place around their kitchen table. The atmosphere is easy, busy, and loose—children and grandchildren underfoot, helpers working in the basement, typists floating in and out, phone calls, interview requests, juggling of appointments. Phyllis is in a wheelchair, the result of a fall down her home stairway some months earlier.

What emerges from the Yorks' experience is how it's possible to capture national attention almost in spite of oneself, if one has the right issue; how one can blend freedom of spirit with firmly enforced traditional values; how irreverence, humor, sometimes dark humor, can nourish and sustain one's vision; how community members can do what agencies can't; and especially how helplessness and utter despair can be used as tools for change.

*

PHYLLIS: Nineteen seventy-one, nineteen seventy, something like that, we moved into an area we didn't know anything about. We had never lived in a bedroom community, we had never lived in a suburban community, and we were very out of touch. Lansdale [Pennsylvania]. It's a community that was old-timey, very hard to get into, nothing much for us there personally.

We were very involved in work. And coming to a place without friends, without community, our kids really got into a lot of trouble. We were not aware of all the stuff that was going on, we didn't have a good handle on it at all, and people who knew didn't tell us. The police department was extremely blaming, the juvenile officer in particular at that time was very blaming of parents. We also didn't know what to do when our kids got into a lot of trouble.

And we saw other families going through the same exact trouble that we did. We saw them professionally. And we didn't find the help in the community, we really didn't; they didn't know what to do either.

So when our daughter was arrested, we felt so alone that we needed to reach out. And we didn't reach out to the professional community, which we had been doing before, but we reached out to friends, and this person [Mary, a long-time friend and colleague sitting in on the interview], and the one in the basement that you met. We keep them locked up around the house, you know.

She was eighteen when she got arrested. And I think we just reached out to people who would go in and be surrogate parents for us, 'cause we decided at that moment that everything we did was wrong. I mean if it got that far, and we did so many stupid things, that we had to stop. We had to get other people who would actually be willing to go in and do—not professionalize.

INTERVIEWER: Can you remember the moment when you said, "We have to do something different"?

PHYLLIS: Yeah. It was the moment she called up for bail. She said, "I'm arrested, and I need bail," and both of us stood there and we knew that we've got to do a different thing. We can't put up the bail, we can't run down there, we can't do it. And we knew. But we didn't know what.

DAVID: It's the sense of being totally devastated.

PHYLLIS: Yep.

DAVID: And totally destroyed, in terms of valuing myself . . .

PHYLLIS: In terms of saying, "I can do it myself, mother."

DAVID: Feeling that somehow whatever I did didn't work or didn't help, and wanting somehow to do something different, but not knowing what. So calling up people who were friends—they were professionals in the field, both of them—but we called them up more as friends, not for their professional expertise.

PHYLLIS: We said, this is what happened, our daughter's in jail, would you help us out, would you go see her? Please go down and see her, please see what we can do, what we need. That kind of thing, 'cause we're doing everything wrong. So that's what they did. They went out and did actual work. They didn't sit and talk.

INTERVIEWER: How did things move from calling up a friend and getting support from a friend to broadening the network?
PHYLLIS: It took a long time. It took time.

DAVID: We were doing family therapy at a drug and alcohol rehab for adolescents, and we were doing a lot of training around Pennsylvania. And one of the things we were getting at was that you could talk to parents, what you think they should do, and how they should say no, but the fact was that most parents really couldn't do it. Because it was too hard.

Finally, someone we knew in this local community called us up and said they were having trouble with their son. He was seventeen. And they wanted him to graduate high school, but he was really getting into a lot of trouble, and could we help? That was funny, 'cause this kid is a very social, nice-looking, tall, blond, you know—

PHYLLIS: Wonderful person.

DAVID: The kind of model American kid that—everybody knew him, and he's so polite. Like when we first met him, and he started to talk to Phyllis, "Oh, I just took my SATs," and he's giving her all this stuff.

PHYLLIS: He would tell these grandiose stories all over the place. I knew he was stoned out of his mind the night before (laughs).

DAVID: So we invited him over to our house, and talked with the mother and the father, and this kid and his sister. And nothing much happened. The kid took off. He took his father's camel hair coat, and his whiskey, and did a whole number on him. And now the father says, "Now what do I do? I don't know where the kid is, he's somewhere around, but we don't know where he's living."

So we said, "Call up the people in your community; call up your friends, your neighbors, and get everybody together, 'cause we know your son's living somewhere in this New Hope vicinity. Let's see if we can track him down and cut off his resources." And so they got thirty folks together, and that was our first *TOUGHLOVE* group.

We all got together at their house. We planned pretty much how we were going to present ourselves in this meeting. So all the things we'd been doing, all the training and other things, were really helpful.

PHYLLIS: Plus our own experience, with our kids. We had the double whammy.

DAVID: Yeah. And we always wanted to have groups in the community, not facilities where people go to, but rather you stay in your own community and solve your problems there. So it all fell into place for us.

PHYLLIS: A lot of people came, I'll tell you that. And then some people came that heard from other people, whose kids were in trouble. So when we went in—

DAVID: We talked about our kid, you know, and our experience, and what helped us. And then we said, "Dave and Linda have invited you here, because they're having trouble with their kid.* They need your help. And we really need to help each other."

PHYLLIS: And then people said, how could they, they were having trouble with their own kids, and that they always thought that Dave and Linda's kids were wonderful. They went into this whole thing.

And then one person said, "Oh, God, he stayed in my house three days, and told me you were fighting, and he couldn't come home." It happened to be a very volatile couple, everybody knew there was spaghetti on the ceiling.

And somebody else said, "Okay, I really like that kid, I'm going to hunt him down, I think I know where he is, I'll talk to him." And somebody else said, "I would like to talk to the juvenile officer because he's already been involved." All kinds of stuff was going on.

And what happened was that he became very visible in that community for what he was doing; and people by the next week had told him, look, you treat your parents like shit, you can't stay in my house. If you're hanging with my son, my son's in trouble. So, that kind of thing went on. The police department was extremely interested in what we were doing, they couldn't figure it out.

DAVID: What we knew we were going to try was to get some folks together who'd be willing to support this couple in tracking down their kid, and cutting off whatever resources they could. That was our goal, out of that meeting. Phyllis didn't mention, but of course there was that one-third to one-half who looked at us and said, "What are you, crazy?" You know, "My kid isn't anything like that, and I don't know what I'm doing here," and so on and so forth. They didn't want to be involved in it. So that was all right, they dropped out, and then others began to come in.

I think we weren't quite one hundred percent sure what we wanted out of that meeting, to tell the truth. We just knew that we were going to try to organize the community in some way, and not quite sure exactly what that was and how that would be.

PHYLLIS: Right, yeah, that's what I feel too. [It was] definitely improvised. As we went, we thought about things during the week, and began to plan for the meeting. But we certainly did not have a preconceived notion or any kind of steps.

One thing I learned is that you have to get people together with a problem they feel is common to all of them. It doesn't have to be the same

*Names of these and other group participants have been changed.

exact problem. But if there's commonalities, people will come together, and that's what will make a program.

And I knew that, and I knew that we had enough people with this kind of problem with kids, and kids were important enough in families that people were going to come together around it. That was always in my head. Still is. The way I think of things . . . does this problem have enough links to enough people? Not to get together to solve this problem, but get together so that they become a community, that would link them.

INTERVIEWER: That's an important point—can social change happen without a social problem precipitating it?

PHYLLIS: I think you have to have a problem. I do.

DAVID: I think so. I think so. Yeah. And it has to be one that you have a lot of investment in. Not just a simple ordinary problem, but one that's really critical to your view of who you are, and how you value yourself and are valued by others. And today we're very valued by the kind of parents we are.

PHYLLIS: I think the thirty people kept coming back for at least six weeks. But then there was a group of twenty people, core people, who just stayed, for a whole year or more, and are still involved.

DAVID: Well, it's funny, because good things happened almost right from the start. I think after the first meeting that we had, people had stereos and all kinds of things dropped on their porches, you know, that they didn't even know were missing, or other things that other kids had taken and "borrowed," or whatever. And they couldn't understand, how come this is getting returned? What's going on? And so they really got excited about the changes that happened immediately.

PHYLLIS: That's the reinforcement.

DAVID: And of course, so did we. So it's almost like instantly things happened, and the group got turned on.

Gee, I can't remember what her name was, but the one who used to come home and her kid would have beer parties in the house? She'd come home after work, and the kids would all be there. And she'd call the kid into the kitchen and say to him, "Look, this is really terrible, can't you get your friends to leave, I don't like what's going on," and so on and so forth, because she didn't want to embarrass the kid. And he'd keep having these beer parties. So she came home one day, and got out of the car, and said (military tone), "You—get over here and pick up these beer cans! You—get out of here! You!" And she screamed and yelled at everybody, and told her kid, "Don't you ever have a beer party in my house again!" And that was the end of it, you know.

So like crazy things went on and people would hear them and laugh, and that would get everybody really charged up.

We knew we had a thing to move on now. We knew something was happening. And we of course got very excited and very involved, and knew that we needed support too, to carry on with whatever the hell was going on with us. We didn't see ourselves as trying to start a movement, lead a movement; we just saw ourselves building something in our community that would help us.

And since we came into it with whatever it took to keep this thing going and getting it together, we became like the leaders of this group. That was okay for a while, but after about seven or eight months, it got to be really tiring, to go every week to this meeting. This was like doing group therapy, for no pay. So we sat down and said, look, we have to get out of this, what can we do? We said, what do people need to know so that they can run their own meeting?

And we began to put a manual together, and write that material out. We shared it with the group, and they said, yeah, this was good, that no, that's not; they corrected our grammar and did everything else for us.

PHYLLIS: Exactly. We wanted to give it to people. Other people were talking about having it in their community. There were new people all the time in the group. I don't know how it did it . . . people came from New York, New Jersey . . .

DAVID: People would come in and say, oh, I heard about this from somebody who worked with somebody . . .

PHYLLIS: Oh, Linda and Dave went on a cruise, and they met these people from New Jersey who were having the same thing, and they came and brought their mother-in-law and their aunts, and then the Drug and Alcohol Commission wanted to see it, and they brought in twenty people from Warminster . . .

And every meeting is between twenty and sixty people by now. Within a year, probably six hundred people went through that group in one way or another. I don't think we had any publicity. There was no organization.

DAVID: Oh, didn't Walter put together a couple of posters?

PHYLLIS: Right. One of the things we saw, if the group met in somebody's house, there was too much coffee and cake and socializing. This went on too long. So we decided to go to a firehouse, in a public place. You want to socialize, do it after the meeting. But the meeting was to work at, and you're not in someone's home.

Nobody wanted to publish the manual. We couldn't get it published; so we were Xeroxing. How many did we Xerox? Six hundred?

We didn't have a name until a friend of mine read the book and said,

"Oh, this has gotta be called *Tough Love,*" because we wrote it constantly in the manual, but never thought of it as a name. So we named it and that was it.

Then we Xeroxed our brains out. And we were going to the poorhouse from Xeroxing this thing. But then we get Ted Wachtel.

DAVID: When we were doing training around Pennsylvania, we had people do videotaping for us. And the fellow who did it couldn't come one time, so he said, "You want to take my friend along, he's a schoolteacher, he's trying to start an alternative school." So he came along, and we got to know him, and sort of liked him, and so we began to kind of work together with him.

He wanted to publish the manual and sell it out of the foundation, 'cause that would help support what he was doing.* And it seemed like a good deal all around. So we got involved with each other, and he gets $5000 from his father, and he printed the manual, he started to sell it.

PHYLLIS: So, okay, we have the manual out, and Jerry and Diane take it to Yardley. We start our second group. And we go in there and do ten weeks training.

DAVID: People would come to the Yardley meeting and say, gee, I'd like to have this in my community, and so they would bring us over to do it there.

Then we started to do one in Cherry Hill, New Jersey. And we also did another one in a synagogue, in Elkins Park, and there was a couple there whose aunt wrote for the *Philadelphia Inquirer.* So she went into the *Philadelphia Inquirer* office, and was just talking about what was going on with her [nephew and niece]; anyway, the editor came in and heard her talking, and said, "Write that up, because everybody talks about the problem, nobody talks about the solution. Write that up; that sounds kind of interesting."

So she put that together, and it was practically the whole magazine section of the *Philadelphia Inquirer,* the Sunday magazine section. And so that came out, that was November of '79, and Phil Donahue called us, almost right away.

PHYLLIS: Yeah, well, it had gotten into seven major newspapers by that time; they had bought it.

DAVID: So Donahue saw it; he invited us on his show. And we of course said no (laughs). No, we were like—oh, my God, you know, it's wonderful.

---

*The Community Service Foundation, started by Ted Wachtel, was the early institutional base for *TOUGHLOVE*. This relationship has since ended, and *TOUGHLOVE* now operates independently.

PHYLLIS: Yeah, we had already been on "AM/Philadelphia," locally, we had like 125 phone calls immediately.

DAVID: Well, it's like, wow, this is really something. It's exciting; it's getting national attention.

PHYLLIS: Maybe we're doing something (laughs).

DAVID: So we knew we were on to something exciting, but basically we just saw ourselves doing a lot of groups in this general area, where we lived. And then writing this up as a model that we would then publish in some professional journal.

But what happened when the *Philadelphia Inquirer* picked it up, and it became national, like we then no longer had all the time and energy to work on the local group. It's almost like it then began to just snowball.

PHYLLIS: Ann Landers put it in.

DAVID: Well, I think after Donahue, *Time* magazine interviewed us. And the gal that interviewed us had a hard time getting it published; they didn't want to publish it. They thought it was too radical a movement—

PHYLLIS: Kicking the kids out.

DAVID: Yeah, it runs against the common trend of the poor kids, you know. These kids are suffering from terrible parents, and—

PHYLLIS: It's a common disease.

DAVID: And who the hell are these parents to be talking about getting really tough on their kids?

PHYLLIS: It's a flash in the pan.

DAVID: And she said they had a bet in the office of who we voted for in the [1980 presidential] elections.

PHYLLIS: Both sides were wrong; we voted for Barry Commoner* (laughs).

DAVID: Yeah, so there was that kind of attitude towards us in the media, to begin with. And there still is that attitude. You know, that we're the group that talks about kicking your kid out. That's what we hear all the time.

PHYLLIS: 'Cause they have bad parents and we want to make them feel better (laughs). We're either Phyllis Schlaflys, or we're communists. Nobody can decide. We still get lots of flak from the old-time establishment who think that guilt is the way to go with parents. We get God-fearing letters a lot of times, that we are godless people.

DAVID: Yeah.

PHYLLIS: Because we are (laughs). All you need in life is Seventh-Day Adventist or Christ or whatever, and they're sure we'll go to hell.

---

*Commoner was the Citizens Party candidate that year, considered on the political left.

God, we were so excited. We got about five thousand [letters] from Donahue, and we sold the first five thousand manuals in a month. Then when Ann Landers put it in, we got fifteen hundred letters a day for I don't know how long. Ten days, we got fifteen thousand letters. With all the same kid. Over two thousand phone calls in a week. At this little office in Sellersville, with one person, one maniac person, working.

Ann Landers called us, and said that she couldn't believe the response. She said it's the biggest response she ever got to anything in all her career. She said she was inundated; that was April; in June, she was still getting something like sixty calls a week. . . . .

INTERVIEWER: What kinds of changes did that mean for yourselves when that happened?

PHYLLIS: I think good ones.

DAVID: Well, we became—

PHYLLIS: Celebrities.

DAVID: Yeah, celebrities, doing a lot of television, traveling around. Then we started to do some training, weekend training stuff; folks would come in, they'd pay us to do a two-day training session how to do *TOUGHLOVE*.

PHYLLIS: And start groups.

DAVID: So doing that. And again, our experience of all the training kind of things we had done prior to that professionally really helped us in on that one. I think our first workshop was in Philadelphia, and we had, I don't know—

PHYLLIS: One hundred eighty-five people from twenty-two states.

DAVID: —come to that one. And that was kind of exciting—

PHYLLIS: To say the least. We enjoyed the whole thing; I still enjoy it. I love the notoriety; I love the celebrity. I like the conflict. I like the controversy. . . . I like being heard. . . . And I like to work with very large groups, one hundred and two hundred people. I enjoy it. I like to motivate. I like power, you know, that sense of power that you get.

And I also think I can give something that's good. That pleases me. . . . And we've made more money, without ripping anybody off. I think there wasn't one negative thing that came out of that.

DAVID: I don't think so.

PHYLLIS: Tired—we're tired.

DAVID: By now, our kids were grown, and so there was just Phyllis and I, and we could pick up and go and do, and it was fun and exciting to do that.

PHYLLIS: And then you have to watch your ass. 'Cause you get involved in believing what you say (David chuckles). And that's dangerous.

PHYLLIS: We didn't feel we needed the system at all. Except to mold it to where we were. We had a constituency right from the [word] go, which were the parents. We knew with enough parents we could influence any system. Basically, we didn't feel that we needed anybody. We didn't need money from government. We didn't need the political system in any way. We said, "You want to join, you can join; you don't want to join, don't join, that's it."

DAVID: We perceived ourselves being set up against the system. We were anti- the system the way it was working. And that's changed with us over the years. We began to feel like, okay, we're now recognized, we have some clout, we have some power, we can now begin to talk to you on more semi-equal terms. Because I don't think the professional community ever perceives you as being their equal. But, you know, so what? They began to see that we had something that worked, that helped, that made a difference. We softened our tone, more to saying how can we co-opt the system to make it work for us.

PHYLLIS: We finally got enough parents together to say, okay, you can begin to teach the system what you're about. The system didn't really talk directly to us at all until we went on Donahue. But I think parents were having a very hard time in the community, and we began to say to them, you need to get cooperation. Now you can cooperate [with others]. So we asked them to invite people in, so the system became very interested. And we have what now, twelve hundred groups? It's hard to ignore.

Yeah, the thing about us, I think we've always been outside of the system . . . to a degree, felt alienated, just as people. But I think that's part of us. I mean, when you think about Goddard [where they worked in the sixties], moving out of New York, just fringy kind of stuff. . . . Even the counseling was in the drug and alcohol field, which is new and not part of a system.

INTERVIEWER: Okay, so maybe there are some morals here about the proper relationship between the agency and the community.

PHYLLIS: Yes. Yes.

INTERVIEWER: Which are?

PHYLLIS: I don't know (laughs).

DAVID: Well, the agencies represent the status quo. And if you're coming in attempting to create change, you're viewed as the outsider, you're viewed as someone who doesn't have all the information, isn't smart like the people on the inside. And I think there's almost a need to batter the walls down, in order to begin to be heard. So it's almost an essential part of starting a movement to really have to attack the establishment.

I don't think you can get that cooperation until you become part of the establishment itself. And that's what's happened to TOUGHLOVE; we've become the establishment now, or becoming more and more the establishment.

PHYLLIS: So we'll have to kill it.

DAVID: Probably.

PHYLLIS: Or it'll die by itself. Right.

DAVID: People aren't going to let you in the door. The social work agencies weren't going to let us in the door. You know, who the hell were we? We're just parents. In fact, we had a social worker call us up and said, "Do you mean you're going to allow parents to have responsibility to raise children?" That was eventually the comment that she came out with.

PHYLLIS: Oh, yeah, our daughter was in jail, and the worker said to us, "She's a really nice girl." I said, "How do you think she got into jail?" She says, "No, it's wrong, she doesn't belong there." And we were all wrong.

INTERVIEWER: So is it a given that the agency is going to represent the status quo?

PHYLLIS: Right. And once a citizen group or parent group becomes an agency, it's again going to represent the status quo, and then you got to bang it down again. Right. I think that's an absolute, yes.

INTERVIEWER: To shift gears for a moment from the agency to the community—you both mentioned in your book your concern with community support, and using TOUGHLOVE as a model for a type of caring community that you would like to see.

PHYLLIS: We probably didn't write it, and it's another person (laughs). Go ahead. What did we say?

INTERVIEWER: "Our dream is that TOUGHLOVE can model a new approach to other kinds of local needs as well."

PHYLLIS: This is terrible. Oh, God, hardly anybody does that to us.

DAVID: Being held to your written word, that's what's wrong with writing.

PHYLLIS: We think there should be a lot of support groups which are both community-based and political. Coming together and getting what needs to be done on a political level, but also being able to help one another in each other's homes.

DAVID: We're saying that people have to begin to cooperate on the things they do believe in, and not use their differences as excuses for not helping each other.

PHYLLIS: And I think that you can bring people [together], if it's in their community, if they see it, visually—if they see things torn apart, and affecting them personally. I think you could do anything on ecology if you have Love Canal in your back yard. Also, we don't respond to massive things that much, even Vietnam, if you consider that. We respond to what happens to one little child who needs a heartplant. We respond much more readily to that than we will to other things.

I think out of pain and emotions, you could start something. And I think the bigger things make you feel too helpless. And one thing people want to avoid is helplessness, as much as possible.

INTERVIEWER: So on the one hand, people want to avoid helplessness; on the other, it takes a crisis which could make you feel helpless to mobilize you.

PHYLLIS: Yeah, but you have to feel helpless before you know you are. Okay, people avoid that feeling at almost any cost; they will go on denying what's happening or will see things that aren't there.

INTERVIEWER: You have to feel helpless first?

PHYLLIS: Yes. . . . Yeah. I did. You just have to say, okay, everything doesn't work, I'm helpless, I don't know what to do.

INTERVIEWER: You really felt helpless?

PHYLLIS: Ohhhhh.

DAVID: Absolutely.

PHYLLIS: Devastated. Helpless. Horrible. Right. Helpless, before you can reach out.

Yeah, you know what the difference is between us and other parent organizations? One of the differences is that everybody [else] came from the mode of prevention. How do we prevent what's happening? Well, I don't think you do. I think you have the problem, then you work with the people who are in trouble. And then after they get out of trouble, or begin to, they develop the community. 'Cause it's community you need. But working the other way around, you can't do it.

*

Recently the Yorks have been taking new directions, David says, making audiotapes and videotapes, and writing other books. They've written a manual for teenagers, and brought *TOUGH*LOVE into schools. They've also been doing a manual for spouses of cocaine abusers, since 800–COCAINE kept calling them. "We wrote it over the weekend, and yesterday," says Phyllis. "It's not hard; it's formula writing, really."

There's interest in *TOUGH*LOVE in England, Australia, New Zealand. David wonders about applications to business. The next weekend they have thirty people coming to their house from across the country to begin a *TOUGH*LOVE trainer system, to formalize, strengthen, and extend the organization.

Phyllis: "It may work, it may not. If it doesn't work, it doesn't work. We're just trying it because we felt like it got too unruly already. And probably, we're tired (laughs)."

*

PHYLLIS: We want to go on to other fun. I mean, if you want to ask that question. Either death or fun; it's one or the other.

INTERVIEWER: What do you think you have left to learn?

(General laughter)

PHYLLIS: Not a goddamn thing. No, what do we have . . . This is the way training runs, too—there are usually two or three people who leave, automatically, when I open my mouth. They're surprised—but actually very few.

That, by the way, is very freeing. There's a whole group of people who say don't use dirty words, it's terrible for your training. And then there's about three-quarters of the group that says, "Oh, I wanted to call my kid a [deleted] bastard for years" (laughs). That empowers people.

But what do we have left to learn—how to manage our business so we really make money, how's that? That's one thing. I'm serious.

DAVID: Phyllis has to learn humility.

PHYLLIS: We have to learn if *TOUGHLOVE* really works, in a way.

DAVID: Yeah. That's an important question. Does it really do what we think it does?

PHYLLIS: Are we only getting good feedback? I don't know.

DAVID: NIDA is talking about doing something with that.*

PHYLLIS: They wanted to do a three- to five-year evaluation, and I think that's good. We didn't want to do it ourselves. We need to see how far it can go, and where it branches out to, and who's going to take it where. Are we? Yeah, that's the other question.

DAVID: One of the things Phyllis and I would like to do at some point is write a generic self-help book, kind of using *TOUGHLOVE* as a generic model. We'd like to see if we could organize a national self-help conference of all the self-help groups, to get them together, and to try and determine just what is self-help, and how does it work, and how can we make it more effective for all of us that are involved in it?

PHYLLIS: Personally, we'd rather write a novel. In fact, we're thinking of doing one on serials. The old-time radio serials—making those characters alive, and saying, whatever happened to Mr. Keen, Tracer of Lost Persons, and Stella Dallas, and all those people? So that's the next project (laughs).

DAVID: There's that, and I would really like to look into psychotherapy and its effectiveness and what it does.

(Laughter)

PHYLLIS: Oh, David, tell the truth, you want to tear the [deleted] thing apart.

DAVID: No, I'm reassessing, whether that's really reasonable or not. To

---

*National Institute on Drug Abuse, a federal agency.

really look at that and write a pop book about it. Basically that says, you know, what the hell do we think we're doing, going to people who supposedly have all the answers to everything, and what is it we're looking for and—

PHYLLIS: Would you like something to eat? No? All right. You're sure?

INTERVIEWER: What else would you like to add?

DAVID: I've always wanted to say this: Now is the time for . . . (laughs).

INTERVIEWER: Anything else you'd like to get on the tape?

PHYLLIS: Um—I'm sorry I said all the things I did (laughs). I didn't mean a god damn thing. My name is not Phyllis York. . . .

(Laughter)

James Baca, *Denver Catholic Register*

Lupe Anguiano (right) congratulating a graduate of the Colorado Women's Employment and Education program.

If we said we're going to do everything in our power to help you become self-supporting, that would be the greatest gift anyone could give a person.

Lupe Anguiano

NATIONAL WOMEN'S EMPLOYMENT AND EDUCATION

S HE wants to change a different system: the national welfare system. She is working out of a couple of rooms in a former public
school in the East Bronx with a staff of four and a budget of $116,000.
These rooms are the offices of National Women's Employment and Education, Inc., Lupe Anguiano founder, president, and chief executive
officer.

She has a model for changing the system, which she developed and
began using a dozen years ago in Texas. It is simple: AFDC (Aid to
Families with Dependent Children) mothers get job training, enter
prearranged jobs, receive follow-up support, leave welfare, and become
self-sufficient.

The President wants to overhaul the welfare system (again). Massachusetts has a nationally recognized model for doing so ("ET," for
Employment and Training). Lupe Anguiano's program is similar; but
it came first, and she built it on her own.

Her story begins in 1970, when she was working as a Civil Rights
Specialist for the Department of Health, Education, and Welfare,
and sat listening to congressional testimony on the Equal Rights
Amendment.

*

I heard American women look within themselves and say they were not
satisfied with the images society had about them. They saw that they were
not satisfied with their lives, and that they wanted greater expression,
greater participation, the utilization of their talents.

I was in Washington, and I was invited by Secretary Elliot Richardson

[Secretary of HEW, 1970–1973] to participate with a group of twenty-five women, to recommend to him what should be done to improve the status of women in the areas of health, education, and welfare. And because there were no poor women, Hispanic women, women in poverty represented in the congressional hearings, I wanted to go out and see what they were thinking.

So I had an opportunity to visit with low-income women, with Hispanic women, all over the United States, as part of my job. I went to seventeen sites, and what I heard the women say was the following: number one, we hate welfare. Our privacy is being infringed upon. I heard them say we want jobs. We want people to get off of our backs, not constantly coming around and seeing who we're sleeping with, how much food we're eating, et cetera; we want to be free from this system.

What I did was go back and study the policy. And I still remember it today, I can still feel it, a gut reaction that I experienced when I started to read it. And I think the word that just insulted me the most was the word "caretaker." In the AFDC policy, the woman is referred to as the caretaker. Not the head of the family, the family provider, but the caretaker.

So I'll never forget going to bed thinking about "caretaker, caretaker." Well to me what that inferred was that the woman wasn't even in possession of her child, that she was taking care of the child for someone else, for the state. And it angered me. And made me feel that here we have in the United States a law that does not provide the woman with a support system to enable her to get a job, to be in fact the head of the family, to be responsible for her children.

Then I started to examine why it is that the women aren't working. The barriers were basically, number one, the lack of information that a job is available to them; number two, lack of skills training; number three, lack of child care and transportation—in that order.

Then I found that you come into a welfare office, and immediately you're given a form to fill out, to qualify for AFDC. And to qualify for that public assistance, you cannot work. The law does not allow that social worker to talk about employment. But you know, when you're divorced or your husband leaves you, you're in a highly emotional state of mind. Trying to get yourself together is not easy. And so the fact that a woman didn't know that a job was an alternative to her was something I struggled with.

Everybody wants to be self-sufficient; people want to be self-supporting. I would say that was the single factor that stirred me the most to do what I'm doing.

I see both public and private institutions serving the poor as being very patronizing to poor people. The poor are asked only to receive; they're not asked to give. They're there as "recipients"; I hate the word "recipient."

You find groups, organizations, agencies, who are always desirous of giving, but they fail to see the dignity of that human person, and that giving could be enhanced by assisting that person to become self-supporting. I think that if every institution in this country [said] we're going to do everything in our power to help you become self-supporting, that would be the greatest gift anyone could give a person.

Well, I started to promote the idea in Washington that AFDC should be changed from income maintenance to providing a job, skills training, and assistance for the women. And of course I couldn't get anywhere. People in congress, they know welfare is a problem. It's such a mind-boggling system, they know it needs to be changed, but they don't know what to do about it. And here they have the experts telling them about income maintenance, and then here comes Lupe Anguiano, like a little voice, talking about, hey, this whole thing needs to be changed to provide a job, skills training, et cetera. Well, needless to say the Brookings Institute and [Senator Daniel Patrick] Moynihan won out, and I said, well, you know, trying to change this thing, you can't do it in Washington.

So Archbishop Flores was in Washington because some bishops wanted to close their office for the Spanish-speaking, and he needed an executive director. And so the Archbishop says, "If anybody can save the office, you can, Lupe, so why don't you come to San Antonio and do that?" And I said, "Well I'll go only on condition that welfare reform be my priority issue, if I can do what I want to do. I'll still do your churchy things, but then I want to do this."

So we agreed. And so in April of 1973 I moved to San Antonio. And moved right into the housing projects. The housing authority would not rent me a room in public housing, so the women invited me to come and live with them. That worked out very well, because they could have a guest for a month, and so I moved every month from one housing project to another.

It was a very rewarding and a very great experience. I experienced the degradation of the welfare system. At night, for example, in Alazán Apache during the heat of the summer, it was so hot you couldn't get into the house, and we never went to bed until maybe about two o'clock in the morning. And then getting up early was something; you just didn't get up. Then at night in the wintertime, it was so cold that I remember just putting on everything that I had and being in the bed to keep warm. So one of the things I learned was why it is that living in public housing under those conditions, you couldn't work even if you wanted to. I had a hard time dealing with that myself, keeping a job.

The beautiful thing about that experience, which is really the most important, is the fact that I was in communication with the women. The housing projects are filled with leader women, who know the system backwards and frontwards. And the issue of we want a job, we want to get out of this depressing welfare system, became so real to me. We'd get together in circle sessions at night, in one apartment or another, we'd talk about what we wanted to do with our lives, and how it is that we wanted to survive. And immediately, the idea of a job. And so the idea, okay, let's go after a job.

The most important thing was that they started to see they were not the only ones experiencing the struggle. There were a lot of other women who wanted a job, who wanted to become self-sufficient; so bringing them together enabled them to find strength within the group. They began to see, it is possible for us to find a job. Okay, what are the barriers that hinder me? What are the solutions? And out of the women themselves—they know more than anybody else what the barriers are, and they know more than anyone else what the solutions are.

I didn't have difficulty at all. See, the majority of women were Mexican-American, and I'm a Mexican-American. Then the majority are Catholic, I'm in the bishop's office. And then I've worked with low-income people in my life, and I've lived under a lot of those conditions, and so it didn't seem awkward, or such a big deal.

This went on from housing project to housing project, and finally on November the 23rd [1973], we just declared a Let's Get Off of Welfare campaign. The women decided they were going to take their checks back and say, hey, we don't want welfare, we want jobs. Some women were going to be taking care of the children, and some were going to be working, and they would pay these [other] women, while they worked. The women just made arrangements for all of this. And so we placed the women into jobs, because I had already lined up jobs. It wasn't something that was meticulously organized. I did not expect the event to be such a highly visible thing, you know, but it just caught on.

My big goal was to reform the welfare system, and the women said they wanted a job. You ask these women if they'd be willing to take that check back if they could get a job. That isn't a difficult thing. It isn't difficult at all (laughs).

The redirection of social services in this country to me has to be the nation's priority. Otherwise, you know, we're in a lot of trouble. As soon as you start an agency or an organization, for the survival of that organization they need somebody to depend on them. You can talk about being generous, about being caring, and that doesn't mean a hill of beans, unless you really are enabling people to help themselves. And what they need is a job.

My biggest criticism of social service agencies is that they have a soup line, a constant soup line, where they're constantly giving, without really doing something about stabilizing that person economically. Also, we have so many agencies that are living out of providing social services. What would happen if you took this fifty-six percent of families living in poverty and headed by women, and had them working? You know, you'd have a lot of agencies no longer needed.

So when it comes down to the bottom line, agencies are more interested in preserving their jobs than they are in the common good. Isn't that horrible?

Social work agencies and the schools of social work focus themselves more on counseling, and providing social services. They're training people to be very patronizing to poor people, without meaning to. The problem I see is that they're not trained to really deal with self-sufficiency. How easy it really is, to deal with poverty issues, *if* you focus on self-sufficiency.

Well, the following day the Kiwanis called us and said, "Lupe, we like what you're doing! What can we do to help?" And I said, "Well, the women need jobs, and they need training." So with very little ado, we started a cashier's training program. Training the women to do a particular skill could be done very easily and in a very short period of time. What we needed to do is get them into the door—the entry-level position—and that required a certain skill, such as knowing how to work a cash register. Then the good companies promote always from within.

Forty-five women wanted to go into the cashier training. Of course we needed child care, so the Kiwanis provided the fifty-dollar scholarship for the women. They provided the instructor. And Sister Maria Carolina provided the transportation to get the women to and from the class. So in four weeks . . . forty-two of the forty-five women graduated. Isn't that great?

And after they graduated, they got jobs right away. Primarily because before we adopted the cashier training program, we already had jobs. We already knew that HEB was opening a store, and Handy Andy was opening some stores, and we already had the agreement of the employer that they would interview our women. And so it was a matter of preparing the women for those jobs. It was really very easy, you know.

That's how the model works, and that's where I learned the process. What I started to do from thence forward is go out and find jobs, entry-level jobs, that were going to be available within a month or two-month period. I knew the jobs and the entry-level requirements. For example, Southwestern Bell said, "Lupe, we'll hire ten of your women in customer service if they can type twenty words a minute." Well, teaching the women to type twenty words a minute isn't such a big deal. . . . And so they gave us some equipment. And then San Antonio College—we just used their classrooms.

I didn't market our women as charity cases—hire this woman because she needs a job. I said, "We have a qualified woman to work for you; and her working for your company is going to make a big difference, because you're going to have a motivated, well-screened, prepared woman who's going to stay in your company." American companies today, their greatest problem is the high turnover rate. So what happened is that we provided a solution to a problem that they had.

Actually moving the women from welfare into jobs has never been a problem. It has never been a problem. What's amazing is that not more people are doing that.

The program kept growing, and it kept becoming more popular. And so the demands on my time were more for the employment program than for the bishops. It became very obvious that my major concern was the women, rather than the office for the Spanish-speaking. So in 1979 I just decided to leave my position with the bishops and I incorporated. I really decided this is what I'm going to do, and this is how I'm going to do it. And I just started to build this National Women's Employment and Education with a goal of dealing nationally with a policy. That has always been my goal.

Society has looked down upon a woman working, and I think that's a wrong that needs to be made right. The truth of the matter is that forty-nine percent of American women with children under the age of three are working. And why aren't the rest working? Socialization has imposed on women ideas that are not actually true. And that is that your best place is in the home, taking care of your children.

But economically and socially, you'd better find out what it is you want to do and become self-supporting, because there's nothing that guarantees you that your marriage is going to last. Or that when you have a child, somebody else is going to support that child. Those are the hard realities, you know.

Then the governor's wife asked me if I would form a corporation that would manage $600,000 in reforming the welfare system in Texas, and they would hire me as a consultant. So I put that together. But because I did not accept their terms, they didn't hire me. They took it away from me, even though I had it developed and everything, because I did not agree to give up [organizing] New York. It was the prerogative of the governor, because the governor wanted Texas, and he felt that I might be using Texas money to come to New York.

I knew what I wanted. I'm after national welfare reform. If national welfare reform is going to happen, it's going to have to happen with the leadership of New York and California. Texas: What can Texas prove? Texas hardly gives welfare. The real test was going to come in New York, because of the 337,000 families on AFDC in the city. So giving up that money was not difficult for me. Everybody was surprised that I gave up $600,000. And I was surprised that they were surprised. They did not recognize that my goal was to reform the welfare system. They thought they could keep me in Texas with $600,000. I was furious that anybody would ask me to give up my national goal just for six hundred thousand dollars.

Giving that up just had me go completely without any money, so I lived one year with practically nothing. That was really rough. I had a house payment, I had to eat. And the way I survived was that some of the women would come and take me to breakfast, and take me to lunch. To this day, I don't know how I survived, you know. I said, hey, I'm still living on charity myself. No one was going to place me in that position again. That's when I decided I'm going to really get into business for myself.

My eyes were still in New York. And then I worked harder to try to get there. I finally landed a consultantship in Albany, working for the state, helping them to develop a home health aide program. That's how I got to New York. I was a year and a half without working.

I received the Wonder Woman award when my consultantship with the state ended. I received seventy-five hundred dollars, and with that I started the [employment] program. I moved in with my niece and her husband in Staten Island. I said, "I have only seventy-five hundred dollars," but she said, "Well, Aunt Lupe, why don't you come and live with us?" And so I said, "You're kidding. Sure." And we made her living room into our little office, and she helped me, and so we started the program there.

That was the program. Me, you know. Keeping me alive (laughs). I just concentrated in doing the program. And what expenses do you have? . . . Finally Manufacturers Hanover gave us five hundred dollars, then Equitable gave us some space.* Then Equitable decided that we're going to tear down the building, so I needed another place to house the office. So Community Board Number 2 told me, they had turned the school into a multiservice center, there was space available here, and so I applied for it, and I got it. I started it in New York City, December of '83, using all the resources that I had, everything that I learned.

*

It's 9:00 A.M., and Lupe Anguiano is stringing Christmas lights and winding tinsel on a Christmas tree. Today is a party for the second graduating class. They have just completed the training program; most have job interviews lined up for tomorrow.

Thirteen young black and Hispanic women look stylish and smart.

---

*A New York City bank and insurance company, respectively.

Many are wearing red corsages. Some have brought their children with them. But all of them are glowing, and glowing conspicuously. I am not used to happiness and pride pulsing out at me; but I feel both now, no doubt about it.

In the classroom, there's a big banner: "We Can—We Care." On newsprint, students have written their names next to each skill they've mastered. During the party, the graduates keep singing the Carpenters' "We've Only Just Begun." Spontaneously; many times. Outside the school building, dogs lie asleep in the middle of the sidewalk.

The job training program takes three to four weeks. Today's graduates will be interviewing for clerical positions at J. C. Penney, Chase Manhattan, New York Telephone. Of the twenty-one graduates of the first class, eighteen are still working. If Lupe and her staff can keep training fifteen to twenty women a month, they'll place two hundred a year. If they can expand their operation, by attracting more corporate and foundation support, they believe that policymakers will have to take notice. By 1989, they hope to have the government adopt their program as a replacement for AFDC.

Lupe Anguiano herself could be your traditional aunt, except that she is also president of Lupe Anguiano and Associates, a private consulting firm which assists other communities to develop similar programs (in at least five states so far). She is the daughter of migrant workers who has written a series of six manuals on her job training model. She is an entrepreneur who spent fifteen years teaching with Our Lady of Victory missionary sisters, and a social service worker who has little regard for most social services. At one time, I might have labeled these contradictions, but now I see more clearly that contradiction, if that's the term, is part of our nature.

Positive thinking is a theme of the conversation, and perhaps central to her achievement. Off the tape, Lupe says she prefers not to dwell on what she calls the negatives, the competition for attention, and the anguish involved in the effort she's making. Instead, "I do so little, and the women do so much."

Then, her work raises broader issues: Will local success really lead to national change? How far can positive thinking actually carry you? Can one person's positive thinking, parlayed with local success, redirect a $12 billion annual federal outlay?

✳

The technique I've always used [in class] is what we call the observe, judge, and act technique. You observe the situation, you determine whether it's good or bad, and then you act upon it. That's a technique that I've used as a teacher, all my life. Another technique which I found really helpful is the circle sessions. You create a circle, you introduce a topic. That topic must always be on a positive line: what is the greatest experience of my life, or the happiest day of my life? There's no putdowns, everybody has a turn, you have a leader, a summary, and then you close the circle session. And so, I've adopted that in the training.

And it's magic—it really is; what happens is that you create a safe atmosphere where people can be themselves. And then people start to talk about positive things. I make it a very strong point to have the women deal with issues on a positive level. For example, divorce; the women are devastated by the divorce in their lives. So I challenge them to think about the happy times that they had when they got married, the happy times that nobody will ever be able to take away from them. You know. And deal with it that way. So try to dwell on the positive factors rather than let the negative factors destroy you.

Another method I use is what we call the twenty-minute meditation or concentration, where I have the women deal every day on focusing: number one, relaxing, breathing; and then focusing on the job of their dreams, the job that they want; or seeing themselves, allowing their beautiful selves to come forward.

Of anything I insist on, it's that, on a daily basis. Primarily because success is within you, you know. I don't believe there's anyone that can really change anyone else's lives; I think that has to come from within. And that factor, the strengthening of the innermost self, is the most important thing that anybody can do; you have to do that every day. Developing a positive attitude isn't something that comes naturally. You have to work on it. It's something that has to become a habit.

So you ask the participants to meditate?

Oh, that's a must. I mean—well, how else can you deal with your innermost self? And I tell the women, "Hey, it's not Lupe Anguiano, or the National Women's Employment, it's you who's going to get you a job."

This isn't prayer. It doesn't have anything to do with prayer. It's a technique of enabling you to recognize your positive strengths, to deal with positive elements about you. I have the women look at the mirror; that's their first homework, to make a note of all of their positive strengths. . . . I have beautiful eyes. Okay, work on that; come to terms with the fact that I have nice-looking eyes. And deal with that, and strengthen that. Or I have a very nice complexion, you know, I have a very nice smile. . . . Some of the women in the class told me that they went home and they had their children work with them about themselves. They're allowing their positive energies to come forward.

I'm a facilitator. I tell the women we're partners in this thing. I don't believe in having people be too reliant on others for their success. It has to be the person themselves. Nothing becomes real to you unless you own it. And then I believe very much that we need to feed our innermost positive selves every day. See, we give our body food every day, but we do very little to feed our psychological energies. We don't do it as a country, as a people—and particularly New York, the city is crazy. I have to work on it every day myself. And maybe, to be very frank with you, maybe the reason why I'm so good at this is because I need to reinforce myself (laughs). I have to constantly struggle at that, at looking at things in a positive light and all.

So when you work on yourself, do you use the same meditation technique as people in the class?

Oh, I try. Sure. Of course. I mean, how else can you accomplish something, particularly if you're changing an 11.8 billion dollar system . . . to be a positive force in the lives of three-and-a-half, three-point-seven million women, families? The only way to do that is by being positive, by being strong, by being determined. Oh, meditation is part of my life, has always been part of my life. Isn't it part of yours? How else can you be positive?

We have so many applicants, you know. When we graduated our first class, this phone wouldn't stop ringing. And we have a lot of jobs, too. Our only setback is having enough money to fill the classroom every month. Because we pay for the child care, for the transportation, and the lunch. And then we need additional staff,—a job developer, an outreach counselor—every one of us right now is doing two jobs.

The *only* thing that I don't like about what I'm doing is having to ask for money. I'm very tired of asking companies to support my work. I don't have anybody in the office to do it except myself. And I don't have full time. I hate it.

AT&T just turned me down, and it just annoys me, you know. . . . What's five thousand dollars every year for the next five years? It's nothing. . . . Why? You want to see the envelope? They give to United Way, or some silly reason . . . (sighs). I feel very annoyed by that. It's almost like a welfare system that I despise so much. . . . And so I'm going to do something about that.

That's the frustrating thing; I wish that there were a way for us to lick this problem. You know, people are giving, and they are generous, but people more readily want to give for social services. All of the pitches for charity are about feeling sorry because somebody doesn't eat, because somebody isn't clothed, because somebody is on drugs, because children are being abused. You make a pitch that will give self-sufficiency and a job— that doesn't have such a strong emotional appeal. Isn't that funny? Isn't that funny? . . . Am I being very pessimistic?

Enabling people to do for themselves. That's the one thing that Reagan has done, in spite of all of the criticisms. His action is forcing us to deal with our strengths in ourselves, and that's great. I love that. We can't depend too much on the government to do things for us, and government just does not know how to do anything right. And I really tried it. I'm really convinced about that, that the Reagan policies are going to, in the long run, help poor people more, because it's going to force us into self-sufficiency.

I'm fifty-five, and I'm beginning to be very concerned about my retirement, and I don't have . . . I have a John Hancock retirement, and I need to take care of that. I never really gave much thought to it until the experience I had with Texas, $600,000, where I found myself with no money.

I was appointed by President Johnson, I worked under the Nixon administration, for Carter, I belong to President Reagan's Council on Private Sector Initiatives, I won his volunteer award.* Under Carter, I received the VISTA volunteer award. And . . . I'm still not the master of my own destiny, financially.

And lately I have forced myself not to work on weekends. I used to just work around-the-clock. When I worked with Cesar Chavez,† I used to work twenty-four hours a day almost, and Cesar used to have a thing where the organizers that could stay up to two o'clock got into the nitty-gritty of the organizing, and so I stayed up till two o'clock. Because I wanted to be in the midst of the action, you know. I can't do that anymore. And so I make it a point to organize myself, to have the weekends off. And then I encourage the staff, because I believe you have to enjoy what you're doing, otherwise you're not going to portray the enthusiasm.

Did you see the women [inside], how positive? Yeah. And that's something that you have to have within you in order to . . . it's contagious, it is. And it's so great, because that's what makes life . . . you see, people are really basically good; our nature is made up of good, love, happiness, enjoyment. And I tell the staff that we need to have that. If the women are going to succeed, we need to be the models and examples of that in our lives. I'd rather have the staff not come to work if they're not going to be in that state of mind. Or me: I'll just lock the door and not let anybody in if I'm not in that state of mind. 'Cause that's what needs to be done. And see, again, it's within all of us; it's within you, it's within me, it's within everybody, and it just needs to be brought out and encouraged and reinforced.

---

*The President's Volunteer Action Award, given since 1982 to about twenty individuals and organizations annually.

†"As a volunteer. Five dollars a week. I was our organizer—I was in the Coachella strike—and then Cesar sent me to Detroit, and then I worked on the grape boycott."

I feel very great about who I am, and my future, and what I want to do. I'm stronger, and I have more determination. I think New York has brought the best out of me. But there's a lot of things that I want to accomplish. And I find that the only way to really do that is by having a strong determination to get the job done. I'm very single-minded. I have a purpose: to reform the welfare system. And whoever's interested in helping me, whoever it is, you know—I'm just interested in getting that job done.

So I think the possibility of this succeeding is very good, I think we're going to reach our goals in a five-year [period], and if not we will have made such a major impact that I could move on to other things, and I'm training staff to be able to handle this.

What I'd like to do is . . . to get into business for myself. I'd like to start a manufacturing plant. Yeah, to design clothes for the Southwest—I'm from California, you know. I'd like to go back home and then start a profit-sharing business, where everyone in the company shares in the profits, everybody. I think that's the only way to do business now—in a dignified way. And that's what I'd like to do. Because I've done social services, I've worked with organizing, I've dealt with political issues, and I'd like to just make some money.

My idea of a manufacturing company is I'd like very much to deal with the beautiful colors of the Southwest, that are very Mexican and very much alive. And then designing clothes that are appropriate for women. And I think the thing that I'm going to enjoy the most is that I'm going to be reliant on Lupe Anguiano and whoever's going to come in partnership with me—not having to depend on a Manufacturers or Chase Manhattan contribution, but actually to be making that money, and producing and reaping the benefits of that, and then sharing that with all of the people who are working with me, from me to the janitor. And make it in a way that people are going to be happy working, and being creative, and being productive, and challenged, and all—that's my vision of the future.

So that's what I'd like to do. I'd like to make a million dollars next (laughs). I'm serious about that. I would like to get out of this whole thing. I've also started to talk to some people at home, you know. (With real excitement) Home, I'm coming back! Yeah, my family's so delighted.

The only way to understand our program is seeing it as a miniature Welfare Department. This is what the public policy should be; and what we're saying, very loud and clear, is "Welfare Department, you could be doing what we're doing, so that we need not be here," you know.

I think that there has to be a job for everyone who's willing to work. And I think there has to be elimination of a lot of the barriers that hinder that, such as the AFDC welfare program. The welfare program needs to be changed so that it supports that working woman, so that when the woman goes and applies for a job, she is offered child care, transportation, or whatever she needs. The woman's salary would be doubled, and we would even be saving government fifty percent. That's what government needs to do. The idea is workable. I guess the whole issue of turning this into public policy is the challenge now. And so to that I say, let's wait and see. . . .

So what I'm saying is that I think the most important contribution that could be made to anyone is enabling people to deal with their inner strengths, with their humanity, and that is not something that can be imposed on a person. It has to be realized from within. . . .

Lois Gibbs (right) with Mary Castle at a protest in front of Rollins incinerator, Baker, Louisiana.

I still get outraged at what I hear. And that's what keeps me doing what I'm doing, the outrage. The outrage and the anger.

Lois Gibbs

CITIZEN'S CLEARINGHOUSE FOR HAZARDOUS WASTES

L OIS GIBBS is the woman who in the late 1970s led the fight against toxic waste dumping at Love Canal in Niagara Falls, New York. She was a housewife, a "hysterical, dumb housewife" to her critics, but who became nationally known. There were partial victories at Love Canal, her own book, a television movie; that story's been told. But in 1981, she divorced her husband, left Niagara Falls, and moved to Washington, D.C. There, working entirely from scratch, she started the Citizen's Clearinghouse for Hazardous Wastes; and that story is worth telling here.

I had wanted to talk to Lois Gibbs ever since I'd heard her speak at a psychology convention some years ago. Someone then asked her what had made her successful at Love Canal; she replied, "Motherly instinct." That has implications, for there are more than fifty million mothers in the United States.

Not all mothers are Lois Gibbs, which may help explain why motherly instinct is rarely encountered in the community activism literature. On the other hand, if you were a mother, or father, who was steadily accumulating cancer risk and whose children had become sick while living atop a toxic waste dump, would you simply sit back? Maybe we really do need a crisis to mobilize us; and maybe, as Lois Gibbs and others suggest, crisis does bring out our best.

On the other hand again, a lot of parents at Love Canal actually did do nothing, or next to nothing; so it could be that there are several explanations of action, multiple determinants of behavior, which probably makes sense. There's always room to dig deeper. The ultimate causes of human behavior are knowable, separable, and elusive, and it's a lifetime pinning them down.

The Citizen's Clearinghouse looks like a big success when we do meet in its small suburban Washington headquarters. Money is continuing to flow in; newsletters are continuing to flow out; there are triumphs to report, and more skirmishes on the horizon. Organizations and programs have takeoff points, when they become truly airborne, and this one seems near its cruising altitude. The Clearinghouse seems here to stay, like toxic waste itself.

Lois Gibbs is still the mother, though. School has ended, and day camp hasn't started, so her kids are hanging out in the office, building Lego towers upstairs, banging on the ceiling when they want attention, which is frequently. Lois fends them off stoically. At the same time, she is folding newsletters and sticking labels on envelopes, by hand. She does her own copying, I notice later, and she is barefoot.

News items:

New York Times, March 10, 1985: "The threat from toxic waste that faces the nation is much more serious and will be much more costly to resolve than the Government has estimated, two Congressional research agencies have concluded."

Time, October 14, 1985: "[In] a poll taken last month for *Time,* when asked, 'Would you be willing to pay higher state and local taxes to fund cleanup programs in your area,' 64% answered yes."

Everyone's Backyard (Citizen's Clearinghouse newsletter), Winter 1985: "On 11/6, CCHW's Director Lois Gibbs gave birth to Ryan Alexander, at 7 lbs., 14 oz., healthy and beautiful. Last year, Lois married CCHW Science Director Steve Lester. This is their first child."

New York Times, October 18, 1986: "President Reagan, expressing some reservations, today signed legislation providing $9 billion to continue cleaning up toxic wastes over the next five years."

*

After Love Canal, I received lots of phone calls from people who needed help, wanted to know how we won evacuation, wanted to know how to get scientists, and basic information. Other people fighting the same problem wanted the same answers to the same questions I had back in 1978, and I clearly could relate to them.

So I decided that I needed something to answer these calls. You know, we should set up a way that would take the resources that I have, that other folks have, and put it out there. So that was kind of the initiation of the Clearinghouse.

My biggest problem was, okay, we're going to start the Clearinghouse—so what? Where do we do it? How do we do it? And that whole process was somewhat painful, in the sense of how much is it going to cost to do this. I can't do this from Niagara Falls. How can I do it when there's no resources there? I was told I should do it from New York City. And all I could think of was, "I can't move my children to New York City, that's a zoo. I mean, I just can't do that." So the confusion over where we should have this and how to set it up and where we're going to get the money—eventually I decided to do it in Washington.

It was a frightening decision. I mean, I had a lot of insecurities about moving. But I had no problem moving, 'cause I hated where I was living. I had become a local celebrity. Based on that, I had absolutely no private life, at all. Going back to my roots, I was always a very shy, quiet, private person. And I didn't like my personal life interfered with by other people.

So I would go into a store and it would be two hours buying a loaf of bread; we'd go to dinner and these strangers would join us at the table and offer to pay our tab if they could stay. I mean, virtually everything I did. It's still like that; we went to the Fourth of July parade last summer in Buffalo, and they asked me if I would ride on a float. I sat through the parade with my two children and never saw one float, because everybody came up (in sing-song voice) "Oh, hi, Lois, how are you doing? How's the Clearinghouse going? What are you doing these days? I heard about Love Canal. My aunt's got a dump, my uncle's got a dump . . ." It was like there was absolutely no private life.

So I wanted to get out of there, in the worst way—not because I disliked the city, the people or anything, but because I wasn't me anymore; I didn't even know who I was. I was very confused over that. It was like, I don't want to be this public figure; I'm not that type of person; I don't like it; I don't want to be interfered with; I did what I had to do because I had to do it; it's over with . . .

In any case, I had twenty thousand dollars from the movie CBS made on me, and I decided I would just go to Washington, start talking to people in Washington, put up shop there for a short period of time to see if I could make it. And if I can't then I'll go back home.

That whole thing, with my family, was just awful. My mother was crazy: "You're nuts, you can't go to Washington by yourself, with those two little babies! You can't do that. What are you doing? You know nobody in Washington, you're not going to make it in Washington, you're crazy." Despite all her chasing after us and [being] behind the U-hauls trying to stop us when we drove off, I came to Washington and began setting up the Clearinghouse.

I had some friends, and my lawyer, and they said you submit a proposal. "Here are some people, I got a proposal writer who will write your first proposal for you." So we went to her, and she gave us our first one free, that we submitted to a whole bunch of foundations. But I still didn't have any money. I mean, I was turned down by every single one of them, mainly because I'm trying to start a national organization from a community base, and people didn't believe I could make it.

They only perceived me, mainly it was through the media, as "the housewife" of America. And how can a housewife and mother run a national organization, with no prior experience? I mean, the media was always good about saying she was a graduate of high school, she was a shy, intimidated person—so the thing the foundations all read was that. And they said, "Fat chance!" I mean, she did wonderful on a community level, but national's a whole 'nother situation, and there's no way a person like that is going to carry it off.

Last year, exactly at this time, we were in the basement of my home, a rental home. We had a part-time typist and a bunch of other volunteers. We had two telephones, a touch-tone and a rotary dial, and one phone jack downstairs, so we were forever fighting over the telephone. We would unplug the phone, go over there, use the touch-tone, dial out, then put it on the rotary line. It was a zoo.

Our copying had to go out, because we didn't have a copy machine. It was all volunteers. It was crazy. There was no air conditioning; we were dying. We had no budget. I had no salary. The only one who was getting paid was our typist. And that's where we were a year ago.

We got our first grant, I guess a year and a half ago. Five thousand dollars. And that's what we used to do our first newsletter and stuff like that. Up until last August, when we moved in here [her current office], we got salaries of $150 a week, all of us, equal, and then we started to raise more money and grow. Raise money through our membership, raise money through our foundations. . . . But doing it out of my house, I mean it was just awful. It was just a zoo.

We did wind up with foundation money, and we have a budget of $197,000 at this time, which will be even larger next year. We have nine staff people total. Sixty percent of our budget comes from private donations: publication sales, membership dues; forty percent comes from foundations. Private foundations. No money comes from industry, and no money comes from government. I prefer it that way. I don't ever want industry money, although foundation money in reality is industry money, washed. But it's washed. . . .

So essentially we established a Clearinghouse. I mean, that was my intent, and that's basically what we've been doing. And we've been doing wonderful. We've been very successful. We fund eighty-five different communities; we do our newsletter and stuff four times a year; action bulletins; we've done a lot of good out there.

And we're still growing . . . to the point where we've got more work than we do manpower in the office, and we need to hire more people to do the work because the need out there is just so much. People are calling us all the time, because they hear through word of mouth how helpful we were to community A and community B.

We don't do any major major outreach work, telling people here we are, this is what we do, mailing our brochures around, or stuff like that. We only work with community-based grass-roots leaders. That's a lot of fun! I mean, in addition to the work load, which is pretty incredible, it's also a lot of fun. Because although we can't take credit for what people do, we do get to share in the victories and stuff like that.

People will call and we'll help them out at a local level. And then they will call back and they'll say, "We won! We just stopped BFI.* I thought you'd want to know." And so we can get a lot of the ups, without actually experiencing the work energy and stuff that had to go in to accomplish that.

I'm still very shy, and I still have this respect for authority. It doesn't appear it, but I am and I do, and it's something that I haven't yet gotten over. I don't have the respect for authority I used to have. But there's something about them that sometimes intimidates me, or authoritative figures in general.

It's like the lawyer says this and that, and "Yes sir, yes sir, yes sir. Okay, I'll do that." Or when you go into a foundation, and you're asking for money, and you're doing an interview, it's like I just get very intimidated; they're just regular people, and they're one of me, so to speak. Yet I just sat there, got very shy, got very introverted, and I would bring all these other people (laughs) so I wouldn't have to talk, and it was very traumatic to go into this, and you go out and buy a three-piece suit, and put it on—

Yeah, me! Buy a three-piece suit, and go in and act like a lady, and try to sound intelligent, because I mean we're talking about years and years of people telling me I was a dumb housewife, of Love Canal—even though I know better than that because I proved I was not stupid.

---

*Browning-Ferris Industries, a waste disposal company.

There's something that it does to you. And so when you walk into this place or that place, and you have to wear a three-piece suit, and heels, and you sit there, the first thing is, "Oh, God, I'm going to open my mouth and I'm going to sound just like a dumb housewife," just what they expect to hear from me. And so, it was very difficult, on the onset. Not anymore; only because I know most of these people now. And I know how to play the game (laughs). I know what they want to hear. But most of them I realize since then are really very much like myself. It's kind of the fear of the unknown, more than anything else, that I have difficulty with.

Which is a whole new thing that I was forced to learn, as administrator of this organization. How do you administrate? You know, how do you do this, how do you do time sheets for projects? How do you project out your time? I mean, all of these weird things you have to . . . there's a whole new managerial thing. Definitely different [from Love Canal].

Or I have to figure out whether to buy a computer, and whether to buy an IBM, an Apple, Texas Instruments. I mean, it's very strange. I know they're silly things, but they're difficult when all you had was HBO all your life. Now you're making a decision on a three- to five-thousand dollar computer.

And what are our needs? Gee, I don't know. I never asked. At Love Canal, I never had to sit down and figure out what our needs were. You know, we need this right now, and we either get a donation for that, or we would go and buy out of somebody else's pocket, or something. But here, if we need a five-thousand-dollar computer, it's going to take six months of fund-raising, and then after you raise the funds you have to figure out what to buy. Who do you trust? Where do you go? It's very different.

At first I was very uncomfortable, and very insecure. Very insecure about making policy decisions. And would make a decision and then call everybody I know to make sure that decision was correct. And say, "Look, this is what I've decided to do, and here are the reasons I've decided to do it, and do you think I made the right decision?" Very very insecure.

Because I'd never done it before. I mean, One Hundred and Ninety-Seven Thousand Dollars! When you come from a house, and a budget of ten thousand dollars a year, total, for everything—house, car, children, family, food, clothing—I mean, I can't even imagine that. I still can't imagine it. I can see the numbers and figure out where it all goes, but I could never imagine that kind of money. Lump sum.

Now, because it's become a way of life, it doesn't bother me. But it was just a big adjustment, to go pay $550 in rent, for a house, when my house payment in Love Canal was $64.44. That's over five times what I was paying for my house. I mean, all of these things. . . . You know, my mother would say, "Well, $64.44, why are you throwing your money away in Washington? You're paying that kind of money for a house?"

So you like this better?

Oh, yeah. I ain't dying here (laughs). Yes, definitely it's better. And it's because I'm personally removed. I still have the anger in the sense that people call me up and I get angry. I still get outraged at what I hear. And that's what keeps me doing what I'm doing, the outrage. The outrage and the anger. When people call me up, which they often do, and they say what they're experiencing, that is the motivation that makes me want to—kill, get outraged, and go on, and what keeps my heart into this.

It's not as intense, and it's not every single moment of every single day. I mean, there's nothing to compare with living with it, and feeling it every single minute. You look in your children's eyes and you say, "God, I got to do something." But it's enough anger that I want to go out and do something about it, that I want to make sure the Clearinghouse is addressing those needs.

But there are many more parts of this that are also fun. I mean, there's an awful lot that's also work. And work is not necessarily fun. I mean, doing direct mail is not my idea of having a good time. But it's just that I guess I'm personally removed . . .

I don't have to do all the work to make it happen. I can go out and help people, to do what they need to do, by advising them, by being there, by helping them think it through, by a whole host of different things. And then we get to share in the victories. All I have to do is spend three days there. They do all the work.

But when I go out to a site visit to a community, I won't usually even wear something like this [slacks and blouse], but rather I'll put jeans on and a T-shirt, or a jean skirt and a low-key polyester top—I'll dress like they dress. So then I'm not this Washington lady that's coming in as a professional, but rather I'm one of them, and they can immediately relate to me.

I mean, that's one thing that I have that none of the other environmental groups have, and that is, I've been there. And when the Lois Gibbses of whatever say, "I can't do that; you're different," I have the advantage of saying. "Uh-uh. Cop-out. You can't say that. I mean, I was what you are. I was worse than what you are, 'cause at least you know where city hall is. I didn't even know that."

And I have an advantage in playing off that. You know, (with emotion) "You have a responsibility. You know more than most people, and you have the responsibility to share that, and you have the responsibility to pull these people together. And you have the responsibility as a parent to do something for those kids! And every time you say you can't do it you go over and look your kid in the eye. When you go look your kid in the eye and tell that kid you can't do it, then I'll believe you."

And then just talk to them, you know: after giving them this hard rap and putting them in shock (laughs), then we just talk. In teaching people, I don't talk to them, I make them talk to me: "What do you feel most insecure about? What is hardest for you to do?" And we'll go on and say, "Well, how do you think we can overcome that? Let's talk about it. You think somebody's going to slam the door in your face. Okay, let's go over there and we'll practice. You knock on the door, and I'll slam it in your face. And then we'll see what happens." And you know, it would be a silly thing, and we'd all be giddy and laughing which would take the tension out of it. "We're going to slam the door in your face, let's go!" And they would do it, and I'd slam the door in their face, and I'd open up the door and I'd say, "Did you lose your nose? Did you lose an arm? Did your pants fall down? And what happened?"

And then help them think that nothing happened; the door got slammed in my face. "So now what are you going to do?" "I'm going to go to the next door." "Right. Who cares? And that person's a jerk. Let's move on."

I would just throw out what my fears were on the table, help them in knowing their fears—yeah, yeah, yeah, I feel that way; yeah, yeah, yeah, I feel that way—and I could immediately connect with them, and then help build them. I'd say, "Well, I felt that way too." And do it in a way that's funny, fun, at ease, not structured, not intimidating, and they learn without knowing that they learned.

It's a head game. It's a head game, and it's trying to get people to think about what they have to think about, to do what they have to do. And we teach them how to set goals—most people do not know how to set realistic goals; how to figure out strategies.

I just have this real weird sense for people. Everybody calls it weird. I don't think it's weird; I think it's the biggest asset I have. But I do have this sense where I can generally pick things out in advance. It has a lot to do with intuition. . . . And I don't know if you're born with it or where it comes from, but it's just a wonderful asset for folks who have it, although I think everybody has it; I just don't think people use it. I think that's their biggest downfall.

The technique is absolutely useless, if you don't have the intuition. I mean, if I want you to do something, I need two things: I need [the intuition] to figure out where you're coming from, and how this would be in your best interests, and then the technique to get you to do what I want. But it's two different things. And they go hand in hand. Technique is no good without intuition.

You can't get people involved unless they feel affected. If they're not affected, for the most part it's going to be very difficult if not impossible to get people involved. Once you find the self-interest in people, you have to trigger the anger in them to get them moving, and you have to keep them informed enough that they understand, so that they can continue their anger.

And I guess the other thing people need to do is to feel some type of ownership, and I think that's real important; that not only am I angry about this issue, and I understand it through this educational process, but I own this issue. This is part of me, and I've been working on this for so long that I'm going to see it to the end.

And that's very hard, to build the ownership in, and it takes a tremendous amount of patience on the part of people who are trying to organize it, because it's so easy to let three or four people go off and do all these things. It's easier, it's less hectic, but it doesn't build the ownership, and therefore, in the long term, the results are not as good, because you don't have as many people involved.

I firmly believe you can get people organized around anything. Some are easier than others, but you can get them organized on anything if you use the right strategy. I don't think you have to have a death or a life-threatening situation. It wasn't a tragedy that happened, that made Love Canal become a nationally known thing. But rather it was the public recognizing the tragedy.

I mean, since back when the first car was made, drunk drivers were running over people. Wastes have been dumped for over twenty years. Woburn, Massachusetts, happened before Love Canal; nobody heard about it. It was the educating of the public that made Love Canal what it was; the education is the problem, not a single tragedy in itself. It goes back to self-interest. How is this going to affect you?

Do you feel that since you switched your focus from a local situation to national, that you're having more of an impact now?

Well, yes and no. My goals are different, so the impact is different, I guess. I mean, certainly I had as much impact as you possibly can have at Love Canal. And on a national scale, I think we're having a lot of impact, in helping people to organize themselves, basically learn from what other people have learned in addition to myself. There's only one landfill's been sited since Love Canal. A lot of that's being attributed to our work.

I guess it depends on the issue. I personally would say that a person should be involved on a local level, not the national level, because I think the impact of local effort is much bigger than national effort. On a national scale, we're doing wonderful things. We're changing industry's practices, we're making them stop and think, regulations are changing, that's great. But—what good are laws on the books if there isn't anybody at home to make sure they're enforced?

So much can be done at the local level that could never be accomplished at the national level. You can pass your own regulations; you can pass your own laws; you can do your own local ordinances to ban hazardous waste from your local community; you can manipulate elected officials, which you can't do on a national level.

I mean, how do you get to Ronald, right? You can't reach him. How do you get to Ruckelshaus?* You can't reach him. Locally, you can get to the local state health department—the local DEQE in Massachusetts, DEC in the State of New York. You can go to their offices, you can sit in. You can picket them, you can protest, you can hold public hearings. You can do so many things and change things—community efforts are always, always much more effective on a local level.

But here you are sitting in a national clearinghouse, which is not local.

Right. But we work with ninety percent local groups. We don't do anything on the Hill. We don't do any lobbying, we don't do any regulatory work. Because we know that's not where the power base is. The power base is back at home. If local communities all organized around issues, then this would be a democracy of the people. Now it's not a democracy of the people as we'd all like to believe it. But rather it's a democracy of the powers, the powers being—it changes with the issues, but mainly goes back to big business.

We had the power locally to get President Carter down there, to get sixty million dollars to get people evacuated. If that Love Canal fight was fought from a national level, we would have lost. We had no targets, we had no people. And that's why we literally do not go into Washington unless it's an agenda item for local grass-roots people.

We tell local grass-roots people not to do things on a national scale. We advise them not to organize beyond their state. That's where their power is, and anything beyond the state, they defuse themselves, and they're powerless, or have limited powers. And so my feeling is, everybody should organize in their community.

---

*William D. Ruckelshaus, Administrator of the Environmental Protection Agency, 1970–1973 and 1983–1985.

I'm very optimistic; I'm an optimist, about everything, unfortunately (laughs). I can't draw the line. The people who organize around this are very much like myself: the blue-collar workers, the farmers, the rural people—people that don't forget. It brings people together from all classes, all races, all parts of the country; there's no societal boundaries to hazardous waste. And in this issue, people who organize never forget, because their churches are involved, their community's involved, and they're stable—they're going to be there, they're not going to disappear. I think that's a value in this organizing effort more than any other one. So that's where my optimism comes from.

And, above and beyond that, when they resolve their local issue, for the first time in their lives they've realized that they have power. They have been empowered. They're not going back home and sitting there, like they would have done ordinarily. But rather, hey, we already know this game, you know. You are here to represent my needs, my desires and wants, and that's what you're going to do. And they just go on to different things, where before all they would do is read the newspaper and bitch and complain. And never move on it. Now they've been empowered, and they know they can move on it.

Although it's interesting, most of them deny that that's what they're doing. Most say, "I'm too burned out, I'm not going to get involved anymore"; and yet the next thing you see is they're trying to put up a stop sign at the local corner. "Well, that's not really being involved, it's just a stop sign." And they don't usually admit that they're still involved in community efforts, but in actuality they are very involved. Because they can no longer sit back and watch it.

Why me and not someone else? The only thing I can attribute why me is 'cause I've always been a fighter, by nature. A middle child of six children (laughs), you learn to fight very early in life. For virtually everything—from the food on the table, to bedroom space and seating. I mean, you have a couch and two chairs, and somebody gets the couch, and somebody else sits on the floor. Who gets the front seat of the car, when ma goes shopping? These were major issues as a child.

Even as a child I was very, very shy. I didn't communicate much with anybody. I didn't have a whole lot of friends. I stayed upstairs until my mother called me, played with my dolls and did my sewing. And that was it. I didn't do social things at the school, I wasn't involved in sports, I wasn't involved in extracurricular activities, I didn't go to dances on Friday night. I mean all of those things I just chose not to do, for whatever reason, I have no idea.

But when one of our neighbors told my sister and I that we couldn't walk on her sidewalk, my sister and I went down and sat on her sidewalk all day. . . . Why I did that, I don't know, because normally I wouldn't even talk to anybody. Whether it was just to be defiant, I don't know, but we just sat on her sidewalk, and we ate Popsicles all day. So we would run home, get some more Popsicles, and we'd come back, and we'd sit in the hot sun on her sidewalk just to aggravate her.

And when it was in reference to my family, I had no shyness, okay? I always was a family-oriented person, and I always would fight for my family. [It was] more motherly instinct than anything. So I would talk to a complete stranger and say, "Off my case. Get out of here, lady."

Maybe it's a humanistic thing; you can't go around torturing people, and that's what I felt they were trying to do, literally torturing my children and my family. And that sort of motherly whatever said, "No more. I'm not going to do this anymore; I've got to do something."

Being a fighter as a child may have helped me to do what I did, but I really don't know that that's the reason. I don't know what it was. I mean, I was outraged. Was I more outraged than the rest? Was I more angry than the rest?

In Washington, everybody's a public figure practically, and everybody think's they're important, so I'm just another face in the crowd, which is wonderful. And I totally enjoy it. I can go into a store and do things.

A couple of times I've been very frustrated: when the children went to school recently, they told the teacher about Love Canal and stuff like that, and I went to school and she sat there and talked to me for fifteen minutes about Love Canal and hazardous waste and what wonderful things we did, and how much she admired—this is a fifteen-minute teacher's conference, that's all you're allowed. And it was like, "How's my kid doing?", you know? So in that sort of way, when people do find out who I am and what I've done, I don't want to hear it. I want to hear about my kid, I want to hear about how that child is doing in school, and where the problems are. And although the person is very pleasant, I just get very annoyed by that.

I am a public figure in the sense that if I go to Times Beach, Missouri, every TV camera in Missouri is there. People pay fifty dollars a dinner to come hear me talk for a fund-raising event. People walk around and say, "Oh, wow, it's Lois Gibbs," sort of like a Ralph Nader or someone in that kind of public role. But that's okay, 'cause I know when I got out there, I'll be out there three days, it's my job; and I will come back [home].

So I am still a public figure, but in a way I can control, I can handle. I leave here at five o'clock, and I don't care if the whole world is collapsing around me. But if I were ever an actress, I would go crazy—those people following you around with cameras. I mean I had this much [indicates small amount] publicity. And I went crazy. I just don't understand how people live like that. Unless they enjoy it. But even that gets old.

I guess the other cost would be more on a personal basis, which is the loss of friends. The loss of family. I found it very difficult to make friends here. And mainly because I'm not a professional, in their sort of way. I don't wear a three-piece suit, I wear less dressy clothes, and I don't play the games they play. And in many cases that's going to Washington and kissing everybody's ass.

I don't feel I have to do that. Nor will I ever do it. Just in my own philosophy, they are my employees. They work for me, I pay them, I put them there. People I represent pay them and put them there. I'm not going to go in there and kiss their . . . And so they can't deal with that. And therefore they can't deal with me. Because I'm a different breed of person.

I really miss my friends, though. I go back often enough, it's not that far; it's an eight-hour drive. I think the children have paid more than I have, losing their school, losing their friends, losing their grandparents, losing their father, losing a lot of things that meant security to them. The house, and all of that routine.

Certainly I'm much more (laughs) educated than I was before in the sense of how the world works. What politics are, what taxes are, what communities are, and all those other things. My personal priorities have changed. I no longer want to save money for that someday trip to Disneyland, or whatever it was, but realize that at any time I or the children could get cancer and at any time I or the children could die. And if I have five hundred dollars now I'm spending five hundred dollars now and having a good time. So my personal priorities have changed a tremendous amount.

But as a person I've changed, and I really don't know how to put it in words. . . . I've become obviously more professional . . . more organized, and more independent than I ever was before. Less shy, less intimidated. (Chuckles) Less of a good housewife, 'cause my house is always dirty. I don't know, I've just changed totally as a person. I'm no longer what I was at Love Canal. . . . I'm just very different.

I'm going to be here for the next three years, five years. I figure I only can take three years at a time. But, I mean, I have no reason or intentions of leaving.

In five years? Well, I'd like to stabilize the organization, in the sense of getting it through this growth period, and broaden our work in communities across the country. And actually do some outreach. I have all these plans for outreach which I've never been able to put into action.

On a personal basis, I'd like to spend less time on the road. Although I enjoy that, I'm still very much of a mother, a person that would like to be home with my children, seeing that my children are getting old now and will be leaving home. Michael's in junior high school now, so he's only got five years or so.

And I'd like to settle into a nice house somewhere and not be Dolly D., as my mother would say—yeah, Dolly Domestic, that's what she used to call me. Not to go back to being a housewife or homemaker full-time or anything like that, but just have less time on the road and more time at home, to do those family sort of things—they're real important.

And I've always wanted to get an education in something I wanted to do. One of my original ideas back at Love Canal was to be a nurse. I really liked the profession; I worked as a nurse's aide, and I worked with senior citizens, who I also enjoyed very much. I'm optimistic that my personal goals can be accomplished, stopping landfilling, helping people, cleaning up America. So when the mother earth's cleaned up, I can go do something else with my time. . . .

I just didn't know that there could be problems or conflicts or challenges—I didn't think that far ahead.

Candy Lightner

MOTHERS AGAINST DRUNK DRIVING

THE last interview poses an issue: local level or national? Lois Gibbs makes a case for investing civic energy locally: "The impact of local effort is much bigger than national effort." Perhaps she is right, or at least justified. Even if she's wrong, most of the time you have to start locally anyway.

But if you make it big locally, and if the media catch your eye, or vice versa, there's every pressure to leave home folks behind and be bound for glory. Whom do we know who had a shot at national exposure and turned it down? We fly to fame like moths to light, except that in our particular case we have something the world must know, and much as we'd like to, we can't in good conscience turn down the opportunity.

Once you've made that move, you become an ex–local hero, an alumnus, strictly speaking. You're on a different playing field, the competition is tougher, you may not measure up. Celebrity—recognition, even—changes how others see you, or how you see yourself. And it's hard to go home again.

But, also, are you doing more social good out there, and how do you measure the good you're doing? These questions recur in chapters to come.

Lois Gibbs, the Yorks, Candy Lightner in this account, all crossed over that bridge from local to national, while others stayed put. Candy Lightner crossed over and then some, for she is the founder of MADD, Mothers Against Drunk Driving, which by her calculation is one of the largest nonprofit organizations in the country, and by most standards among the most successful grass-roots initiatives of the 1980s.

Lightner and Gibbs, from opposite coasts, had fates in common:

women about the same age; divorced mothers of school-age children; naive at the start, without very much formal education or training; involuntarily affected, angered, and eventually mobilized by an external crisis, which in Lightner's case was her daughter being killed by a drunken driver. Do these characteristics predict success? I believe they do. In any event, both women came out of nowhere, then through originally local actions shaped both national legislation and national consciousness.

There are differences. For Lois Gibbs, travel is a necessary part of the job, and you sense she'd truly prefer to be at home. Candy Lightner seems more to enjoy the hopped-up pace, the moving about, the plugging into power structures and shaking them around. She is more entrepreneurial (she used to sell real estate), a businesswoman and proud of it. You can have related backgrounds and related accomplishments, but unrelated styles.

The account here differs from the others in that it was taken from a public lecture in March 1985 at the Kennedy School of Government at Harvard University. (The tape was used with Candy Lightner's kind permission.) There are about ten people in the late-afternoon audience. Candy is relaxed, sharp, funny, engaging, pointed, eating an apple. She can talk; when she's warmed up, she's nearing 270 words per minute.

She's introduced by a former colleague who says, "I don't think I've ever met anybody who had as much raw instinct for how to make an issue public, and to make things happen." Instinct again, and comments such as this must be taken seriously. Yet heroism is not in the genes (we don't think). The social researcher looks for causes in the environment, and in this account there are many of them, contributory if not sufficient.

Causes aside, when I'm listening, what comes through to me most is a woman whose whole being is saying "I have a *lot* of drive," and also "Don't tread on me."

✳

When I first started MADD five years ago after Cari was killed, I had no idea what I was going to do. I didn't think in terms of legislation, I only knew that I did hurt, and people needed to know about this problem, and other children perhaps would be saved.

It was the second time that my daughter had been hit by a drunk driver, and finally it had cost her life. Also I had two other children that I was very concerned about, so I had a paranoid fear, and also I was very angry and very bitter.

And yes, I was thinking revenge, I say that with absolutely no qualms, no guilt at all—I wanted the man who killed my daughter punished. I did think of killing him, actually, and I attempted it, but somebody took my gun away.

But I also have a philosophy of life, and it's no great philosophy, and it's no big words of wisdom. [As a child] I grew up in the military, and I've been through all kinds of things, and I've always believed that something good always comes out of something negative. And when my daughter was killed, and when I finally sobered up and realized what had occurred—'cause I did get drunk after she was killed, I just didn't want to deal with the pain— my first thought was, you know, something good has got to come out of this. I was going to donate her organs.

So I called the hospital, and they informed me that her body was so badly mutilated they couldn't donate any of her organs. And the frustration of (a) losing a child, and (b) not knowing who it was—it was hit-and-run at that time—and (c) knowing that nothing positive could come out of this—I have to tell you overwhelmed me. And I couldn't deal with it. I was just so angry about that. But come hell or high water, there was something good. At that time, I didn't even know what it was.

[The driver] was arrested four days later, and I learned that he was drunk. Ironically we went out to a bar that night, and as we were waiting to be seated we were all having a drink and I said, just out of the blue, "I don't know what it's going to do, but I'm going to start an organization. I am just going to do this, because I'm so *angry.*" And my girlfriend piped up, she said, "We'll call it MADD, Mothers Against Drunk Driving"—just like that. That was her first word, it took her two seconds to say that, and I knew when I heard the name that it was destined to be.

And I have to tell you, from that point on, things just fell into place. And still do.

The press called me for about the first three or four years "the little housewife" from Fair Oaks. I was not really a very typical little housewife. I was a full-time realtor, and I had a full-time job and a career. And hadn't been a housewife I guess for some time.

However, in some ways they were correct in that I was extremely naive: I was not a registered voter; I didn't know a Republican from a Democrat; and when I first decided to start the organization, one of the first people I went to was a very old and dear friend, and he said to me, "What is it you want to do?"

And I said, "Well, I've started this organization, and I want to do something."

And he says, "Do you know what?"

And I said, "Not really. What do you think I should do?"

And he said, "Well, I think you should go see your assemblyperson."

And I said, "Who's that?"

And he said, "Well, what district are you in?"

And I said, "I don't know."

And he said, "Well, what are you, a Republican or a Democrat?"

And I said, "I'm not either."

And he says, "Well, don't you vote?"

And I said, "No, I don't."

And he got so angry with me he sent me out of the office, and said, "Don't you even come back until you're registered to vote." And I didn't know how to register to vote.

And I say this to you so you understand how naive some people can be about drinking and driving. So in the beginning, besides going through the grieving process, I had to learn political reality, I had to learn how to register and vote, I also had to learn about Assembly operation, and I also had to learn what drunk driving was all about, and then find solutions to that problem.

I realized [drunk driving] was a socially acceptable form of homicide. The laws we had in the vehicle code were totally inadequate, and I sat in the courtrooms and watched judges not even dispensing the laws that we had. I watched a judge one time, he gave straight probation to a *seven-time repeat offender*, a drunk driver who had continually been given straight probation and had continually violated that probation.

And I remember going back and talking to him about it and telling him who I was and what I was doing and how could you do this? And he said, "Well, nobody's ever said anything about it; nobody's ever asked me not to do it." Well, this little housewife from Fair Oaks thought that we needed to go and get some tougher laws.

So I went out and I started meeting with lobbyists, talking to lobbyists, and the California Highway Patrol, and various different individuals. And what they did is they gave me a yellow sheet of paper, and they said, here, write down the kind of bills you want to see. And I thought, oh, this is going to be lots of fun. A yellow, legal-sized tablet, you know, have a ball, let me tell you.

I was mandatory everything. I was like, three years of jail on the first offense, I mean, can you believe this? Ten years on the second, forty . . . I mean, you just name it. And I would take this around to various members of the Assembly Criminal Justice Committee, the ones that I could get in to see, which at that time weren't very many, and they would say, "You're too tough, you can't do this, it isn't going to work," and blah, blah, blah.

And I remember I walked into one legislator's office, and I was telling him the problems that we were having in the courtrooms, and his very words to me were, "What is happening right now is fine. You don't need to mess with it. And if you don't like what's happening in this country, little lady, you leave." I mean, you just go—not change it, not improve it, but leave. This was an elected official.

And then I went from that office into another office, and I couldn't see [the legislator], but I saw his aide, and [the legislator] happened to hear me and he says, "Well, I think what we're doing right now in drunk driving is fine." And I said, "Well, sir, if I were to come into your office under the influence, and I were to have a gun, and I were to shoot at all your staff members, and miss, would you like to see me get a fifty-five dollar fine?" And he says, "Well, no, I wouldn't." And I said, "Well, that's what happens in drunk driving cases." And he was so impressed with my logic he walked away.

The third office I went in was a woman, and I thought, well, at least I'll get some sympathy. And I sat down, and for some reason, as I was telling her the story of what I wanted to do, I began to cry. And she picked up the phone and stayed on the phone. So I thought, well, I can't see any progress here.

So anyway, finally, I had to learn to do something that was very difficult for me; I had to learn to cope with myself. I had to learn to give here, give there, you maybe get here, you get there.

But I was pretty lucky because when I first started, and being so naive, I managed to surround myself with very good people. And I was just—tell me what you can; tell me what I need to know; tell me what to do; help me here and help me there. I had a whole group of lobbyists, and people that were just super-good with people, that really cared about the issue.

I mean, they didn't know me from Adam. I could have been a hysterical nothing. I could have been a fly-by-nighter, and some of them thought that, and they stayed away, but others didn't. And I went back around with this bill.

Anyway, we went forward. We didn't have money, and we didn't have power, but we did have the media, which was very interested in what we were doing. And we went out to the public, via the media, and via our little newsletters. We didn't have a membership list, we weren't doing fund-raising, we were really grass-roots.

We were still working out of the den of my home. We had only a few volunteers, and by that I mean a few—two; my father and my best friend. But somehow the media had gotten out the word about this massive public education grass-roots organization with hundreds of members all over the state of California, which was totally untrue, but far be it for us to correct that.

We were trying to start chapters. I mean, John Doe would call us and say, "Hey, I'm interested in this, and I live in Santa Barbara," and I'd say, "Fine, you're a chapter." And I'd never see John Doe again. I mean, we were real grass-roots.

But when we went in, the day that we introduced the bills, we did a little strategizing: we had a demonstration at the capitol, my daughter's friends came forward with paper flowers, because we wanted to present to the legislators something they could see. And these darling little teenagers made up their own picket signs and picketed back and forth, and we had a petition drive calling on the governor to form a state task force on drunk driving.

At that time, [Governor Jerry] Brown was more interested in the environment and flowers than he was about children, and I could not get in to see him. So we started a petition drive. This was again trying to catch and keep the eye of the media, who in turn would help catch the eye of the public.

We had done our homework, though. We had done a lot of lobbying. We met with our individual representatives. We went out with our newsletter in their districts asking people to send telegrams, write letters. The chairman of one caucus said they had received more mail on this legislation than any pending legislation. So really what we did was act as a catalyst, I think, for the people of California. Basically they realized they'd had enough of drunk driving; here was a way to do something about it, help change attitudes, change the laws, get tough. And eventually save lives.

Our bills passed out after a year, and it wasn't an easy process. There were a lot of ups and downs. It's so political; I'm sure you realize this. We were going through a time period where the Senate Judicial Committee didn't like the Assembly Criminal Justice Committee, for some dumb reason. But our bills got caught up in the middle of this.

The bills were introduced on the Assembly side, so the Senate Judicial whatever-you-call-it decided they weren't going to hear them. And Jim* had called me one morning and told me the problem, and he said, "If we don't get the bills out by midnight, tonight, we're down the tubes." And I went into total panic, and Jim, as usual, said, "Don't worry, we'll see if we can find a loophole."

It just so happened that right after he called, NBC news magazine called. This is when, you know, they were on TV. And they said, "We've gotten very interested in that, and we'd really like to do something on you, and is there any committee that you're going to testify before, so we can come up and cover it?" And I said, "Well, as a matter of fact, there is.

*A former California legislative aide and a colleague of Candy.

There's the Senate Judicial Committee tonight at nine o'clock." [The testimony] was originally scheduled for nine o'clock. And they said, "Well, we'd really like to come up and cover it."

So I called Jim back, and he said, "Call the head of the Senate Judicial Committee," who was also running for Attorney General. He said, "act like you don't know that I called you and told you they weren't having the hearing." So I called Omer Rains [then chair of the Senate Judiciary Committee] and said, "Oh, Omer, guess what? I'm so excited! NBC news is coming up tonight, and they're going to film us testifying, and they want to do an interview with you! Isn't that just great?" And Omer said, "I'll call you right back."

And five minutes later he called back, and said, "Oh, Candy, we're going to have a special hearing on your bills, tonight, at nine o'clock. Isn't that wonderful?" And I said, "It certainly is." NBC news showed up, and they never interviewed him. But we got our bills out of committee, and that's all I cared about.

And we went forward, finally got the bills passed, finally did get the bills signed. That was our first attempt on the local level, working with public legislation.

✳

From Candy Lightner's den, and from the first legislative forays, MADD has grown into an organization with 300-plus chapters and 600,000-plus donors and volunteers. Liquor consumption has dropped nationally. Laws against drunk driving have stiffened, and so have public attitudes. MADD can take credit. More to the point, though, there's some evidence that drunken driving fatalities are down, though all data are not yet in.

Another goal is a minimum drinking age of twenty-one in all fifty states. Meanwhile, MADD is working with kids, and with liquor outlets, aiming to build alcohol awareness. (Candy started SADD, Students Against Drunk Driving, at the same time as MADD.) MADD has had corporate sponsors, including breweries, though most funding comes from direct mail. If you land on their mailing list, you'll get lots of fund-raising appeals; MADD is very tenacious.

In 1985, their budget was about $1.9 million. "I think it should be more than that," Candy says. "We should be raising some money."

✳

MADD is far more than legislation. It is victims assistance, it is group support, it is public education, it is court monitoring, trying to change the system, and it's trying to change attitude and behavior. MADD is considered the model grass-roots organization, and we are looked to by a lot of other organizations.

It's something that you can actually get involved in and see how that involvement makes a difference. You see laws change: there have been 360 new laws introduced in this country, introduced and passed, since 1980. There are fifty governor-appointed state task forces in this country. There is, or was, a presidential commission, and there is now a national commission, against drunk driving. Plus the statistics have shown that lives are saved.

So we're talking about major legislative changes, and people can see that. And when I go out to the public, get my little direct-mail letter that somebody else writes for me, and say, you know, twenty-seven states haven't passed twenty-one,* we need to pass twenty-one because it saves lives and blah, blah, blah, people are very willing to give because we will *pass* twenty-one in those states, and they will see that, and we do it because of their contribution.

A lot of people don't know how to strategize. I didn't set down goals and objectives, but I did strategize with the media. The problem is that you have to keep the issue before the public eye, [which was] one of the easiest things for me to do then, which is not easy now.

I had so much anger, emotions, it was very easy for me to go out to do a hard thing on an issue—call a judge a jerk, or say the governor is blah, blah, blah. Because of the emotion that I had; I no longer have that anger and emotion, and I'm much more reasonable than the rest of them. I'm logical and rational now; so when I go out to the public eye, I have to do it on a reasonable basis, but still keep the media interested—and I do that through the chapters.

It's a matter of constantly finding issues that the media is going to be interested in. Everybody said after [the early legislation] passed, what are you going to do next? You know, what is there after laws? Well, what we did next was start on the twenty-one issue on the state level, and build up on the twenty-one. Plus we got into court monitoring, as you know, which was very controversial; for several years it was in all the major newspapers, because our people were being thrown out of courts by judges and things like that. When we did twenty-one as a national issue, that kept the media alive on twenty-one for at least a year, and it's still going. Everybody said after twenty-one, now what are you going to do? And happy hour came along, you know.

Sometimes I don't always feel that an issue is an issue that MADD

---

*The reference is to a minimum age of twenty-one to purchase or be served liquor. Only six states had not passed such legislation by early 1987.

should participate in, but at other times you see the media visibility of an issue and you say, well, wait a minute, it can benefit us to some degree, because it can keep the issue before the public eye on drunk driving, impaired driving—so you go ahead and take advantage of it. So it's just a matter of knowing what's going to happen as far as your issue, and constantly throwing out new things to the public. And a lot of groups don't do that.

We get a call every single day from someone who would like to start a group and wants to know how we did it. And one of the things we'll teach them is how to keep an issue visible. You can't just say that people molest children, you have to do something about it; you've got to keep something before the public. You've got to keep solutions before the public.

And to me MADD is very solution-oriented. We always identify the problem, we come up with a solution. When we wanted a task force, we didn't want a task force to *study* the problem; we said, "We want a task force to *solve* the problem." It's the same when I went after the presidential commission; I don't want a presidential commission to study the problem; we want solutions. And if you read the presidential commission report, it's forty solutions to the problem of drunk driving.

Plus, we're victims. And it's true. The media will always pick up on that. We are victims. Whenever we started a chapter, it's usually a victim.

But I am not your typical victim, 'cause I never attempted to go public with my pain. What I attempted to do was go public with the facts, and talk about the solution. And I felt that MADD was a part of that solution.

You read in the newspapers every once in a while about the internal problems of MADD. They're there, they're very real, we go through a lot of growing pains; but I'll tell you, they roll over and something better comes out of that. Something better seems to get resolved from whatever internal is going on. We learn something and can go forward; it's one of the beauties of the organization.

I was sitting with a group of corporate people the other day, in New York, and they were thinking about funding us, and they said, "Now tell us, what is your five-year plan?" And I looked at them, and I said, "I don't really know what it is," you know, I mean I was trying to think of something real quick, and I said, "Well, I'm not really sure."

And they said, "Well, what is it that you have down for goals and objectives?" and I started laughing, and I said, "I started MADD without a one-day plan. And we're here five years later, so I have to be real honest with you." I said, "We are going to put one together, we're doing our first two-year plan this next weekend, but we just go on day-to-day, and do what needs to be done."

We're flexible; we're not government. My board has given me total authority—I can do whatever I want, I can say yes, no, get up and lobby, say I don't like this bill or what. I'm very fortunate in that respect. I don't have to wait and go see a board and deal with staff and blah, blah, blah. I always say, it wasn't a democracy, it was a dictatorship.

I still have a lot of good people that I surround myself with—I may not always take their decision over mine, but I still listen to everybody, because everybody has something to say. But if an issue comes alive I can go forward with it without checking with fourteen other people, and that keeps us totally flexible. And that I think makes a lot of difference.

Yes, we're a cause, (in soft voice) but we're also a business, and we have to run as a business if we want to be institutionalized. The local chapters are still very much into the cause aspect, and they don't realize that we have staff, and budgets, and comptrollers.

And when I say I'm CEO, people think, you know, oh yeah, you're the one that goes on "Good Morning America." I also run a business. I also manage the day-to-day activity of the organization. I do the budgets and the planning and the objectives and the marketing and the fund-raising, and the chapter development—and all that. You see, the chapters just can't grasp that. Many of them, not all.*

There are thousands of parents whose kids get killed by drunk drivers, but most of them grieve and get angry and in one way or another let it go, and go on with their life. You did not. So I'm wondering what you think it may have been in you, as opposed to the others, that led you to act.

[It was] complete naiveté. If I knew then what I know now, I would not have done it. Most people were more politically aware, more educated, probably of a different background than I had. Because when I first did this, I talked to the mothers and parents who had gone through this experience and had wanted to do something, and said to them, "Why didn't you?" And they said, "It'll take too much time," and gave me a multitude of reasons; they were very valid reasons, but I didn't understand, because those things made no sense to me.

I was so stupid. I just didn't know that there could be problems or conflicts or challenges—I didn't think that far ahead.

Also, it's my Arab heritage, I think. It's true, we're taught to protect our children. That's real strong in the Arab world, do you know that? Protecting

*In October 1985, Candy Lightner was replaced as chairman and chief executive officer by MADD's board of directors, in an apparent dispute within the organization.

your children is just the ultimate thing that you can do. And when one is killed, it's like you didn't do your best to protect them.

So the naiveté was an advantage in a sense?

Absolutely. Oh, but this is my way of doing—I get up and just do things, and don't put a lot of thought into it. Sometimes it works out well, sometimes it doesn't. In this case, it worked out well. . . .

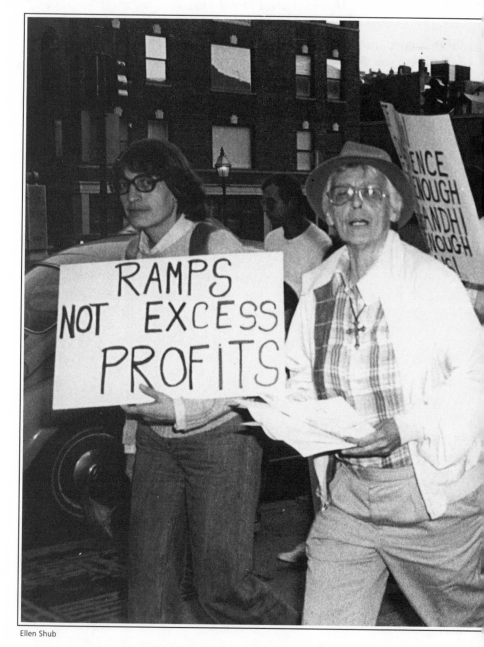

Ellen Shub

Fran Froehlich (left) and Kip Tiernan on the march.

The only way I know is to do what you do passionately.

Fran Froehlich

POOR PEOPLE'S UNITED FUND

S HE is an urban minister, a term she's preferred to nun. Her order was Sisters of Providence, dedicated to service. (She left it in 1985.) She used to live with roommates in an apartment in my home town. I'd see her on the bus going in to work, with parka and backpack.

Fran Froehlich is cofounder and now codirector of the Poor People's United Fund, which raises money for small groups directly serving the poor and dispossessed in Boston. "A raggedy little philanthropic alternative in this vast sea of need," their literature says. Among its beneficiaries: the Boston Food Bank; Families and Friends of Prisoners; Massachusetts Coalition for the Homeless; Disabled People's Liberation Front. The Fund also lobbies for these groups, does research for them, serves on their boards, organizes benefit concerts, runs a coffeehouse, walks the streets, demonstrates, advocates for the poor throughout city and state.

The Poor People's United Fund relies mostly on private, individual contributions, nearly one hundred thousand dollars in 1986. So does Fran, who has chosen to draw no salary from the fund, has no private income, and depends on donations to her personally. She left a job as Director of Religious Education at a local parish—salaried and titled—to start the fund: "It was like jumping into the abyss." For a while, she tried teaching at driving schools to earn daily expenses, but that didn't work out.

From the Fund's newsletter, Christmas 1984:

In four years we have seen the face of affluence become more bloated, more self-satisfied, more insensitive to the needs of the poor. . . . It has become easier to buy gourmet popcorn and chocolates at $7.00 a pound. . . . On the eve of the birth of the Redeemer, we at the Poor People's United Fund once again commit ourselves to help feed the hungry, shelter the homeless, clothe the naked, set at liberty those who are oppressed, and also to educate, to theologize, politicize, to activate, to confront and, if necessary, go to the wall.

Fran speaks slowly and deliberately, with frequent pauses and manifest passion.

*

This is going to sound very trite. . . . It has meant so much to me to be a part of this community of people. Because not only have I discovered different facets of myself, I have learned through them, and because of them, to love different parts of myself.

Like at Rosie's Place [a shelter for homeless women in Boston], a lot of that happened there, I think. There are women there that are crazy, drunk, drugged-out, you know, homeless poor, depressed. In learning to love them, and being able to embrace them, be with them, in learning not to be frightened of them—in learning not to keep myself from embracing them when they're dirty or buggy or whatever—I think, and I hope to God I'm not finished with this journey, and I know I'm not, I've learned to embrace those same parts of myself that get depressed—that's crazy—that's unlovable—that's abrasive—that's too humble, that's whatever—all those qualities.

And an interesting thing happened when that happened: I was able to tolerate more people, because the boundaries of what was acceptable to me were stretched, more and more, and the more people I could encompass, the more I liked myself in them. It just seems like the boundaries keep pushing out.

On the other side, however, I do kick limousines. I yell at people who drive Mercedes. So there are some people I haven't yet learned to accept too much.

The Poor People's United Fund is probably six years old [in 1984]. It was informally constituted by a couple of people who were concerned about what trends they saw in the community—like foundation money being fed into small community groups was now being cut or lost. Or going to be cut or lost. So it was just a way of trying to answer the trend that you saw.

Then Kip and I kept running into each other at different organizational meetings around the city, about other issues.* And she started talking to me

---

*Kip Tiernan, codirector of the fund, and also founder of Rosie's Place.

about Poor People's United Fund and maybe meeting and wanting somebody else to go in on it with her, because it needed more than one person to kind of watchdog bills in the legislature, to read more newspapers and magazines, to try to nail down what the trends were.

So I agreed to do that. We started together. We knew that we didn't want any state money or city money or federal money, but in order to go in any direction we wanted to we thought we should formalize, as far as getting IRS status. So we did that.

It took a while. We got some of our friends to work on stuff for us. One thing we've always tried to do is to use and abuse our friends who are more than generous with the skills they have. A lawyer, an accountant, people who have particular skills and want to be able to contribute something— their services—because they can't contribute their full-time attention to that kind of work.

And over and over and over again we said to ourselves that what we wanted to do was to try to help some groups that were working in the very grass-roots level stay alive, because the services, the things that they were doing, the way they worked in their communities was utterly important to values of surviving. Real community kind of values, people really caring about people in an intense, compassionate way. So though we knew we wouldn't be able to raise programmatic money for them, we decided to try to raise rent money, phone money, stamp money, Xerox money, so that what they were doing would be supported.

It was scary. I was motivated, but it was scary. I didn't know how I'd support myself. I knew that there wouldn't be easy access to money. There was no institutional security. There was no program. I had a lot of anxiety about not knowing what I was really getting myself into. Just the fear of the unknown, wondering about my own creativity in that situation, because I felt it was going to call on a lot of resources that I hadn't really tapped.

And all I had was Kip's word saying "It'll be fine, it'll be fine (laughs). Don't worry, it'll be fine." And I believed her, but at the same time . . .

Was there an official event that started you off?

Well, we told all our friends (laughs). And we stole every mailing list we could get our hands on. We wrote a newsletter and we sent it out to everyone. Here we are.

It was very personal. We talked about our attempt to be a voice for the voiceless and not to be bought out or owned by anybody—to be able to say what needed to be said. To maybe help in some small way. To offer some financial assistance to some small community groups, at that time to the tune of about one hundred dollars a month—into five groups, groups that either Kip or I had some kind of association with and knew.

We did it. We raised just about that much, about seven thousand dollars that first year—gave most of it away.

Then by some fluke we heard there was a woman minister at Old South Church. We just called this woman up and told her our plight. She said, "Okay, I'll see what I can do." The next day she called back and said, "Why don't you come on over, I've got a couple of places in the building to show you." We got an office—donated space.

We believed, personally, that what we were doing was a ministry, but we had some misgivings about being in a church. Some people wouldn't care how ecumenical it was—if it was in a church, they didn't want to have anything to do with it. But we made it clear that there was no association really between us and the church, it was just donated space. It seemed to work out.

And then we just made it look like a ghetto (laughs). Within ten minutes we had files everywhere, papers everywhere. It was a mess. We kind of had a disheveled office space. I think it's a plus. We know where everything is, and it's funny, because I'm a person that likes order. There's a kind of chaotic creativity that seems to take place in that space.

And now I remember, what was causing me anxiety was that I was not letting go. I hadn't really jumped off. There was a certain kind of trust that I hadn't yet developed. Then once I got into it and started meeting some of these people, just getting more into it, unbeknownst to myself, I think, I just opened my hand and let go.

It was important for us not to be in the office all the time. If groups needed us at a demonstration, we were at the demonstration. If they needed us at a hearing at the State House, we would testify. If they wanted us to go to a meeting with them to a foundation, we did that. We wrote letters for them. We spent a lot of time just walking around downtown Boston actually.

We spent a lot of time reading newspapers—we bought every newspaper that we could, just to stay in touch with whatever trends were happening. And it's amazing what you can see. We would tear out articles and file them and use them at the next hearing. We spent a lot of time on the phone, networking with people, interconnecting things. It's very incestuous. . . .

We spent about one-third of the time doing fund-raising and the other two-thirds just networking and advocacy. We're actually going to try to shift that a little bit, do more fund-raising. Also, the manner in which we wanted to do fund-raising—we didn't want to write proposals. We wanted to do things that would also bring people together, like have concerts, like support the arts, because we feel that art is a very powerful medium and speaks to the people at a deeper level than maybe rhetorical things do.

Because of style, too, I think, we didn't want to go the foundation route. At the beginning we went to a couple of the bigger foundations. They didn't want to have anything to do with a coalition, and we were the first formalized coalition of groups. We said, "We are fund-raising on behalf of these groups, because we learned that they spend thirty-three and a third to fifty percent of their time doing fund-raising—that's fifty percent of their time they don't get to do what they were founded to do."

They said, "Well, that's a lot of baloney, that's not going to work." So at the beginning they didn't want to see us, they didn't want to give us any money. Since then, since us, since the Boston Women's Fund, since Community Works, since a couple of other things we helped start, the foundations realized that coalitions are a very good way to go—it does do something positive. Now we think we might have more luck, so we're going to try it again, small corporations actually.

Last year I think we made close to thirty-five thousand dollars. It increases about seven thousand dollars a year, which is really a very good growth pattern, though we still call ourselves the "spare change foundation," because in comparison to a lot of places it's peanuts, you know. We are able to give the groups like two hundred dollars a month now, at least, and other times if groups are in dire need we can give them five, seven, eight hundred, a thousand dollars for a particular project. But it's money they don't have to waste time on; they don't have to send us a proposal, they don't have to thank us for it, they don't have to *do* anything for it. It's a straight donation.

I loved it actually. I had a great time. This is the best time I ever had in my life, still. Knowing that I do have confidence in my personal resources. . . . You know, like Kip and I were saying after the concert, a day later, who the hell did we think we were to even conceive that we might be able to get seven hundred people to come to a concert, that we might be on with Joyce Kulhawik?* It's that kind of thing. It's that kind of attitude where you really believe you can do it.

Well, I've imbibed some of that, I think. I really have the confidence now that you have to take risks. Risk-taking is the most important part—and also it's fun taking risks. You develop your humanity somehow. You become more a part of the human community just kind of throwing yourself out there and saying, it's gonna be all right.

And even if it isn't you laugh. More than anything else that we do—

---

*Fran and Kip had just sponsored a well-publicized concert of women's music. Joyce Kulhawik, the entertainment reporter for a major local television station, featured the concert on the late night news.

more than fund-raising, more than advocacy, more than networking—the thing that Kip and I do the most is laugh, and usually at our own expense. Like we've just been complaining that we have too many meetings to go to and somebody else calls and says, "We're the hunger task force, can you come?" "Oh, sure," you know, because it's needed and because you believe in it and because there's this wonderful motivation that seems to be constant.

In that sense it was easy. And it was fun. I wasn't sacrificing anything, really, once I was in it. I had the best of everything, it seemed to me. Because I was running into all these people who were miserable: they hated their jobs, they were depressed, they were burned out. I was where I wanted to be, doing exactly what I wanted to do.

An experience I had just last night, and, you know, there's nothing profound about this at all: I went to a meeting in Dorchester [a section of Boston where many poor people live]—the Dorchester Women's Committee. These are incredible people to me. One of the things that keeps me going is the sense of awe I have of being with these people who are so down-to-earth somehow. They cut through all kinds of bullshit and they just get right to whatever the issue is about. And that's how they deal with one another.

I go to meetings sometimes, and it drives me right up the wall. You go and you hear, "What I hear you saying is . . ." or "What I heard you thought that I said that you said that she said but that's not what I actually said. . . ." At the Dorchester Women's Committee, somebody at the meeting will say, "Well, I think next Saturday we should do this because I have this idea." And somebody across the table will say, "You're full of shit! You said that last year, you didn't do it last year, and you're not going to do it now." And the first person says, "Yeah, you're probably right."

They're very politicized people, incredibly politicized. Their analysis is right on target and very practical. It has to do with what's happening in their community.

Where do these women get their talent?

I think it's from having to deal with survival issues. They've lived in poor neighborhoods all their lives. And learning how to survive with dignity, even though they have no money—some of them are being abused, women and kids, physically and sexually. . . .

It makes them a better person?

It makes them a better person to be poor? That's a hard question. I think if you're honest about it, it's a hard question.

And yet you want to bring them out of poverty?

Oh, absolutely. Yeah. I wouldn't mind getting my awe some other way. Because it's at their expense that all of this is happening. Yeah, right, I would give up that awe pretty easily, I think, if it meant getting them off the street. It's a sucky way to get your awe.

There's nothing blind on the part of people who are poor. They just know that it ain't gonna happen tomorrow. This is going to take some time. All those greedy people ain't gonna go away. So you just relax and enjoy yourself, because it doesn't have to happen tomorrow. "Now don't you worry about it, honey. Call tomorrow. You don't have to call tonight, call tomorrow." They have a sense of long-term issues, whereas I think middle-class white liberal types have the sense of urgency, that I've got to do it today: I've got this list of fifteen things to do; I've got to call these people right now; I've got to get to them get to them get to them get to them. Because by 1990 I want these five things to happen. I have these long-term goals that must be satisfied. I have these expectations.

Poor people just say, hey, listen, maybe 2016 it'll happen or something. We don't know what, maybe something. We're going to work like hell for it—that doesn't mean it's a laid-back attitude; it's just that there's a different way, a different pace, a different style of dealing with it because they know it's long-term. They *know* it is. We really believed in the sixties that it was gonna end, that it was gonna turn around, and people walked away disillusioned and fell by the wayside, and many people in the sixties sold out because they had the wrong set of expectations.

Can you accept that there will be poor people twenty years from now?

(Softly) I hate it, but I think it's true.

And you'd continue your work still?

Yeah. It's the struggle. It's the struggle. It is a struggle. It is *the* struggle.

As opposed to saying something like, "We're going to wipe out poverty"?

Yeah.

What has made us successful—one thing definitely is passion. Really . . . really caring about it. There isn't anything else I want to do. I don't know how to describe passion, except passionately caring.

The sense of outrage I have is tremendous. You know, when you read in the paper, like there's another program that's cut—it really makes you mad, angry. Not because it's another issue, but because you can see, you can picture, you can picture what it means. You can practically picture the faces of the people, or you can see the person sleeping on a grate. These are *people.* And these people have children. That's what keeps you motivated; that's what keeps you going.

And the humor, that's absolutely crucial. That's partially what has made it successful for us; that's what's made it work for Kip and me. And bringing other people into that laughter. I would say celebration is very important. That's part of it, that whole laughing, that whole being together, that whole saying, "Well, we've been here for an hour, now let's go to lunch."

One thing we would like to do at this point is to develop a fund-raising strategy, about how much money in a given period of time we'd like to raise, and I think we're at that point. We're trying to think of ways to increase the amount of money we give the groups for special projects. We may still go to some of the corporations; we're not sure about foundations yet.

And we're thinking of other creative things. We'd like to buy a building partially to do some of the arts work, to make it available to artists for rehearsals, and for poetry readings, whatever, just some kind of space that could be used for guerilla theater, plays, smaller kind of concert things. And I want us to get a computer. . . .

So we think we're at a growth point, a significant growth point. We didn't talk about boundaries, but I would say probably seventy-five to one hundred thousand dollars a year would be a substantial and for the time being end point. We'd probably increase the number of groups we helped out.

I'm very worried. The political times are very, very harsh. We the people who care about what's happening can see that greed is helping to kill people, literally kill people in the streets, and it's dehumanizing all of us.

You know, people feel that the spirit of the country is growing. That's a pile of crap—the spirit of the country is being corrupted by people just not caring about other people. It shows itself in greed, and in selfishness at a very basic level. Food programs being cut, Social Security programs being cut, making it harder to get on general relief, making it harder for somebody to get on a kidney machine, for crying out loud.

They are going to close—today I just heard—they are gonna close the drug programs at the major hospitals. Do you know what's gonna happen? In the streets? And nobody, you know, will give a damn until it comes to the suburbs and color TVs and video machines start getting ripped off.

There are yuppies out there, many young professionals making a lot of money, who in appearances really don't care a lot—now I'm not talking politics, I'm talking human compassion—who don't seem to have a sense of what's going on. They don't want to see poor people around, or think any further about *why* are these people there, am I contributing to this, how can I help, what can I do?

Okay, so how do you go about changing that person's consciousness?

Yeah, well. . . . I don't know. I don't know if you can, actually.

The only way I know is to . . . do what you do passionately and hope that that comes through in a way that it speaks to that person. That it touches them somehow. I don't know. I don't know how else you do it. Some people are particularly eloquent, and can really get inside people with words. Other people have to speak by what they do. And maybe at some particular point something strikes them. I think that's usually what happens.

It's very slow. And you know . . . I think I used to really believe heavily in education . . . and now I don't depend as heavily on that. I can't, I can't do that. It was energy-depleting for me to do that. So my new tactic so that I can keep going, okay, is that I just do what I think I have to do, and hopefully people will see that I care. I just have to go and do what I see. And I want other people to see that vision or whatever, and I'll talk to anybody who will listen, but I also have to just go along; I can't spend all my time and energy educating. Let somebody else do that. I think it's necessary, I think it needs to be done. But I can't do that anymore. Let somebody else deal with Bernard Law.* Fine. Go talk to him. Do your little thing. But I am not going to spend my energy trying to convince him that what the church needs to do is social justice.

I can tell you the personal frustration I have—some times—I get very frustrated sometimes at not having any money. That limits what I can do. I'm learning how to deal with money. It's been five years for me. It still frustrates me.

On a practical level (laughs) there's no problem (laughs). I mean, food's not a problem because I do have money, there's a personal benefactor, benefactors; basically they contribute money so I can help pay the rent. I live with other people; that's one thing I do that's practical; I couldn't survive otherwise.

If I fall short somehow some month or something like that, it's not a big problem, because we all contribute. I stopped buying clothes. Oh, I buy one or two things. I seem to do all right. You know, when I look back I say, yeah, I still go out to eat once in a while, things with friends, I'm not really hurting. I'm not suffering like you don't have much food. We have plenty to

---

*Then bishop of the Boston diocese, now a cardinal, considered conservative by some.

eat, we eat well. It is worrisome, because I don't like the feeling of not having my own source of income.

But God deliver me from people who say I want to work with the poor. I really hope I'm not one of them. Those people make me real suspicious, for some reason. . . .

Does it make me special? No. No. I mean just recently people have said things to me, like they couldn't do what we're doing. I don't know what that's got to do with it. Sometimes that person is a mother of six; well, I couldn't do what she's doing either. I'm doing what I want to do. If that makes you special, doing what you want to do, well, fine. But that doesn't make you better than anyone else. Somehow, I have to do this.

The reason I joined a religious community was because I wanted to do something for God. Well, as my religious development changed, and I saw the transcendental God become a more immanent understanding of God, God among us, I thought more that what I wanted to do in my life was to be a seeker; and somehow to always keep willing to take risks, to become more a part of humanity. And thereby, finding God, being with God, doing whatever, I don't know.

And somehow, for me, Poor People's United Fund is part of that. It is who I am. It's all the same thing to me. That's what my faith is. I don't know how any longer, at least in this stage of my life, to separate my faith from all these things.

So the faith is woven into the passion?

Yes, it is, they're the same words.

Could someone do the types of things you've done without faith?

Without traditional religious faith? Sure. You can do it. You can do it a long time. But I think they have a certain kind of faith. I don't know if you'd call it religious faith. But I wouldn't presume to describe what that faith is. . . .

*There's nothing wrong with being an outcast at first, as long
as you do what you say you wanted to do.*

Curtis Sliwa

THE GUARDIAN ANGELS

I F the Guardian Angels are controversial, you'd not know it by following Curtis Sliwa through New York City streets. In his red beret and red-on-white T-shirt (wings of the angel, all-seeing eye), he is both visible and visibly admired. "Hey, there's Curtis Sliwa." "Hi, Curtis." "Keep up the good work." Later, in Harlem, "Hi, brother, how you doing?"

Sliwa founded the Guardian Angels, a volunteer civilian patrol whose primary mission has been to prevent urban crime. Many of the Angels are under twenty-one; many in New York are black and Hispanic. The Angels began by riding subway trains in New York City, in groups, and they still do. Since then, they've branched out nationally, and into above-ground patrols and other civic activities: escort services, food distribution, drug prevention, self-defense seminars. They are, in theory, a visual deterrent to crime (they will also grab assailants and make citizen's arrests), and while firm statistics are hard to come by, many feel this theory is borne out in practice.

If they are controversial, it may be partly because crime is controversial. Crime touches us without warning and without our consent; it arouses powerful and conflicting emotions, based ultimately in our biology. Our views on crime may stem from anger, hurt, fear, memory of violation, revenge, compassion, desire for even-handed justice, all these blended uneasily, and differently for different people.

The Angels may also be controversial because Curtis Sliwa seeks controversy out. It's fair at least to call him outspoken. There have been wars of words between Angels and city officials, Angels and cops, occasionally between Angels and their public. And in the New York "subway vigilante" case in 1984, when Bernhard Goetz admitted shooting four youths who he said accosted him, Sliwa said the victims "were sleaze and slime, and this guy was doing what he should. . . . If he can fight . . . maybe we can light into these thugs and punks." Tough language here, from an avowed opponent of vigilantism, founder of an organization whose members can carry no weapons. Public statements like these seem almost calculated to grab attention and stir debate.

Curtis Sliwa in person, at least on duty, is lower-key. He leads an Angel patrol through a mile-long Manhattan street fair, believing that its visibility is helping to deter pickpockets and street criminals. There's no doubt he has presence. His manner is quiet, highly self-assured, notably polite, almost regal. His detractors might add arrogant, or grandiose. The police on the corners look the other way.

We take the subway to the Angels' office in Harlem, given to them by the owner of the *Amsterdam News*. Sliwa says their previous office was torched by drug dealers who didn't want them around. On the street, he is stopped to autograph a book: "Nine out of ten people come up and they treat you like a doughboy come back from the First World War." The newly-acquired office itself is piled with sofa cushions, desks, and miscellaneous debris; it needs a lot of work.

During most of the interview, Sliwa talks with his beret on. When we finish, he escorts me back to the subway, right to the turnstile, as though that were his duty. Several weeks later, a hand-autographed picture arrives in the mail.

As a teenager, Curtis Sliwa turned his front yard into a recycling center. President Nixon honored him as one of America's top newsboys. He won an American Legion award as Outstanding High School Student of the Year, was elected student government president, and was expelled from school shortly thereafter. He comes from a somewhat different mold than most of the Angels he has recruited.

✳

My mom worked as a volunteer in a nursing home for orphans, slipped on some vomit, broke her back, was laid up for three years. I'll never forget the home; they didn't want to pay for many of the medical expenses, ended up costing us. Yet my mom will always have good to say about that. So when you're dealing with people like her, that are giving so much of themselves, it just ingrains itself into you. You think of it as being a normal parcel of growing up. I consider myself very fortunate in that I saw my parents get pleasure out of helping others, and not out of accumulating money or property or real estate or things of that nature.

I grew up in an upper-middle-class, middle-class, predominantly Italian-Jewish area, Canarsie, Brooklyn. I didn't have to fight my way out the door nor fight my way back in. Parochial school education. I had an opportunity to get involved in Little League baseball, Pop Warner football, piano lessons, martial arts lessons. I surely didn't have to worry about where my next meal was coming from.

So who would have thought with the opportunities I had, this would have been probably the last area I would have ventured into. Because number one, not having been born and raised in the midst of it, number two, there being no financial incentive that can arise from it, and number three, clearly having to accept headache upon headache upon headache where maybe you could have become a doctor or lawyer and gain stature in a professional field.

But when you grow up in New York City, you can't escape the realities of crime and what violent crime can do to the way people live their lives. And I think it was just a process of gnawing a little bit each time, having heard of the crime, having seen the victim, having traveled through a neighborhood that was deteriorating and crime-ravaged, and listening to the political and police officials, the so-called know-it-alls, tell us don't go out at night, don't do this, give up, don't go downtown, travel in a group of a thousand, don't, don't, don't, don't—literally reshape our whole life because of the problems of crime. And I just said, *no way*—there's got to be something different. And it essentially got down to somebody had to do something that wasn't violent, that utilized the laws that already existed, that developed the positive role model effect that I believe is the crux of the problem, and did so in a multiracial way so as to embrace all communities and not just the few and the chosen.

I got pleasure out of school, I got pleasure out of sports, I got pleasure out of extracurricular activities, but I didn't get any fulfillment. It was very ephemeral; it was very surface-oriented. I'd say probably about the age of twelve things that were happening in the world began to affect me, and the first area was the area of environment. What bothered me was the tons of garbage that seemed to be strewn about—all these things came from somewhere—and if you take all of that and you don't return any of it, it's like walking into a bank, stealing the money, and running like a bandit.

Having had a grandfather who lived with us, who was out of the Depression years, who even to the day that he died would take a buggy wagon out and pick up scraps of metal, aluminum, copper, brass, old bedsprings, newspapers, bottles, rags, and long miles of a journey walk—and here's a man who is bent over, who had problems of hardening of the arteries, cataracts—for a few cents. When I'd ask him, "Was it worth it?" he'd say, "It's not a question of worth, it's a question of worth*while*. This should not be, and I feel in some way that I'm offsetting all the damage that is being done to the earth."

Then I began to collect materials, when it was not fashionable or in style. I remember I used to put bimetal cans in old refrigerators, in old car hulks, not getting any money out of it, but just so that they would be reprocessed through the system. My grandfather even looked at me at that point and said, "You're nuts; you know, at least I do it, I get a few pennies." I'd collect tons of newspapers, of bottles; I was so caught up in it because just the mere fact that there was garbage, that there was waste product and nothing was being done with it bothered me tremendously.

Now we're talking about the age of·fifteen, sixteen—in high school, active in sports, academic life, involved in student government—but *none* of that excited me. Collecting actually became my key interest. Not just doing it yourself, you know, but getting other peoples to do it was not only a turn-on, but also something I saw as practical, reasonable, that was desperately needed.

I'd bring it to places; I'd have to collect huge amounts to have the industrial contractors pick it up. I made up leaflets and flyers; I got some community newspapers to put in advertising that on such and such days of the week people should leave their bottles and cans and newspapers out in front of their home. I made it a point to try getting the community involved. I started getting some of the younger kids in the neighborhood involved in processing the materials along with myself, so that that became more efficient.

Here it was: I was using my room in an upper-middle-class surrounding—literally turned it into a junkyard. The basement was packed with papers; the front yard was packed with tons of crushed glass in barrels, tons of cans that had been smashed and were awaiting reprocessing; and I mean the place looked like the Sanford and Son junkyard.

But now, in 1971 I believe, the bottom fell out of the economy. You couldn't *give* the materials away; the truckers wouldn't even come and pick it up. So that literally knocked the wind out of the sails, and showed me that although you could build a mechanism, that unless it could perpetuate itself on natural means it really was only meeting a need temporarily, it was still subject to economic control. It was a failure for me because it didn't perpetuate itself. I began to see that if anything was to be effective, it would clearly have to be outside of the norm—independent, autonomous, and able to run on its own.

I'd say seventeen is when this realization really was striking me. I decided not to pursue my education, although I had scholarships to·Brown and

Princeton, academic and athletic. My parents dealt with me very severely; they were hurt and very obviously shocked. They said, "Well you have to pay rent, each week, or out you go," and figured that would be an incentive in itself to go to school where everything was being paid for.

I went out and I got a job pumping gasoline at night with the glorified title of night manager, in the worst neighborhood of the city. Nobody else wanted the job. I was making about 170 dollars a week after taxes, working seven days a week, ten hours a day, but getting held up every other day. It really began to teach me about real life. Now I'm working with people who are doing it not just for pocket money, but for life and death.

I didn't lose sight of volunteer service, getting involved in various different programs, sampling them and beginning to find my own niche. But in all the programs that I would check out, they all seemed to be trying to come up with a plan so they could send it to Washington, get some federal funding, develop into other areas, and not really concentrate on what they originally started on. I saw this tremendous bureaucracy that was developed. It always seemed to have political inclinations, and those involved in the program always seemed to be using this as a stepping stone to go from point B to point C.

Most of these problems that I was looking at were community-level problems. And it just seemed to me there was a laziness on the part of people in general, who just didn't want to get off their duff and deal with it. When I'd look at the drug prevention programs, well, it was the sons and the daughters in that neighborhood that were selling it and taking it—why should there be a federal agency? Why should there be those zillions of dollars spent? Why should we get people who had no sensitivity to that particular area dealing with it, when it was such an easy thing to deal with, it was so community-oriented?

Most of the things—the trash problem, sanitation problem, dealing with elderly people—it was because we ourselves as people didn't want to deal with it; we would rather export the problem out to somebody else. I said to myself, gee whiz, this is the real problem: it's not the problem of Democrats or Republicans, it's not the problem of capitalism or socialism, it's the problem of us taking responsibilities that maybe in previous times would have been considered the norm, 'cause we had no choice.

So I learned, not only from my mistakes, but from others' mistakes, others' successes, and essentially I was like a cook who was traveling to distant lands, taking different recipes, eliminating some ingredients, keeping some ingredients, and knowing that I ought to keep all these experiences in the back of my head for those things that I would like to get involved in and create, although I wasn't really sure at that point what that was going to be.

Twenty years old, and I take on a position of an assistant manager of a McDonald's in the Bronx. They weren't looking for an assistant manager; they were looking for a bouncer really. This is at the time of the gang problem in the Bronx. It was real bad there—places burning down—it's the hottest place in America. But they placed me in one of their largest stores as the night manager.

And it was there that I began to literally go through culture shock, because as part of my duties I'm having to deal with social problems. Guys playing three-card molly [monte] right in the lobby; pickpockets and jostlers fleecing customers on line; gang members coming in, looking to wreak havoc right in the store, this obviously being an extension of what was taking place in the street. Walking the streets, knowing the neighborhood, and seeing the deprivation that existed, the complete hopelessness that seemed to surround me, I realized that this was where there *were* no programs, nothing seemed to be working, and that along with working here that I had to begin addressing some of the problems.

So I formed a clean-up group called the Rock Brigade, which got young people involved, voluntarily cleaning up the streets of the Bronx. I mean this was nasty work, 'cause that is a dirty place. I'd have Hispanics from the West Bronx, blacks from the East Bronx, whites from the North Bronx, about seventy in number. We'd target areas on the weekends, and then late in the afternoons and in early, early morning hours we would hit main commercial areas, like Fordham Road, 149th and 3rd Avenue, over by Yankee Stadium.

It was very difficult, 'cause this is like the last thing anybody would want to do. And at first it was almost impossible—I had to literally go out there myself, get down, and start picking up the garbage in the street. And it built very slowly, one, two, three. Always had to be there myself. If I wasn't there, they weren't going to do it.

We had our shirts: "Rock Brigade—Work for a Cleaner Bronx." I visited different schools, put on different assembly programs. Something like that, you get universal support, it doesn't rub anybody the wrong way, you have open access to all existing community, political, and educational organizations. And slowly and surely I was able to attract people—not football stars, class valedictorians, or mister and miss popularity in school. Then when we did begin to get some attention and recognition, even more came in.

What I learned was that if you plant trees, you clean streets, you do the dirty work, everybody loves you. Politicians were now wanting to set up meetings with us, wanting to give us awards. I had a whole wall at the McDonald's just filled with awards.

But then once again, bureaucracy steps in. We're collecting tons of garbage now, putting it on the corners in plastic bags that are being contributed by McDonald's, Con Edison, merchants' associations. But the Sanitation Department is going through fiscal cutbacks, laying off people, machinery not being used. They approach us and say, we can't pick up this additional trash; you'll have to get private contractors. Five dollars a bag they wanted; merchants weren't willing to pay that.

So what we had was a process where the city was telling me that with all the work we did, sweeping up, canning it, bagging it, trashing it, that they would not pick it up, they would rather see it all over the street. Yet they had asked the Rock Brigade to pick up the trash in Times Square, their showcase. I said, "What about the Bronx? The program already exists there; it hasn't cost you a plugged nickel; all we're asking you to do is pick up the bags of garbage. And you refuse to do that."

So that was the first instance that I ever came to rubbing heads with City Hall, and it left a very bad taste in their mouth, and definitely in our mouth.

All during this process, though, as the group was growing, people would see us in the streets, they'd thank us for what we were doing. But they'd say, "But what about the human garbage?" you know, and the train was right there, the IRT, the Number 4 train, the mugger's express. You couldn't miss it, an elevated line. And folks would say, "Can you do anything about the *crime*?" "Gee, you cleaned up the streets, but clean up the criminals."

For a period of a year and a half I thought about it, I tried to put together different ideas of how that might work, and some of my time that wasn't devoted to the Rock Brigade, I'd literally go out and ride the trains with another friend of mine, another night manager. Just minding our own business, riding the trains, but sitting in the last car, and ending up getting jumped, and mugged, because we were riding some of the worst lines. You'd have gangs coming on board, literally just beating, hitting, savaging all the people. And they just seemed to be feasting on particularly the elderly, the women, and the children. The cops, they were just hanging around at the doughnut stands. The people were helpless.

I didn't know what could be done. The first thing that comes to mind is the images you see in the movie theater, like Charles Bronson, you know, vigilantism, and your first inclination is to beat the shit out of these people. But you realize that in the totality of things, that would be just as bad.

I had a lot of contacts now in the Bronx. And I began to bounce this idea off church organizations, about getting a civilian organization out there patrolling. And naturally they threw up this traditional block watch and crime watch, and what good is that? All you're doing is *watching* the crime.

We watch sports events, we watch theater, and now we're going to watch crime too. I'd say, in the Bronx, the cops aren't going to get there—you need somebody who's going to be a visual deterrent, somebody who can be a positive role model to the young ones. You need to get these young blacks and Hispanics involved, so that they're not just being put in the negative stereotype of always committing the problem.

There were two individuals, a Mennonite minister and a Catholic priest, and I began having long conversations with them. I began piecing together the different kinds of philosophies I might utilize. Didn't know exactly what it would be called yet, didn't even have a mechanism to it, and I'd say it took me about seven months of putting down different ideas, experimenting in my head, experimenting on the train with myself and this fellow Don Chin [the other night manager], and essentially coming up with an idea that formulated into the Guardian Angels.

So all told, a year and a half of thinking, writing, testing, bouncing ideas off of people before we even tested it out, before I approached anybody about getting involved.

We're now in about March of 1978, and I begin approaching people that I know in the community. Ninety-nine out of every hundred looked at me as though I had my nuts and bolts loose. I went to the local community newspaper editor, I bounced the idea off him. He said, "Hey, that's a vigilante idea—that's crazy. What's happened to you, have you gone nuts? Are you off your bird?"

I approached this church organization, and I made a presentation about a civilian group to ride the trains. Mentioned some of the ideas: to have a uniform, no weapons, pay their own fare, utilize only the rights that citizens have to begin with. And I was universally looked at as if I had a case of terminal herpes or syphilis. No one wanted to come near me.

I was being ostracized. Oh, man, you'd of thought that I was Attila the Hun. And I was getting calls while I was working at this McDonald's, a lot of pressure was building up. Calls were being made to the boss—this guy was beginning to go off his bird. Cops were being alerted on the trains to look out for me and this guy Don, because now they were beginning to get an enormous number of citizen's arrests. . . .

Yeah, they couldn't figure it out. The very first time we enacted a citizen's arrest, I'll never forget . . . I'm walking into the back car of the train, and this old man, he's up against the door with a broken coke bottle under his jugular. Two little punks, must have been up to his belt. But these guys had gumption. I grabbed both of them, threw them up the reverse window, knocked the bottle out of their hands, and smacked them in the back of their head, held them there. Next stop, wouldn't let the train move. Pulled the emergency brake. They hate that.

The conductor comes: "What are you doin' pullin' the emergency brake?" "I just seen these two guys, tried to kill this guy, they stole his wallet, I'm waiting here till a cop comes." "You don't pull the emergency brake. . . ." The guy's giving me a hard time. I say, "Hey, the train ain't goin' nowhere, buddy. Get a cop."

Cop runs in, "Uhhh, uhhh, what's goin' on, what's goin' on?", immediately thinking that I was an undercover cop 'cause I had these two guys there. I said, "I'm making a citizen's arrest." The guy looked at me as if I was talking a foreign language. "Citizen's arrest?" he says, "This ain't the movies. You can't do that. There ain't no such thing." I said, "Whaddya mean? I witnessed a crime, he attempted to *kill* this guy, they stole his wallet, I saw that, I'm filing a complaint. If he doesn't want to, I am, and I'm making a citizen's arrest."

Cop takes out his radio and steps out on the platform: "Sarge, you better get down here, I'm discharging this train, nobody's goin' nowhere from this train, 'cause I ain't goin' to touch this with a thousand-foot pole. We got some guy here claiming to make a citizen's arrest." [Untranscribable sounds of sergeant replying]

We're waiting there, they tried to discourage me, threatened to arrest me, said I'm off the wall, you can't do this, you have no rights, you'll be sued. We go down to the precinct, they have me in a separate room with detectives. Now some of the brass is coming down, I could tell, these are guys with gray hair, raincoats, coffee in one hand, cigarette in the other, obviously pissed off because they got woken up out of bed. They're coming in and threatening me with arrest or whatever, and I stood to my guns 'cause I was really enraged now.

Five hours later, after the entire incident took place, the guys were placed under arrest, attempted felony, you know, robbery. I was the complainant, the old man was too scared to press charges, practically had cardiac arrest, and I followed it through. Took seventeen times, I went to court, ended up being thrown out, dispersed in the system. But I know why it went seventeen times. They were trying to prove a point: Hey, wise guy, you're going to be a wise guy, you're going to say it's a citizen's arrest, well now you see what's going to happen.

I just stuck to my guns. In the course of riding the train, we made some other citizen's arrests, a lot of them were just going to and from where I was staying at the time. It wasn't difficult at all—the first hour you'd run into something. I mean the last car on the mugger's express was where this would happen. And you'd run into the same characters. Towards the end, after we had made about twenty-six, twenty-seven citizen's arrests, one cop came on, we had grabbed a guy who was breaking windows in the back car. Cop lets the guy go. He takes his gun, right, he points it at me, he says,

"This is the third time I've run into you doing this shit. You trying to play cop?" He's pointing the gun at me, and playing macho man, and, "If I catch you out here again . . ."

Then I realized at that point I was getting too individually involved, almost becoming possessed by it. I wasn't helping anyone else to think, "Well, maybe I could do this too." I realized that I had to create a mechanism where we didn't have to grab people necessarily, where we would deter by just being there.

That's when I really began to put my energy into getting a group out there that was more of a visual deterrent, and a last-resort measure of physical interference and making a citizen's arrest. Now we're in October of '78. That's when I started putting the last key elements together, and I mean it was around-the-clock.

I would get people pumped up into doing it, talk to them hours at length about the philosophy, the ideas behind it. These were essentially people that I knew, people I had developed a reputation with. But I had to spend an hour or two with these people each time just convincing them of what needed to be done. And then they would go home and tell parents or loved ones or friends, and they would unconvince them and defeat all the arguments.

And the main thing, "Oh, you're going to get shot and killed, and who's going to worry about you, and the cops are going to harass you, and you're black and Hispanic, and the cops are going to give you a hard time 'cause they're mostly white." And then the police themselves—it's being reported that if I am going to try this new idea, the police are going to do everything within their power to stop us. So the parents are having a heart attack.

This is before we've even started! Don't even have a beret yet, not a uniform, all we've had is training sessions, and in the Bronx it's become an explosive thing.

We're involved in physical training, a lot of mental preparation, how you would patrol the trains. So in civilian garb, just going through the motions of what a patrol would look like, a three-person patrol. What your position should be, what the signals might be in case you had a problem. How you would signal your partner that everything was all right, how you would move from car to car, station to station, platform to platform, how to do a patrol log, how to write down incidents, how to get help—all the variables that would exist in an environment that at times was chaotic. We were ready in February of 1979. All the loose ends had been put together.

And then in February of 1979, our first actual patrols.* Five days before

---

*As the Magnificent 13, the forerunner of the Guardian Angels.

we actually patrolled we made the public announcement. You'd of thought we were Jesse James and the outlaws. The *New York Post* had done a story on it. This was considered very bold—"My lord, you're printing your name, and who you are, and where you're from—they'll come in and they'll kill you right there." I must of got more calls at McDonald's, I'd say it was ninety-eight percent against, two percent for. You know, "You're a nut, you're crazy!" (slam)

Cops were threatening to arrest us. Cops would come by, they took their breaks at the McDonald's there: "Oh, you crazy kid, now you've really gone and done it. You shoulda stayed cleaning the streets, you would of been all right. But now, that's it, you guys out there, that's it." The union president [of the transit police] had cardiac arrest, 'cause there was a series of transit police layoffs. And he just jumped on me: "See, see, now they're going to have these kids out there, in sneakers, and they'll think they can replace us." The mayor started with the vigilantism. . . .

And the people, the riding public, were terrified of us. Because we were predominantly black and Hispanic, from the inner city, they looked upon us as some new form of gang. The gangs read about us on the front page one day, vying to put us on the first line of the obituary column the next day. "We're going to ride the trains and look out for these red berets," 'cause we would stick our head out at each station.

So you had the whole city that was ready to condemn us, package us out, and ship us to the graveyard. And you can imagine what it was like for these thirteen, between the eighth of February '79 and February thirteenth '79. Whereas I had to spend two hours each day pumping them up and getting them fired up, I had to spend five now.

I felt strong about it. I felt positive, 'cause remember I had been subjected to all the arguments. And I realized, hey, you know, I have to make a clear-cut choice. Am I going to deal with a realistic problem, or am I going to continue to go on my merry way with the clean-up program, take all the accolades, you know, get all the pats on the back, or really deal with the meat and potatoes, the crux of the problem?

What a lot of people fail to realize is, I didn't look at the Guardian Angels as a bunch of crime fighters. I knew that would happen. But I was looking for the thing which I felt did not exist in this society, the positive role model effect. And I said, the only way you're going to be a positive role model is to be a real person, out actively and visually doing everything and anything that you're speaking about. Particularly for the young blacks and Hispanics, to fight against the stereotyped role model of the pimp, the pusher, the hoodlum, the gangster—a Mr. T., a Michael Jackson, you know, people that were not negative, but were not real. And the one thing, an interracial group, because I felt with an interracial group we would be defeating all the stereotypes that said it just couldn't be done.

Those were the positive things that I was looking forward to. I knew it could be done. But I also knew that I was going to have problems.

Slowly but surely after the first few months we were beginning to win public support. Crime was beginning to drop. We were very noticeable, we were being given credit by the riding public that manifested itself in letters to the editor, letters to the local political and police officials, and increased public coverage for what we were doing.

It was easy to have a great deal of visibility and be effective with a small group. And since it was so new and unique, anytime they'd see you for the first time, it was something they'd never forget. "Oh, it's them!"—a lot of them at first having a negative reaction, but then developing into a positive as they saw how we worked and how we were able to withstand the verbal abuse and the physical intimidation. I think that's what shocked people the most. We'd be in a car surrounded by twenty or thirty punks, and be able to stand there and take the kind of verbal abuse that they would dish out, without responding. I think that's when we really began to win a lot of respect.

But there just seemed to be mounting and mounting hurdles as we continued on. It was the constant emotional grind of pumping people up. So I would literally have to make our members feel guilty, by explaining to them, "Hey, you go back to your community, you complain about the mugging, the raping, the looting—now you have a chance to really do something about it. Finally a young Hispanic can look at you and see another young Hispanic doing something positive to replace Julio the junkie on the corner or the Savage Nomads or the Young Lords or half a dozen other organizations that had defamed their own unique individuality."

I'd nearly have to get individually on the cases of our people, 'cause they'd come back from a patrol and they'd be ready to quit. Many of them would say, "I've taken more abuse than I would take with my old man. I'd of knocked my dad out by now. I can't stand it. I can't stand it being dressed up, like a lollipop, in a sea of humanity, people making fun of me." 'Cause let's face it, berets and T-shirts were not very macho. In comparison to what gangs would wear, hoodlums would wear, this kind of garb was (laughs) very sedate. You'd almost expect somebody to come up and check your bags with you, take it up to the hotel room. So there were so many things to overcome. But I think in the beginning the success was support from the Hispanic community, but also individually my sitting down with people and talking.

It was like, drip, drip. Very slow. Then there came that period of time where it could no longer be a small fraternal group where everybody knew one another. Now people wanted to join who didn't know us personally, who were from other areas of the city, like Brooklyn and Queens and Manhattan. They'd see us on patrols—they'd come riding the trains looking for us, and come to the McDonald's where I worked. Sometimes there'd be a whole line of them.

At first we had to tell them no—we didn't know who they were. The recruiting was that you had to be recommended by someone who was in the group. We had no way of screening them and finding out. And that's when we had to develop a universal kind of screening, reference check program, interview system, and training program.

We had to make sure that in expanding our services we were not cutting our throats. So it was once again the old problem: do you expand and take risks or do you stay with the status quo, and my attitude has always been where people want to help themselves, you gotta go out and reach out to them and help them help themselves.

And in some of those instances we got burnt. A lot of wrong decisions were made, so you failed in many instances. The key thing was just being able to move on, and the secret was if you succeeded in one out of every ten things you did, accentuate the positive and forget the negative. That's the only way you can keep a sanity to yourself and stay out of a depressive mood or a negative mood, 'cause you always had to be upbeat, you always had to be positive, you always had to be a motivator, a catalyzer. And if you were having problems or if you had made mistakes, you had to be very conscious of not letting others around you be aware of that.

It wasn't fun at all. In fact it was very tense. It was hard to eat sometimes. The tension was unbelievable. We were afraid every time the telephone rang that it was one of your guys either messing up on patrol or a police officer harassing your people. I would say now it's more enjoyable, although you'd think the pressures would be greater with so many groups and so many places. But I've experienced just about everything that you're going to experience in this, and I feel comfortable now in it just being part of the norm. But back then everything was so different, so new, the smallest thing would set you off.

*

The group grew slowly, in size and public credibility. On September 4, 1979, Curtis dissolved the Magnificent 13, changed its name to Guardian Angels, and started to accept applicants from different neighborhoods in the city. For the first time, the group went above ground, patrolling Central Park. An organizational and training structure, with borough and individual patrol leaders, began to take shape. By that time, there were about sixty members.

Two key events spurred growth outside New York. In 1980, the

Angels were invited to Atlanta by a black congregation to help residents defend against the killings of young black children there. And in May 1981, New York Mayor Edward Koch, an original opponent, signed a memorandum of understanding giving the Angels official recognition as an independent safety patrol. Local precedent was set, and national publicity followed. This was followed in turn by contacts from other community groups. A Los Angeles chapter was established. Curtis left McDonald's.

*

Today we're in fifty-one American cities, and four cities in Canada. We have about close to five thousand members. No dues, they don't have to pay anything in. But they are responsible for the cost of their beret, their T-shirt, their own food, their own transportation, their own clothes. Each city has its own chapter leader, its own mechanism for perpetuating itself; it's all structured within the same rules and regulations, answerable to the national organization.

We're nonprofit, tax-exempt, the Alliance of Guardian Angels [in Brooklyn]. We have to raise monies locally in each of the chapters just to sustain the cost of telephone, utilities, transportation, postage, mailings, dissemination of information. For all of 1983, we raised eighty-four thousand dollars to sustain, at that point, thirty-eight chapters that were in operation.

No foundations, no government. We would not accept money from corporate or government sources. Individual donations of five dollars, ten dollars, twenty-five. We have some direct mailings, we've had cake sales, bake sales, car washes, button sales, those types of things. No one is salaried. The tenet of the organization is that no one person, *nobody*, will ever receive a penny from the Guardian Angels. It will remain volunteers throughout and throughin, regardless of your position in the organization.

Our only private income is from my wife's modeling. She's a professional model by day, for Zoli, and an Angel by night. And that affords enough to live in a tenement in the Lower East Side of Manhattan, 225 dollars a month rent. We don't go to restaurants and movies, we don't have a car, we don't have children yet, so the expenses aren't that great. I guess if I had children and those other responsibilities, it would be ten times rougher than it is now. I have a certain freedom now—probably a little later I won't.

But I think the beauty of the group is when everybody was trying to fight for federal grants—hey, if there's no money, it can still run. How many great ideas and programs have gotten to a level where they depend on funding, and without the funding they fold? I certainly didn't want to see that happen to the Guardian Angels.

Figure five days out of the week [I'm on the road]. Different chapters, or areas wanting to start groups, or forums. Their request. We're backlogged. There's interest not only from around the United States, but parts of Europe, Guam, Philippines, Australia, places we may never get to for another few years. We have to go to the places where there are people not only interested, but willing to do the nuts and bolts, and where there is a chapter near so that we can offer some kind of support.

On the road is like barnstorming. You know how you're going to get to the first destination, and what your plans are there. Everything else is freestyle. It's physically very tiring. Sometimes you miss your flights, you don't get your hookups, they don't have a car, you gotta hitchhike. You're out there at twelve o'clock in the morning [midnight], you're Curtis Sliwa, supposedly the founder of the Guardian Angels, you got thirteen cents in your pocket, and you're hitchhiking on Interstate 75 in the Smokies. I don't know how many times I've been dragged in and summoned for hitchhiking. You'd think, gee, the least they could do—the last thing I should have to worry about is getting from point A to point B. It's very frustrating. But you accept it.

What you try to do at times like that is to just blank out your mind. 'Cause all you're going to do is get yourself riled up, you're gonna end up kicking a tree. You try to think of other things. In my position now, whenever I have that free time, when nothing's happening, you gotta use it to be thoughtful, contemplative, and think of the future, what things can be done. Sometimes it's good to be out there and away from everybody, 'cause then you just have time to think.

So I'd say it's like a roller coaster at times, in terms of emotions: there are a lot of highs, and a lot of lows. You can't get much higher, you can't get much lower either.

Lead by example, that's the main thing. Leadership I have found is sheerly by what you do. Most people are looking to you, and they will be what they see.

If they see you as a leader violating the rules, or you as the leader cheating, or you as a leader saying one thing and doing another thing, then you can bet your last dollar in your pocket that you're gonna have a group that does essentially the same. Any good group is a reflection of good leadership. And their example is their leader.

Are you a charismatic leader?

I'd say so, in the fact that I don't do things in the traditional manner. I try to adopt the way people talk in the comfort of their homes, where they say what they really mean. And I've always had an ability to essentially talk right off the cuff, which enhances your ability to lead, 'cause many times you're walking into a situation where you have no information, you can only go based on your instincts, based on what has been your experience in this kind of thing, and you got to shoot it right off the cuff, in sometimes a very hostile atmosphere. And, knock on wood, I've been very fortunate.

I think the charisma comes from trying to get people fired up. A lot of people get very lethargic, and they get very caught up in their I and Me. Because you're dealing with a concrete block when it comes to We and Us. When you talk about We and Us, it goes in one ear and out the other. The only way you're going to get people fired up is to show them how it affects them individually, but also affects the whole.

It's harder now?

Much harder. Much harder. Because people seem to be more selfish, indifferent, or more into themselves. We are in the instant society. People want to feel that they're instantly achieving something. So you have to meet today's needs, and I created the Guardian Angel program with that in mind, so that with the beret, with that T-shirt, you can go out there and ride on a patrol. You haven't done nothing but just stand there, and all of a sudden you're just like walking on cloud nine.

A lot of other organizations have not been able to adapt to that, the mentality of the eighties, and I think you have to provide a little juice, as they say, in the caboose to modernize it, to make it glamorous, to make it attractive, to give a personal feeling of achieving something, instantaneously, yet also having that long-range goal, that positive role model effect, preventing crime.

As I get older, it's obvious that you get less militant. Now when I do things I can't just think of New York. I have to think how are they going to think about that in Des Moines, Iowa, or Omaha, Nebraska, or Sacramento, California, or Fort Worth, Texas. It's a whole different way of thinking. It's not that I feel less militant; I have to be more cautious. And I don't like that. Yet I realize that is a fact of life, that when you grow and you become more worldly and you reflect more different kinds of thinking, you can't be locked into doing things the way you've always done.

And not selling out, and not creating a bureaucracy, I think that's the key. As you grow, your needs become greater, so you're going to have to end up compromising along the way. As long as you can maintain the essence of why you started, your purpose in existence, and not become a machine. . . .

But compromise is essential?

If you intend on growing, yes, 'cause remember there's fifty-one groups right now. It's impossible to know everything that's going on or to cope with everything that's going on.

But it's possible to compromise and yet keep one's essence?

On your terms, yes. As long as you're willing to suffer a lot in order to do so. If you compromise initially without any suffering, then you're going to lose it. If you suffer and do it on your level, and compromise so that you don't disenfranchise yourself, then you'll have a successful ongoing program.

In traveling the United States I have run into literally thousands of people who have developed programs in the very same way that I have. Busted their butts, forty times longer than I have. Sunk their life and soul into it, ended up giving up a career, living in a level of poverty, and, gee whiz, these people have had to deal with ten times more than I've had to. Never had *any* recognition, or attention, gone to their graves having to explain why they donated so much of their life to that service.

And that's the real crime that I believe exists, is that we're so quick to give attention and recognition to really stupid things. I mean, out of all the things we've done in the Guardian Angels, we've had more attention and recognition paid to really minor things, but they were controversial and they had attention paid to them; whereas other peoples can do things that are very conventional, kill themselves, and yet not have any attention or recognition, which makes it very hard to perpetuate what you do and catalyze other peoples into doing similar programs.

I think for the Angels, we got to set up a method of perpetuation. We're already five-and-a-half years now. Many of the people who were originally with us are no longer with us. It's a whole new breed of person. Things can never be like they were in the very beginning.

For the Guardian Angels to continue, they have to be adaptable, they have to be reflective of the needs of the community. It may not necessarily be only in a patrol. For those that graduate and go beyond the program, it may be in a wide variety of volunteer programs, whether it's tutorial programs, food distribution, or services that are just lacking or nonexistent. For those who are no longer Guardian Angels in the red berets and T-shirts, they have to become the leaders of the future.

Your own plans?

I'd say to lead in that direction, 'cause it's going to require even more leadership than in the actual formation of the group.

It takes a lot of strength?

Ehh. . . . It takes strength, but it takes a moral conviction to hang with it. There are so many other distractions—you reach a certain level and then there are a thousand different ways you can go.

So your plan is to stay?

Oh, yeah. Absolutely. As long as I'm physically able to do it, mentally able to do it, fiscally able to do it, and don't have the typical types of pressures that a person growing up might have, I don't see any problem with it.

Always remember, if it was so easy to do, it would have been done already. But if what you feel needs to be done has never been done, the main thing is go for it. You certainly can't lose, and even if you fail you will learn so many new things that will help you just in the course of your life.

You should never be afraid of mistakes. Like I said, in the Guardian Angels I've made nine mistakes out of every ten things I've tried, failed nine out of every ten times, but the secret is you don't know what those nine things are. That's the only secret. And when they are brought to my attention, or when I'm asked to comment about it, I'll not deny it, but I certainly am not going to pay any time on it, because I don't want to dwell on the negative.

I felt that if there was one thing I could do that would really make me feel good, it was in showing folks that you can do it for yourself—don't wait for nobody else. That, I would say, is the only self-serving thing. And not in a Reagan sense of getting the poor to help the rich, I'm not talking about that at all. I'm talking in the sense of self-reliance.

If I got a problem here, it's everybody's problem. Because everybody's in my plight. If kids are on the corner with a dope problem, that's for *us* to deal with, not government, not an agency. We have to be the first line of dealing with that, because once it gets to that agency or to that level, it's beyond being solved, it's going to perpetuate itself.

The value of volunteer service, and it's not just a cliché, it is the most valuable work you can possibly do. It is one of the few areas you can instantly see results. The freedom of being a volunteer is that you can make decisions on your own. You can go for it. The pressures are greater, but the rewards towards the self and the community are far better, because it makes the community become more self-responsible.

Government programs, outside help is fine. And I don't knock it; we're certainly not getting enough of it now. But most of the problems in the community are problems that we in the community can deal with, ninety-nine percent of them. Absolutely. The merchant problems, to the transient problem, to the elderly problem, the drug problem—it's all a community problem, it's something that we have to take charge of and deal with. . . .

Heroism in Modern Society

What Is Meant by "Heroism"?

How best to characterize the stories so far? Suppose you are a gracious reader, prepared to agree with my own biases. So, together, we admire the tellers. We are touched by their spirit, impressed with their accomplishments. We hold them up as models for others, perhaps even for ourselves.

But are the tellers heroic, in a true sense of the word? *Local Heroes* is an easy phrase, but is there substance behind it? Are the subjects here heroes if "hero" is taken with full gravity? If not, then who is? And if they are, then what social implications follow?

To tackle these questions leads unavoidably to a discussion of heroism in modern society. We need first to set standards for heroism, and then to decide how to apply them. It's safe to say this is hard to do. The word "hero" today is so diversely applied, so widely attributed, that common meaning eludes us. We're soon in a tangle.

An illustration may help. Here are some responses of participants themselves, when asked for their own heroes:

My own heroes? . . . (sighs). Hmm . . . God . . . I don't think I have any. That's a real good question, but I really can't answer it.

Who are my own heroes? I guess the saints are my own heroes. I have my Jesuit heroes. . . . Oh, yeah, nobody knows about them. . . . I'll have to think more about heroes. I never think of that.

Wonder Woman. No, no, I gave her up. . . . One was Wonder Woman, literally, in the guise of my grandmother, the union organizer. So, I don't know. Who else? Mario Cuomo. . . . Richard Widmark. Rita Hayworth. That's the truth. Stanislavsky, I like. . . .

Well, I admire Cesar Chavez a lot. So he's one of my heroes. Let me see, who else? Of course, you know, the center of who I am is really Christ. So Christ is, and Cesar.

Well, there's me, and whoever's second (laughs). That's a great question you asked, who are my heroes? I don't have any heroes. Wish I could find a few extra truck drivers—I like them best. Those are the people I respect. Those are my heroes.

I don't have any heroes. I really don't. . . . Nothing impresses me (laughs).

People I work with; people that you're interviewing; people who I've met through the Service Employees International Union, who have been very effective organizing their workplace.

I read a book in the fourth grade—she started the Mount Auburn Hospital in Boston. . . . Dorothea Lynde Dix, I think. So that left an impression early on. And another hero in that sense would be B. B. King. And, my sister's an idol. . . .

Heroes? (laughs) I don't know what you mean by that. I used to look up to my oldest brother. . . . No, I don't have any.

Johnny Mack Brown (laughs). I . . . I don't have any heroes, but I always look up to somebody that is helping somebody else, which can be a man, a woman, a child. So that's my hero.

I don't have any. It was really horrible to discover that I don't have any. . . . A few people I've met in nursing homes are more heroic because they've done brave things in honest ways with little reinforcement. If you take away the reinforcement, it's tough to do something brave. That's of the heroic nature for me.

Well, I have to say Jesus of Nazareth is number one (laughs). I continue to read about Lincoln as an American. I'm quite taken with him. I have to say I love the Red Sox, though (laughs).[1]

The scatter of responses is clear. The level of agreement is low. The meaning of heroism is confused.[2]

To end all confusion is beyond our hope. But by calling attention to it, we might lessen it a little. Analysis can help, and in analyzing the term more closely, we can specify three approaches toward describing heroism today.

Some Current Viewpoints

One point of view is that heroes have vanished. There used to be heroes, but not anymore. The term is outmoded.

From a local newspaper article on high school youth:

> Sociology teacher Carol Siriani shakes her head after a class discussion in which a student told her, "We don't need heroes: that's the difference between you and us." . . . . "Heroes," [a student] snickers. "They went out a long time ago."[3]

Or from a recent special edition of *Newsweek:*

> It is said that we live in an antiheroic time. . . . Our official heroes have too often been spoiled for us by officeholders corrupted by power, by athletes and entertainers drunk on drugs and money, by space shots that no longer seem to work.[4]

Or from a *New York Times* essay, a little while back:

> We kill our heroes nowadays; as too much admiration fixes upon them, a killer emerges. . . . Afraid of what will happen if we admire somebody too much, we look a little to one side. . . . We have so much bitterness to put behind us that we laugh at all solutions.[5]

All of which is consistent with a short cultural attention span, and with a dark and possibly masochistic streak in us which cannibalizes heroes as quickly as they are manufactured.

There's partial truth in these quotes. We do dispose of heroes swiftly; attrition rates are high. But the same *Newsweek* feature goes on to profile one hundred new American "heroes of everyday life" ("as ordinary to look at as the neighbors next door"). Many of the high school students cited above do name heroes: Springsteen and Prince, or Mary Lou Retton. And while one-fifth of young people in a recent national survey failed to mention a hero, the remaining eighty percent did.[6]

Most of us, I'd suggest, can identify personal heroes—at least with reflection—and we do. The question is who these heroes are, and why.

At another extreme, heroism is broadly distributed. Almost everyone can be a hero, and sometimes everyone is.

"The mass of men," writes Phyllis McGinley in her book on saints, "live lives of quiet heroism."[7] And in the mail not long ago came a brochure for a weekend workshop called "Here I Stand Ironing—the Heroism of the Ordinary." This was a chance for participants to learn about and affirm the heroism in their own lives, whether ironing or otherwise. Housework, the promotional copy implied, is not necessarily less heroic than a winning touchdown or electoral triumph. Some events might get more media attention than others, but intrinsically, or morally, or heroically, they are on a par.

The President confers heroism generously: "You can see heroes every day going in and out of factory gates."[8] And sometimes to be called heroic, you don't have to *do* anything at all. At Stanford University a few years ago, more than four hundred students gathering for a conference on "entrepreneurs in the public interest" were told by no less a public service authority than John Gardner: "Some people strengthen society just by being the kind of people they are."[9]

But the most pungent expression of this viewpoint I've encountered comes from a columnist who works for my metropolitan daily, and writes straight from the lunchbucket:

> Most of the good in the world is done not by those who set out premeditatedly to do good but by less awesome folk whose first concern is ordinarily earning a living. I am thinking of every postal clerk and "T" changemaker who conquers the urge to despise and abuse a heedless public. . . . .
>
> In the words of an old song, it ain't what you do, it's the way that you do it. A decent omelette or pizza does more for humanity than most bureaucracies.[10]

The problem with this line of thinking is that it trivializes public service and reduces heroism to nothingness. Distinction is conferred for going through the paces. If you go to work with five hours sleep, or fight off a cold, or manage a smile, or get your reports out, or drive home considerately, you might be heroic, like the rest of us.

We can respect these efforts and call them virtuous names. But the omelette makers of America are not heroic, or even distinctive, not if that's all they do. To call ourselves heroic—with all the emotional charge the word still confers—simply for getting through the day, means we have nothing left for the person who seizes the day, illuminates it, is able somehow to pull off something more life-enhancing and more socially consequential.

For heroism to stay meaningful and useful, its boundaries must narrow. We can all aspire to it, and many of us can achieve it; more of us should, though few of us will. Heroism is equal-opportunity at the beginning, but selective at the end.

So the third point of view, and it's the traditional one, gives the hero protected status. Only a very few of us will be called heroes. Who are they, and by what criteria? In earlier times, it was common to point to the gods, the saints, the figures of legend. We're less likely to do so today; instead, we have modern polling techniques.. And if recent surveys on heroes have not been exhaustive, they are indicative nonetheless.

In 1985, a cover story in *U. S. News & World Report* announced the results of its own commissioned survey. A national sample of young adults, ages eighteen through twenty-four, was asked, "Who are your heroes or heroines—that is, what public figures living anywhere in the world do you find personally inspiring and would you hope to be like in some way?"

The top ten:

1. Clint Eastwood
2. Eddie Murphy
3. Ronald Reagan
4. Jane Fonda
5. Sally Field $\Big\}$ (tie)
   Steven Spielberg
7. Pope John Paul II
8. Mother Teresa
9. Michael Jackson $\Big\}$ (tie)
   Tina Turner

No hero or heroine—19%
Don't know—3%.

Seven out of ten were Hollywood celebrities. Though in 1973 almost sixty percent of young adults declined to make any selection at all, "today's young adults," the report summarizes, "clearly seek to pattern themselves after people who, for the most part, are boundlessly rich or successful." As sociologist Amitai Etzioni observes within, "Now, it's O.K. to have heroes. We're back yearning for leadership."[11]

Note that the *U. S. News* request was for public figures. When this condition was removed, in one survey reported in *Psychology Today*, both college and elementary school students tended to choose their own parents. Among college students, "Moms got six times as many first-place votes as did any other heroine, and dads got twice as much as any other hero." The report notes also, "Mother Teresa was a top contender for heroine, along with Jane Fonda, Amelia Earhart, Marilyn Monroe, and Madonna."[12]

But mom and dad scored less highly in a 1985 reader poll in *TeenAge* magazine. Ninety percent reported having a hero or heroine; "Twenty-nine percent of the respondents indicated that their hero was someone they know personally" (and here friends outpolled parents two to one); but "the majority of them cited media figures as their heroes," though no one person drew more than a two percent response.[13]

These results are age-limited and may be methodologically impure, but they are consistent both with each other and with less quantitative views of popular culture. This is a country of "Entertainment Tonight" and *People* magazine. Celebrities are national reference points. The *National Enquirer*'s circulation matches *Time*'s, and the *Star* outdraws *Newsweek*. *TV Guide* sells more copies than all four combined.[14] In an anonymous society where local connections are frail and hometown culture is fragile, how could it be otherwise?

As Richard Schickel writes in *Intimate Strangers: The Culture of Celebrity*:

> The lives of the celebrities create a sort of psychic energy field that surrounds us and penetrates us, binding our universe together. . . . Celebrities have become, in recent decades, the chief agents of moral change in the United States.[15]

And celebrities, for Schickel, are a kind of social compensation. Those of us without close community ties can have vicarious family, and friends.

A Critique of Hero-Types

If the hero-as-celebrity is an easy target, it's still fair game. The key point is that substance is missing behind the reputation. There is talent, more often than not. There is fighting one's way up the ladder. But as for heroic deeds, deeds beyond artistic performance, heroic action by any imaginative stretch, those are absent. And inevitably so: whatever one's deeper strengths or noncommercial potential, celebrity washes them over. If there is talent, that talent must be practiced and expressed; and whether talented or not—especially if not—the celebrity strives to keep in the public eye, which is a job in itself. For there's only so much room at the top, so many culture-figures who can be assimilated; while pressure, constant and talented pressure, surges relentlessly from below.

It's not just that celebrities gobble up media attention, for many of us attempt the same. And it's not only that celebrities may have little to offer besides their names. It's also that we may hand over to celebrities, simply by virtue of their celebrity status, duties we might otherwise assume ourselves. We're powerless against world hunger: but rock groups aren't. Who can help the farmer? Maybe Willie Nelson.

Through investing in celebrities, we may disempower ourselves. Some celebrities realize this and act accordingly, even with noble motives. "Citizens have such limited means and access to the media that the only way their views can be heard is through actors or celebrities."[16] This was Ed Asner (formerly "Lou Grant" on television, and former president of the Screen Actor's Guild), commenting on his legislative testimony on behalf of Salvadoran refugees.

Asner may have a point. Some celebrities may wield social power, and his own intentions may be faultless; yet his underlying assumption, by siphoning individual initiative, may work against our long-run best interest. Not so long ago, says Schickel, when celebrities didn't exist, we took on far more community responsibility.

As young adults mature, their heroes are less likely to be entertainers; political or spiritual leaders are more often named. Quantitative data on adult heroes are sketchier, but one clue comes from the annual Gallup survey of most admired men and women. The top ten 1985 choices in each category were:[17]

Men	*Women*
1. Ronald Reagan	1. Nancy Reagan
2. Pope John Paul II	2. Margaret Thatcher
3. Lee Iacocca	3. Mother Teresa
4. Jesse Jackson	4. Geraldine Ferraro
5. Billy Graham	5. Princess Diana
6. Edward Kennedy	6. Jeane Kirkpatrick
7. Desmond Tutu	7. Betty Ford
8. Jimmy Carter	8. Queen Elizabeth II
9. Prince Charles	9. Jacqueline Kennedy Onassis
10. George Bush	10. Sandra Day O'Connor

Granted that admiration and heroism are not identical, the results are still suggestive. Of the twenty choices, more than half have been prominent in U.S. national politics, through election, appointment, candidacy, or marriage. And though we don't know precisely why these particular figures were admired, a reasonable guess would focus on (*a*) their titles, or positions, and (*b*) their media exposure, as well as (*c*) their substantive actions.

The substantive action, the admired deed, is sometimes harder to discern. Liberals and conservatives, Republicans and Democrats, all make the list if they are in power. All presidents from Truman on (except Gerald Ford) have topped the Most Admired Man list at least once. Jesse Jackson and Barry Goldwater, Menachem Begin and Anwar Sadat, Spiro Agnew and Sen. Joseph McCarthy have each made multiple appearances, though what they did to merit those appearances seems secondary. Raw exposure usually increases favorability, and it may be unfortunate but true that exposure pure and simple helps you make the list.[18]

There are others we have called heroes: sports figures—paid employees actually—as transient as this year's statistics; military leaders, mostly limited to wartime; explorers, though there's less territory left; captains of industry, especially if tough-talking; superheroes, as in comic books; historical figures, real or legendary, although yesterday's heroes get little mention in the modern survey data. In one very early poll, ninety percent of those most admired by young people were historical; but today's heroes, it seems, must be in the news.[19]

Then there are heroes who are physically brave, a quite different category. As a child, I read *Real Heroes Comics* (that name, or close), full of boys and girls leading strangers to safety, or running into burning barns to save the horses. A modern case in point: On January 13, 1982, an Air Florida jet, its wings possibly ice-laden, crashed into the Potomac River near Washington, D.C. A government clerk named Lenny Skutnik dove into the icy water from ashore and dragged a young flight attendant to safety. That was front-page news; Skutnik received thousands of letters, was deluged by interview requests. At the State of the Union address two weeks later, Skutnik received a standing ovation when President Reagan called his action, "the spirit of American heroism at its finest."[20]

Skutnik's act was brave; but heroic, perhaps not. Like most acts of physical bravery, it was a reaction to the unexpected and unchosen. It was apparently impulsive by Skutnik's own account, rather than a consciously thought-out decision. And it was a one-time occurrence: Skutnik is unlikely to meet another fallen plane in his lifetime; he certainly won't go looking for them. Nor will we.

Acts of bravery possibly, and of heroism almost certainly, must involve choice. Consider the fifty-two Americans kept captive in Iran from November 1979 until January 1981. On being freed, they came home to a star-spangled heroes' welcome: ticker tape, motorcades, White House receptions. *Newsweek's* response was typical:

America was a suddenly, extravagantly happy land last week because it had discovered not one hero but 52—and because it had needed heroes so badly for so long.[21]

But were they heroes? I'd argue not, and against confusing survival of captivity with heroic acts. In these (and later) cases, the hostages neither chose to be hostages, nor to remain hostages. And they were powerless to do anything but be hostages; like any prisoners, they could only sit and wait. Their attributed heroism, I believe, stemmed in large part from the American public's need for self-assertion, and for justification of a noxious political situation.

Similar reasoning applies to the seven astronauts killed in the *Challenger* explosion early in 1986. They too were eulogized as heroes by politicians and the mass media. ("We mourn seven heroes," said the President.[22]) But cold logic tells us that their primary credential for heroism was their death. Had they lived, both crew and flight would soon have been forgotten, possibly excepting Christa McAuliffe, as "first teacher in space." The space shuttle had previously flown twenty-four consecutive successful missions; but who recalls one crew member on board?

America, it might be, has played out its hero cards. Americans may be missing inspiration. Those we've called heroes, on closer examination, lack heroic substance; or they're on stage for barely a moment; or they're well paid for their roles; or they bear some disqualifying moral scar; or they are entrapped, never having wanted in. To all the hero categories considered so far, one or more of these marks apply.

And all these types are media creations. The media built them up, proclaimed their heroism, and made it next to impossible for them to behave heroically. Once created, the new media star usually likes the spotlight; but the spotlight requires makeup, and the spotlight reveals flaws, while flawless others seek the same attention. The same media which builds up also chews up and finally spits out, all at an apparently quickening pace.[23]

As a result, the confusion surrounding heroism in American life is fully predictable. Heroism is so weakly anchored and so loosely defined that anyone can lay claim to the word, and sometimes does. In my alumni magazine, I learn that I can be a hero by supporting the Challenge campaign. A recent popular best-seller tells women readers how to recognize seven types of Junk Food Heroes (men, tempting on the outside, empty within).[24] The movie ads a few seasons ago asked readers to "celebrate Washington's Birthday with another American hero"— Eddie Murphy, in _Beverly Hills Cop_.

When a word of such grandeur and moral power is so eviscerated and demeaned, the cultural mood becomes one of exhaustion. And with that exhaustion comes cynicism, powerlessness, and a turning in upon the self.

The Local Hero

Yet we do need heroes, or their nearest equivalent. They play a role— an essential role—in cultural transmission and cultural growth; some might extend the claim to cultural survival. If you feel "hero" is too strong a term, try substituting "role model" for now. And then you might agree that we need people we aspire to be like, whom we revere, whose values we internalize, and whose actions we emulate.[25] I'd agree too; this is one basis of human development.

All children have parents as prime role models, fortunately for civilized society. Considering their impact, it's not surprising they're called heroes (and not altogether without justice) in one survey previously cited. But by our working definition, they don't really qualify. They're fulfilling a role, no matter how skillful or loving; they're shaped by standard role obligation; once the child is born, they have little choice but to play that role out. What's more, parental actions as such affect the child alone; there's little impact on the larger society, real or intended.

The child needs other models as well, known personally or admired from afar. The coach, the minister, the teacher are among sanctioned local providers; yet they are living out their role assignments too. It's possible, though, to extend the role: the coach starts an intercity league, the minister heals racial divisions. And it's possible to stretch the role beyond normal recognition, so that it becomes a new role entirely.

That new role creation might be heroic. It's also possible to call forth a new hero-type who does exist, if rarely; whose role is self-designed; whose actions transform the community; whose personal qualities move us; whose service is inspirational; and whose social achievements can be imitated, and deserve to be. This is the local hero, and here is what one looks like:

Motive

The primary concern is for others. The fruits of accomplishment will go to those with less opportunity, or greater need.

The primary goal is service, as contrasted with profit. Service comes first; it's not a by-product. The service will empower others, building community strength.

The service proceeds from choice, rather than from role obligation or other external compulsion. It is voluntary.

The primary rewards are intrinsic; they're often intangible. And much personal cost may be absorbed to gain them.

Setting

The scale of action is local. The local hero grasps a local issue, and aims for a local solution. The focus is on one's own community. There's no great reach, nor initial attempt at export, though success may prompt expansion later.

Resources

The resources at the start are minimal. As a rule, the local hero has no dollar subsidies, specialized skills, nor outside supports at the onset. The slate may not be completely clean; prior assets are put to use. But most resources are created and developed along the way.

Process

The local hero is stirred by a perceived community need. Others may not perceive it yet. The need may vary widely, as we have seen.

The hero organizes a response to that need. This means initiation, not just reaction to crisis. There may be hesitancy, doubt, less than total willingness; but the hero is the one who takes the first step.

Risk is undertaken—personal, financial, social, or otherwise. Sacrifices are made, especially the sacrifice of time. The risk will not be life-threatening, and the stakes may be affordable, but still there is a conspicuous leap into the unknown.

Obstacles are encountered—apathy, or active resistance, or both. Apathy must be turned around; resistance must be rendered harmless.

Help is sought, to overcome the obstacles. Helpers are recruited; backers are solicited; funding becomes an issue. And with these actions, the service goes public, possibly for good; it's hard to go back now.

Accomplishment

Success is achieved, in terms of original goals. All agree on distinctive accomplishment, which frequently is unique. Typically, success goes far beyond outside expectation; there's a striking mismatch between starting resources and what grew out of them.

The service is sustained. Often it becomes institutionalized; the service becomes a program. Spin-offs may occur; replicas may arise elsewhere. The founder continues until the program is securely grounded, and commonly stays well beyond.

This is a beginning definition. Even when refined, it would allow for wide variation in heroic personality, and in the content, location, and sequence of action. We've also not yet addressed the inner conditions of success—what it takes inside the person to make the service succeed. That is a major agenda item (for the concluding chapter), since not all actions get off the ground, and flight is one of our criteria here.

To live this role has costs, which may cut deep. The local hero may be ragged at the edges, or ripped along the seams. It's not a balanced life, according to the Greek ideal. Still, it's not a life which must be always on the limits, or sustained forever in the same way. For those of us not yet ready or willing to match this definition, approximations will do.

Yet local heroes are worth defining, and worth promoting, because they embody our highest social ideals. The local hero's achievements wear well. Locally heroic actions are available to all. This hero-type has traditional roots, which we now explore briefly. And the local hero is especially suited to our times, to which we'll turn shortly.

Historical Roots

Anyone can posit a hero-type; and as we've seen, it's been done. But if the designated hero is to be more than a convenient fiction, if that hero is to have visibility, and then credibility, and then motivating power, then that hero-type should have a cultural history, a grounding in tradition. The local hero does.

In his classic synthesis, *The Hero with a Thousand Faces*, Joseph Campbell describes that tradition. His method is to collect hero myths from all cultures—Icelandic to Hindu, aboriginal to Greek, Native American to medieval Christian—the broadest range available, and to search for common themes. He finds them. The hero's common path, Campbell says, is one of separation, initiation, and return.

> *A hero ventures forth from the world of common day into a region of super-natural wonder: fabulous forces are there encountered and a decisive victory is won: the hero comes back from this mysterious adventure with the power to bestow boons on his fellow man.*[26]

This pattern varies little; it appears to be a cultural universal.

The body of his text elaborates on this pattern, and with elaboration more parallels emerge:

The hero may embark on the adventure by what seems to be chance.

"A blunder—apparently the merest chance—reveals an unsuspected world. . . . [But] blunders are not the merest chance. They are the result of suppressed desires and conflicts."[27]

Eventually the hero comes to a threshold, which must be crossed. The crossing is risky.

"The adventure is always and everywhere a passage beyond the veil of the known into the unknown; the powers that watch at the boundary are dangerous."[28]

The hero has helpers, guides, or mentors to help him traverse the regions of the unknown.

"The first encounter of the hero-journey is with a protective figure . . . against the dragon forces he is about to pass."[29]

The unknown has perils. The hero is tested.

"[The hero] must survive a succession of trials. This is a favorite phase of the myth-adventure. It has produced a world literature of tests and ordeals."[30]

One by one, resistances are overcome. The hero triumphs.

"Dragons have now to be slain and surprising barriers passed—again, again, and again. . . . When he arrives at the nadir of the mythological round, he undergoes a supreme ordeal and gains his reward."[31]

Finally, the hero returns, and confers good upon society.

"The hero re-emerges from the kingdom of dread (return, resurrection). The boon that he brings restores the world."[32]

The local hero does not undergo quite the same ordeals; there may not be a smoking dragon, nor the same high drama. Yet even in the community stories here, there's a similar sense of adventure, a restlessness leading to a quest, a departure from ordinary life, a passage into uncharted territory, a struggle, and a return with something of social value. No other hero-type mentioned earlier fits quite this pattern. The genealogy, to me, is clear.

There are parallels too in the character of the hero, as well as in action. The legendary hero challenges the status quo. The hero takes the initiative. The hero is someone of intrinsic moral superiority—of "gentle heart"—a theme we'll return to later. And finally, "The hero, therefore, is the man or woman who has been able to battle past his personal and local historical limitations."[33]

The local hero is a descendant, not a replica. The mythological parallels should not be overplayed, though more parallels are found than can be cited here.[34] But what Campbell's scholarship reveals is a "marvelously constant story," and that is the story of the heroic quest. That quest is redemptive; it teaches us of life renewed. For through character and deed, the hero reopens our eye; he illuminates; he represents "the nuclear moment when, while still alive, he found and opened the road to the light beyond the dark walls of our living death."[35]

In the beginning, in the earliest creation stories, heroism belonged to the gods. With the passage of time, in Campbell's view, "The heroes become less and less fabulous, until at last . . . a period came when the work to be done was no longer proto- or superhuman; it was the labor specifically of man."[36] The hero became more earthbound, and in early society without mass communications, more local. And so Campbell concludes, not hesitating to take on the great themes, "The cosmogonic cycle is now to be carried forward, therefore, not by the gods, who have become invisible, but by the heroes, through whom the world destiny is realized."[37]

Suppose Campbell is really speaking to us right now; suppose that our destiny really does rest on the heroes among us. What do we do with that realization? Who are these heroes to be?

Modern Branches: The Hero as Community Builder

They could be close by. The case can be made that what deters social action is not simply inertia, but also powerlessness, the felt inability to make a difference.[38] Big social problems can cause personal paralysis; institutions cannot (or will not) solve the problem, so how can I? And it's not just average citizens who feel this way: for instance, Vin Quayle: "I am not going to go down and picket in front of the White House, because I don't think it will do any good." And: "You gotta deal with an issue that's specific, immediate, and realizable, and that's what I believe in."

But if you can't affect national (or international) issues—or think you can't—you can make a difference on local ones. If you can't sway the White House, or the state house, you can get something going in your own neighborhood, or on your block. Local action is desirable not predominantly from moral advantage; nor even because it is necessarily more impactful, ounce-for-ounce; but precisely because it is more specific, immediate, and realizable, and fulfilling as well. Local actors can pinpoint goals, start right in, chart real progress. Local actors can stimulate each other and form personal bonds. Local action will arouse some of us who would otherwise be immobilized. Very few of us can be heroes on a national or international scale; but on a local level, the possibilities are endless.

And the local hero is a community builder. The local choice is not only practical and strategically sound, but also timely. In an era of cutbacks, individual citizens will, by default, bear more responsibility for community life. If they want change, they'll have to make change themselves. If institutional supports are weakened, they'll have to create their own, if community life as we know it is to survive.

Community virtues—cooperation, trust, self-reliance, belonging— need strengthening, and no one is in a better position to strengthen them than the local hero. How shall they be strengthened? Largely by example. Who will provide the example? Those among us with the courage to risk the unknown, and the character and the ability to triumph over adversity and bring back new ways to serve the people.

That's why the local hero is a heroic model for America approaching the twenty-first century. Compared to other hero-types, there is substance as well as rootedness. There is personification of cultural values. Since local action seems more feasible, there is strategic wisdom. There is the likelihood of results—specific, immediate, and real-izable—which may spur other community efforts. There is personal satisfaction too.

And the local hero's action can endure, insofar as any personal action endures, which ultimately may not be for long. A new crop of heroes must always rise in place. Campbell once more:

> The boon brought from the transcendent deep becomes quickly rationalized into nonentity, and the need becomes great for another hero to refresh the word. How teach again, however, what has been taught correctly and incorrectly learned a thousand thousand times? . . . That is the hero's ultimate difficult task.[39]

So, shouldering that task, how do we foster local heroism in our society? How do we advance the local hero as model? How do we establish conditions so as to maximize our own heroic potential?

No single solutions here, as if that were surprising. Institutional change is one direction, and so is bootstrap development. Media promotion is another road to take, and there are persistent (and varying) allusions to this in the accounts that follow. We'll return to this question in the last chapter, and aim for integration. In the meantime, there are other stories to tell, each of which raises further issues about local community work, and taps further dimensions of local heroism in action.

Interviews

PART TWO

Bob Blanchette

The annual Christmas dinner at the Elks' hall.

*You want to know somethin'? Only one person can do it.
You. Or me, or him. The other guy can't do it.*

Frank Bowes

A CHRISTMAS DINNER

F ROM the *Arlington* [Massachusetts] *Advocate*, beginning in the late
1970s, and appearing with variations around Christmastime each
year since:

TO THE EDITOR:

Hi. Will you have Christmas dinner with me and my family?

I have a special reason for asking. From the time I was a little kid
Christmas, with the toys and the tree, was the greatest day of the
year. Then, when we got married and had five kids, and now have
nine grandchildren, it just kept getting better and better. What a perfectly super, joyous, happy, warm-feeling day.

Then one day Gi-Gi and I realized something. It wasn't the true
spirit of Christmas to keep all this love and happiness to ourselves
without sharing it with you. So, we decided to invite anyone in Arlington who would be eating Christmas dinner alone to join us for
that day.

This will be an old-fashioned, home-cooked meal, served family
style.

There is only one requirement to attend our party. It does not
matter if you're a millionaire or on welfare. The only requisite is that
otherwise you would be eating alone that day. If you have your own
spouse and family, you should be with them, otherwise you're
invited.

The Arlington Lodge of Elks donate their hall to me and all cooking and serving will be done by fellow Elks.

If you want to come, simply call me at [xxx] and ask for Frank
Bowes so I'll know how many are coming.

The Christmas dinner Frank Bowes started has become a tradition in my home town. You can be a local hero with simpler gestures, like this one, I think. You don't even have to enjoy what you are doing.

Frank was born in Canada, and used to be a truck driver and meat cutter. Now he owns one of the largest real estate agencies in town. He lives nearby, but my notes show it took a dozen contacts over five months before we could get together. He's not eager for publicity.

When we do meet, his family's on vacation at their summer place; he's back home alone, working. It's an August evening; he's chain-smoking; it's very quiet inside the house.

*

I remember something from our first phone conversation; you really seemed to believe that one person can make a difference in today's world.

You want to know somethin'? *Only* one person can do it. You. Or me, or him. The other guy can't do it.

Because a lot of people really believe that they are powerless, that they're unable to take action—that the world is too big, and they are too small.

No. No. No. No. Only one person. . . . I said [once, to my oldest son], "You gotta realize one thing; you can't change the world." You know what he said to me? "Dad, only I can change the world." That was a very astute, deep statement. Only I can change the world. You see, we learn from our children, as much as they learn from us.

And it's what I hope you are trying to do. Make that your number one message.

Only I can change the world.

Only I can change the world. Isn't it true? Reagan can't do it. Khrushchev can't do it, he's dead. Do you hear what I'm saying? And it's true. *Only* I can change the world. Only I can do anything. . . . And if I do it, I might motivate you to do it.

I was sitting and talking with a bunch of guys. And someone mentioned that the biggest day of suicide was Christmas Day. And I realized—it's one thing to be alone on July 14. But if you're alone on Christmas, then you're really alone.

And I said, well gee, that's true, there's a lot of people in the world just like that. And I said, well, fine, I'm going to give them a place to go. I don't think anyone should be alone on Christmas Day. I'll run this thing, just so no one will be alone. I don't care if they're rich, poor, old, young, it doesn't matter.

A lot of people call this my taking care of the senior citizens. Well it's true, a lot of them are senior citizens. But that has nothing to do with anything. I didn't want anyone alone on Christmas Day. 'Cause my Christmases were always so good, that I suddenly realized, everyone doesn't have this same thing I've had all my life. So I said, fine, I'm going to make it work for the other people. That was my whole motivation for doing it.

I wish I never started it. 'Cause once you start it, you got a tiger by the tail, you can't let it go. I mean, I hate it right now. Well, after, you know, seven years it's—oh, Jeez, I got to do this again. The first time was a real great thing to do. Now it's something I have to do.

But I can't let anybody be alone on Christmas Day. It's not fair. It's not right. And if you see something that you can give to somebody else, then you have to give it to them. That's been my thinking all my life.

We have an obligation, to everyone in this world, in fact it's part of our nature to help anyone that needs help. You're running up the street, a woman in front of you falls down, trips—what do you do? Without even thinking? You pick her up. It's human nature, to help anyone who needs help. You know, I found people that needed help. So I said, fine—if I can help 'em, I'll help 'em.

If I see something that should be changed, then I think, I have to do it. I can't expect you to do it, or Joe, or Fred, or whoever. I can't complain that you didn't do it; I have to do it myself. I've always believed that. . . . I think I've spent a lifetime doing that.

I pick up kids bumming rides. I pick up anyone bumming rides, except girls—that could be a problem. I figure, if someone puts their finger out and says, "Can you give me a ride?", how can I say no? It's not going to cost me anything. I'm going that way anyway. How can I say no? "Kid, you walk, I'm gonna drive." I just can't do that.

Well, I've been doing it all my life; nothing ever happened yet. It may tomorrow. I should be scared now? I should be scared to cross the street, people get run over all the time. I think most people are too concerned with what could possibly happen that would be bad, instead of saying what can I do that would be good.

I think I'd feel very bad if I drove by someone bumming a ride. Now, if I pick someone up and I had a problem, probably 999 times out of a thousand the worst thing he'd ever do is take my car and my money. Right? That's not a bad gamble. Cars and money, they come easy. As opposed to letting someone walk, when I'm riding. I don't think I have the right to refuse to give a ride to anybody.

That's all I have [my obligations to others]. My honest truthful opinion, and I'm not bulling now, my only reason for being in this world is to make it work for other people. And I do that because I'm a selfish person.

I'm a selfish person; you know why? If I made it work for other people, I feel better. If I drove by someone, I'd feel bad. I want to feel good. So I pick 'em up. I do it for selfish reasons.

When I go to this Christmas party, everybody wants to polish my halo. "Oh, Mr. Bowes, you're so wonderful, oh, oh, oh . . . oh, what a great guy you are." And you know something? I get more out of that than they do. Right? I feel like a million dollars that day, because I run this party. So, that's my reason. I'm a selfish person—I want to feel good.

I think that people are cut into two classes. And only two. Ninety-nine percent of the people in this world are exactly alike. They're willing to help anybody—they want to help everybody. There are the other a-holes that say, "Wait a minute, what's in it for me?", or "Why should I do that?" But they're in the minority. A very teeny minority. Very small minority. I can name both of them (laughs). No, but seriously, it makes sense.

This doesn't make me different from the guy next door or the guy across the street. No, we're all alike. All of us would help the other guy. But when someone doesn't, that becomes magnified. . . . That's the ones we see on television, or read about in the paper. That's the exception, that's not the rule, in my opinion.

I realized that there was a problem here. I never thought there were people alone on Christmas—well I'm sure I knew there were, but I never thought about it before. So then I started the old wheels turning, I said, I'll just run a Christmas dinner for all these people, and invite everyone in town. I couldn't take on the whole world—in fact, the first year I limited it to thirty people 'cause I didn't know if I was going to get two, or two thousand.

So I went to the Elks in October or something—I'm a member there— and I asked them, "Can I use your facility?" They're closed on Christmas Day. And they said, "Of course, use our facility. We're closed."

But now how do I get the people? I figured I had to tell people about it. So I sat down and wrote a letter to the *Advocate*, inviting everybody who was going to be alone on Christmas Day, regardless of age or financial ability to pay; I wanted them to be my guest. I didn't want anyone alone on Christmas Day. So I took it down to the *Advocate*, gave it to the girl, and I said, "Put this in as a letter."

The girl says fine, she took it—it was just a letter to her. So I get a call from the editor that afternoon, and she said, "This letter you want to put in the paper; what's it all about?" So I told her. And she did something entirely different: I wrote a letter; she took the letter and wrote a story about it.

And she repeated my whole letter; she'd take a sentence out, comment on it, take another sentence out, put them in quotes, you know. It ended up on the front page of the *Advocate*. Oh, what beautiful ink! (laughs)

So that's what she did. And the only funny part of it, the day the *Advocate* came out—and again I'm going to prove my point— I remember I got thirteen calls that day: only three people wanted to come; the other ten wanted to help.

The first person that called me—there's a fire lieutenant named Coscia, his wife was the first caller. And she said, "I read your article, and there's one thing I'd like to ask you. You've limited it to thirty-nine people; if you get two or three more than you can handle, please, can they come to my house?" And the funny part about it was, I thought she was a woman living alone; just like everyone thought about me—most people thought I was some widower living alone, that needed some company on Christmas. And I thought the same about her.

She gave me a name and phone number. So before Christmas I asked her if *she'd* like to come. She says, no, I have my husband and kids (laughs). But again, that's human nature.

I didn't know how many people were coming, so the only thing I put in the paper was please, if you want to come, just call Frank Bowes at [Frank's office phone number]. Right? And that's how people come—they call and say I'm coming. Now, some people just expect they're going to come.

I'm sure there are people who would love to come, but they think they're not qualified. A young fellow that works for Raytheon, Wang, or whoever, the thought of going never occurs to him—you know, I can't go to that; that's for poor people (chuckles). Everybody would love to come, but they don't call. That's one of my biggest problems, getting to people. I want to see if the editor can get it across to people that this is for you, if you're going to be home alone on Christmas. Your family's in Ohio, and you're a millionaire—who cares? You can't go home? Come down here.

All you have to do is call me and come. And I don't ever ask why. I've actually had people call me and say, "Well, look, I'd like to come, but I can afford to pay for it." You know, they want to come, but they don't want to accept "charity." . . . Well, I guess in a sense it's a form of charity too, but it's nothing to do with money. You see what I'm saying, or do you?

Oh, the first [time] it was total confusion. Gunny [the custodian at the Elks] was walking around in a suit, and everyone was calling him Mr. Bowes, because he was all dressed up, and they figured, well, he's the host here (laughs). And I was in the kitchen, running around in a T-shirt, mashin' potatoes and slicin' turkeys up to my ears, and everyone thought I was a janitor or something.

In fact, the first year we found out we didn't have any knives or forks. Christmas Day. So Tiny Flynn, who has always been one of my biggest helpers, went out scouring the town for the Melrose Spa and these little stores that were open, trying to get plastic knives and forks. Pandemonium. It's getting a little better now.

There were people I kicked this around with down at the Elks, 'cause I couldn't do it all myself. There's people who leave their families and come down to help for four, five, six hours, whatever. And quite a few guys, they brought their kids and their wives, to help; to prepare the meal, and serve it, and then the hard part—cleaning up afterwards (laughs). It becomes a family thing.

I've never asked anyone to help me. Everyone wanted to help—they wanted to be part of it, to the point now where they kick me out of the kitchen, they won't let me do anything. Every year there's got to be, oh, ten, fifteen, something like that. They all know that's where they're going to be Christmas Day. . . . It's unbelievable.

But there's a perfect example of what I'm saying. There was one guy, he used to go out and eat on Christmas Day, that's not easy. And I asked him, "Why don't you come down and have dinner with me?" "Nahhh"—that wasn't his cup of tea. "Yahh, what are you, crazy? Yahh, blehh, blehh, blehh." He wouldn't come. And so after the first year I was talking to his roommate, and I said, "Jeez it's a shame that Billy wouldn't come." His roommate goes to his daughter's house [for Christmas], he's got no problem. He says, "Look, if you want Billy to go, ask him to help you." I said "You know, that's a good approach."

So before the next Christmas rolled around, I says, "Billy, I want you to do me a favor. I need a little help with my Christmas party. Will you come down and help me on Christmas?"

He says, "Yeah, on one condition."

"Sure, what's the condition?"

He said, "I'll do all the cooking."

I said, "Okay, fine, hey that's great, Bill." I said, "I'll tell you what we do—like we did last year—we partially cooked the turkeys on the day before Christmas, 'cause these are twenty-four-pound turkeys, and if you're going to eat at one o'clock, you got to get them started the day before."

And, "No, I'll do it Christmas Day."

"You're crazy, Bill," I says. "You'll have to put them out at five o'clock in the morning."

He says, "Yeah, that's what I figured."

And every year since that first year, they've opened that Elks at five o'clock on Christmas morning to get those turkeys on so they'd be cooked by one o'clock. Everyone's like that. That's what people are all about. . . .

A lot of people come together [to the party], but, you know, not husband and wife or things like that. Although occasionally we get a few of them. But you never say no to anybody. They call and ask you to come, you say sure, come on down.

And I've had people come down there and, well, they're chiselers, they want a free meal. People see these things, and they comment on it, and I say, "Look, it doesn't make any difference. That's what Christmas is all about. That's what turns them on, let them do it; it's there; let them have it."

I had one woman that took some apple pie and ice cream and put it in her pocketbook; she was still there an hour later (laughs). I don't know what her pocketbook looks like, but there was a few comments on that, because people were sitting at the same table. I said, "Well, look, what do I care? If she ate it, I wouldn't have minded; if she took it home, I wouldn't have minded. The fact she sat there for an hour and ruined her pocketbook, what do I care?"

It was easy. I'll admit it was a hell of a lot of work, but I never doubted for a minute it was going to be done. . . . No, I mean, I just knew it was going to work, and it did.

There's no other real highlights; it's all kind of routine. People come down and enjoy themselves. And I hope, I know—well, they all think it's a great time for one reason: they're all happier being there than they would be if they weren't there. They'd be sitting in a room someplace, with nothing to do. And no one to do it with.

I have one rule: under no conditions will I accept anything to pay for this. I insist on that; you can't pay to come, you can't even make a contribution toward paying for it, because then I prostitute it. Just like if I put my company name on it, I'd prostitute it.

It's not a hell of a lot of money, please believe me. But I mean, I just— that's the way it has to be. You just can't accept money for it or the whole thing is out the window. I saw on television some guy in South Boston, owns a bar, raised money from his customers to run a Christmas party exactly the way I'm doing; fine. In fact, quite a few [television stations], either [channel] 4 or 5 or both, wanted to televise it, and I won't allow it. I figure if I did that, it would be, again, prostituting it.

I'm not looking for self-aggrandizement. I don't want any personal publicity out of it.* I don't want any recognition for it; as long as I know what I do I don't give a damn if you know what I do or not. I'm not doing it

*True to his word, Frank was the only one of the interview subjects who preferred not to have his photograph included in this book.

to entertain the television audience, or to get me, "Hey, what a nice guy he is." I don't want any of that.

I'd rather spend three hundred dollars of my own money feeding people on Christmas Day, than spend three hundred dollars in taxes to the government to feed someone that didn't want to work. Sure. I don't think the United States government or the federal government or the city government should have the programs they have for so-called "disadvantaged" persons. I don't think anyone in this country should ever be hungry. . . . But I think that's their only right. Mothers for Adequate Welfare demanded certain things. I don't think anyone that's asking has a right to demand. You take what you get.

I don't think anybody should be hungry. And if it's in my power, no one will ever be hungry. If I ever saw a hungry person, I'd feed them. But I don't think I should be feeding people who just won't work.

See, welfare, it's a shame. I think everybody should get adequate food and shelter. I have nothing against welfare or unemployment. I'm concerned about the abuses of it.

Well, in fact if you want to get involved in politics, which I really didn't (his tone so indicates), we have two factions in government. Reagan is spending much much much too much money on defense. No not defense, war. The Democrats want to spend too much money on giving things away to people. They call these "social programs." They're both wrong! Why don't they make sense?

Are there things you would have done differently with the project now, Frank, in retrospect?

What, the Christmas party? Yeah, I never would have started it. It's a pain in the ass (laughs). No—

No, let's follow that, okay; because one of things you said at the beginning was that you hated it.

I do. I got a tiger by the tail. What can I do? Can I stop?

Let me call you on that. I mean, how facetious are you being?

I'm not being facetious at all. I wish to Christ I never started it. But I can't stop now, can I? Can I just not have it next year?

Well, I guess you could. You could say . . . (both laugh)

No, no, no, I have to live with me, you know. I have to live with me.

The only thing I worry about is if I did stop, and said, "Okay, Elks, you do it," what would happen? It would die. Of course. No one is interested in doing it. No one's going to put all this work and effort into it. Who puts work and effort into things like that? "Okay, Joe, you're chairman of the Christmas party." "Okay, fine." You know. It wouldn't be done right.

'Cause if I don't do it, it doesn't get done. Maybe I've never learned to delegate. Or no, maybe I just don't think anyone else can do the same job. . . . No, uh, what you have to do, you have to do.

It's become a lot easier. Naturally, anything is with experience. [The numbers have] gone up and down ever since. I don't think I've ever had over one hundred, but I don't think I've ever had less than forty-five.

But I constantly try to figure out something that will make it better. Like I was looking for entertainment; or people will suggest that I have people bring gifts for each other, you know, two-dollar gifts or something, and I kind of pooh-poohed that; and the idea of having a Santa Claus, that never turned me on. But really, if someone could give me any kind of an idea that would make it a better time, I would incorporate it.

No, I have no plans to discontinue it, change it. [I'd] change it only in the sense that I can improve it. If I can find a way to improve it, I will. My only problem is getting to the people who don't think they qualify.

You know, this Christmas party—everyone thinks it helps other people. But I get more out of it than anyone does. 'Cause as I said, I'm a selfish person, I only do things so I'll feel good. I love to shave in the morning, I'm proud of that bastard; that's why I can't steal or lie. I wouldn't be able to shave. I'd have to look at that guy in the mirror. . . . Without mirrors, I could be any kind of a rascal.

That's right; I want the halo there. I don't really like it, when people want to polish my halo, openly, to my face, or even behind my back. I just want to wear that halo. I want to feel good about myself. I'll be honest with you. I don't really care what you think about me. As long as I feel good about what I'm doing, then there's nothing more I can get.

Like the greatest thing I have in this whole world is my own family. It's a big one. They're very close. They're close to us and they're close to each other. I don't care if I leave them twenty million dollars. More important, I left them each other. . . . They're friends. Ahh, it's a nice thing to leave behind you. . . .

It would be nice to be able to create that same family feeling among people in general.

That's the whole idea—the only thing we have is our association with other people, whether we know them or not. That's what religion is all about. It's based on my relationship with everyone I meet, every day. Well, so my Christmas party is doing my religion, isn't it? (laughs) Picking up the hitchhiker, that's my religion. It's not a bad religion. You know, I get a lot more out of that, a better feeling out of that than going to Mass (chuckles).

You can only teach by example, and the only way that the example can help is if enough people know about it. Because that can trigger a thought in someone's mind who will do the same thing.

In one way or another, we all have to learn—and eventually we will—that the only way we can make this world work for ourselves, the number one premise, is to make it work for everyone else. And then it works for us, automatically. I don't know of any other way to do it; in fact, I think it was two thousand years ago, a guy tried this. . . .

*

From the *Arlington Advocate,* December 25, 1986:

People with no place to go for Christmas dinner or who are unable to be with families and friends, can find free home-cooked turkey dinners at two places this Christmas.

Carrying on the tradition started by Frank Bowes and his wife GiGi several years ago, the Arlington Elks Lodge is preparing for approximately 100 people expected at the lodge on Pond Lane for Christmas dinner. . . . The Rev. Peter Miano will host another Christmas Day dinner at the Calvary United Methodist Church.

George Reynolds, *Los Angeles Daily News*

They started walkin' up to the front, I knew they were coming up to fight. And they got halfways up to me, and that's when I started singing.

Wally Olson

"THE SINGING BUS DRIVER"

I F Frank Bowes broadens the definition of local heroism, Wally Olson broadens it further.

In the Los Angeles area, he's known as The Singing Bus Driver. He sings to his riders, the old standards mostly, on the Number 8 run for the Santa Monica Municipal Bus Company. He's been known to pass song sheets down the aisles.

All the others in this book started some community program, broadly speaking; usually a lasting organization, designed to deliver some specific helping service to a target group. Generally, these services became formalized, institutionalized, in the best sense of the word. We've not spoken so far of persons whose very actions or very being *are* the service, or at its heart—people like the friendly store clerk, the cheerful mail carrier, or the pharmacist who personally delivers the medicine late at night. There's been an implicit judgment that the more programmatic, more codified acts have broader and more enduring social value, and that's a choice I'd normally defend.

But every once in a great while someone comes along who not only makes the very best out of a routine job, but who turns it into a transforming experience for everyone in the vicinity. I've heard about a toll collector who dances all day in the booth, and I've personally watched a self-appointed greeter and maître d' at the Registry of Motor Vehicles (an amazing display), and they approach what I mean. But if you can get a busload of rapid transit commuters singing "You Are My Sunshine" before 8:00 A.M. on their way to work, that's in another league entirely, that is transcendent, and it's worth more than feature-page reporting to learn how such events come about.

I wonder what Frank Bowes would think of Wally Olson. Frank loves his neighbor, but there's a cloudier side. Love and obligation are

mixed with human limits and human failing, with a flintier understanding of the world, maybe closer to the truth. Wally's love, I think
you'll notice, is of a different order: more explicit, unpasteurized, purer
in its way. When Wally says, in essence, "I love everybody, and I want
everybody to love me," repeatedly and emphatically, there's no evidence
of guile and every reason to believe that's the very center of the man.

So how far can unmixed, unadulterated love take you in community service? And, if any distance at all, how do you cultivate it?

Wally looks like a bus driver, a guy you'd see in Greyhound com-
mercials (to which he once aspired). You'd feel safe as his passenger.
He's a big man with a big resonant natural stage voice, which solidifies
the impression.

✳

To be honest with you, bus driving is the hardest job there is. Everybody
thinks it's easy. But I've seen young healthy men at twenty-four, twenty-five
come and work one year and end up in the hospital with bleeding ulcers.
I've seen heart attacks at thirty. I've seen men completely go out on nervous
breakdowns.

It's a very hard job. Because if you do your job right, you've got to drive
safely; you've got to keep good track of your customers in your bus; you've
got to drive in different weathers; you've got to watch the other drivers;
you've got to watch everything outside; and today seventy percent of the
drivers on the road are terrible.

I mean, if my father lived today and watched these drivers . . . thirty-five
years ago if you drove and made a mistake, you'd roll down your window,
"I'm sorry. I apologize." Today, wrong or right, they give you a finger. And it
isn't the men, or the young kids, (with passion) it's old women, old men,
young women, young men; it's rich and it's poor. They got no patience, and
there we're going back to the main word again—no love.

They got no love. And when you've lost love, in the majority of the
people, they become bad drivers. And I'm going to tell you, the drivers today
are bad. They're very bad. But if you have a [bus] driver that keeps
everything within himself, he's going to get sick. So you have to expel it
somehow. And that is a secret to driving.

So, what are you going to do? Well, some guys sit there whistling,
which is all right. Or some guy starts twitching, you'll see some drivers there
twitching, they're moving all over that chair. Or they get nervous, you see.

I don't do that. I think about singing a song. Telling a little story, see. But
it all goes on love again.

I just started singing the first day I went on. Just singing out. I think the first song I sang was "When Irish Eyes Are Smiling."

To begin with, I had a fight that first day. One of our worst lines is Pico, going into Rimpau. When I first started, I had to do that run. Well, I caught that line on a Friday, and going down to Rimpau—if you've never been there, it's rough. Two guys stood up in the back of the bus and hit each other, and it sounded like broken bones. Like you take a chicken in a bag and hit it. And I could see the blood just running down their faces, they just stood there and they belted each other three or four times.

I pulled the bus over, and I says, "Folks, I want you to know, I love you all. And you guys back there fighting, too. Now listen: you don't know me, but my name is Wally Olson, and there's things I don't like on the bus. I don't want you to smoke, because I'm against smoking, and it's against the city ordinance. I don't like you fighting, because you might get hurt. Now if you want to fight, wait until you get off my bus. I don't want you picking on little kids and old people, and I want you to show a little love for one another. Now if we do this, we're all gonna get along."

And everybody said, "He's crazy!" You see. That very first day, on the Pico run—it was a blood run, I want to tell you. We had several drivers beaten up on that route, right in the seat. So them two guys said, "You're crazy," and right away I knew what was gonna happen—they come walking forward.

Everybody was frightened. I was just as scared as anybody else. And nobody wants to help you, you know, when you're getting in a tight spot. So everybody was looking straight ahead.

Well, they started walkin' up to the front, I knew they were coming up to fight, you know. And they got halfways up to me, and that's when I started singing. I'll never forget the first song, "When Irish Eyes Are Smiling." And everybody clapped. And I said, "Folks, now let's all sing a song together—'Take Me Out to the Ball Game.'" Them two guys started singing. They listened to "When Irish Eyes Are Smiling," but when I started "Take Me Out to the Ball Game," they started singing. They went out to the back of the bus.

I just go to one thing—that everybody has a little love in them, and you can develop it and bring it out in them. Even them two guys fighting. Do you know that them two guys—I never signed a complaint, I never did nothing to them—both those guys were on my bus eight, nine times, and if somebody lit up a cigarette, or somebody did something, they stood up and says, "He don't allow it in the bus, 'cause if you do it, I'm going to ask him for permission to throw you off." They were on my side, see?

Well, it got around. The next couple of days were smooth, I just kept singing. They all loved it. This one girl says, "Do you do this all the time?" and I said "Yeah." "Oh that's nice," she said. "I like that. Peace and quiet, a little song, you know."

I usually get down to work here at 6:00 A.M., and sign in, and then I set up. Punch my tickets for the day. And have a little cup of coffee, maybe walk out to my bus about 6:30. I set it up, you know, the seat. Clean it up. And by 6:40 I'm all ready to roll and then I deadhead to Westwood and Wilshire. There's where I start my run, coming into Santa Monica, at six minutes to seven. I start coming in, I pick up the kids, and the real early ones, going to their different jobs in the morning. I greet everybody. And I always greet them saying, "Hello, I think it's going to be a pretty day."

Now (sighs) I've been told many a times, it's starting to rain, I say, "I think this is going to be a lovely day." And the man looks at me, he got on the bus and he says, "Now, Wally, how can you say that—it's raining! Every day is a nice day to you." "Well," I said, "we need rain. If we didn't have rain, this country'd blow away. So I'm happy today it's raining. It's going to be a happy rainy day." See. I mean, just start 'em off in a positive way. And he said, "Boy, you already made me feel good. I was kind of down and out this morning." See. Then I always like to go into "Pennies from Heaven," or "April Showers," if it's raining.

Like this morning, I sang "Oh, What a Beautiful Mornin'." And then "There's a Rainbow 'Round My Shoulder." You know, and songs like that. And now of course there's older people, that like particular songs, they say, "Wally, will you sing 'You Are My Sunshine'?" So I do it, you know.

And then there's a girl gets on said, "Will you do 'Love Me Forever'?" That was one of Elvis Presley's songs. I just know not too many of his songs; I liked a couple of them. And if there's one that gets on that wants this and that, if I know 'em I sing 'em. But if I don't know 'em, I just start singing another song. See?

In other words, if somebody says to you, "Will you please do 'Donkey Serenade'?", and I really forgot all them words, I'm not going to fumble around. I say, "Hey, I got one for you," so I do them "South of the Border," see. Or "Mexicali Rose." "Donkey Serenade," "South of the Border," "Mexicali Rose," they're all the same, you know.

Yeah, I do the light ballads, the old standards. I like a lot of Frank Sinatra, "All the Way," and all those songs. So if somebody asks for something, I don't believe in criticizing what they like. Now that's one very important thing, 'cause you're going to be making an enemy. So if a kid gets on and says, "Hey, do you know that bop and boll and boll and bop?", I say,

"No, but I know 'On Top of Old Smoky.'" (laughs) Or I'll give 'em some other song. And they just laugh: "I never heard that one before," you know.

And they say, "How do you like that Stone music?" There's a bunch called the Stone, the rock and rollers, the Stoners, or whatever it is [Rolling Stones?]. I said, "I guess they're real good," you know. I just say, "I *guess* they're real good." But I ain't gonna criticize them, 'cause maybe the kids like 'em, see. But then instead of criticizing, I'll just sing out one of my songs.

I sing to little kids. I sang a song like . . . "You Were Only Fooling, but I Was Falling in Love," and a boy about ten years old and a girl about eleven said, "Man, that's a good song; is that new?" And I said, "Yeah, that's brand new." He went home and he told his dad, and his dad said, "You tell Wally that song's about one hundred years old." (laughs) But the kids loved it, they never heard it. And I sing them old ballads to the kids, and the kids like it, the old people like it, and they all like it.

I tell you, since I've been in Santa Monica, I've had so many children, their parents go to work, and they leave a first-grader on the bus stop, to get to school. It gets pretty dark. I can see the kids, they're standing there worried. And I'd talk to them. I'd say this is fine. Sing 'em a little song, and calm them down. And I'd say now, "Lookit, when you get out of school, I'm going to be waiting for you." I got kids that went to first grade here, now they're in high school, and they come and remind me when I sang to them. They said, "Oh, you made me feel so good." It relaxed them.

One girl, who got married now, she found the bus I'm drivin' to introduce me to her husband, because she said I made her feel so happy when she went to grade school. That's love, you know, giving them a peace of mind. Doing something for them, see.

Well, you can't sing all day, because you'd get worn out. But I've been singing for ten years. If I drive for twenty minutes [without singing], and somebody rides the bus that long, they come and say, "Are you sick? Don't you feel good?" "Why?" "'Cause you haven't sang a song." "Oh," I said, "I was just thinking. But thank you for reminding me." So I'll sing them a couple of lines of a song, see. But they'll think I'm sick.

Do people join in?

Well, I've got them really good on "Take Me Out to the Ball Game," and "You Are My Sunshine," and "Let the Rest of the World Go By," that's a good one. And I try to get 'em on most, but those are the main songs.

Of course, I like (sings) "If you were the on-ly girl in the world," they like that song, now that's an old one, you know. And there's one lady in

Brentwood always asks for that song, "Smile." That's a good song. And "When You're Smiling,"—(sings) "When you're smi-ling, when you're smi-ling." And then of course, I like all of Jolson's . . .

✳

He knew Jolson, when Jolson was on tour. Wally's been around a while. He was stage manager at the Palace Theatre in Minneapolis and at other theaters around Minnesota, his native state. That goes all the way back to the 1940s, when there was a movie, and a stage show before the movie, and when Wally was producer, emcee, and sometimes star.

He's been around, and restless. Theater manager in Iowa, Korean War vet, singer at Eisenhower's first inaugural ball, staffer at Harold's Club in Reno, a Greyhound bus driver in fact, a short stint as a restaurateur, a drive-in movie manager, a flea market founder, then a driver for Universal Studios, where he met a few celebrities.

He is not shy. He carries publicity stills in his briefcase, four different poses, giving his height (6'3"), weight (200), and eye color (blue). He sings at weddings and anniversaries on the side, and is available for bus charters. His three daughters are married, and he lives with his wife and "a couple of bad dogs." The bumper stickers on his Toyota van read "I ♡ Simi Valley," and "I ♡ Big Bear Lake."

✳

But anyway, I started to work here, and I started singing, and after being here six months, the talk was going around they're going to fire me.

I got called into the office. There was some letters sent in, compliments. So the bus line naturally thought, well, maybe all I was doing was singing out there (laughs). So they says, "Now lookit, that's nice you're singing out there, but are you driving your bus, and taking care of your business?" I said, "Yes sir, I'm taking care of the customers, I'm driving the bus, and trying to do everything in nice shape." They said, "Well, we're going to check on you." So I'm sure they sent checkers out, because I had no complaints.

I had one man, and he says, "When I get on the bus, I don't like noise, I don't like singin', and you sing, and I don't like it." He says, "Just shut up and drive the bus." So all right. Well, he sat down, this particular man, he was about seventy, very cranky man. Here comes on a young girl and says, "Wally, you going to sing me a song?" A school kid. I said, "Not this time; I got a man and he don't feel too well and we don't want to upset him." (said without sarcasm) "Ohhhh—which man?" I said, "Now never mind—leave him alone." So he heard the girl.

Pretty soon some older people got on—here comes this lady, and she walks with crutches, she drags both of her legs actually, she's up there about seventy-five. She says, "Wally, sing me a song." And I said, "I'd like to, but I . . ." She says (plaintively), "Why not?" And I says, "I have a gentleman on the bus, and he asked me not to sing." "Oh," she said, "would you tell me who he is, I'd like to speak to him." I said, "No, I wouldn't do that." So she hobbled on her crutches, she just turned around and she says, "There's a lot of people on this bus, so I don't know who you are, and Wally won't tell me, so I'll just say, whoever it is, I wish you would say that he could [sing], because it makes me feel good."

He didn't say anything. Nobody said nothin'. Then he walked up behind a seat and said, "Can I have a schedule?" I said, "Yeah, there's a schedule right there." He bent down to pick it up. He said, "Wally, go ahead and sing a song for that lady." He didn't want anybody to know it was him, you see. All right. So I said [to the lady], "I think maybe the gentleman wouldn't mind if I sang one song for you." So I sang her a song, and she thanked me. And when he got off the bus, he said, "I'm sorry, Wally. I think I was just worrying too much about my own problems. That was very nice what you did." Now after that, every time he got on the bus he said, "You're going to sing for us today?" He felt bad about it.

Then I had a lady once that came on and she says, "Every time I get on this bus, you're singing. Now everybody might like it, but I don't. I don't like it." Well I said, "Now, I am sorry." And I apologized. "I don't like to upset you." So I said, "I tell you what I like to do. I'd like to sing one more song for you, with your permission, and I'll never sing for you again. I want to say I'm sorry." And she says, "Okay, one more song, and never sing while I'm on this bus again." So. Okay. So I sing (sings), "I'm sor-ry, please for-give me, I didn't mean to make you cry." And at the end of the song, you know, it ends, "Let's be sweethearts again"; I changed the line so that it said, "Let's be bus pals again." Sang that song and she just sat there, didn't say nothin'. When she got up to go on out she said, "You know how to work a person." She said, "It's okay, you can sing for me."

Now over ten years, there've been three people [who complained]. One other person, one lady. She was very polite, very dignified. And this lady never changed. . . .

The drivers around here are liable to say, "More power to you, but you're crazy. You're nuts; how can you do it?"

Now, I'm going to tell you, the first couple of years at work, there were some drivers that said, "Don't talk to me, I don't want to be seen with you." And they even did things to try to get me in trouble. They turned me in and they went to the supervisor and said Olson's doing this wrong, that wrong; they were trying to get me down.

One driver, particularly, that turned me in, that was riding me and everything—I walked up to him and says, "I don't care what you say." I said, "You know something, when I found this job, I was looking for a job, and I love people, and I'll find another one. I'm not worried. But I'm not leavin'. If they believe you, I'm just gonna tell them you're okay, I still like you." See. And it got to him. He talks to me now. A chief supervisor told me about eight years ago, maybe they're jealous that the people like you. And I hear a lot of times, "Why don't you train these other drivers?" You got a bunch of other drivers that are so cranky. They're so mean—they tell old people sit down and shut up. "Have you got a schedule?" "Shut up! There's one there, and don't be fooling around in this bus."

Well, I tell you, that's the whole thing like I told you at the beginning— [fervently] the trouble with the world today, eighty percent of the people, and now this is a big percentage, has no love for their neighbor, not much love for their relatives, not much love for any man, woman, and child.

I'll go up and say "good morning" to this bunch, and that bunch and every bunch, and if they don't like it, I don't care. In other words, if somebody told me that you didn't like me, I would remember that so I'd be very careful, and if I seen you I'd say, "Hey, good morning, Bill (sweetly). I hope you have a nice day." I'd keep working on you. When you come home, I say, "Hey, I hope you had a nice day." And if you would say to me, "I didn't have a nice [day]. Shut your lousy mouth and mind your own business." I'd say, "I'm sorry." I'd leave you alone.

It bothers me, it does bother me, if somebody don't like me, because I love people. And I work on them, and then when I see it's no use, then I forget it—but I don't forget them. I forget trying to do something. But the time always comes. Everybody's got a sensitive spot, I don't care how tough they are; and through illustration you can get to most people.

Do you get a sense of the effects of your singing, and the way you drive a bus, on people?

Well, I think talking to them, they know I have no hidden dislikes about people's race, creed, color, or anything like that. They can feel that. They can feel that. And I think they can also feel when I sing a song that I'm not just singing to be cocky or funny or anything. I'm singing because I love music and I love people.

Now I think that showing love . . . I was on the 2 line in Venice here, over on California Avenue, at nine o'clock at night, and this gal was real mad; she pulled a knife on another person in the bus, she's going to gut him out. And I said, "Please don't do that on my bus. Think it over before you do anything like that, I like you both," you know. And it just got her wrong, and she jumped up on me and she says, "You gringo, I'm going to get you good." She stood up in the front of the bus with her knife (laughs), she's going to get me.

So I talked to her and I says, "You know," I says, "I'd like to sing you a song." She says, "No. I think, you gringo, you better pray." And I said, "I'm not going to sing, but I pray all the time, because I need help. I need help, so that if I get help, maybe I can help you. I need help every day. And I need help right now."

"Well," she says, "I'm going to do it to you." I knew now nothing was working. So my mind completely went around, and I said, "Do you have any children? Please tell me if you have children." She says, "Yeah, I got a girl and a boy." I said, "I think they ride my bus, I think I sang 'em a song the other day." I says, "I think I know your children. I think you got real sweet kids. Do you spend much time with them?" I talked real fast, and I said, "You got sweet kids."

She started cryin', she put the knife in her purse, she went and sat down, and she said, "I haven't been feeling well lately." And I said, "I know you haven't." And she said, "Are you going to report me? If you report it they'll come and get me." I said, "I'm going to promise you, that if you never do this again, I ain't gonna report it. But if I see you do it again, I'm gonna tell them you did it twice." She said, "I won't do it again." I said, "Good."

Well, this lady—from then on she got on the bus and went to work and says, "Good morning, Wally." She was so sweet and so nice, you know? And I could see, she's changed. She used to drink a lot. I think she took dope, or whatever she was takin', she was high that day. She quit bein' high, I could see it; her appearance was cleaner, she looked better. She started saying little things like "I took my kids to a movie," and "I spent time with my kids." I said, "Now you're talking."

Now I think a lot of people need correction, and I believe if somebody takes a life deliberately, their life should be taken. But she just needed a little chance, a little love, you see. You don't get too many experiences like that. But in ten years, I've had no trouble. I could have wrote a book myself (laughs). . . . Yeah, I could write a book on everything that happened, I really could. . . .

From the time I was young, my dad and my mother taught me how to love people; and you can't do it unless you show it, and demonstrate it, by doing something, in maybe helping that person.

Now I can just sit right here, talk to you, and smell my mother making homemade cookies and bread. And I used to go in the kitchen there when she was bakin', play with my trucks and cars on the floor—I was six or seven years old. And my mother said, "Play over there now, don't get in the way." But she said, "Now the first pan that comes out, I'm going to give you a cookie if you're good." My mother had real love. I'm not saying the women today should have to make these things, but parents got to show love for their kids.

There's only one thing I really look forward to now. This is the longest I've ever been in anything, heh, heh—it's ten years driving. But now, I think I'm right in a position that what I really want I can really have. My plan is, in the future, I'm even looking for my spot, I'm going to have my own restaurant-theater.

I'm not going to be in it to get rich. And take a lot of money. I won't be open seven days a week, day and night. I'm going to be open four days a week, maybe from four till one. I'm going to serve food, and I'm going to have a theater entertainment, a restaurant theater, I should say. I'm only going to hire retired entertainers, people that don't want to work no more, they're lonesome, they want something to do, they want something in life. There you get true love out of them and good quality.

The show on the stage will be good. But in there I'm going to make (speech slows down, for emphasis), you, the public, my show—that's what I like. Really getting the people to show love and expel this love where they never expelled before. I want them to feel that this show is *theirs*.

Now, this is hard to do. I love it. I'd go out in the audience and I can pick out people, take them right out of their seats, and I can find out what they can do, and I'll have them do it. See. And they'll do it. They'll say, "I never knew I could do it that way." "Well," I'd say, "you're great!" You know, they're relaxing, they're really them that's coming out, really the true them.

So I'm going to retire from driving whenever—it's going to take me another couple of years. It takes a lot of money, and I'm trying to put it together. You see, I'm no king—I'm nothing. But I know thousands of people in this whole area. I know them in Thousand Oaks, I know southern California. And all I want to do is make people happy and see happy people. I want to make the people part of what I want to do.

If I had to do it all over again I would have wanted to drive a bus, but not as long as I have. Okay. But I consider myself still a young man. The only thing is, if I'd have done it ten years ago, and not worked here, and not got all this publicity, they wouldn't have known who Wally Olson was.* So I love driving and everything—but now when I hang up my shingle, they'll say, "That's Wally Olson, The Singing Bus Driver, and he's got *you* part of that show, and he makes *everyone* have a good time."

So you see, I don't regret anything I do, because everything I've done was not to build me up but to build love and to have people recognize me for one main thing—that I love people, I care for people, I'm interested in them, and I want them to share with me true love and happiness.

It would be just like this: can you picture this? Here you got a town, and a lot of blood and guts going on, the police work and everything. And over here, on the side here, you've got a beautiful little valley, some stores and some farms, and everybody in their own profession, and everybody's happy. Everybody loves one another, and everybody recognizes one another. In the morning, you say, "Hi, Tom," "Hi, Bill," "Hi, Wally," and everybody's happy.

See? That's where I'd like to be. Where everybody's happy. . . .

---

*Wally has been featured in Los Angeles area newspaper and television stories, as well as on National Public Radio.

We realized that we didn't have the faintest idea of what to do.

Ellen Cassedy

9to5

I USED to argue with a friend who was directing a meditation center. I would say, "If society needs changing, go out and change it, no matter where you are inside." He would say, "To change society you have to change yourself, so that society will more likely accept what you have to offer." Over the years, I've come closer to Howard's point of view. This book, in fact, is a testament to it.

Yet even so, much of the time, character takes a back seat to action. We can radiate love down every aisle, be loving in our every gesture, and in many eyes that still counts less than somebody who goes out and *does* something. This is our Western way of acting on the world, of salvation through works. Eastern philosophy, Taoism for example, says "The way to do is to be," but for many of us, most activists included, that's a postponable lesson.

If we do elect to be saved through works, in whole or in part, we might as well learn how to work at peak effectiveness. And it could be this means planning, rational thinking, that whole apparatus. That's what they teach in business schools; but planning's not patented, and it's open to use by homelier enterprises.

The stories in this book vary in their approach to planning. People like Henry Ware, Ray Shonholtz, Chick Colony and his associates were conscious planners, their paths mapped out most steps of the way. Lightner and the Yorks, those who were "victims," dove right in and started swimming; but so did Fran Froehlich and Marti Stevens. People like Frank Bowes appear somewhat in-between, and to Wally Olson this dimension hardly applies. We might conclude you can do great things whether or not you've thought of all the angles.

Which is not to say that planning doesn't help, a lot. 9to5, the association of women office workers, is a case in point. The people who started 9to5 in 1973 were in fact secretaries, junior-grade secretaries actually, barely out of their teens, and you don't get from the typing pool to the national mainstream by good intentions alone. The women's movement gathered momentum through the 1970s, so the times were in their favor. But the feminist landscape has its own tombstones, and survival depends on more than dreams.

Ellen Cassedy was one of those secretaries, a cofounder of 9to5, an early and a continuing leader. She has directed 9to5's research and educational programs, and was Executive Director of its affiliated Working Women Education Fund. When we meet, she is working out of shared office space in downtown Philadelphia, moving her operations base from year to year to stay ahead of rising rents. No executive suites here. Our conversation, as it happens, is punctuated by typewriters clacking a few feet away.

Her story—the early days are emphasized here—highlights the value of step-by-step planning as well as the deliberate use of technique. Just the basics, carefully applied; many lessons inside for other organizations. And several other themes make a reappearance here: the role of parental influence; the use of the media; the long haul.

One further theme is newer, which is the value of a core group in getting started. All social initiatives ultimately rest on individual actions, but where other programs have been more personally attributable, 9to5 was closer to a collective creation. Group influences can dampen individual responses, but can stimulate them too, and 9to5 shows clearly what can happen when high cohesion, mutual support, and a sense of injustice—and planning, and excitement—are jointly at work.

Ellen was working at a clerical job in 1972 when she and a coworker, both dissatisfied with the treatment and pay they received on their jobs, attended a weekend workshop for office workers at a Boston-area YWCA. At the workshop, they heard grievances worse than their own.

✳

I graduated from college with a degree in American history, and what was I going to do? There weren't jobs for people with degrees in American history. I didn't know how to think about a career. Before I had a college degree, I had been a clerical worker. And now I had a college degree, and I was a clerical worker again.

So I couldn't begin to think what I was going to do with my education, what I wanted to do with my life. And I think that's true of many women; we look around at the jobs most women are doing and say, well, I guess that's what I'm going to do too.

I think that's going to be true for a long, long time. We have to improve those jobs, not [just] try to convince women that they can be aerospace engineers, or go to work in coal mines. Many, many women are going to remain in women-dominated jobs for the rest of their lives. That's where we're focusing our efforts.

Let's see—after that [YWCA] workshop, people signed up, saying they wanted to get together again. We started meeting at somebody's house, and . . . I think the main thing was that we were very excited. We didn't know what to do. There was the context of the times, which was that many women were meeting in consciousness-raising groups and sharing things. But the mere fact that we were together in this group seemed like an incredible step to us.

We spent a lot of time talking about how we got to the group, what made us go to the workshop in the first place. We did a lot of going around the room and describing our jobs and our backgrounds, as a slow warm-up. We did some informal research, and we got in touch with people who were doing similar things in New York. Maybe we read a couple of articles about clerical workers in the economy. But mostly we just talked.

And one of the smartest things we did was not form the organization right away. We realized that we didn't have the faintest idea of what to do. So rather than go public, and say here we are, everybody join us, before we knew what we were doing, we spent a number of months just talking. Then eventually we decided to put out a newsletter. That's when we decided on "9to5."

We got the newsletter printed up and went out on streetcorners to hand it out before work. We had to get up an hour earlier than usual to get out there in the freezing cold. We made a lot of mistakes. I remember standing in front of Liberty Mutual, which is one of the largest insurance companies in Boston—I got there around 8:30, maybe 8:15, and I stood there at the front door. Here's this enormous building, and I would say maybe forty people went in in half an hour. And then as I was leaving I noticed there was a side door, with people pouring in, *streaming* in, to go to work (laughs). There were other places where we'd get there at 8:10, only to find out that work started at 8:00. . . .

But we divided up the city and went out to these places and stood there handing out these newsletters. We did that for a year. And we went out there with our prejudices. For example, we thought that people who were not quite so dressed up would be more interested, because they weren't playing the game as much; probably young people would be more interested than older people, things like that.

But in fact, a lot of people who were dressed up were deeply involved in their jobs, and really interested in changing them. And there were older women who said, "Finally! I've been waiting for fifteen years for this kind of thing to come along. Tell me how I can get involved." One woman in her fifties came sweeping into our office one day, wearing a cape, like an apparition, and saying "You are braaave warriors!" . . . And we got lots of letters. So there was a lot of support out there.

And where did we get the money? We raised it somehow. We wrote up a fund-raising letter and sent it around to people we knew. Some of these people were involved with churches, and others had been involved in progressive causes. Then we had to call them up and ask them for a donation—this was very difficult. But people would give twenty dollars, twenty-five dollars.

The next thing that happened was we heard that the Midwest Academy, which is a school for organizers, was going to be starting its first session. We decided to send me as our emissary, to find out about how to organize. Why me? It probably had something to do with my perception of myself as someone who needed training. I felt like an apprentice in a lot of ways.*

The tuition seemed astronomical; it was five hundred dollars. I used some of my own savings, and I went around to my friends and hit them up, and women in the group each gave ten dollars. Then I went off and learned about community organizing for the first time.

The Midwest Academy would describe campaigns. Well, I had never heard of a "campaign," you know. They would go through all these various steps, put out their timelines—all these things I'd never heard of before: timelines, work plans, strategy, tactics. And we would draw charts up on the wall, and how do you get from here to there? . . .

I think it taught me two things: one was the actual nitty-gritty skill of having a little index card file where you put the name of everybody who was interested, and then little notes like, "She seems to be particularly interested in pay issues," or "She's willing to pass out the newsletter to her coworkers," that kind of thing. Organizing, in the sense of organizing your desk.

Then also, there was the whole concept of setting a goal, and planning the steps to get there. Before that, I had been sort of vaguely propelled by a feeling that things should be different—that if we raised issues, spoke up about things, then maybe people would take action. At the Midwest Academy, I learned about much more specific tactics: let's hold a meeting;

---

*Ellen in fact was a cofounder of the group, together with Karen Nussbaum, who is now executive director of the national 9to5 organization.

let's call the press; let's put pressure on this company; and here are the ways, here are the allies we can get, here are the tactics we can use.

What I knew about was demonstrations in the peace movement, where people who really didn't work together day-to-day would come out on one day to do something. Now I was learning about community organizations whose members went to committee meetings all the time, and did outreach, and talked to people—a much more intense level of organization, that had completely passed me by.

My parents taught me to be concerned about social issues. And I guess I had a number of experiences that taught me not to take things at face value and to be critical of unfair conditions. And also to know that there were ways to change things.

I remember, for example, that I experienced school desegregation firsthand. All of a sudden there were black children in our classrooms. It was 1956, right outside Baltimore. My parents sat me down and explained what was going on and said integration was a good thing.

My father drove me around mixed neighborhoods at that time, and said, "The white people in this neighborhood were very disturbed when they heard that black people were moving in. But look at these houses: does it look to you as if this neighborhood is going down the drain?" And it didn't. So at the age of five or six I got some very specific training in learning to step outside and take a good look at things, and a strong belief that everybody deserved equal treatment.

The peace issue was very important to me also. Starting around the age of ten, I was extremely worried about nuclear war. My first feelings were that I was sure that my parents were not going to build a bomb shelter. Everybody else was going to be saved, and we were going to be out there dying in a nuclear war, just because my parents wouldn't get it together. I started looking around for some way to do something about this fear—what could I do to handle this? So I started reading about radiation and how atomic energy worked. I read books about isotopes and electrons and all this kind of thing.

So I had the experience here and there of talking about social issues and doing something about them. Then when I ended up in an office, my natural thought was, "What's the matter here?": (a) what's my critique of it?; and (b) what can I do about it? Rather than, "I'm here and I just have to accept whatever happens."

I got back [from the Midwest Academy] in August of '73, with a whole new view. Now it was time to start the organization, because now we knew how to set goals, and keep card files, and all that.

It was August, and hot as hell, and I was full of plans: we should prepare for a public meeting to get the organization off the ground; we should print leaflets, we should move into an office in the YWCA, get into the newspaper, announce plans for our action program, meet office workers who would introduce us to their coworkers, meet with the Chamber of Commerce and present them with a series of demands about the status of clerical workers in Boston. I was ready to jump out of my seat, I was so ready to go.

We basically did all that. We moved incredibly quickly after I got back. It was great. I quit my job—I hesitated back and forth; I was afraid to take the risk—but I did. We started raising money again, and we got a Presbyterian church grant of $3500, which went to pay my extremely small salary for a while. We did get an office at the Y; I went in there and told them they should do this; much to my surprise they agreed (laughs). We held our first meeting in mid-November, and 125 women came.

At this meeting, we gave everyone a stack of questionnaires to hand out to other office workers. This was really an outreach tactic. It was also a way to find out what people thought about their jobs. People would put their names on the bottom, saying "I want to hear the results of this survey," or "Please be in touch with me about other things you're doing." That was how we'd get more names.

We were looking for examples of people who were doing things to make changes in their office, whose experiences we could publicize. We were looking to create a snowball effect. If you heard that some women over in this office have asked for maternity leave, well then, maybe you can do it too. It's always been important to show that regular people, just like you and me, have opened their mouths and tried to get a promotion, or asked for a general pay raise, and they got it.

Well then, we had these 125 names. So we started going out to lunch with as many of them as we could. Of course I'd gotten instructions from the Midwest Academy about exactly how to go to lunch and what to order—"coffee, pie, and a small sandwich" (laughs)—the point being not to order some huge meal that means all you can do is eat, rather than concentrating on the person you're talking to.

We learned about all the cheapest coffee shops, all over Boston. You would meet the person and then you'd have your coffee or whatever—we often ate at least two lunches a day, by the way (laughs). We started out by asking people why they were interested, what brought them to 9to5, and what it was like in their office. We'd draw out what the problems were, and how other people felt, to see if there was the potential for getting a little group together and making some changes.

Then, at the end, we'd say, "Here are the next three activities 9to5 is doing; would you be able to do any of them?" They were things like: "Can you take a few questionnaires to pass out to your friends or coworkers?"; or "Can you come to the next meeting?"; "Can you make some phone calls for the next meeting?"; "Do you have any friends we could get in touch with?"; "Will you help plan the upcoming meeting with the Chamber of Commerce?" We had learned how to plan by then, you know, and how to involve other people in doing so. . . .

This was one of the most exciting periods of my life. I had a sort of entrepreneurial feeling, like working at a church bake sale in a way. You know, "Buy these cupcakes! They're really great!", and getting totally absorbed in selling every single cupcake off the table. It was like that, trying to get through this stack of 125 names.

There was an incredible amount of energy involved, finding out more and more, and getting more and more names. We kept a log of every phone call that came into our office, and we'd all rush back from lunch to read what had happened, and compare notes. So we were full of high hopes.

At the beginning, I had to acclimatize myself, to . . . working myself to the bone. It was hard. You had to sit down at the table and make phone call after phone call after phone call to people you never heard of. I mean, it was like being in an assertiveness training class, all day long, all the time. I was often doing something that I was a little bit anxious about.

For example, when I was a teenager I had a fear of making phone calls, and in fact when I had to call a movie theater to find out when the movie was playing, I would write out my half of the conversation ahead of time: you know, "Hello. Could you please tell me when 'The Parent Trap' is playing?" (laughs). So there was a lot of desensitization going on for me. Here I was, meeting strangers for lunch, and sort of being in charge of making it all flow, and all that. It was hard.

These things weren't *extremely* difficult; I could do them, but it made me anxious. Even passing out the newsletter wasn't that easy. You'd be surprised, if you've never done it, how hard it is to stand out there all by yourself, and hand things out to people. People say all kinds of things to you, slightly hostile things, like "What are you sellin' today?" You feel a little vulnerable, in some ways.

By this time, we had met hundreds and hundreds of women. Every two weeks we would have an evening meeting at the YWCA. There were usually about fifty people at each meeting—sometimes more. And early on we got into planning what we called our public hearing, which was going to be held in the spring of '74. What it meant was passing out all these questionnaires, tallying the results, and then calling up people who had gotten involved, or who had written particularly interesting things, and saying, "Would you be interested in testifying here?" and "How many people can you bring?"

And hundreds of women came to that meeting in the spring. We had people from the Equal Employment Opportunity Commission and other agencies sitting on the stage listening. We had women from all different industries testifying: publishing, universities, insurance, banking, temporary work, law firms. They talked about what their jobs were like, what was bothering them—very personal stories. Then everyone signed a petition, a bill of rights for women office workers, which we had made up: the right to equal pay for equal work, the right to equal promotion opportunities, grievance procedures—ten different items.

And then after the hearing, we started working specifically with different industries. I worked a lot with a group of women in publishing. This was a good example of being in the right place at the right time, because publishing in Boston at that time was just incredibly ripe for change. We did a little survey of women in the publishing industry: women who had been working there for many years were making thousands of dollars less than men who'd been working there for two years—the same job, the same background. Classic discrimination-suit material.

The network spread like mad. Publishing was a small enough industry that it was pretty homey. Everyone knew a lot of women in other companies. And it was one of those industries—universities are the same way—where there was a lot of talk about the life of the mind and all that. It made people feel very exploited if they weren't part of it, which they were not.

So we held a public meeting about the publishing industry itself, where we released the results of our survey. The big honchos in the industry all came, all trembling in their boots. We ended up going to the Attorney General of Massachusetts and filing suit against three of the largest publishing companies in Boston, and settling for several million dollars in back pay.

And it transformed the industry. People who were involved in the group were getting promotions by the dozen. Companies were changing all kinds of policies, instituting job posting where there had never been any before, instituting training programs. . . . It was fantastic.

It was the pressure from women in the companies that did it. It just became too costly to the powers that be to have these women riled up all the time, not to mention the threat of discrimination suits. It was getting pretty scary for the publishing executives. I guess probably some of them who changed their minds realized that, gee, I suppose these girls do need some better employment policies. But mostly I think the pressure got so strong that they figured the easiest thing would be to contain us, by giving in to some extent. They were very worried about unionizing. And in fact one of the three companies did end up unionizing.

So in terms of the techniques you were using, what would you identify as being some of the most effective?

Well, one thing was to reach as many people as possible, and to have a lot of those people come out publicly in trying to change things, which would embolden others. And women did become leaders, even if they hadn't been formally elected. Eventually we did elect a steering committee— a representative from each publishing company.

Another technique was to put out demands right away: job posting, training, job descriptions, raises. What we found out, to our surprise, was that money was the easiest thing for the companies to give; they had plenty of money. What they didn't want to give up was control over their policies. They didn't want anyone to think that if you screamed about management prerogatives you could change them.

Then, we always had suggestions for things that could be done about problems on the job. Most of the time, people couldn't think of anything they could do about the problems. But we'd always have five or six ideas. We would suggest, for example, trying to meet with management, or writing up a letter and sending it to the boss. Or we would ask: "Which would you be more comfortable with: writing a letter, or meeting in person?" Things like that. So we would have this list of things that other people had done, which were often things people hadn't thought of before.

So we really got a feel for what people were concerned about, and we tried to remain very close to that while also presenting a vision that things could be different. A lot of times when people think about organizing, they think the organizers will go in and tell people what's wrong, and then tell them how to change it. But everybody knew what was wrong. It was really a question of putting the tools in their hands, and showing them how to use them.

Today I think, gee, I was twenty-three when I was starting 9to5. It seems more amazing than it did at the time. At the time, I didn't feel too young (laughs). Today, if a group of twenty-three-year-olds wanted to start a citywide organization, maybe I'd wonder if they were old enough. . . .

✳

Twenty-three is old enough. With twenty-five national chapters, fourteen thousand members, and activity in one hundred cities, 9to5 is now out front on virtually every workplace issue of the day: job stress, fair pay, comparable worth, pensions, office safety, automation, VDTs, maternity leave, day care, part-time work, career advancement. They need to be: there are eighteen million clerical workers in the United States, and most have little job protection.

More than a decade later, 9to5 lobbies, researches, advocates, organizes, much as before. Do the same strategies that worked locally work for a national audience as well? Ellen is patient.

*

Feeling that we're reaching thousands and thousands of people—that's really important to me. There are people all over the country who are committed to 9to5. It's also important to me that we're building something that has some kind of permanent structure. It's not an ad hoc project, it's an organization with years of history, and years ahead of it.

I think we've stumbled here and there, searching for what actions people would find it possible to take. I think we're still searching. The fact that we have fourteen thousand members rather than fourteen million means that the right vehicle has not yet been found. Part of it is that people need a lot of support. If you had an organizer on every block, I'm sure you could get people taking these little steps. But we haven't found the small steps that millions of people could feel comfortable taking on their own that would get them rolling.

But, you know, these are huge goals—eliminating the wage gap, or bringing women into every level of the labor force. It takes an awfully long time for those things to happen. When we first got started we thought maybe it would take five years (laughs). And then after five years we said, all right, maybe five years more.

What intrigues me at this point is using the avenues of really massive publicity. We've had our hit song; we've had our movie; we have our book.* I've been interested in things like a [syndicated] newspaper column; and we've done a lot of national TV, but there are still national TV frontiers we haven't crossed. I'm also really interested in what I consider to be the lost art of public speaking. When you hear good speakers, you realize what you've been missing; it's an art, like opera singing or something.

At this point, though, most of us who are actively involved feel that it's going to be a long-term effort. It's taken decades and decades to organize other kinds of workers. Nurses and teachers, for example, began organizing long, long before office workers were even thinking about it. We're really

---

*The movie *Nine to Five*, starred Jane Fonda, Dolly Parton, and Lily Tomlin. The song, of the same name, was recorded by Dolly Parton. The book is cited in references following these interviews.

right at the beginning. We aren't going to organize office workers in a day or a decade; it's going to take a long time. You have to be persistent rather than merely frenetic.

And I can see the progress of our organization in many ways. The climate of public opinion about women and women's work has changed a great deal in the past fifteen years. We haven't wiped out the problems, but that doesn't mean we haven't made some progress. We're preparing the groundwork for achieving our goals. It's a question of time, and a question of history.

So five years down the road, another five years . . .

Oh, by then we'll have our fourteen million (laughs).

No, I don't know what I'm going to be doing in five years. I do feel very strongly that I want to be doing a job that helps to change society. I don't know if it's going to be within 9to5 or not, but I expect to be intimately involved in changing people's lives for the rest of my life.

I've always felt that I was in this for the long haul, and that I have to pace myself. I pay attention to relaxing after work. I don't take a huge amount of work home, and I don't work like crazy every single minute; I work a reasonable amount that I can tolerate over a long period of time.

And I'm not going to change the world this week, or even eliminate the wage gap. I'm going to start a campaign, or hold a press conference. So the goals are attainable.

I think for a lot of people the hard step is not necessarily confronting the boss. That's one hard thing; but it's also hard to go to your coworkers and start a new kind of conversation: "Okay, we've griped about our problems long enough, now let's see what we can do about them." I think that step is scary for a lot of people. It was scary for me.

So one of the things that we try to do is to show people that it's not so difficult. It's not as if you have to change your whole personality, to become the office organizer. It's often a question of giving people the tools to express what they already feel. There's plenty of pent-up energy out there. And often it's just a little nudge in the right direction that will get people started and accomplishing great things.

Right after the *Nine to Five* movie came out, I was on a bus, and I heard one woman saying to another woman, "So I said to him, 'I will not make your coffee! I just saw *Nine to Five* and I'm never going to make another cup of coffee again!'" It was great. And I think there are a lot of things like that. . . .

You find yourself talking to your children about what you could have done. That in itself should be enough to kick you into action.

Mimi Fariña

BREAD & ROSES

Y OU can script your calls to movie theaters, as Ellen Cassedy did, yet later on bring corporations to their knees. You can sit all day with your dolls upstairs, yet carry the fight at Love Canal. These aren't contradictions, we ought now to realize, but aspects of the same personality. They seem incongruous, but incongruity spurs change. If there are parts of your self you don't care for, you can compensate for them, and maybe change them, by taking action in the world.

Mimi Fariña brings this point home again. She started Bread & Roses, which brings free professional entertainment to institutions—hospitals, prisons, convalescent homes, and others—mostly in Marin County, north of San Francisco. She's candid about what were her own insecurities; the direct connection between them and her community work is clearly stated. Once more, inner conflict brings out best performance.

There's more, of course. Mimi Fariña is a folksinger, and folksingers are supposed to have a social conscience. She grew up in a politically aware family; that's also a factor. Yet it's one thing to put some energy into a cause, and quite another to create an organization that delivers dozens of free institutional shows each month, to stay on top of it for more than ten years, and to subordinate your own singing career in the process. So we keep looking for underlying sources of action.

Mimi Fariña has quick humor and a big laugh, and you sense that the structure of the Bread & Roses office holds her antic self in check. (She's been an actress in an improvisational comedy troupe.) And she's into the structure right now, in earnest: she talks at length about boards of directors, leadership styles, and job descriptions—this even though Bread & Roses had hung on for many years, if somewhat shakily, with not much structure (or planning) to speak of. There are questions, which surface in the interview, about whether the tighter structure is a sign of organizational maturity, as Ray Shonholtz suggests, and whether there's a spiritual price to pay. Mimi has ambivalence.

The office itself seems pretty serious. Fund-raising is still a dominating issue. The tenth anniversary banquet is coming up, and invitations are being mailed out—the kind with envelopes within envelopes, as in weddings. It's one hundred dollars a plate, which is serious money, and they're running behind schedule. Lunch is friendly and short.

Mimi doesn't go home at 5:00 (though sometimes she's away on tour.) She's single, perhaps with fewer outside agendas, to use her phrase. She has a stiff neck from pushing herself, and she's going to a masseur. She returns phone calls herself, and handwrites her own thank-you notes.

*

When Bread & Roses started, it was a great place for me to have a scheduled time off the road. When you travel, and when the plane arrives in San Francisco, and I go home—then there's empty space, and how to deal with that for me was always very threatening. And I think it is generally, for people; it's a time when I suspect people do the most drugs.

So how to organize those weeks and those days always kind of threw me. I mean, I would fall into one kind of emotional depression or another, and be confused as to how to deal with the time. So inventing Bread & Roses gave me a place to be, and gave me a structure when I got home. And it has always remained that.

I have remained involved for so long because it serves that purpose for me. I don't lose interest in what we do. And the performers in the institutions are a constant reminder to me—to come back and hear music and watch jugglers and see people relate in a way that I wish would happen on stage in the commercial field, it's always kind of a relief, and it reenergizes me.

[In the early 1970s, Mimi had a dispute with her record company, eventually leaving it.] I had run into antagonistic feelings with the industry and could not for the life of me understand how art and business were supposed to be connected. It just never made sense.

People would interview me and talk about, "How's your recording career?", and "Are you going to have a hit single?", and "Gee, we love to hear you sing, but we don't hear enough of you on the radio." I was supposed to be veering into a commercial career, but I wasn't as successful as I wanted to be, didn't know how to be, didn't want to what we then called sell out, and be as commercial as the record companies wanted. It was always irritating me.

So this opportunity came up, through a cousin of mine who was at the time running a halfway house. He said, "You're in such a state of confusion over your singing, and what you seem to be complaining about most of all is the commercialism. Why don't you try singing somewhere where that doesn't exist and see if you enjoy it?"

So I said, "Yeah, not a bad idea," and did that at his halfway house. It was a . . . kind of uncomfortable evening, you know, with agitated uncomfortable people, mental patients, for lack of a better term. And they kind of half-listened, and they were not very responsive. It wasn't a great sense of joy in the performance. But on leaving I began to think what it might have meant to be able to perform without the pressure of being in a club and having to impress someone in the audience—just the pressures I wasn't ready for, and was putting myself under.

So this became an idea, and I would talk about it at interviews, and answer questions, and the more I talked about it, the more I convinced myself.

I came home from a tour, must have been I think about a year after I had the idea, the seed had been planted. And I was sitting and staring out the window feeling lost, you know, knowing that I had several weeks of nothingness in front of me, and being very aware that it made me feel kind of sick and lost and directionless and meaningless, and I don't have terrific self-esteem to begin with.

So I was in that slump of just arriving home, and I went for the phone, picked it up, and started calling local convalescent homes and said, "I'm a performer, and I'm interested to know if you'd like to have some music brought for no cost. . . ."

And it was . . . it was a wonderful sensation; the difference between being passive about being depressed and being active about it is a major jump. I knew when I was picking up the phone that that's what I was doing. I'd been in therapy long enough to know that it was "probably the right thing to do at the time (laughs)." And the fact that I was utterly alone and that it simply came to me and I wanted to do it at that moment, all made it feel very much my own. . . . That would have been early '74—must have been summer, yeah.

Well, the institutions said, "Oh! Sure!" Some of them knew my name and others didn't, but it sounded good, and they would turn me on to what they called the "activities coordinator." I had no idea how these places were run. Then my cousin said, "Why don't you go to the volunteer bureau and

Marion Kelley knows everything about the county; she'll tell you which places to go visit." In Marin [County]. So I did that, and they were very excited about the idea, and gave me a list, and some hints, you know. So I was mildly prepared.

That week I must have seen ten or so institutions. Those were just visits. Just to see what they were like, if institutions had stages or platforms or pianos, or equipment, or who was in them and what could I expect to take to those people to be entertaining. I became more and more knowledgeable with each institution. I just kept going, to one after another, and being moved.

And those are still some of the most significant moments for me, when I think about why Bread & Roses got underway. I really was not with any education, any background, anyone guiding me in terms of what's supposed to get done. It was really my own. My premise didn't have to be messed with anyone else's idea of what ought to be happening. I didn't have to compare myself to anyone or anything, which is always a problem. So I felt inspired.

My main premise was that people who are isolated and lonely probably would like some music, and joy in their life. Everything I saw verified that. I wasn't discussing it with anyone yet, so everything I saw from a very pure solo point of view. I'd see a blind kid sitting in a room with a red sock and a white sock on, listening to the radio, and I'd go home with that image, and it would feed on me. And each institution seemed to leave its own impression, and kept feeding on—the more I do this, the more I feel involved, and I can't stop. It became a snowball; I couldn't slow down.

So I got my fill of seeing underdogs and little vegetable kids who probably wouldn't live long, and leukemia, and old folks slumping in their wheelchairs. And I started calling friends, three or four friends I thought of, who seemed organizing types, or who had been involved with sixties political events. And one said, "Oh, you won't believe this, I was just thinking yesterday I've got to find something to do and I'm really up in the air." And she became the cofounder, and a better girlfriend than she had been before.

I found a place, through my cousin again, a room in Larkspur, and the day we were having the phone put in [my friend] brought her typewriter over. I'd been scribbling ideas down, but Lucie was much more eloquent, had gone to college for one, which I hadn't, and she was interpreting my thoughts in a very appropriate manner. So we were developing a brochure. And that was exciting.

There was no furniture; we were on the floor, sitting here and writing stuff and typing things.* Then after we got phones, we decided to go to the local radio station and ask for volunteer help. I had help from the beginning. We had meetings with a local group called Public Media Center, went over to their place and sat around and brainstormed a lot of ideas about how this place might be run, essentials like where do we start getting our nonprofit status, what do I need a lawyer for—all the things that wouldn't have occurred to me, 'cause I was not a planner, hadn't grown up in a business world at all.

I really was never a goal-oriented person, and the lack of education, of college education, made me feel pretty inferior and insecure. So I did need those phone calls to people to say, "Hi, I have this idea, and I don't know what to do with it. And where do I take it next?" I did need to rely on friends.

So the name went from Reach Out to Interchange to lots of things that sounded like highway signs, and then Joanie calls, my sister called, and said she had heard the phrase Bread & Roses on the East Coast, and wasn't it pretty.† And I said, "That's real nice." So it was actually her phone call. And I had a dream of some roses and some wheat, and we eventually put that into the logo (laughs).

Then we have to fund-raise. Our first proposal was written by a friend who had just come out of prison for protesting the war, and we started shopping it around. The San Franscisco Foundation, and smaller foundations—I can't remember if they were in the foundation book or if it was advice through friends, probably both—and approaching them with this proposal that we had. And after a while, people started answering.

And we started off in bars. I said, why don't we as a group learn how to produce concerts by doing local, really small stuff to get the experience of production? So local people would [perform] in bars and restaurants, who would lend us their place; and the bar would take, you know, the liquor money, and we would take the rest, the door. Then local clubs started letting us come in, very small, maybe three or four of them. We kept doing one after another just to bring in more cash; we had no concept of a budget yet.

It wasn't till '77 that we did benefit concerts. I think our first major event was at the Berkeley Community Theater with Bonnie Raitt and Maria Muldaur and the Grisman Quintet. And that went smoothly. We learned

---

*Mimi is describing their present Mill Valley office. She and Lucie moved from Larkspur shortly after they began.

†Joan Baez, her sister. "I would say that due to my sister I have met many people in the social change world, and therefore have places to turn, should I want to."

how to take out ads—we did that with [the rock concert promoter] Bill
Graham. His advice was forget the cause; put the name on the ad, and
that's what people are going to come and see. It sounded very crass at first,
but I'm convinced, however, that he's right.

These [shows] are the fund-raisers for the visits. The visits are going on
the whole time. I did the fewest, I must admit. But auditioning performers,
and then taking them to different institutions, I guess in the beginning I did
a lot. I would sing myself or else I would take somebody, try out different
experiments, you know. I'd know an actor who could read poetry, and I'd
say, "Let's go try that."

So I was finding a place for myself, and all of that was very satisfying
and exciting. It wasn't hard, because I was so caught up in the energy of it.
And it really was the first sensation of success that I was feeling. I wasn't
somebody's wife or somebody's sister. I had direction in my life, and this was
for me.

And people were always asking me along the way, "What are the main
problems?", da da da da. And I was either blind to them or they didn't exist.
I never saw any. I was in such heaven, just moving so fast, and getting so
much support, and doing this work that was turning out to be fun and
great. There just weren't any roadblocks; everyone thought it was a great
idea.

But that energy has to dissipate, at some point. The struggles came
later, with funding. To sustain what we had created.

Another person might have taken the tack of expressing anger
about the institutions themselves, and saying, "These people just can't
sit here all day," or stuff like that.

I started out doing that. I remember watching a TV show that I had
been interviewed in, saying something about how these poor people sit
there all day long, and the nurses don't seem to care. Well, it was a very
naive statement, because many of the nurses, and even more so the
volunteers, are very caring, and have a horrible job. And you get used to it;
you get used to dying bodies and fecal material on the floor, and you get
hardened. You're not as social-worky and lovey-dovey as you may have once
intended to be.

I think the institutions need to exist. I think they need to exist. Not
forever, perhaps, but the way things are now, if they were suddenly, radically
taken away, number one, all the people would simply drop dead. Where
would they go?

The prison institutions—the prisons are such a part of some people's
youth—kids from the ghetto are familiar with prison as part of their lives,

from birth. So it's not such a big deal for some people to go to prisons. They're set up for it from an early age.

My original feeling was, "Locking someone behind bars? (shocked tone) How could you?"; then beginning to get acquainted with inmates, how they respond to life, what they expected out of life in the first place, where they see themselves, how they could possibly integrate back into society, and how terrifying that is. Getting out may be more horrifying than going in for [some] people.

So those things I've learned to consider, where I didn't know them before. I had my charitable missionary point of view, which had very little to do with being there and understanding the situation.

You're less of a missionary now?

No. It's just I know more.

I'm sure you've heard this before—the Band-Aid criticism, that you're just going in, doing something, going out in two hours, and people go back to their TV sets or whatever they were doing before.

Oddly enough, I don't take that as a criticism. . . . I'm usually very ready to be criticized, and feel belittled. But I have such a firm belief that this is an appropriate thing to do, that there's nothing wrong with it. In the scheme of things, it's a plus all the way around. There aren't any negatives. If I could do more, I would be doing more. I don't know how right now.

I would like to see us not be just a social service agency, I would love to see us be a social change agency; I don't know how to do that right now. One day I will. And there have been ideas, like a conference on life in institutions, for families of people who are institutionalized. There are things we can do when we have the money.

And there's nothing the matter with taking entertainment in and leaving. It's better than what they've got. So it's one step in the right direction. And I have always seen this as a stepping stone for something that's going to happen in the future. I don't know what it is, and I don't have grandiose ideas or visions either.

But would you rather be a social change organization, rather than a social service organization?

No. Not one or another. Both. And who knows what that means, anyway? You know, it's a matter of degree. I think they're both pretty much the same. Social change, from the sixties anyway, implies radical change, rewriting a script somehow and changing the blueprint; but I think change is gradual, and takes a lot of forethought and time, and I think we're doing that.

And if it takes ten years to get wealthy rock-and-rollers to think they should come here, because we're a place that can maybe do things having to do with social change and music, then that was ten years well spent, not trying to be too aggressive about changing, but establishing ourselves as credible.

The staff has been like a family—and I've used them for that too much so in the past. I have been aware that this has been my social life, and my family life, and we have changed all that very consciously.

When we started out and were a small collective, we behaved like a family. We would get together over meals and think up ideas and come to decisions and go out and do a benefit. And our dreaming and our scheming and our inventing of Bread & Roses was created through the process of very family-like get-togethers—meetings at people's houses, meetings over meals, staying late at night, the way everyone did in the sixties. So in time, that has had to change.

Why?

I think when we created enough structure—in other words, forty-five shows a month; a three-day weekend benefit, a humongous show once a year; and the newsletter—there were things that began to be expected of us. You know, the public was waiting for the festival next year, and forty-five institutional shows were waiting for us.

And so when that became so organized, we then had to become more organized. So how are we going to fund that, to keep that going, in an organized way, and not just, "Oh, let's throw another benefit."

Yet when you talk about people having meals together and sitting around with each other, that sounds nice.

Yeah. I miss it. I was interrelating like family, for sure. And it was imbalanced. I was a family member coming and going, going off on tour, coming back; they were here doing a job, coming in the morning and leaving at night. And they had other things in their lives, generally speaking, and I didn't.

So that dependency, I think, was not healthy. And if I were to do it all again, I loved that initial stage, and I'd probably seek that in some way again—cause that's a real high. And I do miss it. But in order for us to survive now, we are an organization that hires and fires and acts like grown-ups, that awful state of being (laughs).

When our festival lost money [beginning around 1981], the energy in the office went way down. It was, "Ohhh, noo"; it's not us, the famous Bread & Roses kids anymore, it's a big situation where all of us may not get our paychecks. And it got to be serious, and this is a job, and we're out there doing that benefit in order to keep our paychecks coming in. It all became much more realistic. Much more tangible. It wasn't such a party.

When we were in such trouble, I called in a consultant. Here I am empty, you know. What's happened? How did Mimi mess up? What went wrong? I was really spinning. I felt pretty out of control. I didn't know how to be a director. I had this weird title (lowers voice) "executive director," I didn't know what that means, and either I had better discover how to handle all that, or change the organization, or quit.

And it looked as though we could close; financially, it certainly looked as though it could close. But I decided to be tenacious, and I liked the idea of change, because of what I've learned in therapy. I think that it takes a long time, and it's a serious business, and I think it's what we do all of our lives. To me it means progress. I began to sense that it might have to be a different organization in order to survive.

And maybe I should hear what others have to say, and stop being such a kid and such a Committee actress and merry prankster.* I've gotten away with that for a long time; let's see what happens otherwise.

So the consultant came in and interviewed everybody and read through all the files and came up with the conclusion that indeed it was time to mature. She really felt that the place wouldn't be the same without me, that I had certain qualities that would maintain the organization better:

"Mimi, you're the leader. You're the"—oh, there's another one— "spearhead." I always thought that was fun. "Spearhead," I walk around . . . (laughs). Spearhead, a leader—oh, the creative guidance, the creative force, all kinds of stuff that has no tangible meaning for me. I can be sitting at my house and totally depressed and it doesn't help me to hear that I'm a creative force (laughs). I need a job, you know. Outside of the fund-raising events, I'm pretty lost. And I need some direction.

Anyway, what that meant for Mimi was that she needed an associate. In fact, I didn't do things that an executive director does. I don't read a budget. I don't know from a time chart, et cetera. I learned how to write a job description, and I wrote one for an associate director; things like plan, you know, oversee the staff, create budgets, write proposals, everything that I didn't think I could do that ought to get done.

---

*She was a member of The Committee, a local improvisational and satirical theater group.

So I spent a year and a half hiring an associate director, and ended up hiring someone who is very organized, who has all the Robert's rules in her head, that's where she comes from. She also has experience living in Berkeley through the sixties and isn't a total Junior Leaguer, by any means. And so I'm experimenting with that. Luckily, she and I get along very well.

I've always resisted school. . . . The idea of timelines and flow charts, those very words were to me things to be ridiculed. And that suited me just fine. I now find, this year, finally, ten years later, that I'm creating timelines and flow charts, and beginning to be able to read a budget, 'cause I realize it makes sense to be able to do that now. I don't like it, but it's part of growing up is how I'm looking at it.

It's better that way?

I think—it may or may not be, I don't know yet.

Like we have a personnel committee meeting, we have now developed committees for the board. We're developing policies. So I take a deep breath and, okay, it's probably going to resolve problems more quickly in the future, so let's get these policies, let's see what they look like, let's not make fun of this anymore.

So the question the other night was, "Well, Mimi, now do you want your policies to read that people take vacations one week at a time or two weeks at a time? Everyone gets four weeks a year, but how would you prefer it to be?"

(Sighs) I don't know, I don't care, so I'm sitting there straining and struggling and remembering something that the associate has said, which is it's easier on the flow of work when people take one week off. So I say, "Well, it's really easier on the flow of work if people take one week off."

It's not me talking; I don't give a damn, and my true answer is "whatever is going to make people happy," which is a lousy answer for a director. I know that it has to be more organized than that.

I'll try it, it's a new suit of clothes. I'll try it on. And when it gets to where I know it doesn't fit, I put my foot down.

I am aware of what I get out of Bread & Roses. It's given me a level of confidence, that I certainly didn't have. Purpose, that I didn't have. . . . Self-esteem. It gives me a lot of structure, it gives me an identity, it makes me look good, that's for sure; no one would have a clue as to my cynicism and my depressions and my other self that comes through sometimes in my music or in other situations. But this—I mean, look, peachy keen, [I'm] the director of this marvelous organization. It's a great image I built for myself; I was real sneaky about that.

I've found so much contentment here. People always want us to be out there, changing the world, but I think, well, there's so much going on here. It's not as if . . . it needs to be that much bigger. It's still in its youth, it's still learning to be what it is. So to have monster dreams of consuming the world seems silly to me.

I know I'm a perfectionist, so I'm pretty concerned about getting this down, getting this right. I don't think I can handle anything bigger than my own back yard. My sister takes on the world. I love to travel and do international things, but in terms of what I think I can handle with a job, I'd like to learn how to do this well, then I'll be happy (laughs).

There's plenty of work cut out. Conference, banquets, more festivals. And so far, there are enough back burner ideas here that I don't see this coming to a halt and me having to move on to a whole other area.

My hope this year has been that we would be organized enough that the staff could go on a number of prison tours, which means we go on the road. I would very much like to see a book on how to produce benefit concerts come out of Bread & Roses; it's been started and stopped, and started and stopped.

I would like to involve more wealthy entertainers, to do our small shows—those people who care and who hopefully are guilty enough that they're wealthy and not doing much with their lives, seeing us as a place to come with ideas.

And promoting other organizations like this, that makes sense to me—to keep them small, to keep them localized, so they have their own personalities, so that they work with their own communities. And I would love to network, and maybe have a convention once a year in Kansas, or some part of the country where we come together and discuss what we learned that year and how to improve, 'cause it is still new, it's still a new project.

Another secret ambition—this is more where we're talking legacy, which is more where my mind goes—I've had this dream of creating a situation comedy for television, out of a nonprofit office. This has so many elements—it has performers who come and go, famous and not famous. I mean, I'll be in here trying to read something, and there'll be a belly dancer with baby boa constrictors down the hall doing an audition—it has the most hilarious aspect, that could be very television oriented. There are chase scenes, I mean, "Late to the gig, will we get there on time?"

This is daily. I mean, I sit in here in hysterics sometimes hearing what's going on, thinking this is too good, it's being wasted; God, this is the part that I want to remember, that I want to go down in history—the nonsense of having a nonprofit and the agony of the funding, (mock dramatic tone) and then how we finally pull the banquet together, and all the arguments that go down before you get there. The real human element—what gets glossed over when you become a grown-up. When your organization has matured, you don't talk about these things. But it is so funny, and for me it's so much what is the reality of the situation, is the humor.

But in the meanwhile, the next two years, and I would suspect a couple more, will go into perfecting how to run what we've got, and do it well, and get some stability before we can have the money and the time to leap into other ideas, which I think is necessary in order to keep everyone stimulated. But all of that takes money, which we don't have either, at Bread & Roses or in my life.

So I need to make dough before I dream. And I got a call yesterday that there's some interest at Rounder Records to do an album (softly). They had rejected a demo about four years ago. The same producer calls, and they may be interested in listening to the demo again. I said, "Do it."* I got a CBS contract in '77, made an entire album, it wasn't released. They released me, instead of the album. . . .

Coming back to the community service issue, and going beyond Bread & Roses, there's a lot of room for people to get involved in their own communities. So are there ways to—

Inspire? . . . Well, it always is going to depend on getting someone motivated. Whether it's out of frustration or anger—one would hope it wouldn't have to be, but probably it will be. I think it was easily defined as anger, that I was experiencing from the music industry. But I would like to think that I made a very Gandhian choice, to transfer that energy into something positive, and I really think that can be done.

I don't know; I think in the past few years I've seen less and less of a desire to make [community] improvement. I'm judging that on the interviews I've done for hiring here. Before, it was the hippie era where people would come in and say, "I just think you people are beautiful, and I just want to do anything for you." And that faded with the Me Generation, these pompous kids would come in and say, "Well, what does the job have to offer me?" And I'd think, "Get out of here. What are you talking about? This is social service; what do you have to give?"

So if that's real—

I think it is.

---

*It was done. Mimi's first album in fifteen years, *Solo*, was released by Rounder about a year later.

What is to be done about it?

Flog them; I don't know (laughs). Put them in jail (laughs). I get really annoyed with it, I really do. I think if they can't come here and see the fun that exists, and they're going to come in full of credentials and full of themselves, and wanting a big paycheck, then I'll do it myself.

I do think that it's a matter of media and popularizing. I think it is dependent on what's popular, and Lord knows the work ethic went out the window a long time ago. God, there are very few people who get a thrill out of working. I think my associate does, and she and I can stay here late hours and feel it's what we want to be doing. Everyone else drifts off at five, and I used to resent that years ago. But I don't now.

I just don't know what I would do if I left every night at five; I don't know quite what I would do. I don't have another agenda waiting for me somewhere; no, I do sometimes, but it's off and on. I just feel happy, and it's appropriate, and I like to be needed here; so I like to stay late. But I don't think many people do. . . . And you're called a workaholic if you do. And usually—I don't know, "burnout"—it's made such a big thing of. And yes, it happens . . . but I think it happens to people who are expecting a lot in return.

I'm sick of hearing about burnout, I really am. Either people pace themselves or they don't. I'm learning much better how to (arches voice) "timeline my schedule" (laughs), how to find out when I get too tired. I'm doing a bad job this month, 'cause we took on not only the banquet, but then at the last minute decided to do a video at it, and I'm involved in something I probably shouldn't. I've got a stiff neck and I'm overworking right now, but I love that. I don't think about myself so much.

You love the overwork?

Yeah. I mean, I love to have a purpose. I love to feel that I'm needed to get something done, and I know that it'll be crisis time right before, and then we'll pull it off, and we'll all be able to feel some sense of success. It's like putting on a play, or performing, and in that chaotic world of performing, which I'm used to, I can handle all that. Even though it is tension-making.

(Laughs) It's all in here, in my neck (laughs). No, last week it was plenty crazy. Addressing envelopes, and volunteers in and out, and the newsletter is late, and so hollering through the hall, "Did you want that to get in the newsletter?" It was chaos last time. It's pretty horrible (laughs).

I'm sure that there will be community leaders in any community. How to make them surface or give them a boost or tell them, "Yeah, right on, listen to your heart"—I think that's probably what you're looking to do, and I don't know what to say.

Is it worthwhile to try and inspire people? . . . I would want to answer that of course it is. If you don't try out ideas, they rest with you for the rest of your life. They rest in the back burner area, and you find yourself talking to your children about what you could have done. And that in itself should be enough to kick you into action.

Only I think I would say that at nearly age forty, I wouldn't mind being manipulative in doing that. I think that most of the society is very manipulative; we're manipulated by the media, by Reagan, by—everywhere we look we're being manipulated. And because that has become so natural and acceptable, I would join that, rather than trying to do it grass-roots and through the more honest down-to-earth, one-to-one methods. I would at this point in my life not be afraid of what we used to call selling out. And I would use the media, and I would use stars, and I would use market techniques, sell techniques, any gimmick I could get my hands on before I vomit and it goes too far.

It wouldn't be my choice originally to have to market what you are talking about, but I would say it would be a useful technique. 'Cause I do think it needs . . . sex appeal. Pizzazz. It needs to look pleasurable and look like fun. And it is. People just don't know that. . . .

Here are people starving, and there's food going to waste. See if we can't put it together.

Homer Fahrner

THE SENIOR GLEANERS

H OMER FAHRNER is sweeping the sidewalk by his apartment building when I arrive at 7:30 A.M. Early morning, seven, eight o'clock is the best time to reach him on the phone. The previous day, he'd gone to bed by five. Some mornings, he's up by two.

You want to get up early to be a Senior Gleaner. Midday temperatures in California's Central Valley can easily top one hundred degrees. If you're picking produce in the broiling sun, it is work. Or if you're working in a warehouse at any time of day, that's not what most folks call retirement living.

But that's what Gleaners do. The premise of the Senior Gleaners is that there's an abundance of food that farmers can't sell—the size is off, or the color or shape, or there's a surplus plain and simple. At the same time, some people barely have enough to eat, especially seniors on fixed incomes. Bread first, then roses.

Homer Fahrner, then twice retired, put these facts together. The Senior Gleaners he recruited would pick the surplus, haul it away, and distribute it free to their members. In 1982, for example, six years after they began, the Gleaners distributed five million pounds of food products* to more than sixteen hundred members, and helped feed more than five thousand others in the Sacramento area alone. They now glean food from supermarkets and canneries as well, redistributing it also to food banks and local charities. They own an 8000-square-foot warehouse, plus various forklifts, trucks, and freezer vans. They claim to be the largest gleaning organization in the United States. Though

---

*According to a Sacramento newspaper article on the Gleaners, this is less than the amount of food that goes to waste in California every day.

they receive pledges from members and outsiders, no one has been salaried.

For founding the Gleaners, Fahrner won the Jefferson Award from the American Institute of Public Service in 1981, and the President's Volunteer Action Award in 1982. Some of these medals, and some others Homer can't identify, rest now in coffee cans. "I've been back to Washington two years in a row; enough's enough after a while." He was born in 1902.

He lives in a modest apartment near downtown Sacramento. His directions on how to find it are marching-order clear. Sitting at his desk, in a windbreaker and cap, one sees few clues to his previous life. What catches the eye instead is a nearby copy of *Personal Computing*.

He was a ministerial school reject: "Fahrner, you're more interested in feeding their bellies than in saving their souls." He went through Washington University in St. Louis studying electrical engineering, though on a woodworking scholarship. In 1926, he entered the securities business, later heading the research department of Dean Witter; the company put him through law school (he was valedictorian) during the Depression years. He was president of the Securities Analysts Society of San Francisco; he published, ran, and later sold *The Coast Investor*. He's still active in the market.

In the 1970s, having retired as a stockbroker in Sacramento, he became a stage dancer. In the evening, he and his partner would dance at the state fairgrounds and around town. During the day, he was a volunteer waiter at an elderly nutrition center.

✳

I worked at two different places where they served, and I noticed the meals were skimpy, maybe a thousand calories. They were balanced, but they were skimpy, there wasn't much of it. As a waiter, I got a free meal too, and if there was one left over I got a second meal, and if I was still hungry I could eat three of them. Well, two of them satisfied me, but I could have eaten a third without too much difficulty, put it that way. I'm a big eater (laughs).

And I noticed that a lot of the people, particularly the women, were bringing doggie bags along, and they were putting part of this food in the doggie bag. It was against the rules, but I didn't stop them, and I asked, "Why aren't you eating this?" "Oh, I don't feel hungry." "Well, you didn't feel hungry yesterday." And this fellow nudges me and says, "Don't embarrass these people—don't you know that's all they're going to have? They've got to spread this thing over twenty-four hours." I asked, "Is this so?" "Yes, this is so." And I saw all this food going to waste out on the farms. I thought, my God, if that's the case, maybe we can work something out.

Well, it's just humanity. Here are people starving, actually emaciated and there's food going to waste. See if we can't put it together.

I tried to get several other people to do it—oh, no, they won't do it. I was associating with the people who had it, that had made it, eh. I lived low on the hog, not high on the hog. That's the way I was brought up. I'm embarrassed when somebody tells me I'll take you someplace and I get into a Cadillac. I live low on the hog.

I couldn't get anybody else. Actually, I tried at least a dozen different friends of mine to do it. They never were interested. "I'm too busy with something else." "I want to be with my grandchildren." "I want to take a trip to Europe." They weren't interested. People that I considered my bosom friends—not interested. And I said, well if there's nobody else that will do it, I'll have to do it myself.

So I wrote to the paper, the senior citizens' weekly here, a letter to the editor. This was in December of '75. And I said in effect that the seniors were having difficulty in making ends meet on their income, that there was a lot of food going to waste, and I said if twenty people would phone me, I'd call a meeting and see if I could do something about it. Oh, I forgot to say, the editor of the paper, I had never met him before then, he did more than just print the letter. He says, "This sounds like a darn good idea—I hope it works."

Over two hundred called. There were thirty-eight attended the first meeting, and out of that thirty-eight, thirty were sightseers, nothing better to do. I think they were curious—they were expecting free food. Now the food is free, but the going and getting it is not free—it requires work. But as I say, there were eight of us who carried on, and we got started.

Well, we're working, and gradually getting more and more. Because the paper had encouraged us, I felt free to ask them to give us a write-up every week, what we were doing. And the members started coming in. We'd all meet here [Homer's apartment]. Then it started getting bigger than those eight, so the senior citizen center was a block away, and they invited us to go over there. The first thing you know, we have 150 members, two hundred members and so on.

You'd be surprised—when three people get together, they say you've got to elect a president. It was mostly who's going to be on this committee, who's going to do this? Nobody wanted to work, but they were all willing to meet. We spent most of our time haggling over the name of the organization. And finally, I don't know whether you recognize that picture up there in the corner [Millet's *The Gleaners*]—well, I suggested Senior

Gleaners, Gleaners from that, and Seniors because we were seniors. That's where the name came from.

Oh, I'm telling you, we incorporated in June of '76, but we were well under way long before that. Even then I didn't drive a car anymore—I was in a couple of accidents, by the grace of God I didn't kill somebody. But they would take me around, and we would start out, depending on how far we had to go, just before five, six, seven, eight o'clock in the morning, if it was right around here.

What I did, I had a prospective gleaner take me into a territory, cherries for instance, and we stopped at every ranch where there were cherries grown, and especially if they were picking the cherries. Then you've got to find the owner, the fellow who can say yes, otherwise they'll say no, just to show their authority or whatever it is.

You have to find the fellow who can say yes. And you tell him, in a polite way, that you're representing the seniors, more particularly the seniors who haven't quite made it, on welfare or trying to keep off of welfare. Will there be any cherries left over?

At first we were turned down right and left. They didn't know who we were. They said, "Well, we let other people in the orchard, and they broke the trees. They let the dogs in, or they dropped their beer cans, they did this, they did that, and get out." Or "You could find a job if you really wanted to work, and I pay taxes and to hell with you. . . ." It was really something the first few years. I forgot to tell you, I used to go out after I was turned down, and if I was turned down fifteen times without even a yes, I'd say, "Well I've had it, let's go home."

*

After many rebuffs, Fahrner wangled permission from a big tomato farmer to pick on his land, "so big, you couldn't see across the field." The Gleaners followed the farmer's instructions to the letter. A different group, picking at the same time, did not. The farmer called and said, "Well, we gave the Gleaners a chance, and you blew it." Homer convinced him it was a case of mistaken identity; that mistake was turned to advantage.

*

Two weeks later I got a bulletin from the Farm Bureau—and in it it said that any farmer with surplus they don't have a home for, we recommend you give it to the Gleaners, because we've investigated them and found them on the up-and-up. Anyway, they approved the Gleaners. That fellow turned out to be the president of the Farm Bureau. Well, we were in, because that bulletin goes up and down the state.

From then on, life was much easier. Now, it's very, very seldom I get a cross word. The farmer may say, "No, I don't have anything," but he doesn't say, "Get the hell off or I'll sic the dogs on you."

In one year—one year—a farmer gave us a thousand acres of cherries to pick. This is what happened: the cherries were so thick on the trees that they were breaking the limbs. The farmer said you can have them 'cause there are not enough number 12s [large-sized cherries]. There has to be enough of those number 12s [in a box] so they look big; what's underneath can be anything. But there weren't enough, so the farmer says you can have the whole works. We didn't need to go anyplace else.

This is the important thing—to *go after,* then *ask.* It's a legitimate calling. Now this farmer, I didn't notice then, he wrote us up in the *California Farmer,* which is a big farm magazine here. He told a reporter that we saved his trees, because the cherries were breaking the limbs. And of course a broken limb is not going to bear any cherries next year.

I remember, we had five thousand pounds of sack potatoes, and we didn't have any place to put them. Now the reason the potatoes were given to us—there were a few rotten ones. We stacked them all along this building [Homer's apartment building]; in no time at all, flies (laughs). The whole place was swarming with flies. My landlord [says], "This isn't going to work," but I got him in, he's still with me as a gleaner.

We gotta do something. It attracted the attention of one of the elders of the church, and he said to me, "We've got an empty building over here. You can have that." We found our first home—no rent. And that building had a basement that was dug out of the ground, and it was cool, it was ideal. I mean you didn't have to have refrigeration or anything.

So we're in the building. And then I got to thinking: here I am running this thing, somebody gets hurt—personal liability. Apparently, I was the only one in the whole outfit that had an extra dollar, and so we incorporated. That brought in another organization. I found free legal service, which is again something that the others will not do. They're afraid somebody is going to say no. And I said, "*Of course* they're going to say no, you've got to expect . . ." I went out there day after day. . . .

Always, I've got to have help. Plenty of people who will pick. Plenty of people who will distribute. But there are damn few who will ask.

Ask for anything. Ask for legal service, ask for rent, ask for food. Oh—I went to the school board, a lot of vacant schools around here, and they gave us the use of a school building. You have to ask. I went to the city dads, and they gave us a freezer. Well, a freezer has to be transported, and I mean it's a thing you don't put on your back, a huge outdoor freezer. I tell you, I got one of the outdoor trucking outfits to transport it and put it on the school lot. Outdoors. Then we had to have a fence around it to keep the kids from sticking their fingers in the flywheel. Well, I just got on the phone, and I got lumber, and I got wire netting, and I got the electrical work—one outfit put up $750 of electrical work to handle that damn freezer.

Oh, then I made it a point to talk to every Rotary Club, to every Kiwanis Club. I didn't realize how many service clubs there are; there must be thirty or forty of them. I got myself invited. I spoke to one Kiwanis Club, I said, "Can you give me a list of all the Kiwanis Clubs in this area?" "Yes." So I called every one, and I said, "Are you the fellow who arranges the program for the Kiwanis Club?" "Yes." I said, "I'm Fahrner, I run the Gleaners, I'd like to speak to your organization, let you know about it." "Never heard of you." "Well, then, you ought to hear of us, and so forth, what we're doing." And "Sure, no problem, we'll schedule you. . . ."

It takes somebody who's sales-minded. Other people would say, "Well, it's only going to cost a few hundred dollars to buy the lumber." I'd say, "Yes, but we don't have a few hundred dollars." All the time, I was scrounging for money. But to get that money, that was hard work. If I could get the hundred dollars worth of materials free, that's the equivalent maybe of talking to two or three service organizations.

Most of our members, it's easy come, easy go. "Well, go ahead, Fahrner, you go out and find the money." They are not willing to go; they're afraid of being turned down. Well, you're going to be turned down, and it takes somebody who is sufficiently sold on this thing to carry on *in spite* of being turned down, eh. Now practically every farmer, they all know us now, and if they've got any surplus, they'll call us. They even call me on the phone.

So you must be an especially persuasive person?

No. Nothing. I just asked. Did most of this on the phone.

"Hi, this is Homer Fahrner, I'd like you to . . ."?

No. "I'm with the Gleaners, and we have a problem. Thought maybe you could help us." You have to ask a *dozen,* but finally you find the fellow who says, "Sure."

Could somebody else set up something similar?

Sure. And they do.

That's an important point.

It's *the* important point. You've got to be willing to stay with it and ask, ask, ask all day long. Practically every organization is built that way. The difference between our organization and other organizations is that they won't do it unless they're paid.

*

Fahrner left the Senior Gleaners in 1979. There were differences of opinion regarding the Gleaners' bookkeeping. He went on to found another gleaning organization called Gleaners Statewide, designed to take in a larger territory, beyond Sacramento County. Gleaners Statewide covered a four-county area, working in parallel with Senior Gleaners and a variety of subsequent gleaning operations throughout California. An efficient gleaning operation, Fahrner believes, could feed every hungry person in California without cost.

At the beginning of 1984, Homer Fahrner retired as active president of Gleaners Statewide.

*

I'm President Emeritus—they call me up, I still answer the telephone for them. Surprised there haven't been any calls today—we get about fifty calls a day. Wonder if the damn thing's been unplugged (gets up to check). It's all right. They may be having a meeting. . . .

I thought that finding somebody to replace me would be, nothing to it. I thought there'd be a lot of people, but it's not true. There aren't a lot of people. Damned if I know why. I can't get anybody—my friends who have made it, they think I'm a damn fool, to spend all my time. "Aren't you drawing a big salary?" In fact, the Senior Gleaners thought that I was making twenty thousand dollars a year. I wasn't drawing a dime, but they thought I was, because people who haven't made it don't know how to read figures.

This is one of the weaknesses of the gleaning operation—we attract people who haven't quite made it. We don't attract any executives, lawyers, doctors, things of that kind. People who have made it, they avoid us. The people we do attract are people who have always followed orders. They've always been told what to do. And they're not salesmen, it takes people to be salesmen. We don't attract the right people. I've spoken before the service clubs, the Rotary Clubs, to try to pull those people in, even after they retired, and I've not been successful.

I feel that I have done my part towards helping others. What happened with the Gleaners—they wore me out. They wouldn't help do the work. I had to do everything: I had to find money, I had to find food, I had to run the organization, I had to find the location. I had—oh, that is the hardest work there is—to go out and ask for money, ask for food. To be rebuffed.

So it takes something out of you?

Oh, sure. Even though they say yes. Physically, you get up at four o'clock in the morning, ride that truck all day, and back—for an old man? I used to come home at night, and I'd get pains, knots, and everything else, with my feet. Sit up in hot and cold water. . . .

Sure. It took years off my life; well of course it did. The physical work, and the mental; the mental is just as debilitating as the physical. You've never tried it. You go out and get turned down fifteen times in a day and go back the next day for fifteen times till you finally hit upon the president of the Farm Bureau.

Now I can go to these places—"Oh, Homer, haven't seen you for a couple of years. How are you?" That's the pay dirt; that's all I get out of it. I don't get it from members; they don't say thank you. Never occurs to them. "I'm getting free food; I don't pay for it."

Oh, I have known for years never to expect thanks. I mean, if I were doing this for the thanks I wouldn't have started it. But most of the people who are members think they have it coming to them. They don't care whether it's paid by the county or whether it's given to them by Fahrner. They don't distinguish, they don't differentiate. No, they take it, same as going to the public library.

And that's why I quit, I guess. I figured there ought to be a little fun in it. It was never any fun. I've done business with people, with stockbrokers, they're my friends. I don't think I've got a single friend among the Gleaners. (Softly) It's painful to me.

My mother used to tell me, as far back as I can remember—she didn't have anything, but she used to say to me, "Never do business with people who have less than you have. They'll skin you to death." I didn't see how that fit, 'cause we lived on the wrong side of the tracks.

It's just what my mother told me, I should have known. . . . Her father in his day, he was a forty-niner, came out to California, and he took three thousand dollars back to Missouri and bought acreage. This was right after the Civil War. Anyway, people would come to him, and he would lend them money, and pretty soon he was the biggest farmer there in Warren County. He had no faith in banks, so he carried his gold in his saddlebags. One Christmas Eve, my Grandma wanted to make a mince pie or something, she needed some brandy, and it was quicker to go by horseback than to hitch up the carriage. So Uncle Joe, on his twenty-first birthday, saddled up Grandpa's horse—the saddlebags were on it—put on Grandpa's overcoat, went to town, never got there. He was shot in the back, the saddlebags robbed. 'Cause everybody knew Grandpa wouldn't put money in the banks.

It must have come from that. Now, Grandpa again, he built a church for them, he built a school for them, and yet he was hated. Hated by these people because they lost their farms. It wasn't his fault.

I wouldn't do it again. I think I would do what other charity leaders do, get a paid job first and then I'd say, well, to hell with them, I'm getting paid, forget it. I think that's probably the way it will come. I'm not for it, but I think that's the only way it'll survive.

Are you feeling that one person like yourself can still make a difference in our society?

It would take a million like me, I know. I don't think so. I don't think it makes a damn thing. I think probably five years from now people will say "Gleaners? What was that?"

No, I just think it's one of those things. The real bugaboo is that we're having too many kids. And we're spending more and more money to prop up those fellows like me. We're doing everything to help the weak; we're doing everything to thwart natural selection. We are crowding all the other animals off this earth. How the hell are we going to survive?

If you ask me what I think is going to happen, I wouldn't give you ten years before this damn thing's blown up.

I'm not physically able to carry on with gleaning. I've got to be close to that toilet. I'm pretty well housebound. I'm feeble. If I'm not careful, I'll fall over.

I'm interested in helping my fellow man to the extent of my ability. As I say, I've helped the poor for eight years, and now I'm going back and help the rich. I'm going to offer investment advice to the poor through the same [senior citizens'] paper, and I'm going to offer investment advice to the people who have made it. Don't see anything wrong with that either. This is what I'll do when I get my teeth fixed, my eyes fixed. I got a bunch of aches and pains. . . .

But is is more noble to serve the poor than to help the wealthier people?

Yes. But I'm not physically able to carry on. So what should I do? Sit in a rocking chair and go to waste, or should I . . . See, I have been doing this [investment] research for sixty years. I've developed something which I think few others have. What I would like to do is to find a successor to carry on my work. In the meantime, I'm going to help as many people as I can, and maybe they will collectively find some way of carrying it on. . . .

✴

Homer writes, March 1987: "Since talking to you last the Gleaners have been overly nice to us. . . . Lately whenever I appear the current managers always have something nice to say about me to the members. So maybe I could [tone] down my reference to friends among the Gleaners. . . ."

On his eighty-fifth birthday in May, Gleaners Statewide honored Homer Fahrner for founding the gleaning movement in California.

*I had a vacant lot right behind my house piled with trash
and litter, and I got* very annoyed.

Haroldline Trower

THE POINT BREEZE BEAUTIFICATION COMMITTEE

I MAGINE a neighborhood with more flowers per capita than perhaps any other neighborhood in the Northeast. A tight, clean, and relatively poor neighborhood of low-rise row houses straight out of an Edward Hopper painting. That neighborhood flourishes in South Philadelphia. It's called Point Breeze Greene Countrie Towne.

The flower planting comes from the Point Breeze Beautification Committee, chaired for the past several years by Haroldline Trower. Largely through her efforts, more than fifty vacant lots have been turned into gardens and sitting parks. Vegetable plots grow throughout the eighty-eight-square-block area. More than fifty of these blocks have conspicuous street horticulture—trees, planters, flower boxes. There's also a wedding garden, with a gazebo; a brochure notes, "The bride and groom walk down the slate path amidst climbing roses and Grecian urns filled with cascading petunias."

She didn't work alone. A lot of the impetus and most of the dollars came from a program called Philadelphia Green, a branch of the Pennsylvania Horticultural Society. The Society put up the front money and provided the materials and technical assistance, in a casebook example of community partnership. But the initial request, the starter fee, the actual planting, and the ongoing maintenance are up to the neighborhood residents, and Haroldline Trower pulled them together.

Haroldline Trower is a mild-mannered and self-effacing woman with grown children who's around the house for much of the day. Her home, darkened against the summer heat, is full of plants and plastic furniture covers. It's a setting where you're offered a cold glass of water. When I ring the bell, she says, "I thought that was you parking your car outside." In this neighborhood, you are watched, and if you lived there, you'd feel protected.

Point Breeze is said to have the largest urban planting program in the United States. But Point Breeze residents are probably not much different than most others. They're not chomping at the bit to do community work. They have their own lives to live, their own problems, and their own fatigue, just like everyone else.

Yet if someone gets out front and offers people something to do that has perceptible benefits and modest costs, that seems important and sounds like fun, people will do it. Ray Shonholtz proved this point with neighborhood mediation. Flower planting, beautification in general, is another good choice, because the results are immediate, pleasing to the eye, and, as this story indicates, include unexpected offshoots with lives of their own.

*

I always been interested in my community, but I didn't know how to get off the ground. You look around and you see so much things happening, you know it's not nice.

And I had a vacant lot right around behind my house here, just an old dirty house piled with trash and litter. Let me see, it was about ten years ago, I think. I got *very annoyed*. And I was so disgusted I took pictures of it in color, and carried it to City Hall and showed it to them, and I asked them, would they like to live around [here] and look at that? And (laughs) they told me no.

Well, I think the only thing dirt is good for is to plant flowers in. I just got mad, I called City Hall sometimes three times a week or more than that, and then neighbors would meet me in the street, and I would be telling them how they could do it. Until eventually they came and tore it down, cause it was really just an eyesore. You know, if you complain enough, you'll get some action.

So then after they tore it down, I was sittin' there and I thought, well, it would be nice if a garden was put there, where trash and dirt is. It was just sort of a dream I had in my mind.

Got over by the telephone with Mamie Nichols,* and she said, well, she knew this lady that was working with the Horticultural Society, and she asked her to come up. So after writing and calling and writing and calling she came out, she talked to us, and we began to work on this garden. It took about a year.

Then after we got the garden and other people seen it and liked it,

---

*Executive Director of the Point Breeze Federation, the parent neighborhood organization.

that's when Miss Nichols says, "Why don't we form a committee?" And I love flowers and I'm always messing with them, and that's why Mamie said, "Well, chair it." So after that we got other ladies with us, and we had a lot of people that were organized. It's really something.

We had about eleven other ladies or so, and a lot of them know about gardening, and they carried the information back to their blocks. I told them, "Go to your next block, around your corner, if you got a spot that's there, go to whoever lives there and tell them about what's happening."

You see, if the person cared enough to organize their block, they had to sign, like who was going to be in charge of that block; they had to get most of the block people to sign this petition, that they wanted a garden, or they wanted the flowers, you know, on their block. Like our block, we could have got planters, we could have got pots or window boxes, but we wanted trees, more trees.

So by sending that money, twenty-five dollars, that's all you would send at the beginning, initial fee, then they would hold their own meeting—you'd have a block meeting. When we first started out, I would go to some of the meetings, sometimes someone else would go, you know. And that's how word got around, just like wildfire (laughs).

A funny thing, I never had to worry about people. They came to us, because they wanted the information. They seen it. They seen what was happening, and they wanted to know how to get it. We never bothered with people that didn't want it—people were coming to us.

So what happened, see like you start with one street like here, and then this little street, that little street, another little street, then the next block, another street, another block, and everybody they just want it. Lots of time you'll see people that don't maybe even seem to care, but if they have a little beauty in their lives, it begins to wake them up.

So last year we did about fifty-one blocks and I think it was forty-eight gardens, all down here—not at one time, but that's what has happened in this area, through our Beautification Committee.

And now if we see houses that are bad, real bad, and let's say they're tore down, we try to turn them into a garden. I don't know whether you noticed as you drove down, but all through here, sprinkled around little streets, little corners, you'll find a little garden.

And then like our block, we had I think it was forty-eight [flower] barrels planted on a weekend, one weekend! Last year, one weekend. It was something, it was really something. I think everybody was happy for it.

And last year we had a wedding garden, did you hear about it? And then during the [city election] campaign, the Horticultural Society had all the candidates come and plant trees. And our City Council even agrees with us.

They have allocated money towards helping with gardens now, because it is helping to turn around the community.

Then see we have the art program, children that were taught to help paint murals on the walls, instead of this weird graffiti and foolish things like that. And we have two or three real gorgeous murals. One of them is like a mountain. When you ride by, they say people almost stop their cars because it's a wall with a mountain like in the Alps. It's blue, like the snow and the sky; it makes you look like you're going into a mountain, it's really something, it is.

And it has been a wonderful experience. Because the streets are cleaner. We have days when we clean up the street if it's dirty; you know, we'll get out there every morning and clean and sweep. Now like a few years ago you come down here and our streets were fairly clean, but they didn't look like they look now.

You walk down the street, I see people with little children, walking down with their head up in the air, and most of them don't throw trash around the street, as much as they used to. I keep telling this over and over; but I had got ready to come in the house for something, and this little girl had a banana peelin' in her hand—this street was clean as it could be—so she held it out like this, and her mother looked at her, she said, "Don't you dare drop that—these people around here will kill you!"

In other words, she seen it was clean. Now maybe in another block, the kid probably would have throwed it there, and she would have thought nothing of it.

I'm not going to tell the story everything is exactly like I want it to be, but it's happenin'. It makes you feel good inside. It really does.

And another thing that's happened, our communities are organized: we have block captains, we have block meetings, now that's from our Beautification Committee. And, oh, I think one time we had a meeting, we have over fifty-some block captains there. Now that's from each block. Uh-huh. And they came to our meetings, and they go back, they carry the information.

And like you know we have our crime. I guess you noticed in the window we have town watch here, we watch out for each other. And it helped, because they put those signs in the windows, and they know somebody's watchin', so they go to another block. But in this area, crime has really dropped down. Yes it has.

We have meetings with our police, you never seen people so tickled to meet in a police station. That place would be crowded from one end to the other, and you laugh and you talk and you think you're in like a hotel or somewhere. And the captain, you go in and you talk to him; the fire chief, you go talk to him; I mean, that's wonderful. And he comes to our meetings, and they have meetings and we go to their meetings, and (laughs) it's really something.

You know, the flowers, if you look at them, it just sort of calms you down. I see people walking there on the street, I see the young people, I don't hear a whole lot of carryin' on or loud noise; maybe they do it somewhere else. It's just not as loud as it used to be, it's really not.

And I tell you, anybody that's sick, or anybody that's worried or upset, flowers helps them a lot. It really does. It really does. It's almost, well, it is therapy for people. 'Cause the lady that live down our block around the corner here, she hadn't been out of her house for about a year, she had had a stroke. And she seen so many people coming up the street and they were telling her what was happening about the garden, and you know she got out and come up there; yeah, she did.

And you know, people in the neighborhood, people are coming together, and that's one thing about the flowers—you'd be surprised, how close people are. I've been in this home now over thirty-five years right here, and I didn't know everybody's name, or I'd speak to people but didn't know them. But now people stop and talk to me.

And even people from other communities—like if you're working in a garden, they'll come by, and stop and talk to you. Sometime they want to find out how they can do it in their communities—don't even live in this section of the city. Most people by now know our names and things, 'cause we've had a lot of articles written about [us]. So they will call us. And we even had people come last year from other cities to see our garden.

But getting back to how our community is, we've done a lot of things toward helping our community fixing up homes. Did you notice new homes across the street as you came down? First brand new homes being built in this area in over fifty years.

In a lot of areas now, people rent out these homes and they let them go down. That's what our problem was. We had a lot of people that were not even living in the city renting out houses, and causing property values to go down. But now we're on a turnaround, because we're going to try to help these houses, we're working with our organization.

And people are coming back now. Younger people are coming back and buying homes, and people that have some money, they were getting ready to move away, are fixin' up. And we have a business area that is beginning to come back more, and I hope it will. And I told them at different meetings, I said, "When we fix up our community, people will want to come back to live." And sure enough, we've had people come from Germantown, nice sections of the city, and they're coming back. So we've really turned things around.

I think we've come a long way (laughs), and I think we're on the move really. 'Cause we've got so much attention from other cities and other people that they want to know "What is happening in Point Breeze?" They heard about this Greene Countrie Towne, and they see a little sign up on the post there, it's Point Breeze, The Greene Countrie Towne.

And I figure the most wonderful thing that is about it is that it's bringing people together. We have a lot of people doing things on their own, by just seeing it. It's just sort of like a pattern, it all fits together.

Like I tell Mamie sometimes, I look like I'm so timid and so quiet, but I mean I can speak out, and then nobody knows what I know or what I can do. I don't like nobody telling me what I can't do. Because I say if you make up your mind that you're going to do anything, you can do it, I believe that. The only thing I say is that if I'm going to make a mess I'll probably make a big one, 'cause I try hard whatever I'm doing. You just don't give up. If you can't do it one way, you have to figure out some other way to do it.

I've been to meetings and they have someone that is highly educated come out and tell you what you couldn't do, and don't do it this way, and don't do it that way, and tell you it won't work. I said, but it *is*! It *is* working! And then they wonder, how? Why? But it just does. You gotta wake up. This is our community. I say the same sun that shines on Society Hill shines on Point Breeze too (laughs). You can't stop it.

Well, that's just about what I see. I didn't know I could talk this long. I didn't believe it!

I walk down the street and I see people, I say, "Good morning!" (with conviction). You speak to people. You go down looking like you're angry, that's not gonna help nothin'. But if you help somebody up the mountain, you're gonna wind up at the top yourself.

And if you have good ideas, don't be afraid to share them. Because when you tell them to somebody, it's going to grow, it's going to be better than just sitting back and doing nothing. What do they say, light a candle or curse the darkness? You light the candle (laughs). I don't know what else I could say. . . .

✳

After the interview, Haroldline Trower takes me to a meeting of the Point Breeze Federation, the larger neighborhood organization. A dozen middle-aged men and women are gathered in a dark room at six o'clock on a summer evening. I'm asked to sign in. They talk about traditional neighborhood and American values—home ownership, cleanliness, schooling. There's a feeling of poignancy and universality here.

The youngest woman of the group is a banker, whose emotions are strong and closest to the surface. There's a tradition of sharing and caring inherent in black people, she says: if you don't get it from the very beginning (childhood, she means), it's hard to get it later on. As for her, she has pride in South Philadelphia; she's staying right there; she wouldn't move if her income doubled.

When I leave, Mamie Nichols gives me an invitation to the upcoming Point Breeze Greene Countrie Towne Festival; my name is on it. Also a poster, which I unroll later: it's a picture of a butterfly, and it says, in large letters, "Point Breeze is Butterfly Beautiful."

Bill Sample with a leukemia victim whose wish was to go to Walt Disney World.

The philosophy is so simple. You raise the dollar, you spend it on the child.

Bill and Helene Sample

THE SUNSHINE FOUNDATION

F IFTEEN miles away, in a different corner of Philadelphia, Bill and Helene Sample have a different perspective on neighborliness. They've recently moved ("The old neighborhood turned bad"). They're not connected to their neighbors, and don't know them very well, but they've found another way to give.

They started the Sunshine Foundation, which raises money and spends it on the dreams of dying and chronically ill children—trips, ponies, personal computers, whatever the parents would buy if they had the money. Bill was a cop, assigned to a hospital; Helene worked inside, in personnel. There was a chance encounter, whose effects lingered. They got married. They started Sunshine with their own savings and went into debt; only very gradually did things fall into place. In 1986, they raised over $1 million and helped 2184 children.

They've chosen to help the dying rather than others in need—the dying child is innocent, they feel, the poor and elderly have had some chance. What's made their program work, they believe, is the cause. The dying child is hard to resist; some chord strikes deep inside. We respond more readily to a child's impending death than to welfare mothers looking for jobs, to allude to Lupe Anguiano's example.

So a powerful cause, and simple mechanics: "You raise the dollar, and you spend it on the child." If you've got these two, plus, what?—dedication? staying power?—you're well on your way, or so it would seem. A reductionist lesson: you don't need college education, you don't need management training, and you don't need fund-raising experience. Bill and Helene Sample had none of the above.

Eight years later, in midlife, Bill has retired from the police force and accepted Sunshine Foundation pay for the first time. Helene continues to work for the Foundation for free. They live more modestly and more intensely than it appears they could.

We sit in their back yard, near a truck route, drinking iced tea. Bill, a gentle and bearish man, a self-described softie, is smoking strong cigars. Helene, petite and outspoken, is in shorts and a midriff top lettered "Miami." Inside, there's a piano, which Helene is learning to play, and a mounted animal head from one of Bill's hunting trips.

We'd like the Samples and everyone else to tell us that their days are blessed with the joy of giving, that the meaning of their lives lies in helping others, and the Samples do say so, convincingly, but there's a bitter edge here as well. They have earned it. We're talking heroes, not saints after all. And truth be told, the saints had plenty of flaws. This isn't to advise holding on to bitterness, or dwelling on imperfection, or even accepting it, but simply to appreciate that for almost all of us, service has costs.

*

HELENE: Most people aren't concerned with going out and helping another person. Their first concern is themselves. And their second concern is their family. They don't look outside the door. You don't knock on a neighbor's and say, "Can I do something for you today?" when you know the car has been sittin' there for four days. People don't do that sort of thing any more.

BILL: Today people have changed so dramatically, it's just unbelievable. The helping part of the American public, the closeness we had, has gone. I was born in '35. During the Second World War I guess it was at its height, helping one another, working together as a neighbor, as a part of the community. Then as the years slowly progressed, from the sixties on, people started to go their own way, the neighborhood concept slowly disintegrated, whatever you want to call it. Until today, everybody's out there, dog-eat-dog, grabbin' while they can.

HELENE: Yeah, I've seen a decline [in neighborliness]. I remember when I was a kid growing up, if my mother was sick, the neighbors would come in with soup; if my father wasn't working, our neighbor would say, "I'll pay your electric bill for you this month." I mean, people did do those things. When you went outside and shoveled your walk, you shoveled five walks, you just didn't shovel your own. You shoveled five walks.

BILL: Today people come home from work, they close the door, and they look at their telly. There's no closeness of the neighborhood environment like there used to be years ago.

And just like Helene, I came from a family that was very very poor. They never had anything. And if I had two nickels and you wanted one, I would give you the nickel without any question, without any thought about it, 'cause you needed it, and you said you wanted it. Like Helene just said, we've been giving all our lives.

BILL: In the late sixties I was assigned [to St. Christopher's Hospital] as a police officer, and that's where I first became aware of the families. I'd be standing outside, and families would pull up, and they would drop their children off. And I would talk to them, hold their hand, while the parents went and parked their car, or I would just tell the mother that Johnny, Robby, Carol went up to clinic, and the mothers and fathers would know where to go.

There was a little child I had personal contact with, who had leukemia and had her leg removed. And everywhere we went we took the little girl with us, Rita. She wanted to see Donny Osmond. He was appearing at the Allentown Fair.

And we had an Allentown police officer who had brought his child down to St. Christopher for treatment, and he mentioned maybe he could do something with me. So we made the arrangements. They brought Rita up to the stage, Donny Osmond sang to her, gave her his sweat towel. And this result in a child, just the look in her face, knowing that her dream was answered. . . .

HELENE: She died in January the following year.

BILL: And that's how we handled Rita, and that was the start of it.

HELENE: Well, basically Bill knew a child who was dying, and being at the hospital, seeing that there were other children who were possibly dying too, just put another idea into his head. Well, we could do it for one child, why can't we do it for another? And he asked a couple of people to help; we were just lucky.

BILL: They were employees of the hospital, or outside people we came in contact with, working through the hospital.

HELENE: They thought it was a great idea: "Why didn't somebody else think of it?" But it took Bill to come up with the idea of trying to do it, and everybody getting together and doing it.

Now of course, most of these people have gone by the wayside, but Bill and I stuck with it, we took the seeds and we sowed them, and somebody has to be there to harvest it all the time. Because people are still basically the same way; they have to put their own life and their family first. We didn't do that.

BILL: We would give to others before we would take care of ourself, which has been the same thing going on for quite a while.

HELENE: Our personal gain has been absolutely nil. We were under scrutiny all the time. You know, "What are you getting out of this?" It makes you feel good. You feel good about what you're doin'. I'm not starvin' to death. I don't have to buy fifty-dollar shoes, I can buy ten-dollar shoes; I'm happy with ten-dollar shoes; I don't have to go out and buy fifty-dollar shoes, like your wife might.

BILL: We called it Sunshine right from the start. And we submitted our paperwork, so we've been Sunshine Foundation since October '76. We sent our first child away the next January. And we have been together since, working for one thing, and that's it, since then.

HELENE: [Bill] had a credit union, and all I knew was that when he got paid, there was this amount taken out every week, so I . . . it just never dawned on me. I mean years are goin' by and I said to myself, what the hell is on this thing? Every month this comes out, every paycheck. And here he was making all these loans [for the Foundation's initial projects]. And I was paying for it. More or less. I was working.

BILL: When we first started, we received very little monies in contributions from people, until it started catching on. And in the meantime, as Helene said, I was going down to the credit union, police and fire, borrowing money and borrowing money, and she was helping me pay it off (laughs).

HELENE: I didn't even know it. Then finally I found out, that every time he would go down he would go get another loan, and keep the same deduction coming out all the time. So it didn't dawn on me.

BILL: If somebody wants one [nickel] you give him one. If somebody wants the two of them, you give him the two of them. . . . It's that simple.

HELENE: Yeah, as an example, I got a bill from a department store for a forty-dollar junior raincoat. I didn't buy it. I hadn't been in that department store. And I said to him, I said, "What the hell is this? Forty dollars for a raincoat, what did you buy a raincoat for?" "Well, there was a little girl at school," he said. "It was cold, and she didn't have a winter coat, so me and so-and-so went over and we got her this coat." I said, "And I paid the bill."

And I mean, I could be walking barefoot and he'd think, well, Helene will take care of herself, I'll get this kid a raincoat. And that's the kind of guy he is.

BILL: The monies were in very short supply in the beginning; very, very slow coming in. We were strictly working out of the Philadelphia area. It picked up when we had an article in the *Philadelphia Daily News,* then we were picked up by a radio talk show host here by the name of Irv Homer. Irv had us on the program a couple of times, and people started to become aware of us.

A few people wanted to help, and they came and helped us with various fund-raising events. The first year, we handled a total of fourteen families. And they included children down the seashore, they included going to the mountains; our first Disney child was not until 1978, no, '77.

And from there on in, no child has ever been turned down. We've never said no; that's one thing we can brag about.

HELENE: When we first started, and we decided that we would go nationwide, I said let's write a letter to every pediatric hospital there is in the United States, and let them know who we are and what we're doing, and if there's a child that needs our help, they can refer it.

So I sat there and composed a two-page letter, mailed it out to over fifty-two pediatric hospitals, and we got three answers. The first answer, they wanted a copy of our financial report; the other letter said, we can't help anybody, we're helping enough people. And I forget what the third one said.

BILL: But they're all knocking on our door today.

HELENE: We're working with every one of them.

BILL: So it took us a while to get it started, 'cause we're giving something away for nothing, we're not asking for any return other than a thank-you, a smile, knowing that we've helped. I mean, when you say to somebody, "I'm going to give you a trip to Disney," or "I'm going to buy you a Cabbage Patch doll," and we're doing this for you for absolutely nothing, that's reward in itself.

HELENE: How can you stop doing it? When we began, we never dreamed in a million dreams that it would ever become what it's become today. We just started out doing a few things for the children at St. Christopher's Hospital, that was all.

But when people saw what we were doing, and believed in what we were doing, the only thing we could do was to go on with the things that these people were giving us the money to do. We had to: what else could we do with their money? And that's exactly what we did. It wasn't anything that you really thought of as a sacrifice, it was just you got up in the morning, and this was just what you had to do.

This is the way I was raised, it was a responsibility. I've always been very responsible; sometimes I want to be irresponsible, and I get angry with myself when I can't be that way. When I can't be irresponsible. I want to say, "The hell with it. I'm not going to take care of that, let somebody else do it." And I can't do that, and neither can he, and it's just—I guess you program yourself in a certain way and we can't get deprogrammed.

BILL: Once you see your first child, which we did—the first child was a little boy name of Bobby we sent to the Poconos, and being there with him that weekend . . . We didn't know what to expect, what to do, and we saw the look on his face and the enjoyment that he was receiving, and that's reason enough for not stopping, not saying, no, you can't do something. You make yourself do it.

HELENE: And how can you just close it down? You know, how can you turn around and say okay, kids, we're going to close up shop 'cause we're tired of this thing?

BILL: And especially a child? A child is full of love, a child is full of caring. He doesn't know what he has, why he's ill. Children are special. We do for our own children what we can, but these poor families can't.

HELENE: They're so innocent. They didn't ask to be born. And they didn't ask to have cancer. They didn't ask to have a family that can't afford to do these special things for them. And that innocent child, who would never meet Mickey Mouse, has; and when he's not around, that family has some good memories, not all bad ones. So how can you just not open the mail to that?

BILL: And it made a difference in our lives. . . . That's the main thing. We get more out of helping these families than the families probably get themself at times. We are here happy helping.

HELENE: Some people . . . some people . . . the only way I can explain it is some people love taking from other people. People who just love to take. I mean, people go around with coupons, and rebates, and boy, I'll tell you, if they can save a nickel or save a dollar, or use somebody, they love it. We know those people. They do make me angry. 'Cause they only know how to take; they don't know how to give back.

I can't do that. I never did that. I will never be that way. Bill is never that way. You know, I'll do it for you, but don't take advantage of me. I feel better doing it for you; I don't want it done for me—but that's hard to understand.

✳

Those who don't say no can expect to be called upon. Pressures to expand are hard to resist, for suffering is boundless. The Sunshine Foundation has expanded, its founders have stretched as far as spirit will allow.

Multiple chapters have arisen by the eastern seaboard. A branch office in Atlanta opened in 1985. Sunshine now has paid office staff, though about eighty percent of the funds raised go directly to children and families. More significantly, the Sunshine Foundation has been godfather to dozens of similar organizations which have sprung up across the country.

Sunshine has begun to help other affected children—blind, deaf, retarded, and chronically ill. Children with progeria, a disease of premature aging, are flown in from around the world for an annual reunion. In 1986, the Foundation chartered six planes and five buses in one day to bring 1246 children to Walt Disney World. Sunshine is now raising funds to build its own village, thematically based upon Snow White and the Seven Dwarfs. It will house vacationing families, and will cost an estimated $1.5 million.

*

INTERVIEWER: I'm thinking, though, that a lot of people who get involved in community service work are responsible, and really do want to make a contribution. But for one reason or another they have a whole lot of problems. So was there anything else that you feel was important in contributing to your success?

BILL: A child. The cause. Helping a child, helping a special child, a child that has no tomorrow. A child that may not be here, that would never have a dream or wish answered. I guess that's the closest I can give to you.

INTERVIEWER: So when you had to make decisions . . .

HELENE: We fought, a lot.

BILL: Oh, yeah, constantly.

HELENE: Oh yeah, we fought. I'm sending out the gift application— "You can't ask people those questions!" I said, "I certainly can." "I'm not signing that." I said, "Then I will." Oh, we've had our fights; we were going to get divorced—and "Take your foundation," and "I'm not doing nothing anymore," but. . . . not so much now. I mean, we fought, but we fought for what we felt was right, and fair, and we didn't always agree on everything.

BILL: But things, excuse me, things worked out in the long run.

INTERVIEWER: Going back to the beginning again, when you were getting yourselves recognized and established, were there mistakes that you made that you wouldn't repeat again, and things that—

HELENE: I can't think of any.

BILL: As far as I'm concerned, not that we've done everything right, but to me the philosophy of the Foundation is so simple. You raise the dollar, you spend it on the child. You raise twenty dollars, you spend it on the child. We only have our sights on two things: we raise the money, and we help the children. So there's not that much of a philosophy there, as far as the intricacies go.

HELENE: We often wonder ourselves: I finished high school, and I never went on with my education, and you're just a cop, and I'm just somebody that was working since I was fourteen. . . . How the hell did we figure this out? (laughs). I mean, that we didn't, you know—

BILL: That we didn't stumble.

HELENE: Stumble. We never even had a check bounce. That's how lucky we were. But see, I made sure them books balanced; if he wrote a check for a hundred dollars, there had to be two hundred in there, or I wouldn't take the chance. I mean it was . . . I don't know how we did it. Because we're certainly not geniuses, and we—

BILL: Speak for yourself.

HELENE: And we don't always write the letters with the beautiful correct English, although they look pretty professional because we've learned a lot, you know. We've had a lot of help and advice from people, and we either took it or we didn't take it.

BILL: And it's just the common sense of working with people. We both know people. We both know what we're about. We both know what we're trying to do, what we have done. There's a lot of people with book smarts that just don't have the common sense.

HELENE: Yeah. You could be a surgeon, but you know, you can't write a check. I mean, I've worked with doctors at the hospital, and they didn't even know if they had insurance. "You have Blue Cross and Blue Shield?" "I don't know. Maybe my wife knows." That's not having much common sense, I don't think.

I do the paperwork. Bill is the kind of man, he sees that vision on that wall, and he says, "That's what I'm going to do." And I say, "That's great. But—before you can get there, you have to go here, here, here, and there; so that's fine, but let me do all this stuff." And that's basically what I do.

He was best going on television, he was best doin' the articles, and getting the ideas, and I would just do the follow-up. I'm a planner. I will not jump over there unless I know when I get there I'm going to fall on my feet. I have to fall on my feet. Because my mother died when my son was eight weeks old, my brother was nineteen, my sister was sixteen, and they needed to be taken care of, and I tried to answer them the best that I could.

Everybody always leaned on me. Everybody leaned on me. The whole world leaned on me. He [Bill] leans on me. I get so angry at him sometimes. I say, "Why are you leaning on me? I don't want to be leaned on. I want to lean on somebody." And when I try to lean on somebody, I find out that I can only lean on myself sometimes. And there's things that you just have to do. And . . . I just can't see any other way but doing it the way that it has to be done.

INTERVIEWER: I'm trying to see if I can phrase this right . . . If you want to help people, why focus on the dying? Or if you want to fulfill wishes of people, why shouldn't we go and fulfill wishes of a poor person who's struggling to make ends meet, or a person who's old and ready to die, or some other type of person?

BILL: Okay, when you're speaking of poor people, you're speaking of Helene and I. When you're speaking of elderly people, they should have had their chance, if they've saved their monies.

HELENE: Time afforded them that opportunity.

BILL: But when you're speaking of a child, a child with a terminal illness, a child that will not have a tomorrow 'cause it's going to be taken from him, ripped from him, let's do what we can for him or her while they're here with us. Why shouldn't they have that dream or wish ever answered?

If you and I want to go on a trip, we save our pennies, we go on our trip. But to the child, who's seven years old, and comes down with leukemia or cancer—there's no tomorrow for him . . . there's no adulthood for him. And why should this, this little person, leave us and not have his or her dream answered? It's that simple.

HELENE: Right. And we don't choose to help people who are poor, because they still have a chance at somethin', and the people who are elderly, they had their chance too. But these children, they're not going to have that opportunity.

INTERVIEWER: Do you feel that it's better, or more noble, or more virtuous in God's eyes to help a dying child than to engage in other sorts of community service?

HELENE: No.

BILL: I believe in one thing: we're all God's children. And God will take you when he wants to. We're not trying to—

HELENE: Make points with God.

BILL: We're trying to give the child an earthly pleasure.

HELENE: We're trying to make it easier for him to bear his pain.

BILL: While he's here with us. Before he goes back with God.

INTERVIEWER: So this is of the highest calling, you feel?

BILL: I feel it is. I feel it is.

HELENE: I don't think it's of the highest calling. I don't think that way at all. I feel that it's just something that I chose to do. . . . And I'm happy doing it. And I chose to do it. I'm not doing it because I'm going to make points with anybody, because I don't have to make points with anybody.

BILL: And as far as helping the poor is concerned, I believe there's opportunity. America is still the land of opportunity—there's work out there if you want it.

BILL: Let me read you a little thing here. (Gets glasses) This was at Christmas:

Dear Mr. and Mrs. Sample: This is a very overdue letter concerning Missy. Her dream of a piano came true, thanks to you and your Foundation's efforts. Missy received a piano for Christmas, and played for the first and only time on the Sunday after Christmas. Missy died five days later. She touched many lives, and brought happiness and fulfillment not only to her parents, but also to all those that she came to know and who came to know her. She had leukemia, but she remained out of the hospital and with her parents for the longest part of the illness.

That's why you can't stop.

INTERVIEWER: Do you still feel touched by these kids?

BILL: Oh, yes.

HELENE: Yes.

BILL: Certainly. Sure.

HELENE: I open letters and I cry. I still cry. And I say to myself, why am I crying? I've heard this thing a hundred times, and I'm crying. So if I can cry, you know, the hardest-hearted person has to cry.

BILL: Helene won't go to funerals anymore. We've been to too many. I've been pallbearer . . .

HELENE: See, we used to deal with them on the phone constantly, and we got to the heart of things, and now we have a gal in the office that does that. So we don't talk to the families as often as we used to.

BILL: I'm still a softie (laughs).

HELENE: He's still soft and easy.

BILL: You want my shirt, I'll give you my shirt. I'll give you the two nickels. I haven't changed.

HELENE: I really think that probably what made it work so well was supporting each other in what we did. Fighting with each other, and working together. Now how many people are married and he works there, and she works there, and they come home, and that's the end of it? That's not the way we live. We live seven days a week, twenty-four hours a day with Sunshine.

BILL: You can go home at night and turn off your phone, or do what you have to do. We can't turn off our phone. Our families have our phone [number] from the minute we contact them till they come back from the trip, and sometimes afterwards.

There's a family here, they'll be out in Disneyland the entire weekend. If they have problems, who are they going to call? They're going to call us here at the house. We're always on call.

HELENE: Yeah. Yeah. And decisions have to be made, and sometimes I make the decision, and he's mad that I did it, or he'll support me or I'll support him, and the two of us, like I said, we—

BILL: Fight like cats and dogs (laughs).

HELENE: No, no we don't. No, he's very easy.

BILL: When we come home, we talk Sunshine—11:30 at night, we're there looking at the television, and if a child appears on the news that needs help, we're going to write back to them, this is Sunshine. Then we get up in the morning, it's seven o'clock in the morning until midnight every day. That's all you talk about is Sunshine. It consumes you. But it's happy being consumed that way.

HELENE: I mean let's be honest with each other. Sometimes we look at each other and say, what the hell are we killing ourselves for? You know. But, we know if we weren't the driving force, and we weren't looking after things the way we do, who else would do it? Would it be there? Would it be there? And that's what keeps you going.

BILL: We're constantly under fire.

HELENE: We try and delegate everything we can. But when the bottom line comes in, and there is a problem, people come to me or come to Bill: "How did you allow that to happen?"

BILL: We're always the quarterbacks, we're always the quarterbacks.

HELENE: We'll have a board meeting, and we'll decide to do this benefit, and it looks like we're going to make five thousand dollars, so everybody votes to do the benefit. And then we put it into action, and then we come back to the board six months later and they say, "How did that benefit go?" We say, "We made a thousand dollars." "Why? You told us you were going to make five thousand. How come you made one thousand?" Now, what did they do about that benefit? Nothing. So then you have to sit there and explain why.

And, if people take things personal—they really do, they take them very personal. Just because you like carrots and I don't doesn't mean I don't like you. It's the way it goes. It's a tough world out there.

BILL: Last year we helped over 812 children. We're going to help over one thousand children this year. The Foundation's just going to continue to grow and grow and grow, and nothing is going to stop it, because of the simple fact that there will be children out there who will constantly need their dream or wish answered, and we're here to answer their dream or their wish.

HELENE: The future I see is that someday we will have a nice office, a larger staff, more monies, more volunteers, and I see a lot of the work coming off our shoulders, and having the right kind of people that we can afford to pay to do what we do.

BILL: It would just be nice once in our life to be able to get up in the morning and go to sleep at night and not have to worry about a dollar coming in. Someday, we'll be able to hit it, like Helene says, where we can relax just a little bit. We're never constantly relaxed.

I always worry about bringing money in. I worry about it, constantly. We have no millionaires, we have no large corporate sponsors, we receive no federal monies—so we derive our monies directly from people who want to give us donations, of the one, five, tens, and twenties; from various service organizations that have held fund-raisers; little people in the neighborhood who want to have a block party, a bake sale, a whatever. That's what has kept us going.

So I'd just like one time to maybe get a windfall, maybe get to the point where we can have a national telethon and sit back and then we get some money coming in where we could just (whoosh sound).

HELENE: National telethon, yeah. I want to hold a telethon like Jerry Lewis does.

BILL: The program won't change. We don't want to branch out, we just want to help the children. That's all we want to do. It's so simple. You raise the money and you help a child. It's that simple.

HELENE: And the mechanics are very simple. We get a referral, it comes in, we send out an application, the application comes back, we write to the doctor, we make telephone calls, we make arrangements . . .

INTERVIEWER: Is it fun?

BILL: Oh, sure it's fun.

HELENE: Sure it's fun. It's a lot of fun. You meet wonderful people. We meet all the good people. We meet all the nice people. We meet people who care about other people and who want to help us, and care about helping the other children. Most people that we meet are great people.

INTERVIEWER: Is it hard?

BILL: It's hard. It's hard.

HELENE: Oh, it's hard.

BILL: It's a labor of love.

HELENE: It's fun and it's hard. Very hard.

Once in a while I think, please, Lord, take me away from it. You know, I really believe, personally I believe that earth is hell and that death has to be heaven. Somethin' has to be better than earth. I myself welcome death. I think it's going to be a hell of a relief from what I'm doing on earth (laughs).

INTERVIEWER: But if I take you seriously, I mean, if you say that earth is hell, then you could say, well, these kids who are living on earth, why not just let them be released, let them die, and hopefully—

HELENE: Because you want to take some of the hell out of the earth that they have. And you want to put some pleasure in it for them. Because all they know is that it's hell on earth, they have cancer, they're sick, they're dying. They wanted to be an astronaut, they're never going to be an astronaut. But maybe we can provide them with a seat in a space capsule.

So let's take some of [the pain] out of there, because people make it tough for each other, and if you can make it easier for somebody, it makes it nicer. And wherever they go, I hope to God that they're happy. Because they certainly had a problem here.

BILL (to interviewer): What do you think now, Bill, of the Sunshine Foundation? Personally.

HELENE: Do you think we're really nuts?

INTERVIEWER: No. I respect and admire enormously the type of work you're doing. But what interests me in talking with the two of you is also to see how your life of idealism can coexist with a certain degree of cynicism, which I take as real—

BILL: Yeah.

HELENE: Yeah.

INTERVIEWER: And bitterness and anger about people who are not willing to put out; that's part I think of what makes us human. We have our ideals, but we screw up and act nasty, and I'm becoming more aware of how those things can go together. So that's part of my own learning.

INTERVIEWER: I wanted to follow up with you, Helene, something you mentioned earlier on, about the way you grew up—it almost sounded that to be a caring person it was an advantage to grow up relatively poor.

HELENE: It was an advantage. It was most definitely an advantage. If I didn't have the life I had, I probably would not be the kind of person I am today. And I'm happy with the kind of person I am. Not always.

BILL: I would have much rather grown up with a silver spoon in our mouth, maybe like the Kennedys or the Rockefellers. But then like Helene said, maybe this would not have happened to us, and not enabled us to start the Foundation and continue with the Foundation.

HELENE: Nobody handed us anything. Nobody ever handed us anything. Every good thing that's come our way has only come because we worked for it. And everything we worked for, we enjoyed that much more.

BILL: I haven't been out of work since 1947. I worked since I was twelve years old, all my life.

HELENE: Yeah. I worked when I was fourteen.

BILL: Helene's the same way. That's all we know is work, work, work. I'm happy with it.

HELENE: Right.

BILL: If you enjoy doing what you're doing, that's ninety percent of the job. And we enjoy helping children. . . .

*Everyone thought it was stupid. Everyone. My peers:
"What, go to a nursing home? I mean, come on, let's go
to a party."*

Kathy Levin

MAGIC ME

K ATHY LEVIN has just flown in, and her doorman apartment is
something of a mess. She got back late from Nebraska the night
before, her refrigerator and air conditioning are both on the fritz, and
she's barely had time to catch her breath.

While she was out there, circling spring floods, donating her time,
she was training children to become intimate with the institutionalized
aged. Preteens visit nursing homes, make friends with people seven
times older, and disco dance, write poetry, and play basketball together. It's part of a program she started in Baltimore, called Magic Me.

The Sunshine Foundation helps the dying child; Magic Me serves
the living. The idea is to inspire children, streetwise and tough-skinned
children, to discover magic within themselves and thereby to transcend. When you see yourself in a wrinkled face, you are expanded.
When you have found your magic powers, you can release those of
others. That's the open agenda, a large part of it.

There's more: if the middle-aged are beyond redemption, then start
with children. If caring is scarce, one deprived group can assist another.
If one group helps another, both are served; and both are changed.

And so is the creator. I have doubts that many people in this book
would call themselves altruistic, but Kathy Levin is the most forthright
on the topic. She's given years of time, thousands of dollars of her own
money, but says that Magic Me has nothing to do with altruism. It's
for her, it's her way of expressing herself in the world; she wants to do
it, she *needs* to do it, and to that extent Magic Me is selfish. If she didn't
want or need to do it, *then* it would be altruistic.

Our social task then is simple: encourage others to express themselves similarly.

Kathy Levin had the money to spend, and she had connections and used them. These helped, but cannot fully explain her success; the Samples were as poor as Kathy was comfortable. There's something else pulsing inside, whatever its source. Kathy went from a gleam to a fully operational community program in less than three months, and you can't do that on good fortune alone. Kathy agrees it's important to "care about it a whole lot."

She sounds like she does; no one could doubt it. Animated and youthful (twenty-seven at the time), high-pitched and disarming, she speaks in exclamation points. Her voice radiates excitement. There's no interview here that better exemplifies the role of personal qualities in creating change. Her story is the longest one in this book, and with reason, as I hope you'll see.

*

I feel that my urge to create is an excessive one. There's a little bit of talent, a very little bit of talent, and a lot of urge. Where there are a lot of people who have a lot of talent, who have little urges (laughs). But there's a big crying to be heard, that comes from maybe being shy and sheltered and privileged and something.

Being privileged, generally, being a privileged kid growing up, I never felt that I had to pursue a conventional field to make a living, to prove my identity, to establish a name. Because privileged kids have so much of that at their fingertips, or feel as though that's given, even if it's not. There's that perception.

And my own motivations were a little bit different, a little skewed, from high school. Fortunately I went to a small private school in Baltimore, where one of the most influential teachers taught me Latin; I ended up being a classics major. And my biggest academic and personal reinforcements were from something that was out of the mainstream, something different that I loved for its own sake. It was classics per se, and using language as persuasion.

I'm convinced, if I were a social service major, I would never have done Magic Me. If I were a professional in geriatrics, if I were a professional social worker, I don't think I would be able to communicate all that I do about the geriatric stuff. Somehow, in my ignorance, I think I would have pursued something more narrow. As opposed to having this kind of personal freedom, which is part of why I'm able to do Magic Me. It's [not] keeping a professional distance.

And I think that the hypersensitive, shy little ones see the world differently. For me, it's some combination—I can't pinpoint it—of being hyper-, hypersensitive and shy as a little person. And as you might be able to see, some of the creative stuff that I do is excessive, the painting and the drawing and the music expression; this is all because I'm doing it for me, crying out to be understood.

I stumbled into a nursing home in Providence when I was at Brown. Tripped! (laughs) I thought I wanted to be a volunteer, just in my spare time—there was no reason. I had no inclination to old people, other than I just thought it would be an interesting social service thing to do, on my own. And I thought maybe I could write for their newspaper, because I wanted to apply my interests in persuasion to a social service field; so maybe I'd do some newspaper writing for the nursing home, wouldn't that be fun.

I walked in the door and there were these ladies in light green volunteer uniforms, and they were all excited about my interest, 'cause I went to Brown. They assumed that I was intelligent. So they told me that as a volunteer, I would have to come at certain hours, which instantly horrified me (laughs). I wouldn't have very much contact with the elderly, but I would be able to write and edit their newspaper.

But it struck me as I was walking around the hall touring that the volunteers in this nursing home—I didn't know anything about nursing homes—they were all around fifty years old and bored and boring, in these light green horrible uniforms, and they really didn't want to be there, and there was just no energy. And in college, you know, at this time in your life, this is an opportunity to question everything you see.

Well, I did (laughs): it doesn't have to be this way; it doesn't have to be this way. The worst thing was that volunteers plug into institutions through this system, and volunteering should be a freedom, it should be a luxury. It should be a pleasure, and having to be joyful at the hour that they choose you should be joyful is a job (laughs). That's not volunteer activity.

So I told them I'd like to come at my own time. And that was not acceptable. . . . I then decided not to do the volunteer activity there, and I snuck in the next day (lowers voice), and said that I was visiting a relative, and I wasn't an official volunteer.

And I felt like me, which was insecure, and without the green coat, and without the sticker that says, "Hi. I'm your friendly volunteer." And I was totally naked, emotionally. I was just a wreck, which was the most valuable experience I've ever had. This is the one experience that really motivated me: There was a woman with white hair, and as with most of them to a young person, excessively wrinkled and smelling as if she's been in a nursing home. I was petrified to walk over to her, though there was no reason for me to be afraid of her, because here she is, this helpless woman, alone in a lounge, sort of sobbing into her lap, and I couldn't figure out what horrified me.

And that's become an essential, it's really become core, when I go out and teach Magic Me kids, is this confrontation of your own fears. All the things that bother me are at the center of Magic Me. You see, if I were a saint, if I were really Mother Teresa's daughter, I'd be miserable at this, because I wouldn't be able to talk about all these kinds of problems. I speak firsthand when I talk to these kids now, across the country. Yet this one woman struck me as being horrifying.

Somehow I had a breath of inspiration—I walked up to her and shyly said, "Hi," and she spoke in a language I didn't understand. A few minutes later, she spoke in another language that I didn't understand, and then the third time she spoke in French; it turns out she speaks five languages. She was 105—I looked at her bracelet.

She speaks five languages, in this nursing home (laughs), and nobody talks to her. Well, I was into languages (laughs), I was in heaven; it was just like the best thing that ever happened. And yet it was still pretty horrendous to have to look at her, because I was so used to looking at pretty people. I promised her I'd be back the next day to talk.

I didn't realize what I was getting into (laughs). I knew that when I was there, and fired up, and into this woman, and beyond the wrinkles and tears, that it was very easy and wonderful to be there. When I got back to my college room that night, got out of the place, thinking about the environment was horrifying again. Even though I had pierced through and found what was worth sorting through the wrinkles and tears for—I knew this woman—it still was horrible to think about going back, just the worst thing in the world.

I promised her, so I went back.

She had forgotten everything. I didn't know any of this (laughs). I didn't have any courses in the stuff. For me, it was one big creative inexplicable world. It was marvelous, scary, and emotionally testing, and—there was a man on the other side of the room, and the one thing that led to the next to the next to the next was imagining that maybe this man, who's tapping his toes to no music, except maybe some music that was in his head—what occurred to me is he might be a great dancer. Who would know that this woman spoke five languages? Who would know what he might be? And what she, in the other corner, might be, drooling? And this one, screaming in the other corner, might be something that I could relate to, in a big way. And only by going over to the man who was tapping his toes to some imaginary music and finding another way to pierce through his stuff, his layers of difference, by encouraging him a lot—"I bet you can, I bet you can, come on, try, 'cause I got to find out if you are what I think you might be"— it's for me. Magic Me is not so much about altruism—it has nothing to do with altruism—it's about learning about *me*!

He becomes the disco dancer, I bring in my records, and he and I start waltzing around the room; because a lot has to do with the fact that I kept saying, and meaning, "I bet you can. Come on, you gotta do it for me." He felt sorry for me, 'cause I needed him to perform (laughs). And the process is one for me where I have to unzip, emotionally, and sort of take off the Ivy League coat of excellence; so many of us who are sheltered, and sort of thrust out from this elitist environment, don't ever have to get down and touch and smell and realize how human we are, and how common we are. This for me was like the antithesis of Ivy League education. And it was marvelous. . . .

So that was like the first episode, this high-powered, scary—every day was scary—private experience. This was the experience that really motivated me. There was no one to whom I could talk about it; everyone thought it was stupid. Everyone. My peers: "What, go to a nursing home? I mean, come on, let's go to a party" (laughs). My parents thought it was not exactly what I should be doing at college. And listening to myself talk about a nursing home sounded ridiculous, because I have all of the same image fears and problems that my peers do. But I had by accident discovered something inside, when I still have some problems.

I went back weekly, and did little group activities with some of the people that I had met and felt comfortable with in the nursing home. I wasn't noticed. I imagine if I had been more closely scrutinized, I would probably not have had the freedom and the personal experience that's all been critical, I now realize, for how Magic Me began. Because I tried to create a free, healthy, personal environment, as opposed to a highly organized, singing-to the-elderly, because the Christmas-carol style stuff is not exactly what I had in mind.

So that was how it began.

One of the conscious ideas I had in college was to maybe approach a professional area of persuasion as my first job, like advertising, or P.R. or something, so I could then apply my interest in language and communications to community service. I felt like my real energies, my talents—many of them would be lost by my indulging in the human stuff, inside geriatrics, working one-on-one, affecting one person at a time. I wouldn't be as valuable to communities as I might be if I stayed out of the human services.

So I worked in advertising when I got right out of college, in New York City—and got a terrific job. It was developing products for prospective clients, so that if I could help, say, General Foods progress in their ten-year testing and development of a product, shrink the time of testing, fly around the country and find out what people really wanted in this product, (excited tone) the product would come out sooner, because we help that process.

It was marvelous! It was the most exciting job in the world, and also doing the conceiving of campaigns for different clients in the agency, all the testing and the people contact et cetera, et cetera. It was creatively marvelous. Ideas and ideas and ideas. And yet, I'd been spoiled by this human stuff already.

I was visiting nursing homes in the morning in New York, before advertising, and then going to work. Same thing—teaching poetry writing and disco and stuff that I like to do. Advertising felt like cotton candy. It felt like light and fluffy air; it didn't feel like it was solid in a hard-core way, as opposed to the nursing home stuff. It was a marvelous opportunity. It was fantastic. But there was something else longing. . . .

Then I quit advertising. And spent a year volunteering in a nursing home, and I flew around the country doing some speeches for a charity in Israel, which has since developed from a seed idea to a really important project. It reconfirmed what I had suspected: that I was not going to be working in a conventional way, if I was going to fulfill the things that were important to me.

I came home to Baltimore after I had volunteered a year, and part of the reason for coming back was to get heavily involved in community activity here. I looked around and asked around, I was continuing to visit nursing homes, and there was a woman there, who's paralyzed, who spoke just utterances, incomprehensible sounds, and she became an essential seed voice for Magic Me.

She finally spoke, I know, from my encouragement every day. "Come on, come on, I bet you can, come on," just from the attention in an environment where she was getting very little personal encouragement. And she was telling me what it was like to live inside this body, how miserable it is to live inside a crippled body, and what it's like to have people walk by and not be able to look at you. I never would have imagined precisely what it felt like. So—I thought it would be interesting to teach people like this woman in groups, in big groups, and I had to come up with ways of doing that.

That was fun. It was purely creative, it was just like advertising in nursing homes. And I also began to write articles aimed at fifty-year-olds whom I saw not visiting their relatives anymore, as you know, an old story. And I began to explore the psyche of the fifty-year-old child who for many good reasons has difficulty looking at this changed parent.

The first article that I wrote was printed in the *Jewish Times* and in the Brown University magazine. And I received more letters and phone calls from fifty-year-olds whose chords I struck, I somehow shook them. But what I realized from responding to all these calls and letters by hand, and really getting intimate with this group of fifty-year-olds who responded, was that although there are things they can improve on, so many of them are so deeply, negatively ingrained that my input is minimal.

A fluke! It occurred to me—wouldn't it be fun to teach a group, a little group of kids, who could grow up to be fifty-year-olds who weren't so hung up. Kids who could see through the wrinkles and tears from an early age, who would know this woman Harriet in the paralyzed body, who could come and see her and go into the nursing home and listen to this lady, and really see nursing homes differently. Wouldn't that be fun!

All of this is building a kind of whirlpool inside my body, and it was an urge, it was more important than a creative urge . . . it was a need for Kathy to express what she's evolving into. I needed to know that, since I had trouble my whole life expressing what I was feeling, landing my idea in kids might be a way to confirm to myself that I'm not crazy, that this is valid. If there're ten kids who didn't see it in the beginning, and whom I could communicate to, then that makes me more valid.

Maybe it's out of some big insecurity, this whole thing—ha, maybe. Maybe a fluke isn't exactly right. Maybe it was preordained, that I needed to confirm myself in other people.

It was a very simple idea. It was to create a new generation of enthusiastic young volunteers who could see through the wrinkles and tears. Start all over again! These middle-aged people were like past the influenceable time. And why not kids my own age? Even we are already too preconditioned. Whereas I was thinking if I hit kids like preteens, like ten through fourteen was the original group. Lots of energy. Undirected. Who don't even know what volunteering is, they don't even know what old people are about except that they're icky.

And we could do something about that. We could try to confirm some of their fears, which is important in this whole process, and give these kids a way of looking at themselves and their own lives. It's not so much about the old people, but it's to give children at an early age, oh, a kind of confirmation that what they're feeling in the most human raw vulnerable ways is important, that it's really valid to stay in touch with the part of you that's insecure and scared and weirded out about being mortal.

And Magic Me, in a sense, is a way to keep it open, to keep it raw, to keep us human. And old people allow us to be that way, especially the old and the isolated. They keep us vulnerable and raw, and feeling, and unpredictable. And alive. I mean, to me that's kind of the essence of our humanness. It's scary and it's delightful.

I went to a regional superintendent in the school system, the beginning of '82. It took some courage; now I'm doing lots of things I never thought I would be doing. I was pretty shy about calling someone who had a job like a regional superintendent. And I said, "I have this little idea about teaching kids about themselves. I'm going to call it Magic Me, and give maybe an underprivileged set of kids a way of building self-esteem."

I wanted one to four schools. And I was going to start with four nursing homes. If I could do that, I would be real happy. That's all I wanted, was like this little activity where every year I could affect, say, fifty kids in a classroom. Gosh, if I affected *one* child—it was inconceivable to affect fifty. I wanted a little project, where I could have an end, at the end of, say, a number of weeks, I could see their attitudes change, and these kids could write essays about it, it would be nice! A nice little program, and that was it.

And this regional school superintendent said, "That's a real nice idea. Why don't you talk to this enlightened principal X, X, X, and X, and we'll give you schools that are enlightened, whose kids are difficult ones as well." I'm not sure why I wanted difficult kids at first, but there's some part of me that likes the more dramatic difficult aspect—also, instinctively I thought maybe that difficult kids, kids who felt left out, might surprise us and be really good with old people. There might be a natural connection.

Then I spoke to the principals, who had to work out some logistics when I was going to come, and how we were actually going to get these kids to join the program. I kept insisting I didn't want these kids to have to do it. I mean, it was hard to set up in the beginning, because I wanted to affect the basketball-playing athletic kids who want to be cool. 'Cause then, for my purposes, I would really see some change, big change.

So how to attract the kids was a major problem. The principal said, "Well, during a particular class you could do this," and I said, "Well, then I'd have a captive audience," it didn't feel quite fair. I wanted somehow to get kids attracted by the image of Magic Me, 'cause I wanted Magic Me to be trendy. So I told him I'll come back in a week, and I'm going to give all the kids these neat T-shirts.

Well, that week I had to come up with a T-shirt that looked zippy, that would lure the kids in. So that's it [Kathy displays a shirt]. It's a purple child, 'cause you can be any color, juggling a rainbow, which is doing something impossible. It's sort of the ten-year-old mentality, fun and up, and these are sort of inner-city colors and stuff. And I'd give every kid a T-shirt—well, that would be sufficient reward.

But I wanted them to choose to be in it not merely for the T-shirt, although that is a lure, believe me, for kids who can't afford clothes. So I told the principal that I would write a musical (laughs). That was a fluke—although (laughs) I probably always wanted to write a musical anyway; here's my opportunity.

This would really be what I wanted. It would play to the whole school, like fifteen hundred kids. And whoever responded to the message in the musical, which would be about the possibilities, the unimaginable possibilities, in places as strange and bizarre as nursing homes, these kids would sign up for Magic Me. And knowing that they'd get the T-shirt, well, that was okay, that fulfilled my little ranking inside my body, of being fair.

So the principal said, "That sounds great."

So. Then I came back and sat here and wrote my musical. And wrote and wrote and wrote and wrote. And I realized that I had to know exactly what I was going to do with these kids in a program before I wrote the musical to inspire them (laughs). So I had to design the program, the Magic Me activities in the nursing home, and the training in the classroom, which I ultimately had to do with the kids, in order to write the musical. In a week.

It took me more than a week. It took me two weeks. In the meantime, I have an affiliation with the Baltimore Actors Theatre, which is a private professional children's actors group. I support them, I give them funds, and try to give them some P.R. help and to keep them going. And I gave this musical to them, to work out, to perform, to direct, to rewrite parts of it if they wanted. They played with it, and they came up with a real live performance, I'll show you some clips on the video.

Well, needless to say, I was really excited and nervous as hell (laughs). What this thing was going to be like; whether any of the kids in the audience who were black underprivileged ten-year-olds were going to respond to these white performing kids doing this musical about nursing homes (laughs). And I cared a lot about this, if it sounded really stupid. And my mother and father were thinking, this is just more headaches than any little girl needs in her life, and (laughs) they had a good point.

On top of all this, I get a phone call from a man who says, "Hi, my name is Ozzie Segerberg. I'm a producer from CBS national news; I went to Brown. I read your article in the Brown alumni magazine, and I just think it's the greatest thing I've ever read.

"I was crying," he said, "and I went to the executive producer of the national news, at CBS, and I presented your program—to tap the latent, magical energy of inner-city kids, to actually get them to enjoy going to nursing homes. And the executive producer, Kathy, says we're going to go, we'll be down on Monday, to film the opening of the musical, and the subsequent week to see your first seminars in the classrooms to meet these kids who are petrified of nursing homes. And then when you first go to the nursing home, we'll be there with our cameras again."

Oh, my goodness. The musical wasn't even finished. There was not even a nursing home that said the kids could come in. I didn't even have a specific idea of the program. So I was rather uptight (laughs). But I knew the goal (laughs).

So Monday comes, the CBS crew comes down, and we're ready to roll.

The musical performs. There were fifteen hundred inner-city ten-year-olds, at a big school auditorium, and the musical ran beyond imagination. I credit it all to the Baltimore Actors Theatre, because the three-dimensional stuff made it happen. And many of the kids in the audience were crying, and happy. They were really excited about it. And at the end I said, "Well, everybody gets these T-shirts who wants to be in it." And I suspect that everyone would have raised their hand even if I didn't have the T-shirts, that was the feeling I had. This was like extra. And they all screamed when they heard they got these T-shirts. I didn't have these T-shirts printed. (Softly) I had one; I had a sample. Talk about being over your head.

Well, the kids just thought this was so exciting and challenging and wild and fun and all the things I sort of imagined it might seem to them. The school couldn't believe it. Here are these kids who have little self-esteem, who are mostly flunking out, all excited about this program. Everybody's going to be in Magic Me, and they all want to go to the nursing homes.

Wow. I told them sort of on the spot that the next week I could only handle fifty kids at a time, in a classroom. I had no idea how I was going to talk to them, to actually be able to do some of this stuff. It was a little mind-boggling from the time of the musical to the next week.

The next week is the first seminar in the classroom. So I thought of a cute name, called "What's All This Geri-Stuff About, Man?" And it turned out to be an unrehearsed—I had all this thing planned (laughs)—how to get kids to see through the wrinkles and tears. And I got into the class, and the cameras were rolling, and there are all these officials from the mayor's office, and everybody looking at me. . . .

It was horrible (laughs). I'm subconscious to begin with. This is miserable. I just realized the way I would feel more comfortable is by fielding the kids' questions. And I realized while I was doing this, that this would become the way Magic Me was to be taught.

I started with, "What are your most horrendous fears about old people?" Specifically: talk to me; talk to me; talk to me. And these kids are saying exactly what they need to say. Like, "Somebody's going to die on me." Well, then we have to launch into a discussion about what it means for someone to die on you. And live out our worst fears.

"What are your worst fears about old people specifically?" I knew what was boiling behind these kids' scared faces. Like the smells. So I had to find a way to get the kids to talk about the smells. And I wanted to confirm their fears, and their impressions of how horrible it is, because it is! I don't want to tell them that the way a nursing home smells shouldn't bother us. It does bother us. That's a fact. "Okay, now what's the smell for? What is that smell when you walk into a nursing home?" And the kids say things like "ammonia," and "mashed potatoes," and "it smells like old cooking," and everybody's dying to say "urine," but nobody says it, and then I have to find a way to get them to talk about it. It's so much more effective than my trying to teach or preach.

It's all a fielding of the kids' questions and reactions. "What are your worst fears? What do you hear when you walk into a nursing home that scares you?" "Loud TV's, moaning, groaning, crying I hear," ta-da, ta-da, ta-da, ta-da. "Why do you think they're groaning? Let's imagine, bring it down to a specific person, Max at ninety-six, who's crippled, in a wheelchair, and his family doesn't visit him. What's a good reason that he's crying? Why should he be crying? Would he be right to be just kind of relaxed and happy-go-lucky and, 'Hey, how you doin'?' I don't think so. I think Max is reacting normally in certain ways." You give them a kind of optimistic way to look at everything that bothers them. And yet, at the same time, confirm that what bothers them is real.

That was the approach in the first session, and I found that it worked, it worked. I saw these kids still enthusiastic.

You didn't have a particular teaching background?

Zero. I didn't know how to teach. I'm a miserable teacher! I really am not a good teacher, but I think that what happens with kids in the classroom is they know I'm with them, they know I'm not on a higher level, I'm not a teacher; that I'm as helpless as they are, and scared, and weirded out, and I constantly remind them that I make all the mistakes in the world, so you guys are in at least as good shape as I am. With your creativity, only your creativity, in Magic Me can you do something to bring that person out.

Then I realized that the kids needed at least another session before we could go to the nursing home. I asked the kids what they needed to be able to go in, and they said, well, what are we going to do? I hadn't even visualized. And I realized that what I should go through with them in the classroom would be role-playing, that is to get the kids to actually feel the way, as much as they could, as the elderly do feel with limitations. Bind their hands; put them in wheelchairs; feel how it's like to walk around with weights on their legs; and to be blindfolded, and to have cotton in your ears, and stuff like that. Kids thought it was fun, I mean, all this physicality. Role-playing is great; kids just enjoy it, and really get something from it.

I made up the rules as I went, right: Magic Me never performs to old people, like singing Christmas carols to them, because that reinforces condescension; it suggests they can't sing or perform, so we do it for them. All the activities are participatory. So we're going to show them how to do disco with us. . . . They're just imagining this, they can't wait to go the next week. It was like the big mystery was going to be unraveled.

And we arrive at the nursing home the next week, after this role-playing. . . . The kids like start from scratch, the minute they walk in. They forget everything (laughs). They're horrified at the smell, the everything. And we had talked all about this, and they told me that it was okay, and it would be fine, but it wasn't (laughs). And they were all wearing their T-shirts, going, "I am me that's magic; I am Magic Me. I am me that's magic . . ." Right? Right? (laughs). And we kind of sort of huddled against each other, and walked around the elderly in the lounge who were arranged there, and the music starts to play, and in about seven minutes the kids loosen up.

And I say, "Okay, everybody, move out in front of one person." The music is playing. "Come on, everybody reach up, and if that person can't reach up, what do we do?" Mac, who is ten years old, says, looking at the woman in the eye, "Oh, well if you can't move your left side, it doesn't matter, you got a whole right side!" He had sort of the right spirit and attitude, and here's the street delinquent kid who is looking at this woman and going, "Come on, I bet you can, I know that you can. I mean, I'm Magic Me and you're Magic Me, and it's all cool." And this lady like with no energy, she reaches up and she waves her hand, and, you know, what that child feels I can't even begin to express. It's what I feel when I do it—the kind of self-confirmation and importance and value and that his particular kind of energy is received and matters, really changes that woman's attitude to a smile, something small like that—it is the world.

And it happens again and again and again. And all these surprised kids! All the kids are watching Mac through a corner of their eye, and they're doing it with their own people, and the guy that doesn't have any legs is no longer queer to the children, but he's the creative challenge.

Everybody rushes over to the more difficult cases. It doesn't matter if you don't have any legs—tap your hands on your wheelchair! That's great, you got it! And what happens, many of the elderly stand up, out of their wheelchairs, sort of get motivated to pick themselves up, and maybe three or four or five of fifty elderly are up out of their chairs, crippled, holding onto these kids with the Michael Jackson music and moving and dancing, and needless to say, it was a real experience.

I had to decide, do I take these kids to another nursing home the next week? No, they wanted to go back to the same one, because they were worried how their person was going to be next week. Four weeks, just to begin with. One school, one nursing home. And each week was a different activity. The next was poetry writing, where we sat across the table from the elderly; we need unusual themes that help them talk about what they're going through. So "How would it feel if you were the ocean?" the children would ask. And the children are trained to ask detailed questions: "What color blue are you as an ocean, and how big are your waves, and what do you see when you look up at the sky?"

Every week was another activity. The kids had been going on their own time, in the middle of the week, using their lunch money to take a bus to get to the nursing home before school. And by the last week, the kids were on their own, feeling very comfortable. They'd run into the nursing home, there was no huddling and distance. Each sort of hooked up with a person naturally, kissed and hugged and touched, in spite of a lot of the physical difficulties, and sat at the feet of wheelchairs and things. And the kids brought pictures and paintings and were very relaxed, and had quiet time.

CBS was doing filming in the meantime. I was exhausted (laughs). I was so thoroughly worried out and happy and strange. So I just breathed after these four weeks.

So that's what Magic Me is, that's how it began, and everything that has happened in different cities from this is very much the same. The whole program, even the littlest details, were really thought about, to just be joyful. Because it should be sort of a celebration, as opposed to a duty.

Obviously this was my program, so I paid for it. I didn't realize it was going to be successful, or bigger than a few schools in Baltimore, so it didn't mean that much to me to sink a few dollars in. And then—boy, from this article I wrote for the Brown magazine, a foundation calls me out of Washington, and said, "We'd like to come up and see you," and I said, "Sure, fine." Well, that's neat. I didn't even know how to approach a foundation (laughs); I wouldn't know now how to approach a foundation.

They called me! She said she was so moved by reading this article, the one that the CBS guy read, that she was crying; wow, maybe I should be a writer and forget the whole program (laughs). And she came up, and they ended up giving some money to Magic Me, this foundation did. She wrote the proposal, the woman who worked for the foundation. It's great. But most of the money has been my own, out of my pocket.

Now it's in all these cities, I have to go fund-raise; it's just too much to handle, there are thousands and thousands and thousands of T-shirts, and prizes, and sweatshirts for writing essays and stuff like this, and it runs into money, and buses, et cetera, et cetera, et cetera.

How much does it cost?

I can't even put a—I can't, I can't begin to describe. I don't even know. . . . I have no idea. I was safe when I was counting thousands of dollars, I mean, I knew that it was five or ten thousand the first year. And then lots of little people sent checks, like hundred-dollar checks, which we used quickly, because you can imagine, sending out a hundred T-shirts a week, it gobbles up a couple of hundred-dollar checks.

I have a business, which I run with my sister, my own business [in advertising specialities], and being involved in Magic Me takes up maybe eighty percent of my time. If I were working at Magic Me fifty percent of my time, I would have more money to pay for the Magic Me stuff; but because it's time-consuming, I always feel pressed, money-wise. So it's like as much as I can afford is as far as I stretch the Magic Me program. . . . So far there haven't been too many restraints.

If somebody had your idea, and had your energy and had your spirit, but no bucks to front—

They'd be better off. And I say that because if you don't have any bucks up front, there's no choice—to get the program off the ground, you have to set up a very professional fund-raising activity, even if it's just one grant. And you get that grant for hard things like an office, and a telephone, and mailing expenses, and a budget (laughs).

Better off with no bucks?

Yeah. Because it forces you to be more systematic in the beginning. . . . Or even if you have bucks, if I were smart enough in the beginning to set it up properly, it would have been neater, even though I had a few dollars to chip in.

I have no office; I have no professional organization; I don't—I don't have anybody to take requests for T-shirts and funds for buses. When I'm in Paris doing this, I have to do it from Paris to Nebraska! So I end up with, in a sense, a sloppier organization from the beginning; because I didn't have to ask for the bucks, I could do it out of my pocket, sort of without batting an eye at the beginning.

This year it cost (sighs) . . . (softly) about twenty-five thousand.

It's hard to see this as an official charity, because so much of it is Kathy-luxury. You know, it's like buying ice-cream sundaes, for myself. I mean, it's like spending money on something that's pure joy, for me, as opposed to seeing it as a profession. It's not a great act of courage to put some dollars into something that is this way. . . .

I am incorporated. I'm a nonprofit charity. In the meantime, the last year-and-a-half, I've been sort of tax-free under the Baltimore Community Foundation, which is where I funnel my money through. They're like an agent, a fiscal agent, and then they pay the bills from there.

Now, the reason that that was especially useful was when I went to Atari—Is this the right time to tell you?

I went to Atari six or seven months after the program began, the Warner Communication Foundation in New York. There was really nothing to lose.

They said, "Well, why do we want to hear about your program?" And I said, "Well, it will make your day happy" (laughs). Also the reason they met with me was I said I didn't want any money (laughs). I wasn't looking for money. They were so excited.

I had an idea; I wanted some Ataris, for the Magic Me program, in the nursing homes. And maybe, we could train the kids to train the old people how to use Ataris. They thought that was so novel (laughs).

And this woman in a nursing home in Baltimore—her brother, who lives in New York, called Warner also and said he wanted to be part of this meeting. He was like a testimonial, which is great—how his sister's improved, et cetera, et cetera.

I go and meet him, we went to Warner Communications, and they had a little board meeting. I showed them the CBS film and told them about the program, and they were really choked up. I was really nervous. I said, "Well, what I'd really like is, if you're really interested, I don't know if you have some spare Ataris, a few of those real nice coffee-table games, where on one side there's one player and another's another [player], and they could compete against each other. Maybe the kids could teach the old people and *maybe* we could have a story someplace, in some newspaper, that the old people develop better eye-hand coordination from their Atari game.

"And I know you're receiving some bad publicity about it's ruining kids' brains, and occupying too much of their good time, wasting it on these machines; this could be a way to use it in a very good context. And we could maybe take out the coin machines; it would be free, if you go to a nursing home to play it, to lure other kids in as well as the Magic Me kids. And it would be great stimulation for the old people."

Well, I sort of oversold it. I asked for four games, and I thought that was a lot, 'cause they're like three thousand dollars apiece. I was just a little nervous. So the seventy-year-old man who was there, claiming how wonderful his sister is because of me and the kids, et cetera, he's a businessman. So he said, "Four, no; I think we should have six Ataris." He knew that four was a ridiculous request when you've got them in your hands. These people were just sobbing.

But I thought I'd die. I thought that just ruined it. Six would be too many to ask them. I was the naive one.

They said they would call me back, and I come back to Baltimore. . . . The result was, they gave 250 of those games to the program, and they offered more, but the cost of the freight from San Francisco, which is where these things are stored, to here is immensely expensive. It's an all-glass top, and they're like 250 pounds apiece.

They also offered those big arcade ones, with the like stripes on the side, the lightning stripes; the supercharger, space asteriod. Can you imagine these things in nursing homes? We were imagining the old ladies, in the booth of the video game saying, "Come on, get that bandit! You got him!" and the sounds and the noise, stuff like that, to make nursing homes just more lively. It would be really fun. But I decided on only these [coffee-table] games, because I now know how to pick up the top and recircuit them to make the sound softer, so it's not offensive. You can slow down the action inside, and you can shift the game around so that it's really doable.

So, got the 250 here, stored them in Baltimore, the Baltimore Community Foundation was the official recipient. And we gave them out all over the Baltimore area to nursing homes, orphanages, hospitals, crippled children's centers. We had an application form for any agency in the Baltimore-Washington area that felt they could use these as therapy. And then we sent the rest of them to the Magic Me locations around the country.

The CBS piece that was aired a number of times, like a seven-minute feature, that was the most touching capsule to describe this program that I could imagine. I could never have paid to have that done. And I got phone calls and letters from this piece from the most remote places in the world, including Nebraska. And that was the first [place] I went to, cold.

There was a woman who worked in a nursing home out there, an activity director who was bored stiff. Nobody would come into her nursing home; and it was a good nursing home—she couldn't understand. And by accident she saw this thing on the CBS news and it took her a month or however long to get up enough courage to call me. And would I possibly be able to write a letter, or (in meek voice) maybe come out if I were ever traveling across the country.

I flew out in three days. How all this happened was sort of spontaneous, and ad-libbed. Here I was in a position in Nebraska to set it up all over again. I didn't know how to teach this to people out there: I needed volunteers; I needed the school system, the school board, the nursing homes, on and on and on.

It took a couple of visits out to Nebraska, and today that's the biggest area we have. This one woman who started that first phone call has spoken at all the conventions for the aging out there and to the activity directors. We just had a convention with like forty people who were involved in almost a full-time way as volunteers in small schools who call me and write me for T-shirts all the time.

The program spread into Kansas, and a woman whose child was in it in Nebraska last year moved to Iowa, and this woman started it in Iowa. So, one thing has led to another. . . . In terms of cities, I mean Nebraska alone is like fifteen cities. In each community, there are a handful or ten schools. It's hard to know the numbers exactly, but there's Stuart, Florida; Indiantown,

Florida, which are migrant kids; Baltimore; Old Saybrook, Connecticut; and Cleveland, and Memphis. . . .

And it's already started in three different areas in England.* These were really cold calls. They had not really heard of this. But it helped having received the President's award.† I went there, and set up a program which is very very similar to this one. I thought it would be interesting for my experience to learn about different cultures' attitudes toward the aging. Anyway. . . .

All right, ask me some hard questions.

✳

Kathy shows me a video clip from the CBS show. She is teaching, and she is red hot: she is wired. She says, "Being there is ninety percent of what I do." I don't think so.

✳

It takes a lot of energy. It takes a lot of time. It costs me a lot every time. One of the reasons that the work is appealing to me is that it is challenging in that way. And then another cost is that this work is intrinsically difficult. These people are moribund; they're going to die, soon. And getting attached to them has a built-in huge cost . . . some have died in my presence.

I'm thinking that maybe in the next six months I should hire someone to administer it, so that I can pump new ideas. I like to generate the ideas. The running of it is not so much fun. Now that I'm the administrator, and doing all this stuff, I can't stay here and spend the time with the people I care most about.

[It's] less fun. It's sending T-shirts, by hand; I go to pick the T-shirts up, and take them to the post office, and wrap one at a time (laughs); it's a real pain. And the keeping up with all the different people and their problems and situations all around the country—I don't have a secretary for that. It's a hassle.

But I can't allow myself to be bummed out. If it's a one-person activity, I can't afford to be out of service for two months. What I need to do, I've discovered, is find a way to see what is bumming me out and deal with it quickly, rather than indulging in self-doubt and depression; and that's really an indulgence—yeah, that's a real indulgence. Because there's a part of us that feels good by feeling how low we are at certain points.

---

*The program also started in France around the same time.

†Kathy was a citationist for the President's Volunteer Action Award in 1983.

That's one responsibility I have in Magic Me, is to stay buoyant. In my private world . . . (laughs), a lot of this gets to me, let me tell you. It's all worthwhile, but the depression sticks with me in a big way, and the many many many many many elderly that I see stick with me in a big way.

Because sometimes this work is so tragic—it's just by nature so heavy, because I'm involved all the time. It's difficult to keep enough distance—I really have to struggle to do that, to function. . . .

I have to force myself to be disciplined that way. I have to. Because it's me, and the whole program relies on me at this point. I take that very seriously. I feel it sometimes for a couple of months; I just don't want to deal—I mean, I don't know, I don't think it's a burnout syndrome, but it's a . . . it's dealing with so much overload that I can't express . . . I have to go to Nebraska when they need something. It's hard because it relies on only one person. It's very hard. . . .

But it's still in a forming state, it's still creative, and I'm still imagining what to do with it. It's still a baby. I assume that when it's ongoing, and I don't want to go to any more cities, and I'm just administering it, it might begin to be sort of burdensome or heavy.

And I still find it the freshest challenge to be in a new place, like Nebraska yesterday. It should have been the most horrible thing in the world, just to fly all the way out there in the rain and the floods to talk about Magic Me again, where they're mostly self-sufficient. But it's just so exciting to talk about the subject matter—it's so close to heart.

I have no deep affinity for aging per se. It just happened to be nursing homes.

Most people don't have some strange combination that makes me tick. Not that I'm better, but it's different. I really do have another drive, another urge, that I don't feel from other people. I would do a whole lot more—I'd go 150 yards, for this urge, where most people would maybe go ten. . . .

It feels needier than pleasant. I don't know. It's really a basic need, I have no idea. It might have to do with the fact that I cry at Russian music (laughs). I don't know. It's something very deep. I mean, it's like archetypal, Jungian. (Laughs) Way back.

If we could find ways to have people who are normally ten-yard runners to go 150, that would be a step.

Okay, some things I could identify:

First, identify what it is you care about a lot. If your interest is in the making it happen, more than what you care about a whole lot, it seems to be a more difficult task, because what keeps me going, I know, is the caring about it a whole lot.

Reinforcement helps a lot. I'm first to admit that acknowledgment from others whom you respect is important. So we might not only try to motivate individuals, but enlighten communities around these individuals, to pat on the back, to reinforce, to constantly encourage people for doing good work.

Goals. So much of this stuff is vague and nebulous. It's hard to grasp. If we can get some assistance in categorizing and seeing goals, projects that have beginnings and ends, so you feel like you're covering ground, it helps you breathe at the end, so you can start another movement. If there are no breathing spots, you just get tired of running. . . .

And packaging is critical. In this day and age, where there's so much media bombardment, it might be important from the beginning to hook up with someone who's got a particular media packaging skill, a creative talent, to work with you, if you don't have that skill yourself. . . . I would easily lend my services, in sort of a volunteer, friendly way, to help.

But my premise is that I'm not giving magic to anybody. And I mean this straight. It's my belief that everybody's got it, and it's latent, and I'm taking the cover off a particular segment of kids to let it happen. That's the same as in advertising—hitting the hot button, you know, getting that right spot on someone that allows them to breathe or buy or whatever.

And I really feel like I've found something instinctively that taps people's real desire to transcend. I think that human beings have an ability to transcend their specific lot in life. I mean, an *urge* to transcend, to get out of the mundane, to get out of the self—to supersede the bodily. And people do it in strange ways—they take drugs, they sing, they work hard at a job. Some of us use religion. For each human being, there is something that allows us to get out. The creative arts, maybe art per se, seems to be a quicker way.

To me, I think people need to be shaken, and told again and again and again, in every way imaginable, that you have an ability to see more! We've lost that these days. We've really lost that. We need to remind people that there are ways to get out. Society's giving the wrong message in a big way, or not enough of the right message to most people.

I'd like to systematize Magic Me more professionally than it has been. I should have a staff. It's a big decision, but the numbers are just so big now, I can't . . . I'm not as effective as I could be at this point. And it would also free me to explore some other ideas. While I've been doing this in the last few years, you can imagine, I've had a thousand untried ideas. If I had someone who could organize the day-to-day aspects, I could do some pumping into the cities in which we are already.

I don't want franchises and, you know, headquarters in Chicago and all the major cities in the country. I'm not caring about numbers; I really care about affecting a small community in a big way. I love the fact that it's in Nebraska City. I take one small community at a time. I gravitate to people who have small-town values. I like being around them.

But there's a musical that I've written for New York, that should affect a larger audience. A two-hour, full-scale, original musical, like for Broadway. It's about kids and the elderly, but if there's one message-message—big message—it's the preciousness of time. The reasons to celebrate. It's serious, and entertaining. I hope it's all of this. Right now I'm talking with agents, and I've written some of the lyrics with a partner, and we're looking for a composer in New York—so chatting with directors and producers at this point.

I see more cities, I imagine more cities. I imagine it bigger in Europe; I'm going to hit some third world countries. I'm planning a trip to India and to South Africa, which should be even more bizarre (laughs) than before. So I see it more places. I don't want to imagine too much because I really love the freedom of not having to follow a plan, but being flexible; if India becomes a focus, then focus on India. That's what keeps it fun and inspiring for me. So—I have a list . . .

I don't think Magic Me is any ultimate project; I think it's a good idea. I would love for the Magic Me people who are already involved to take an active role in catalyzing other activities of this nature, unplugging magic ability in their communities, in other fields. I'd like them to help others around them in their small radii, to make effective other people's dreams, to help explore other people's creativity. Maybe that's the biggest value Magic Me can have; I'd like to work at that more seriously.

I don't think it's the program of my life. It's teaching me an awful lot about me and about my world and how to put programs together. It could grow into something that's more ultimate, for my life. It could also stop where it is, sort of around this point, hold its own, and be runable by someone else. And I could go off and start something new. It's hard to see. Right now I feel I have all the energy in the world for Magic Me. I don't know. . . .

What sorts of things do you think that you have left to learn, Kathy?

Um . . .

Maybe nothing.

The field's so big. I'm having trouble talking about it (laughs). Where to start, okay, just plug a hole.

I need to learn how people who don't have my mentality, who don't have my almost selfish community approach, who are genuinely altruistic, how they work. I would love to take in some of that, to absorb some of the more genuine community spirit. I feel like I have a lot to learn in that regard.

Selfish?

If it's not self-fulfilling, I have trouble imagining working at it.

Whereas others are more purely altruistic?

More dedicated to the task, in spite of themselves. I sometimes find myself avoiding areas that I know won't be self-fulfilling, that really might be valuable to the program. I don't venture into [them as] boldly as I should, because I know it's just going to be one headache after another. Somehow there must be something I can learn about accomplishing what I need to accomplish even though it's not self-gratifying at that moment, or even ultimately gratifying.

To be the real community trouper, that's an essential for me.

So you don't define what you're doing as altruistic?

No, I don't. I *really* don't. I really—this is just pure Kathy-fun. . . .

I don't want to change what I have. I'd like to be enriched by being able to be more dutiful. Because I have the freedom to go as I please, and to do what I please, I do! But there's a part of me that would like to be even more dutiful, community dutiful.

You've given a lot of yourself.

(Laughs) Here's my liver, and my intestine (laughs). . . .

Renato Tonelli

It was just a response to a situation. What I would call grace.

Lucy Poulin

H.O.M.E.

I N our last account, we come to H.O.M.E., which literally stands for Homeworkers Organized for More Employment, but which factually and spiritually means much more.

When Lucy Poulin started H.O.M.E. in 1970, it was a crafts cooperative, a place where country people could sell home products to earn a little extra money. You need that money when you live in Hancock County, Maine; average per capita income is about four thousand dollars a year. It's one of the poorest counties in America.

The craft co-op still functions. But now there's also a food co-op, and a day-care facility. There are shops for woodworking and metalworking, for weaving, leather, and pottery, where goods are made and people are trained. At the Learning Center, you can choose among standard high school courses, or study home construction or chain saw safety. Tutoring in any subject is available, as is basic literacy instruction. There is a sawmill, a shingle mill, a homegrown wood industry. Volunteers build homes for poor families; land is assigned to a community trust. Firewood is delivered to those who can't get it. Shelter is given to the battered and homeless. A round-the-clock, all-purpose helping service fills in the cracks.

So jobs have been created; people have been joined. All buildings are raised by the members themselves, and all programs are run the same way. Hard physical labor is part of H.O.M.E., inevitably so, and deliberately. Hard work yields self-reliance; hard work alongside others yields community. At H.O.M.E., under Lucy's leadership, these three elements are fused.

Lucy Poulin lives a few miles from H.O.M.E., on a farm without a phone, at the dead end of a rocky road, one mile straight uphill. When

I arrive, Lucy emerges leading a magnificent horse—she grew up with horses; she teaches work horse management. She's wearing a brown beret, a workshirt, and torn jeans, atypical garb for a one-time Carmelite (now living outside the order). Her cabin, Covenant House, sits by a pond below. She's caring for her mother, who's staying with her, and who is very ill.

She is brief, terse, to the point that I think she's reluctant to talk at all. For the first time I'm almost out of questions. Only on third hearing of the tape do I start to realize her short replies mean there's nothing more to say. When she does speak, it's without pause or ramble, without ums or you-knows. There's a serenity in her remarks, which I've not found elsewhere. And yet she eyes the time closely; she's got other things to do.

Self-reliance and community, spirituality and hard work, serenity and task orientation—if all these pieces could blend in each of us gracefully . . .

We're back again in rural Maine, close to our starting point. Marti Stevens and Lucy Poulin, two single women about the same age, so different in style and in apparent substance. One built a theater, to nourish the spirit; the other made jobs, to nourish the body. But these capsules oversimplify, for results intermingle; both accomplished both ends.

These two women, like others in this book, started from very different places, but in both cases with few resources other than their own. If both had strength, they found it within, and along the way. At the end, both created community, vibrant and lasting community, where community was dormant before. Their work is outstanding, and yet it is duplicable; others now dormant can stand out and join them.

*

I'm trying to understand more about what it was in you that led to your getting involved in H.O.M.E. in the first place.

That's difficult. The question really could be important, or not. I don't really know, Bill. I think that the answers I would give would not be the ones you'd like to hear.

I would say mostly it was a question of grace, of being in the right place at the right time. I think that growing up the way we did, we learned certain things. We learned to work. And to work in situations that people would call hopeless.

I recall my mother having us jack the house when I was nine years old, and making a [cement] form with my brother Tony who was seven. The porch was collapsing, and the form gave way, and . . . I think it was a pretty hopeless situation, for a widow with eleven children, with very little income. But it was an attitude that we could do anything that we got from her.

And I was raised with that sense, that you just go and do it, no matter how difficult it is. And I've never gotten away from manual labor, and I now deeply believe, intellectually, philosophically, and spiritually that manual labor is where the solution is at.

First of all, if you go load wood with your son, you're going to have a different relationship than telling him it needs to be done. Something happens when you do manual labor together. Divisions among us are lost—I deeply believe that. Also, now, based on experience, I've made roof rafters with one group of people who consider themselves Marxist, and another group of people that consider themselves born-again Christian. But when they're pounding nails and building houses for people, and all doing the same thing, those word-ideas that divide us collapse.

I believe that we need to do more physical work: families do; community groups do. The crazy class system that we have—we have an educated type that never gets its hands dirty—is I think terrible, destructive, both for that person and for all the other people that just do the manual work all the time.

And I think one of the things that has made H.O.M.E. succeed is that we have a pattern somewhat different from other poverty agencies. We don't have middle-class people with liberal education running the place and drawing most of the overhead money in salaries. People with that background, we expect to come and work, because it's a privilege to do the work, as opposed to coming in on a salary to direct the place. In that sense, we're different. And that relates to the philosophy I have about manual labor.

Having grown up with that appreciation of manual labor, you could have become a manual laborer—you could have become a roofer, or a carpenter, or some other trade.

Well, I do all those things. I can do masonry, I can work horses. And it's extremely fulfilling, though I'm not bound to it. I can go wash dishes to earn my bread labor, but I can still have the privilege of doing some of these other things I like and enjoy.

I went to a New York City high school, and also a Catholic girls school in Manhasset, Long Island, just because my sister was dying of cancer and I was helping take care of her. In a big family, you go and take care of each other.

What I decided was—I never forgot it because I still believe in it—was that all the ideas that people were learning and collecting and passing in to get grades were meaningless, and what was really important was to take one [idea] and truly live it. I still believe that. Just to get grades really didn't affect or change their lives. So that profoundly influenced me, when I was quite young.

But I think I was also gifted in that I grew up in a family where people read. So when I worked in a factory, which I did for ten years, I would read a book or two a week. And have some kind of a self-education; in other words, though I've never been to college, I don't feel any limitation in terms of education, or intimidated by it. So I think I was extremely fortunate to have that balance.

For a brief time I was a maid in Newport, Rhode Island, with the really rich. And then I was on Long Island with middle-class people, getting on the bus with the black people who were going out to be the maids of the rich people in Manhasset. I think I learned more from those experiences of seeing what society was really made of than what I learned at school.

Then I went back to my mother's farm and I went to work in the factories, and I worked until I was twenty-six. When I left the farm, it was in somewhat good shape, because I started a business there; one of my brothers has taken it over.* And then I joined the Carmelites, who at that time were a contemplative group of nuns who also did manual labor to support themselves.

We did home work. They [the Bangor Shoe Company] delivered the work, 'cause it didn't get by all the union regulations. You know how it works. So we did it at the monastery, and other women did it at home.

When the shoe factory did close [in 1970], two things [happened] I think: one elderly woman came to our door and said that she could make quilts and could we help her sell them—somehow she had the idea that we could help people earn money. And the other thing is that the group of us, myself and two other sisters, thought, if we can make crafts, why don't we sell them and help other people? So that's how H.O.M.E. came to be. . . .

But it turned out to be your idea rather than theirs, and that's what I'm trying to learn a little bit more about.

I think it just emerged and grew out of the meeting. Rather than thinking, well, gee, we've got a brilliant idea, let's go do this—it just happened. It was just a response to a situation. What I would call grace, or what Einstein calls intuition—he never credited his intellect for any great discovery. He said it was the gift of his intuition, in a very beautiful way, and I think those things are gifts, nothing we could credit ourselves with.

---

*Lucy started a successful horse-breeding farm as a high school student. In factories, she cut gizzards from chickens, and packed paper plates for eight years.

Did you have any particular image in your head at the time about what you would like to see happen?

No. No. No, just to have people be helped and be happier. Truly. . . . Then it just grew and grew and grew. And more people came, and it continued to grow. . . . You can see for yourself.

*

What I see at H.O.M.E., a few miles from Lucy's farm, is a nineteenth-century American village. But this one functions for local people; it's not a re-creation. Picture a cluster of buildings in a rough circle off the main road. Clockwise, facing east: office, food co-op, gift store, learning center, weaving shop, woodshop, cows, private home, pottery shop, chapel, cobbler shop with duck decoys. Other work goes on outside the village.

H.O.M.E. is busy and relaxed, not so busy that artisans won't stop to talk. They certainly seem glad to be there. I feel disoriented in time. I'm not sure whether H.O.M.E. is anachronism or harbinger. Possibly it's both.

*

Some people when they're designing programs write down plans and outlines: *I, a, b, c, II,* stuff like that. And I guess other people are more seat-of-the-pants in the way they work, things sort of flow. Do you see yourself as fitting into one or the other category?

I think I fall into the peasant category in terms of how my intellect works. I have to catch up to it, or it has to catch up to me.

You must remember that I came from a family that was very poor, and lived on a farm all my life. And one of the things that struck me [was that] H.O.M.E., and the idea of cooperatives, really excites and thrills middle-class people, or people who are liberals. This new group of people I began to meet, who had all the ideas—I had never met people who had so many ideas. But also, I had not met people whose emotions were out of touch with their ideas.

I had grown and lived and worked with people whose emotions weren't always beautiful or good—I lived with people who were much more gutsy. So I was not exposed to a class of people that bewildered you. I grew up, if it was going to rain you got the hay in. Well, we could sit and talk all day, these liberal educated people; and I guess my push was if they want to join us—and they have made an incredible contribution to H.O.M.E.—they gotta work.

They've got to do work. They all want to come in and teach, they all got all the answers. Their attitude about themselves is one of privilege. They're going to come and teach the poor people. Well, I think they've got to come and learn. Now you see my prejudice.

Were there any particular turning points you can identify that were really important in getting the program off the mark, any events that you especially remember?

I can't think of any, Bill, which is awful, 'cause I think it just kind of grew.

Or if there was maybe one event that stands out for you, or a moment that really made you feel happy, a glowing inside?

Well, we have so many people. It's mostly changes in the people, and the good things that happen in their lives. And there are a lot, hundreds of incidences. . . .

Recently I went with a group of volunteers and cut and split an elderly woman's wood. And she watched us every minute. She could hardly walk, but she sat out on the logs. It's just a thrill—it was a real privilege to be there.

We cut her wood, we stacked it around her little trailer, and she had this beautiful fence where the wood all stacked up. So that was a great event, a couple of weeks ago.

I think money always has been a problem, how to meet the payroll, to do what we need to do. But we always seem to solve that problem. It's always been a crisis with us, having enough money. But we smooth through. Again, it's the only alternative—do something when the time comes. . . .

Oh, we had opposition. We had strong criticism from the town; the local Catholic priest at that time felt we were terrible. He felt . . . that we were different. There was a lot of movement going on here. And whenever you take a quiet community, and all of a sudden something just blossoms up, people are afraid. We're a pretty passive people, the Americans of our age, I think.

Whatever your prejudice is, it's easy to find it with a group of people at H.O.M.E. We're not wearing conventional dress. [If you don't like] the dirty poor, well, we're dirty, and we're poor. So we've been subjected to all those prejudices. But it hasn't prevented us from doing good things that are helping a lot of people. Truly.

The local priest right now is extremely supportive, but it's been thirteen years since we've had any real support from the priest. And that's hard. It makes the townspeople think less of you. And there continues to be real prejudice against us. But also there is community support.

The old Mainers had an openness and a generosity of spirit; and I think our country and our time enormously needs people who are generous in their observations and their spirit. But I think we have a class of people who are now in control who are just reactionary; their judgments are incredible, about other human beings. And I don't know why that's happened.

You mean reactionary not simply politically, but reactionary in spirit?

Yes, I think so. And I can't tell you why. The old-timers weren't—you talk to my mother. It was live and let live, and help someone if you can, and don't judge them too harshly, they have their reasons. Not this group. It's incomprehensible to me, but anyway it exists, and I don't think it's peculiar to Orland, Maine. It seems to be pretty broad-based.

Did you have doubts?

Oh, all the time. . . . I continue to have doubts. Oh, about everything. . . .

How do you deal with them?

I just keep at it (laughs). Let them filter in and filter out. . . .

Do you feel despair?

Sometimes. Not a great deal, but once in a while, I do. . . . I try to hand it over to God. And then I keep working. What else have we to do?

Hand it over?

Hand it over. Why own it? (laughs).

When you were developing the program and helping to make it grow, were you conscious of using any particular techniques, strategies, tactics, in terms of making things happen?

Not that I can think of, to tell you the truth. . . . Well, I think one thing that happened is that we've attracted some extraordinary people.
You see, it isn't just me. Phil Gray, who heads up the construction— I don't think anyone ever thought he was ever a success in his life. And he came to work for us, and he is extraordinary. He's worked with thousands of people to create the village and do the construction. I also think that Phil has an attitude about doing things which is like mine—maybe it's Maine people. People do it, they don't talk about it. It's not [that] we consider something all day. We go do it.
So I think Phil is only an example of many people who came to work at the co-op. I think Phil Gray is an unusual man. I think the woman marketing the crafts is an unusual woman. And extraordinary people. You get a lot of

people around who have some zest and push, and when they work together, then miracles happen.

So then how do you get more systems like H.O.M.E. on a national level?

It's a lot of hard work, and a lot of faith. You got to believe in it. It can't be justified by textbooks, or by rational planning.

The work has been extremely hard, but there was no one stopping us from what we wanted to do other than ourselves. I guess that's what I'm trying to say. I think people have to just push, and make it happen (laughs).

So when I give you a prod to itemize technique, *a, b, c, d,* and you come up with not very much, that may relate to the whole bias of acting versus talking.

I don't know if it's that simple. I really don't. But I think if we were analyzed by an accounting firm today, they might tell us to cut out half of what we're doing. That we'd be sound and healthy if we did.

Rightly so?

I think so. But I think it would kill the spirit of the place. Somehow that struggle, the struggle to do more, and to be more helpful to people, that's very life-giving. It kind of intrigues and fills the spirit. And I think we've let the accountants take over the world. It's not a bad profession, though.

So the making of mistakes is part of what contributes to the spirit of the place?

I think so. . . . Or the risk.

Going out and doing it because it needs to be done, rather than sitting back and planning it—that could be a very optimistic way to live a life.

I think so. Yeah. I think so. I think that I am an incurable optimist, and that I'm always full of hope. I recall someone saying of my mother, "eternal hope"; in other words, they were almost putting her down. But I think that's really a gift she gave us, that we could just make the most of things, and do what you can, and I would credit her with giving us that sense, that we can do it.

I believe most human beings are intelligent, have a real desire to be good, have a real desire to help people and to be part of community; but our society creates, and I don't have all the right words, systems and cultural conditions that prevent us from being good.

Try to drive through Boston: you have to hate people, you've got to run them over and hit them, don't you? The only way I can drive in Boston is to take the old truck down there. I don't want to drive that way, I don't want to run over people. I don't want to go on the subway and push people around. I do believe it's in every human being to be helpful, to be good, to be generous. But our society just cuts that right out.

It destroys [basic human goodness] by competition and by upward mobility, by greed, by money. The greed that capitalism breeds, and there's no other word for it—step on your neighbor to make money kind of thing. It's a sin. I think we live in a sinful society, and now it's just going crazy. I deeply believe that.

There are wonderful people working in human services, doing wonderful and compassionate things, but I don't think that's the real solution. And I think the maze of government programs that came out of the sixties have done little to radically transform the lives of the poor. We've just created a whole bureaucracy of middle-class people and social workers and counselors who serve this other group of people who are chronically poor. Now, what's the difference? I think there's something *fundamentally* wrong.

So I'm trying to envision what the ideal system would be.

The ideal system. Well, I can't create the ideal system, but I think an economic system that had an equal amount of investment in cooperation as opposed to competition, and that put an equal amount of emphasis on the fair distribution of goods and services and education, rather than the unequal distribution we have now.

So if there were a change in the economic system, the human service system would change?

Certainly. Don't you think it would?

So how do you go about creating systems which unlock . . .

Well, I think you have to create community. So if you organize a work to be done, then community happens in the struggle, working for the common good. I guess it's that basic.

Is the desire for community the same here as it would be in an urban setting? Or stronger?

I don't know. But I think that the need for community is a basic human need.

A community like H.O.M.E., or other types of community?

Well, I think it's just being accepted and knowing people, and having friends, and working together.

Same stuff all over the world?

Yes.

Human nature?

Yes.

So how do you go about creating or encouraging people like your-self, as one example, who will go out and do things related to what you've been doing?

Well, I don't know what the right word is, but it would be almost like encouragement, a persuasive encouragement to go try it. For their own sakes; forget about helping anybody else. And then see what happens.

Where does that encouragement come from?

Well, it ought to come from religion. It's the very basis of Christianity, and the problem is it's not lived by any of the Christian churches. To me that's the great tragedy. But if you know anything about Christianity, that's the basis of it; love your neighbor; and what you have, you want for your neighbor, right? It's that simple. The problem is no one lives it, or even takes it seriously. It's too bad, isn't it? It's a tragedy, really. . . . (birds chirp)

Was your position as a Carmelite at the time a help, you think, in terms of getting H.O.M.E. started?

No, I don't think so. . . . But one of the things I took very seriously was the Gospel. And I still do. I think it was a good experience for me to be [in the Carmelites], and it was meant to be in a sense. I feel it was one of those things that's beyond a rational understanding, and I think that was true for me.

"It was meant to be." Do you mean that it was ordained?

Maybe. I don't know. I think "ordained" is an awful word. I think things are meant to be, and you just accept them. Right? There must be things in your life that you just accept. You don't know why—and you just accept them and keep going. You don't think about them too much; they're almost givens.

Is it possible to create an organization like H.O.M.E. without re-ligious faith?

I think so. Because I see there's only a few people at H.O.M.E. who have beliefs similar to mine. But there are many people at H.O.M.E. who have the will and the commitment and the desire who don't call themselves religious. And who are just as generous and just as understanding and just as compassionate as any of the rest of us. And that's very beautiful and very humbling.

They don't call themselves Christians?

Not at all. No.

But yet they have the same qualities?

Yes. . . . God only knows (laughs). It's wonderful, isn't it?

Some people, in choosing how to invest their energy in the world, would put it into something more on a national scale, or even on a global level. Whereas your focus has been mostly local. So I'm wondering how one makes the choice of the scale.

I haven't thought about it much. Only that I think the way I function is at the personal level. On the immediate level. So I guess I can only think in terms of the local level.

Would you be doing more good if you were going around the country teaching other people how to set up H.O.M.E. co-ops in other states?

I don't know. I'd say God only knows.

Or, would it be better to invest one's energy toward creating employment on a national scale?

It maybe would be. But I wouldn't know how to do it (laughs). I'm teasing (laughs). I think again my response is to the people in front of me; and maybe I can't make that leap into the numbers and the causes—it's too impersonal for me.

A [similar] thing I've been thinking of is—I don't feel comfortable with the word, but I don't have a better one—how you "measure" the social good that one does. How do you assess that?

God only knows. I don't know. I don't think about it very much. I personally feel that the way I'm living and what has happened has been quite a privilege for me, in terms of what it's done for me.

So for example, I was reading the sports pages last week, and I was thinking about Joan Benoit as a current example.* She creates social

---

*Joan Benoit Samuelson, the long-distance runner, a native of Maine, had then just won the women's marathon in the 1984 Olympics.

good through her running, because people pay attention to her and admire her for her courage, I guess.

Yeah, I think so.

Is there a way of comparing that to a person involved in social service work in terms of measuring. . . ?

I couldn't. Could you? No, I couldn't.

There's a part of me that would like to say, let's take personalities out of it, that a certain type of work has more social value than another type of work.

You see, I would question making that comparison.

That it's presumptuous?

Well, I think the way Jim Rice conducts himself on the field has great social value.* He's a gentleman. His being a human being of some maturity and some gentleness must be tremendous for hundreds of thousands of young people. That I think has tremendous social value. I think the way he conducts himself is unusual. Win or lose or whatever.

So in terms of making a contribution to society, one could do so—

By who they are. How they live. It tells more about what kind of person you are. How you do anything. Though I mean, if you want to get into measuring prople, and I think that's the realm of the divine and not me and you, certainly to go help people who are cold is more important than playing baseball, or running in a road race. Let's be honest, all right? In one sense. Someone's freezing to death, and you keep them warm, is more important than running half-dressed around the town or doing the marathon, let's be honest. That's what I think.

But people are who they are. And I think what's critically important, is to be who God is calling you to be.

How do you know what God is calling you to be?

I don't know, I suppose every person has to deal with that. I think we know—I think we have approaches. We don't become Richard Nixon overnight. It's a series of decisions. We become the choices we make.

Have you thought of what you might want to see happening three or four or five years down the road for yourself, and your organization?

---

*Rice, the Boston Red Sox outfielder. Just before this part of the conversation, Lucy had volunteered, "I love the Red Sox," and asked about the previous night's game results.

I think that immediately we want to do some of the things we're doing better, and certainly to continue to build more homes—people are desperate for homes. The family violence and abuse is oftentimes related to [not] having a home and space. So I'd want to see us build hundreds of homes and houses. I'd like to see everyone without a home have one.

Of course, we can never do that. What we're doing is a drop in the bucket. But I would like to see that really grow.

I think people should have employment; they should have education; they should be able to have housing, instead of social workers and counselors. . . . It sounds too simple, but I think it is simple. I think that it is.

I think we need to create systems where it's easier for people to be good. And I think H.O.M.E. is such a system, though it's incredibly imperfect; it's kind of an experiment that we fashioned. But it's desperately needed. And I think you turn people loose—and you don't have to give them a lot of monetary rewards. We don't; what do we pay people, the minimum wage? They'll perform miracles. . . .

I keep thinking the time will come when it would be better for me not to be here. But every time I kind of make a little break away, I get kind of called back, as a helper.

Part of you is tempted to make a break?

No, not make a break, it's just to be open to change. But I don't know anymore. I keep thinking it's best not to. I just take one day at a time. Let it happen.

So what is it that sustains you? I guess what I mean is that there aren't a whole lot of people who start something and stay with it for fourteen years.

What sustains me is the people. The friendships, the love and affection, and the people.

And I think that it must be God, and I think it's a mixture for all of us, but those two things are a real mixture. God gives us life: you wake up in the morning, with ideas that are gifts, and with hope that's a gift, and with energy that's a gift, and with enthusiasm, that's a gift, and go out and work on that and give it back (laughs softly).

I almost ran out of questions . . .

(Laughs) Good.

What else should we talk about?

I can't imagine (laughs). . . .

The State of the Art

QUESTION: Suppose someone asked you to summarize, or put in a nutshell, the main lessons you've learned—the things that would be most important for others to know for their own community work. What kinds of things would you say?

MARTI STEVENS: "You can offer sort of tidbits, hors d'oeuvres or samples. But it's got to come from the community. I don't think you can go in and tell the community that they want theater, whether they want it or not. I'd offer that sampling and see if I was good enough to meet what the community wanted. If I was willing to do what the community wanted. And then ask the community to grow with me.

"You've got to say, 'Is this something you need as a community?', without going in and saying, 'You need it.'"

HENRY WARE: "Having role models you can choose from is very important. And of course, you have to have people with the ability, and people with the persistence, and also people who are willing to roll with the punches. You have to be sensitive enough to not be too stubborn—you have to have persistence, but yet not stubbornness.

"And communities change, and every community is different. Don't you think so? Yeah. And I don't see any way of formulating a panacea which can be applied to every community."

VIN QUAYLE: "Whenever anyone comes in and asks, 'How do I begin this?', I say, 'The first thing you gotta do is commit ten years of your life to it.' The rest is easy. The rest is easy.

"I guess the belief that you can do it [also]. That you can make a difference on it. And the commitment of time, the long haul. If you have those two, the rest begins to fit into place, begins to make sense.

"Without those two, if you don't have those two, you got a real handicap startin' out. And then all those other things become important: being able to pace yourself, having fun, dealing on a real issue that people feel. Bring in friends—don't try to do it yourself, you know. Get a couple of others who believe in what you believe, do it together. And then sit down and figure out, where are your strengths? Our strengths were totally obvious—priesthood, church. They were ours. Drawing those supports.

"Barring death and serious illness, I think we can do anything. Absolutely. Any problem that comes up on a community level. I think we can—we can't solve it totally, 'cause it's not a perfect world. But we can make a difference."

CHICK COLONY: "Well, the enthusiasm of the organizers is what made it go, set the pace for it; without that it would have been different. And I think there's a fine balance that you have to strike between overplanning and underplanning something. We planned thoroughly enough so that it would work, but not so [much] that those doing it burned out on it."

RAY SHONHOLTZ: "I don't think it can be capsulized (laughs). We've learned a lot. It's been like going to graduate school and taking ten courses of graduate study. . . .

"Lessons, is that what you're saying? Well, it's definitely increased my faith in the capacity of people. I definitely have a stronger respect and appreciation for the kind of creative genius that people have, once they start working. That there is no limit to what people can do if they feel they are powerful in relation to the work they're doing. . . . That's been a very important recognition.

"I'm trying to think now . . . opportunities to leverage your work should always be seized whenever possible. At all points. All the time. Because there're not that many opportunities, and the opportunities will build on one another, the more often you do it. So you're the captain of a ship, and anything that will enhance the direction in which it's going, all the foreign affairs of it, should be seized. You don't want to be so myopic as to say the work is so valuable, it will necessarily speak for itself."

DAVID YORK: "The first thing that bounced right in my head is don't try it alone. You have to have a support system of your own."

PHYLLIS YORK: "The other thing I thought of, you have to have a problem with enough people connecting to it. Um—you also have to find enough helpless people (laughs) who want to have fun."

DAVID: "And maybe to be stupid enough to believe in yourself."

PHYLLIS: "Yeah. Or just to know that how it's been is no good. It has to be really important to you. Very important. At that time I think it meant to us life and death—I really do."

DAVID: "It's been exciting, which has allowed us to keep going. But when you start out to change communities, you'd better be prepared for an awful lot of hard work."

PHYLLIS: "You know what else I think? Don't worry about the present system. Don't concern yourself with that at all. Just do what it is you're going to do, if you can find people who will do it with you. And the system will have to come around."

DAVID: "Yeah, if what you've got is any good, yes. . . ."

PHYLLIS: "And don't worry about being a charlatan, 'cause you'll certainly feel like one. So . . ."

LUPE ANGUIANO: "Well first, it would be the attitude, the positive attitude. Second, it would be a strong determination to accomplish what you want to accomplish. And third a very very realistic assessment of who you're working [with], and what it takes to make that happen.

"The struggle is always going to be there. The struggle of, you know, it can't be done, the messy welfare system, raising money and all that. You have to be determined that you're not going to let those obstacles deter you from what you want to accomplish."

LOIS GIBBS: "The bottom line is to organize, to talk to people. If you have a problem, talk to people. And people together will resolve it. Standing alone won't."

FRAN FROEHLICH: "Well, I think that it is a long-term struggle. To remember to celebrate, I think that's very important. To not take ourselves too seriously, so that you can't laugh at yourself, or laugh at your mistakes. 'Cause you'll burn out in no time, a couple of years (laughs). And to develop an ability, I think, to take risks, without getting attached to the outcome, expecting a particular outcome. There's gotta be some resiliency, or it'll lead to burnout.

"And in all those things, you know, to take care of yourself somehow; and I think celebrating does that, not taking yourself seriously does that. Some of those problems will take care of themselves if you take care of yourself. Again, or burnout occurs, and then nobody has anything."

CURTIS SLIWA: "In order to be really successful, you've got to concentrate your energies on one thing and to do it very well, come hell or high water, and not giving a damn what anyone else thinks. You can't go on to something else until you have achieved doing what you set out to do. As long as what it is is righteous, and it's not hurting anybody.

"So forget what the mayor or the police chief or your local city council person or your alderman says, you don't need their help to do it. It's just that you have to expect that if it is a new or bold or unique concept, they're going to take the traditional form of being opposed to you. You may not get their support until two or three years down the line when you've proved yourself.

"There's nothing wrong with being an outcast at first, as long as you do what you say you wanted to do."

FRANK BOWES: "You want to sell people on your idea. Okay . . . Tell them that the greatest thing they could ever get in this world is a good feeling about themselves. Is that the nutshell you were looking for?"

WALLY OLSON: "Well I'd say that first of all, treat other people the way you want to be treated. Don't be waiting for somebody to show their love, which everyone in the world does. Forget it.

"If you will go forward and try, to the best of your ability, to make people happy and do things that are nice for people, don't worry. Don't even think of nothing else, you know why? You will be happy.

"You know how I feel in my heart? I love everyone to love me, 'cause I love everybody. But you know something? If no one loves me, that's too bad. But I'm still gonna love 'em anyway."

ELLEN CASSEDY: "The truth is that you can be a regular person, and lead a pretty normal life, and be active in social change. Early on, I thought I'd have to make a choice: am I going to care about myself, or am I going to give up all my personal concerns and dedicate myself to helping other people? It was almost like deciding whether to leave civilization and go off in a wagon train, or something like that.

"But in fact, it's not an either-or proposition. I have a family, and I have many interests, and over a long period of time I have incorporated social change work into a very satisfying life. And of course, 9to5 made it even more satisfying."

MIMI FARIÑA: "I would emphasize individuality. I think people are most successful when they can stay true to themselves, and follow what their personality traits are.

"And it takes a great deal of desire or inspiration. Combined with the technical capabilities of running an office. And I really mean running an office, not getting together and gabbing. Comprehending what suits you—you know, how structured you can be, before it's uncomfortable, and going with that as your own formula."

HOMER FAHRNER: "Well, what they're going to ask you is how do you start a gleaning organization—this is the question I get. I'm saying first, right out, when the crops grow, go out and see those people and *persist*. Because one turns you down, maybe he's got a good reason. Go on, go on, go on."

HAROLDLINE TROWER: "Well, if you can get people that can work well together, you know, get rid of all the little petty things, and just get down to working, I think you can do just about anything you want to do. 'Cause you got good people that care. You're gonna find them everywhere—you don't know where you're gonna find them at, but don't ignore anybody.

"And when you come together, work as a group, instead of just trying to do something by yourself. 'Cause that's a losin' battle, just one person, 'cause you'll knock your brains out. You get yourself a good group of people together, working together, and then you can get things done, that's how I feel."

BILL SAMPLE "Be sincere in what you're doing. Be in love with the work you're going to start."
HELENE SAMPLE: "Care about what you're doing."
BILL: "And like I say, don't just do it for—"
HELENE: "Personal reasons, or your own ego. Put yourself last."

KATHY LEVIN: "Uh (sighs) . . . Nothing really important comes easily. The important parts of it don't come easy at all. The less significant parts are a breeze. And I know that if I haven't struggled, and I've got something that seems to be big, I second-guess it, I assume that it's not what it appears to be and usually I think I'm right."

LUCY POULIN: "I think to trust in people, and in their ability to be good, to be responsible. And to encourage that."

Conclusions

Interpreting the Stories

TIME permitting, an interviewer could fill a small bookshelf with stories like these, perhaps a larger one. That is, there are hundreds or thousands of local heroes who could have appeared in this book, but did not. Each one of them, just as those who did appear, could have offered fresh insight into the nature of community work, or the nature of heroism, or both.

But at some point you need to stop and make do with what you have. The hope is that from the stories assembled, common themes emerge. Though each account may be revealing in itself, together they should also have some cumulative meaning, some collective weight. We would like to generalize beyond these stories, to make broad and penetrating thematic statements that will be useful to others, and to trace out their implications; that is our task here.

It's a hazardous task. Most generalizations need qualification, and ours will be no exception. We'd like to claim the world, but it can't be done; yet we don't want to claim too little either. So it's probably best to get the qualifications fully out in the open before proceeding further:

Since no standard definition of "local hero" exists, we can't be sure that our stories here are representative of local heroes in general. The sample is small to begin with; nor can we be certain what a representative sample would consist of. Would we reach the same conclusions had we chosen another set of people? It's convenient to think so, but we can't know definitely.

And since the subjects described here are thought to be exceptional by definition, we can't be sure that any conclusions carry over to those who are less exceptional—that is, to most day-to-day community workers, and therefore to most day-to-day community work.

Within the interviews, all subjects will choose what they wish to reveal about themselves; their statements may not mesh well with other versions of the same events. We've not tracked down those other versions, nor sorted out conflicting accounts. We've not aimed for a definitive history of any community program, but have instead taken each subject's word at face value.

Subjects can and do change their minds. Their beliefs about community work and their own roles may evolve, which is a natural process. And programs change, too. Had each subject been interviewed a year earlier or later, or three or five, different statements might have been offered; beliefs might have been shaded differently. One interview is only one snapshot.

Finally, while a few accomplishments described were true solo flights, most founders here would not have been founders without a lot of help. The early supporters and the present-day staffers may be just as caring and just as talented; their contributions may have been crucial for program success. We have emphasized the individual at the possible expense of the group, and of other outside determinants.

So having gotten these caveats out of the way, and based simply upon the interviews collected here, what can we learn from these exceptional cases? What distinguishes the local hero from anyone else? And how does the local hero work in the world differently from you or me?

I hope it will come as no great surprise that the distinguishing marks are hard to find.

Differences

The fact is that the differences among those interviewed stand out at least as clearly as the similarities. Local heroes can be, and are, of either sex, of any race, of urban or rural background, of virtually any age or education or occupation. They span the demographic scales. They don't seem to cluster in any one group.

Their approaches to community work also vary widely. It's fun for some (maybe most), but not fun at all for others. It's hard for some, a constant struggle, but for others things come easily. Some had a clear intent at the start, others had an intent that differed from results achieved, or had no particular intent, and were gradually drawn in. Some came from the political left, but others from the political right, others still from the center or from no discernible position at all. Most would do it again; but a few would not.

And having started, they reached their destinations by different pathways. Organization could be loose or tight. Growth could be ordered or haphazard. Funding could be public or private, big or small. Membership could be broad or narrow, or nonexistent. Success could lead to distant chapters, or to imitators in other cities, or to no geographical branching at all. In short, styles and structures vary, a lot.

So the local hero is not of one kind. Detailed biographical interviews, or lengthy questionnaires—neither attempted here—might have yielded more similarities than apparent in this review. The origins of local heroism, of social action in general, may go back to childhood; as far as this investigation goes, that remains an open question.

Yet a good case can be made for the acceptance of differences as real, and also consequential. Experience suggests that if we consider most fields of endeavor—teaching, gardening, bus driving, writing—we're likely to find variations just as broad. Moreover, the particular evidence on citizen action, or on helpfulness in general, does not point to a single personality type.[1] Without attempting to survey all the literature, we can highlight some illustrative examples:

In a recent study of people who risked their lives to shelter Jews from the Nazis during World War II, the authors conclude:

> Up to the time of their heroic deeds, they lived ordinary lives and, on the surface, at least, were very similar to everyone else. The motivations of rescuers cannot be reduced to a formula or explained by any single personality characteristic or type.[2]

Or in an interview with a case investigator for the Carnegie Hero Fund Commission, which makes annual awards for physical bravery, to the Lenny Skutniks of our society:

> If I could deduce a common quality about these people, I'd tell you. But I can't. They're pretty ordinary folks.[3]

Consider also the lives of the saints—human beings, later canonized—who as a group were distinguished community workers, early models of local heroism. In her study of sainthood, Phyllis McGinley writes:

> Francis of Assisi was a gay rake and prodigal. . . . The Portuguese John of God was a gambler, a drunkard, and a mercenary. . . . At once so alike and so diverse are the personalities of my heroes that no pope or bishop or even fellow saint can say dogmatically, "Do this, renounce that, and you will be called blessed."[4]

And commenting more generally on these and related findings, Ervin Staub, a leading scholar on altruism, alludes to varied heroic origins:

> Goodness, like evil, often begins in small steps. Heroes evolve; they aren't born. Very often the rescuers [and other heroes] made only a small commitment at the start. . . . But once they had taken that step, they began to see themselves differently, as someone who helps. What starts as mere willingness becomes intense involvement.[5]

That, in many ways, is how we view the process of social action in this book.

To the extent the differences among heroes are real, they are not very helpful for someone wanting to spot the local hero, as in a field guide. But the lack of external specificity has possible advantage. It means that heroic markings might be internal, and that many of us might carry them. Local heroism may be largely a matter of calling up qualities already inside you and exercising them fully. It's an optimistic view: the potential for distinguished community action might be widespread.

Similarities

Still, in all this variation, certain themes do emerge, in low relief at least, and rising beyond the attributes of the local hero as previously defined. They may not be present in all interview subjects, and they may be neither necessary nor sufficient for success. But they're on the scene enough of the time in enough of the people that we suspect they are not chance visitors, but rather somehow related.

We want to be careful how we introduce them. They're not the only themes, for a complete accounting of similarities would fill its own volume. They are admittedly impressionistic. But they are themes which catch the eye, more than once, and which as a group are also relatively neglected in the community service literature. They deserve more attention. So these relative similarities across our subjects, or themes underlying successful action, are offered briefly here not as definitive facts, but rather as propositions supported by some evidence which are worthy of fuller consideration and of further investigation.

Several of these themes are demographic, based on prior history, and in that sense are external qualities.

Low domestic obligation. Relatively speaking, that is. Of the twenty subjects, ten were then single. Of the ten who were married, only four then had children living at home. As Marti Stevens says, "Just logistically, [community work takes] plenty of time"; she doesn't need to get home to feed the kids. Simple behavioral ecology, but worth restating.

Intimate relations burn psychic energy. Nuclear families take up more. The energy consumed in domestic life is largely the same energy available for serving the broader community. Which is not to say you cannot be a devoted spouse, parent, and community activist at the same time; but in fact it is harder. If you are single and living alone, you simply have more time to give.

Parental influence. These were not primarily life story interviews, but focused instead on the present, future, and recent past. There were no "tell me about your childhood" questions, nor specific queries on family background. So it was surprising to find so many spontaneous references to the influence of one or both parents. These occurred in almost all the interviews, virtually without exception.

Froehlich and Poulin, for instance, explicitly praise their mothers. Olson recalls his mother's love. Sliwa says his mother was a major formative influence, his grandfather too. Gibbs, in her own book, calls her mother "the most precious person in my life." Fathers, as well: Lightner's main helper at the beginning of MADD was her own father. Cassedy's father taught her early lessons about equality.

Few of these parents were particularly involved in community work as such. Their influence appears primarily moral. There's plenty of research evidence describing the transmission of altruism and the similarity of moral values between parent and child, and both seem to be the case here.[6]

Spiritual Background. Survey data indicate that churchgoers and people with strong religious convictions are more involved in social causes and community activities.[7] This sample suggests the same. Poulin is a nun; Froehlich and Anguiano are ex-nuns; Quayle is an ex-priest. I did not know about the latter two affiliations before making initial contact. Nor was I aware until the interview, just for example, that Fariña's grandparents on both sides were ministers, or that Fahrner was a ministerial school dropout.

"Involvement" and "success" are of course two different things. The direct connection between spiritual or religious background and community accomplishment is unproven. And of course nuns and priests have more time for community work by virtue of being single. Yet the evidence is suggestive enough to make one wonder more about the linkages between spirituality, religious life, and community work, and more particularly about whether consciously attending to one's spiritual nature has any implications for success in community action.

Influence of the Sixties. About half the subjects were between thirty-five and forty-five years old at the time of the interview, which means they were students or starting their careers during the social ferment of the late 1960s. Ray Shonholtz is only one of several who spontaneously recalls being influenced by those years. During that time, Quayle was learning Alinsky organizing techniques; Stevens was peripherally involved with the Black Panthers while teaching junior high school; Froehlich was doing antiwar work in the South; the Yorks were trying to bring Vermont college students to the inner city.

Two decades later, they're still at it, and they're not alone. Many who were socially active during the late sixties may have settled into middle-class comfort; but many were freed up and transformed enduringly by the events of that time, with transformation ongoing still. The big chill passed them by; the sixties thawed them out. For them, the social ferment of one period drives community action twenty years later.

A second group of similarities belongs more to personality; they lie close to the service process, and parallel the course of action.

Naïveté. Many community workers start out naive; many here were no exception. They weren't sure what they were doing, and they didn't know where they were going. "Naive" may understate the case; some were innocent as lambs. Gibbs didn't know where city hall was; Lightner, the master lobbyist, wasn't registered to vote. The Yorks took this a step further. Phyllis: "You just have to say, okay, everything doesn't work, I'm helpless, I don't know what to do." Once you've reached that point of utter helplessness, then you can start to move.

We take for granted that community work should be structured and formalized, right from the beginning; but that mind-set can be a barrier, protecting us from involvement at all. The truth is that most of us start out naive, in varying degrees, and few of us know what to expect, or could. How else could it be? There was no way to anticipate that riding the subways would turn into the Guardian Angels, or that going out for coffee and pie would lead to 9to5.

Naiveté, if truth be known, can be more asset than liability. Naiveté can be a powerful advantage. First, because if we really knew what we were getting into, we might not get into it. If we could anticipate the eventual time and energy investment right at the start, we might run like hell.

Second, because naiveté allows you to aim for goals you wouldn't attempt if you knew any better. Since you don't know what you're not supposed to be able to do, you're psychologically free to go out and do it.

And third, because naiveté, especially that lamblike innocence, can be seen by others as charming and winsome. If you show your naiveté to others who "know better," you may attract protectors, skilled people who know the ropes and are willing to help you. Few of us want to see lambs led to slaughter. And smart lambs learn fast; with experience, some community workers get skilled at projecting naiveté—but now we're talking technique.

A caution: There's a time for naiveté to end and sophistication to set in. You can only get so much mileage from innocence. Planning of some kind is essential to keep the work going, though even here there are wide variations, ranging from those who planned everything out before sticking their toes in (e.g., Cassedy) to those who don't like to make plans for anything (e.g., Stevens). Eventually everyone here does plan, but even so, capital-P planning can come later on. The freshness of the idea, and especially the spirit behind it, may suffice at the onset.

Pacing. Beginnings tend to be full of energy. The idea, the vision alone, can keep you in high gear for quite some time, and longer still when mixed with even a little bit of success. But sooner or later adrenalin ebbs, the starting energy fades, and some kind of pacing becomes necessary to stay in the game. This is probably adaptive.

The participants here have all been successful in pacing themselves, though not always in the same way. Vin Quayle and Lupe Anguiano used to take work home with them on weekends, but no more. Lois Gibbs hears the quitting whistle loud and clear ("I leave here at five o'clock, and I don't care if the whole world is collapsing around me"). True, Mimi Fariña still reports working well past dark; the Samples, and Curtis Sliwa, are still on twenty-four-hour call. Yet by and large, people do ease off some with time.

Several different factors are probably operating here: aging, fatigue, greater personal efficiency, better delegation to others, less *need* to work quite as hard if the program is stable. Pacing, and even a slowed-down pace, can be useful both personally and programmatically, especially if the founder is in it for the long haul. From an efficiency standpoint, the best choice is to expend the energy required by the task, but no more. Cassedy puts it well: "I don't work like crazy every single minute; I work a reasonable amount that I can tolerate over a long period of time."

Proper pacing may also prevent burnout. Fatigue may occur, but burnout does not, not in these people. Possibly this sample is atypical; or possibly burnout as a topic has been oversold. For all the literature and shop talk on burnout, we have little hard data on its observed frequency, and my guess is that it's far more exception than rule.[8] In reality, mature and committed people who pace themselves well are not likely to go up in smoke. They might damp down, or char at the edges, but most do keep a steady flame.

Humor. "We're not a great bunch of comedians here," Chick Colony mentioned in passing, and participants as a group were certainly not selected for their comic talents. But humor stood out, both as a cited virtue and as part of the interviews themselves. It bubbled up naturally. Subjects spent more time than I might have imagined smiling, or chuckling, or laughing out loud, and so did I.

This reminds us that humor is a program tool, with multiple uses: it redirects hurtful energy toward self or other; it helps others feel good about themselves; it can persuade the opposition you're not out to get them; it can lead others to respond to you more genuinely, as a whole person; it prevents us from taking ourselves too seriously (and getting burnt out?); it gets you over the rough spots that invariably happen; it soothes pain. A sense of humor, a willingness to laugh at oneself and with others, is a major asset in community work.

And a related theme occurs too, one of celebration, which is partly a structuring of situations so laughter can occur. Part of work itself should be fun, but when it can't be, fun can at least be factored in. So, Fran Froehlich, for whom celebration is deeply woven into daily life. Or, Lois Gibbs:

> We did a lot of partying [at Love Canal]. You know, "Hey, guys, this is great; we got our fifteenth newsletter out." What's the big deal about

the fifteenth newsletter? Nothing, in reality. But fifteen newsletters—
that's fine, that's a reason to celebrate. I mean, I would find any excuse
to party (laughs). Any reason would do.*

Two Major Themes

But of all the qualities the subjects shared, two stand out above the
others. Both of them are internal; and if accurately observed, they are
important to emphasize, because both have broad significance for social
action.

There's no better word for the first of these than "excitement." Our
subjects are energized by what they are doing; they are operating on
all cylinders. Technically, we might speak of high emotional arousal;
colloquially, we might say they're pumped up. The meanings here are
the same.

But it's more than ordinary excitement. The subjects here are not
just attached to their work, but swept in, hooked, immersed, driven,
turned up to a level that most of us do not experience most of the
time—or perhaps more accurately, that we do not try to experience,
thinking that the end result, however desirable, is not worth the energy
price.

Expressions of high excitement occur frequently and spontaneously
throughout the interviews:

"I was ready to jump out of my seat, I was so ready to go."
(Cassedy)

"I'm excited about it. . . . I've carried them along or swept them
along with my enthusiasm." (Stevens)

"God, we were so excited." (Phyllis York)

"The greatest ingredient for someone who's starting something new
is to articulate and transmit the enthusiasm, so that it's contagious."
(Shonholtz)

"The more I do this, the more I feel involved, and I can't stop. It
became a snowball; I couldn't slow down." (Fariña)

And what these words don't convey are vocal dynamics and bodily
emotion, manifest in almost every case. The feeling-tone expressed
often goes beyond excitement in the sense of being involved in, or being

---

*This quote is part of the transcript, but not of the interview text included here.

charged up by, instead more closely approximating total enmeshment in, or passionate caring about. "Passionate caring about," or passion, broadly speaking, is not a quality we display very often in our work, or in our lives. But these subjects had both the capacity for passionate excitement and the willingness to show it.

What goes together with excitement, much though not all of the time, is anger. The emotional charge is directed toward redressing a grievance or correcting an injustice, as well as toward establishing program content itself. This added motivation raises energy level and also fuels it. The anger may stem from personal tragedy or trauma, as in the cases of Gibbs and Lightner. Or it may emerge from a more abstract analysis, without direct suffering. Lupe Anguiano and Fran Froehlich, neither living in poverty, both get very angry at social treatment of the poor, even though in this instance their social viewpoints are quite divergent.

Anger, like excitement, can also feed on itself, especially if initial and typically inexperienced attempts to correct the injustice fail, thus making one even more angry. And as in the case of excitement, what is commonly observed here is not just anger in the sense of being aggravated or upset, but consuming anger, passionate anger, and (a word volunteered several times) outrage:

"I'm going to start an organization. I am just going to do this, because I'm so *angry*." (Lightner)

"I still get outraged at what I hear. And that's what keeps me doing what I'm doing, the outrage. The outrage and the anger." (Gibbs)

"I do kick limousines. I yell at people who drive Mercedes. . . . The sense of outrage that I have is tremendous." (Froehlich)

If there is rage, it's not allowed to strike blindly. It is harnessed, and channeled productively, toward activities to modify the anger's source. The system may eventually yield under pressure, or the activist may reach outside the system altogether to create a new system of one's own. But while the anger may be harnessed, it is rarely extinguished. Several subjects report simmering anger even now, and merely thinking about a triggering event can start juices flowing all over again.

As for the second major characteristic, a one-word definition is hard to find. The closest wording may be belief in and reliance upon traditional virtue. I mean old-fashioned virtue, the kind instilled by parents, taught by Sunday schools and scout troops. Perhaps it is universal virtue, found in texts stretching back through civilization. But in American history, it is virtue linked most closely to the earlier days of the republic, to nineteenth-century industrial expansion, and to the spirit of the frontier.

Traditional virtue, as the term is used here, is a composite of several different qualities, which include:

Commitment to the task at hand, and to the underlying cause.

Hard work, plus the belief that hard work pays off.

Persistence: a willingness to go over, around, or through obstacles; what we once called stick-to-it-iveness.

Considerate treatment of others; practice of the Golden Rule.

Riskiness, not necessarily in the entrepreneurial sense, but rather the readiness to take a chance.

Tolerance for criticism, even for being called "crazy" by one's peers, as several participants independently reported.

Belief in the power of a single person to affect larger events, even if self-esteem were low.

Optimism that things will turn out well; there are very few pessimists here.

The traditional virtue motif occurs over and over again in the interview accounts, almost to the point of cliché. The "nutshell" summaries in the State of the Art chapter, however well expressed, are a series of time-honored beliefs. Consider also these excerpts from the text:

"I think that I am an incurable optimist, and that I'm always full of hope." (Poulin)

"The only way to do [it] is by being positive, by being strong, by being determined." (Anguiano)

"The only thing I say is that if I'm going to make a mess, I'll probably make a big one, 'cause I work hard whatever I'm doing." (Trower)

"I felt confident that it could be done, and I felt I couldn't rest until I could show myself that it could be done. That I could do it." (Ware)

"This is the way I was raised, it was a responsibility. . . . And how can you just turn your back on so many people?" (Helene Sample)

"The only way we can make this world work for ourselves is to make it work for everyone else." (Bowes)

"I love people, I care for people, I'm interested in people, and I want them to share with me true love and happiness." (Olson)

"You've got to be willing to stay with it and ask, ask, ask all day long." (Fahrner)

"Everybody is called to strive for sainthood. Everybody. A lot of people don't realize that." (Quayle)

"Always remember, if it was easy to do, it would have been done already." (Sliwa)

I believe these are fair samples. Similar comments are found in transcript sections not included here. And it's not coincidental that the virtues cited have characterized the American hero throughout our history.[9]

It's wise to take a backward step here, to note that these are not our subjects' only positive or relevant qualities, and also that no virtue monopoly is implied. We all possess these virtues; we're citing matters of degree. But degrees are important, for degrees can make the difference between getting started or standing by, and between the praiseworthy or the remarkable. Compare again McGinley's description of saints:

> The saints differ from us in their exuberance, the excess of our human talents. Moderation is not their secret. It is in the wildness of their dreams, the desperate vitality of their ambitions, that they stand apart from ordinary men of good will.[10]

This quote applies here. Our subjects may never be canonized, but they do display well-above-average amounts of traditional (or saintly?) virtue. This cluster of virtue seems to be significantly correlated with program success. And to the extent it is, it gives pause; for the source of success in community work may then be not only technical, but moral as well.

Implications

All of these personal qualities may be praiseworthy, and they may be powerful, but they hardly break fresh ground. They are homely virtues, straight from the cracker barrel; ordinary, serviceable, satisfying perhaps, but surely not new. They've probably guided intervention since intervention began. They sit quietly in the pantry right now; all we need do is take them out and open them up.

And the same holds true for technique. There is hardly an operating technique cited by the participants (and all were asked) that's not in the catalog of common sense. Homer Fahrner asks for what he wants. Candy Lightner reaches out for advice. Haroldline Trower relies on word of mouth. Kathy Levin applies innocence and charm to get Atari sets for nursing homes. Ray Shonholtz uses his contacts to build credibility, then leverages credibility in one area to expand in others.

And so on, with an occasional clever twist, a variation on a theme. We know these techniques already. Whether we choose to practice them is of course another story.

Our inability to come up with conclusions that extend the frontiers may be taken as failure. The fact is we have few fresh insights to offer. There is little new of the head or the heart. We're always looking for magic, but there is no magic at hand, nothing of revelation. What we have instead is milquetoast. Our conclusions are obvious, and they are dull.

Yet there is a positive side to no-magic, maybe more than one. In the first place, we can use reminders of what works best. Reminders serve a proper and necessary function, by keeping us on course and by narrowing the gap between who we are and who we could be. Behavior change rests on slow accretion; even revelation meets the mind prepared. And so we need (and seek) reminders, whether spoken in church, or spread through the media, or posted on the refrigerator door. If we have flesh-and-blood reminders, who personify desired qualities in their own lives, so much the better.

The failure to uncover the new also prompts us to revalue the old. The value of the findings may lie in their age. The requisite qualities for successful action may have been dwelling in us all along. There may truly be heroic potential within all of us, and that is truly revelatory. The main task then becomes not one of adding on, but of polishing off; not one of mastering esoteric skills—who will stay still to master them?—but rather one of housecleaning.

In a country of nonstop information and souped-up pace, we are so caught up with learning by taking courses, listening to tapes, glancing at the latest, squeezing something in, that it is hard for us to believe fully, and to live a life based on the belief, that practical wisdom can develop in silence, without outside stimulation, by focusing on and refining what is already there. But that may be true.

So if we value local heroism and its near relations, the encouraging news may be that the distinguishing qualities of such heroism are ordinary qualities, already well distributed, and already residing within. They may not be well utilized, they may not often surface in daily living, but they are there nevertheless. And for those who really believe this, who take this as more than a harmless fantasy or entertaining diversion, important policy implications follow. They deal with expanding the frequency and duration of heroic and other helping actions in our society. And not the least of them is that the essence of social action is based on character rather than skill.

Consider what this might mean:

Training. Such character is learned, and its moral qualities can be taught, but moral education in our society continues in eclipse. The moral training most of us have received outside the home, and that most of our children are receiving, is defanged, uncritical, and tolerated rather than sought. It's rarely part of formal schooling, almost never part of training on the job. Instead, it's relegated to sermons, commencement speeches, or recognition dinners. Or it comes from advice columns and talk shows—the media personality as moral arbiter—whose advice we might scrutinize more carefully if we recognized its social power. As for moral exploration and moral struggle, there's hardly a forum. It is far easier, it always has been easier, to adopt current fashion, or at least acquiesce.

If moral education takes a back seat in society at large, it is virtually invisible in education for the social services, where one might assume it should be most prominent. But in fact, such education is devoted explicitly to methods and techniques, and implicitly to learning the professional culture. Instructors transmit content-knowledge and practical skills following course catalog descriptions, but, sotto voce, the student also learns, and is meant to learn, how to use those skills to think, feel, and act like a professional, and more precisely, to succeed on the job.

One could sit through an entire graduate curriculum without confronting values, or virtues, or feeling their weight. And one would have to search far and wide for a training program that deliberately sought to instill moral values in its students, where moral development was part of the *training goal*, and where conscious effort was made to nurture and refine moral sensitivity. (Or, stretching the imagination further, to make such sensitivity an admissions criterion.) But the question here is whether such training goals are legitimate and should be professed.

I believe the correct answer is yes on both counts. And the justification lies not in moral authority, but in pragmatic advantage. If we really believe the accounts we've read, if it is *really* true that success in community action is linked to highly developed moral qualities, then it really does follow that successful training in those qualities should result in community gain. Moral education and practical effectiveness should go hand in hand.

Professionalism. Our findings also have implications for the human service professions themselves.

To begin with, it's probably true that nonprofessionals account for the bulk of community service hours in the United States today. Though we may lack an exact head count, by one estimate there are about 1.2 million community service professionals on the scene.[11] Then, using one recent survey as an indicator, if we have 10.5 billion volunteer hours yearly, that's a rough equivalent of 6.7 million full-time volunteer staff positions, or more than five times the professional number.[12]

And these professionals are not on the scene all day. They are teaching, or grading papers; administering, or meeting in-house; filling out forms, or searching for dollars. Much of the professional's time is spent maintaining the professional system.

But the heart of the matter is this: the personal qualities most apparently associated with intervention success—excitement, anger, traditional virtue—are poorly assimilated into professional culture. Worse than that, professional culture may select them out. Take a closer look:

Excitement, for example. We don't talk much about it in school. We don't see it much on the job. To oversimplify, but only a little, we don't experience it much in our own work, or in our lives. We don't select for it in our students, and we don't place much emphasis in passing it on to the next generation.

We don't particularly value excitement either—when it's too high, we back away. I don't mean simply caring for your work, or being interested in it, or concerned about it. I'm thinking of excitement in the sense of being truly entwined in your work, riveted, enveloped in it, fused with it, and inseparable from it.

People like that seem a little strange, and maybe threatening. They're *so* on fire, so apostolic, that they won't fit well into the department or the agency team. We don't want their waves in our boats. High excitement, in the sense of full-bore passionate excitement, risks both professional and personal costs, for an implicit but powerful part of our professional ethos is not to get too charged up, but instead to be well-mannered, to hold excitement down.

This holds especially true for anger. You're not supposed to get too worked up about social injustice as a faculty member. You're not supposed to rant and rave or get unduly perturbed about the system as a helping professional (or common citizen), or to show with your voice or your body that you are *really mad*. To do so breaks unwritten rules; you'll only make everyone else upset, and if you keep it up you will be isolated or worse, your ideas disregarded, your credibility gone.

So we as helping professionals, and as citizens too, learn to suppress. We bury our anger. We patronize clients and students and community members who show their anger, believing that we are more mature and impartial. Or as researchers, we choose topics which are truly difficult to get angry about, where there is small emotional connection, and where anger would indeed be an inappropriate response.

Anger can distort our judgment, that is true. But the other side is that anger, and more generally excitement, may be predictors of success in community change work. We don't allow ourselves to use high emotion for social good, and we distance ourselves from those who do. I think this is a mistake.

And as for virtue, the same analysis applies. You won't spot virtue in job ad copy, nor will you note it in job promotion reviews. Traditional virtue is nice but extraneous. Instead, is the person "qualified"?—meaning will he or she do a good job, not embarrass the employer, and not start a crusade? Given basic competence, then well-mannered expediency is what gets rewarded; crusaders need not apply.[13]

So the irony—if irony is the word—is that active nonprofessionals may have the same amount of personal qualities needed for intervention success as professionals do. They may have more. They may be equal in overall ability too. They may be better. I know of little firm data bearing on this issue (who would produce it?) though in psychotherapy, for one example, there is solid, though poorly acknowledged evidence that nonprofessionals and professionals are not significantly different in helping skill.[14]

A safer and more conservative conclusion is that professional superiority in carrying out successful community actions has not been demonstrated. At the very least, the best nonprofessionals match up strikingly well. And that shouldn't be surprising, if we take a second glance. The singular attributes of the professional in the human services are not necessarily ability or skill, nor have they ever been. Rather they are attributes of the *position*: (*a*) credentials, (*b*) community acceptance of those credentials, and (*c*) time in one's day.

How to Be a Local Hero

It follows, then, that if you want to be a local hero, the first step is to want to be one. This isn't tautology; the most important act is mental. To the extent the actions described here are legitimately heroic (and I believe they are), they can be approximated by acts of will. Nothing may be needed beyond the reach of the ordinary citizen. The potential has been there all the time. It's there right now.

Technique is important, but we already have enough to get started. When we do start, we'll become more receptive to learning new technique, and we'll also attract others who have technique to teach us. But technique is useless without prior will power, as any appliance sits idle till you flick the switch. When local interventions fail, was it really because the right technique was not precisely used? Or was it ultimately due to lack of passion, or failure of the heart?

The social consequences of this line of thinking are clear and profound: "You can be a hero, too." The temptation is to slide into exhortation, without disguise. Just as neuroscientists tell us that we use about ten percent of our brain's potential, we tap possibly the same percent of our heroic and community-building capacity.

We've begged off the bigger question, though, which is how do we tap that capacity, or how do we get people (us) to want to be community-heroic in the first place? Remember that these are the same people described in the opening chapter, whose need for privacy is compelling, who hole themselves up for the duration, bar their doors, and screen their calls. Or these are the same people who are occupationally or domestically overloaded, or feel they are, and whose life-styles would not be called holistic.[15]

We have a long way to go. A full answer to this question would involve a transformation of American society, and goes well beyond the scope of this book. But we can trace some very broadbrush outlines, beyond the display of personal examples, based largely on the premise that the individual does not bear sole responsibility for change. Individual behavior is shaped by institutional forces, and each institution has a role to play. That is, in a society that wanted to stimulate community-building by its citizens:

Social agencies would work more closely with citizen groups. They'd do more education, give more training, offer more consultation, make a point of nurturing local leadership skills.

Schools would upgrade their local history and government curricula, provide more instruction in civic values, bring more community leaders into the classroom, involve their students in service projects from first grade on up, and honor students with distinguished community service activity.

Businesses would set forth community service goals, expand release time for employees, adopt local community programs, and sponsor competitions for the most creative community ideas.

Local governments would foster neighborhood and block associations, award mini-grants to neighborhood groups, offer tax credits to active volunteers, provide tax incentives to community-oriented businesses, and establish offices of social innovation, responsible for seeking, testing, evaluating, and promoting as many new ideas as they can handle.

These are starting examples—small in scale, low in cost, but potentially high in impact. There are hundreds of others.[16] Since each of these institutions is more powerful than individuals taken singly, the individual actor here must apply maximum leverage on the institution to get it to move, to help it apply its own greater leverage back onto the citizenry. With force applied wisely, the institution will move, at least a little. Many individuals work within those institutions, and that helps. And institutions themselves are interrelated; a splash in one will ripple in another.

Nowhere are institutional effects more powerful than with the media. With only one exception, none of the people interviewed in this book would have come into my own consciousness without prior media attention. The same may hold for those you most admire. And all subjects here allied with the media to get their point across. Sometimes they waited for reporters to track them down. But most of the time, they sought media attention actively, even if they had to muster up some courage or overcome some scruples to do so.

So Vin Quayle picketed banks because he knew the media would show up. Candy Lightner sought new issues to keep the media's eye. Levin, Shonholtz, Cassedy, and Fariña, among others, explicitly stress the need for media coverage and personal media skills. Fariña: "I would use market techniques, sell techniques, any gimmick I could get my hands on before I vomit and it goes too far." Even those who shunned personal publicity, like Frank Bowes, had to write the local paper to get things started.

On a hometown level, publicity is relatively easy to come by, since local media are hungry for news. But if the media also hunger for citizen initiatives, as they should, they may need to take initiatives of their own, through features, contests, sponsorships, and editorial backing. The citizen activist will need media support, if an effort is to reach beyond a neighborhood; not just to let people know what's going on, but also to keep spirits up, to draw helpers in, and to give skeptics the impression you have clout, maybe more clout than you really do. There's a delicate balance: the media may expose you, or overexpose you, and the media may be an uneasy ally. But without publicity, your work can stall, or die a needless death.

However much institutional change is desirable, and however much takes place, there's individual responsibility to be faced all the same. To rely too much on institutions to foster local change is unrealistic if not also dangerous. The individual remains as the frame of reference. Private citizens, in all their imperfection, must act in public for the public good. The wellspring of change must be found within. And if these words sound far too facile, there's really no other choice.

Quality of life begins at home, where people live and spend their time. The way people relate to those around them, in their immediate neighborhoods and communities, shapes how they see the world. Quality comes down to home front action. Ultimately, we control that action. Who else could?

And it has to be more than defensive action, reacting against the latest threat. Fighting to keep the guard on the crossing, or the neighborhood school open, or the zoning unchanged is all important and good, but keeps you only running in place. What's needed at least as much is action where initiative is taken, where something new is dreamed, and where, like the people in this book, some one dreamer is willing to take the first step.

Taking the initiative, taking the step (or leap) is what lifts community spirit. It's that type of community-building activity which ought to be especially encouraged. The initiative need not be grandiose, or even grand, or in any way duplicative of the accounts given here. It can be humble. It can be the tiniest initiative imaginable. But even tiny initiatives are welcome; they take their own form of courage. If you want to have a block party, you have to seek your neighbor, and not be deterred.

Having acknowledged that, the field's wide open for the locally grand. The opportunity for a complete, soul-stretching community workout is always there, where whatever heroic potential may lie within you can be fully exercised. Local community work provides an arena for the cultivation and display of vision, of risk, of adventure, of personal odyssey, of overpowering of demons, of triumphant return, of all the attributes of heroism which have served us from antiquity and which we will need at least as much as we enter the next millenium.

Thinking about the Long Haul

There are limits in community work, to be heeded and accepted, if they can't be transcended. Some change simply lies beyond personal control. Institutional change can be a lifetime waiting for. Parental transmission must take a generation. Individual action can fail, can fail badly if you're honest, no matter how hard you try or how much you care, and even actions that don't fail may teeter constantly on the brink. To keep a community program and yourself going day after day and year after year can take enormous energy and keep on taking it, every drop you have to give. Creative and initiatory service can be a constant struggle—is, usually—and it's in the nature of things for some programs to die. As we've learned, a program need not last forever.

That goes for the founders, too. Nothing says you have to be a local hero for the rest of your life. Some founders may stay with their creations till their working days are over; others may alter their roles significantly; others again may leave their programs altogether, vertically or horizontally, and move to something entirely different. The portraits here, like any portraits, are frozen in time; but those portrayed will mature, grow, wither, evolve, take unexpected turns. As you read this, they probably have. Life keeps serving up possibilities, and we should not expect anyone always to turn them down. They could be the start of new heroic attempts.

None of this in any way diminishes the people who have made these accomplishments, nor the accomplishments themselves. The accomplishments are completed facts; they'll stand by themselves. And, if their makers have been well depicted, they'll help spawn a new crop of local heroes who will take their place and break through the limits we've been referring to. But if we're after more than individual achievement, if we're really speaking of changing the national consciousness, or promoting a new heroic archetype—and we are—then progress may be slower than we would like. Assume inspirational leaders, enlightened technique, sensitive readers, responsible institutions, and persuasive writing: change is still likely to be gradual, incremental, one candle at a time, as it's usually been. I wish I could see a faster way, prophesy some miracle fix, but I cannot. You can die for a cause, with little difference. That's happened, and it will happen again.

Vin Quayle says: "The first thing you gotta do is devote ten years of your life to it." It may not take ten years, or five, but Vin has a point. The strategy of choice may be keeping at it, in individual ways. The preferred tactic may be testing one's limits, evaluating that test, and figuring out where to go from there. The proper state of mind may be staking some faith in the positive evolutionary power of nature, while ensuring that you, as part of nature, will use those powers you are given. If you are not that hundredth monkey who tips the scales, you can be any lower number. You can add your weight. You might be hundredth after all.

"Heroes evolve; they aren't born." So we, as part of evolution, help evolution along. We keep moving slowly along the path, from wherever we happen to be. We are apprentice heroes, waiting for the call. At some point, the opportunity may arise to cross a threshold, from which there's no turning back. Or, heeding some inner call, we force that opportunity ourselves.

For problems of community—for problems of the planet—the technical solutions are already in hand. For building community, technical solutions take second place. The primary ingredient is intrinsic. In first place is personal mobilization; or, in different words, a locally heroic spirit, which grasps a community need, judges what can be done, gathers the necessary forces, then draws fully from within.

As Emerson writes, "Heroism is an obedience to a secret impulse of an individual's character."[17] Which means we need to know our secrets, and trust in their potential goodness. The chance is there to hear them out, risking the price of our attention. The chance is there for us to be heroic within our lifetime. By simple choice, we can join inner spirit with community good. The inner journey will find its community expression, and they will be as one.

Notes

Introduction: How to Build Community Life

1. Responses from a 1983 Roper survey, cited in *Public Opinion*, August-September 1984, p. 25.
2. *The Gallup Report*, May 1986, pp. 14–15. Percentage figures in surveys like these depend heavily upon the definition of volunteerism used. A 1983 Gallup study broadened the criterion of volunteering to include "working in some way to help others for no monetary pay," taking in such activities as helping an elderly neighbor, giving free professional advice, or cooking for a bake sale. With this expanded definition, 55 percent of the population said they had volunteered at least once the previous year. See George Gallup, Jr., "The 1983 Gallup Survey on Volunteering," *Voluntary Action Leadership*, Winter 1984, pp. 20–22.

    Note also that trend data on American volunteerism appear inconclusive. The 1986 Gallup release cited above describes a steady increase in volunteerism since 1977, when the percentage was 27 percent. However, a different Gallup survey, using the broader definition, indicates a drop-off from 52 percent in 1981 to 48 percent in 1985 (1983 = 55 percent). See Independent Sector, *Americans Volunteer 1985* [Summary Report] (Washington, D.C.: Independent Sector, 1986), p. 9. For additional, and also mixed, data, see "Americans Volunteer: A Profile," *Public Opinion*, February-March 1982, pp. 21–23.
3. *The Gallup Report*, June-July 1982, p. 176.
4. For recent summaries, see, for example, Sheldon Cohen and S. Leonard Syme, eds., *Social Support and Health* (New York: Academic Press, 1985), and Mark Pilisuk and Susan Hillier Parks, *The Healing Web: Social Networks and Human Survival* (Hanover, N.H.: University Press of New England, 1986).
5. Figures for 1973 and 1980 from Daniel Yankelovich, *New Rules: Searching for Self-Fulfillment in a World Turned Upside Down* (New York: Random House, 1981), p. 95. Subsequent data from Yankelovich, Skelly and White, personal communication.

6. See, for example, Maryann Bucknum Brinley, "The Ferrell Family's Unlikely Crusade," *McCall's*, January 1985, p. 54+.
7. In all phases of the interview process, particularly in transcribing and editing, I drew extensively upon Cullom Davis, Kathryn Back, and Kay MacLean, *Oral History: From Tape to Type* (Chicago: American Library Association, 1977); Mary Jo Deering and Barbara Pomeroy, *Transcribing without Tears: A Guide to Transcribing and Editing Oral History Interviews* (Washington, D.C.: George Washington University, Oral History Program, 1976); and James Hoopes, *Oral History: An Introduction for Students* (Chapel Hill, N.C.: University of North Carolina Press, 1979).

An Interlude: Heroism in Modern Society

1. Responses are respectively those of Marti Stevens, Vin Quayle, Phyllis York, Lupe Anguiano, Frank Bowes, Helene Sample, Ellen Cassedy, Mimi Fariña, Homer Fahrner, Bill Sample, Kathy Levin, and Lucy Poulin.
2. For a recent popular article confirming the range of hero identification, see Lawrence Eisenberg, "Who Is Your Favorite Hero—and Why?" *Good Housekeeping*, July 1986, pp. 108–110. Further support comes from responses to an author's query in the *New York Times Book Review*. The thirty-three nominations received ranged from a lumberman working with Indian tribes in the Bolivian Andes to a woman who led a crusade against dog droppings in New York City, and appeared to cover all points in between.
3. *Boston Globe*, April 25, 1985, pp. 77 and 78. Reprinted courtesy of The Boston Globe.
4. Peter Goldman, "100 New American Heroes," *Newsweek*, Summer 1986, Collector's Edition [special issue], p. 47. Copyright 1986 by Newsweek, Inc. All rights reserved. Reprinted by permission.
5. Edward Hoagland, "Where Have All the Heroes Gone?" *New York Times Magazine*, March 10, 1974, pp. 20 and 92. Copyright 1974 by The New York Times Company. Reprinted by permission.
6. Susanna McBee, "Heroes Are Back: Young Americans Tell Why," *U.S. News & World Report*, April 22, 1985, p. 44.
7. Phyllis McGinley, *Saint-Watching* (New York: Viking Press, 1969), p. 19.
8. From Ronald Reagan's Inaugural Address, January 20, 1981. In the same speech: "I'm addressing the heroes of whom I speak—you, the citizens of this blessed land." *Facts on File*, January 23, 1981, p. 32.
9. Quoted in the *Stanford Observer*, April 1984, p. 3. Gardner was former Secretary of Health, Education, and Welfare, and founder of Common Cause. See also the discussion in his book *Excellence: Can We Be Equal and Excellent Too?* (New York: Harper & Brothers, 1961), ch. 12; for example, "*And the society is bettered not only by those who achieve* [excellence] *but by those who are trying*" (p. 133; emphasis in original).
10. David Wilson, "Those Little Acts that Help a Lot," *Boston Globe*, July 26, 1983, p. 11. Reprinted courtesy of The Boston Globe. "T" is short for MBTA, Massachusetts Bay Transportation Authority, Boston's public transportation system.

11. The study is reported by McBee, op. cit. All quotes from p. 44.

    Similar results have been found in other youth polls on admired public figures. In the "Seventh Annual Poll of Heroes of Young America" (1986), students in eighth through twelfth grades were asked to choose the people in public life they most admired. The top ten heroes overall: Bill Cosby, Sylvester Stallone, Eddie Murphy, Ronald Reagan, Chuck Norris, Clint Eastwood, Molly Ringwald, Rob Lowe, Arnold Schwarzenegger, and Don Johnson. Cited in *The World Almanac and Book of Facts 1987* (New York: Pharos Books, 1986), p. 34.

12. Elizabeth Stark, "Mom and Dad: The Great American Heroes," *Psychology Today*, May 1986, p. 12.

13. Christine Kole MacLean, "Who's Your Hero?" *TeenAge*, November-December 1985. The first quote is from a press release about the article mailed out by the magazine; second quote is from p. 28.

14. Circulation figures from *The 1987 Information Please Almanac* (New York: Houghton Mifflin, 1986), p. 290.

15. Richard Schickel, *Intimate Strangers: The Culture of Celebrity* (Garden City, N.Y.: Doubleday, 1985), pp. 275 and 29.

16. Quoted in *Boston Globe*, June 5, 1985, p. 70. The larger article gives other examples of celebrity actors as policy advocates. Reprinted courtesy of The Boston Globe.

17. George Gallup, Jr., *The Gallup Poll: Public Opinion 1985* (Wilmington, Del.: Scholarly Resources, Inc., 1986), pp. 292–293.

18. Sitting and former presidents, presidential candidates, prime ministers, and popes have been among the most admired since these polls began in the late 1940s. See *The Gallup Report*, December 1984, pp. 3–7.

19. Poll cited in Daniel Walden, "Where Have All Our Heroes Gone?" *USA Today*, January 1986, p. 23. The poll date is 1898. Walden also cites data (p. 23) indicating that in a 1950 survey of those most admired by boys, Gene Autry outpolled Jesus Christ by four to one. This is a good summary article on heroic values in American culture.

20. Account derived from *Time*, January 25, 1982, pp. 16–17; *Facts on File*, January 29, 1982, p. 45; and *Time*, February 8, 1982, p. 18.

21. *Newsweek*, February 9, 1981, p. 27. See also *Time*, February 9, 1981, p. 12. Copyright 1981 by Newsweek, Inc. All rights reserved. Reprinted by permission.

22. In a nationally broadcast speech. Quoted in *Facts on File*, January 31, 1986, p. 49.

23. This point is developed in detail in Joshua Meyrowitz, *No Sense of Place: The Impact of Electronic Media on Social Behavior* (New York: Oxford University Press, 1985), especially in ch. 14 and on pp. 311–312.

24. Sonya Freedman, *A Hero Is More Than Just a Sandwich* (New York: G. P. Putnam's Sons, 1986).

25. And possibly more now than in the recent past. The *Readers' Guide to Periodical Literature* lists twenty-eight main-heading articles on heroes from 1960–1969, forty-one from 1970–1979, and seventy-one from 1980–1986 alone, an increase not primarily attributable to changes in the number of periodicals indexed, nor to apparent changes in classification terminology.

26. Joseph Campbell, *The Hero with a Thousand Faces*, 2d ed. (Princeton, N.J.: Princeton University Press, 1968), p. 30. Emphasis in original.

27. Campbell, ibid., p. 51.
28. Campbell, ibid., p. 82.
29. Campbell, ibid., p. 69.
30. Campbell, ibid., p. 97.
31. Campbell, ibid., pp. 109 and 246.
32. Campbell, ibid., p. 246. Quotes on p. 246 were originally in italics.
33. Campbell, ibid., p. 19.
34. See for example Campbell's summary on his pp. 245–246. While Campbell's account is among the most detailed, it is, of course, only one of numerous analyses of the historical hero. For some other sources, containing roughly similar parallels, see the bibliography.
35. Campbell, op. cit., p. 259.
36. Campbell, op. cit., pp. 315–317.
37. Campbell, op. cit., p. 315.
38. In a 1986 Harris survey, for example, sixty percent of the population felt that what they thought didn't count very much anymore. The Harris "alienation index," a composite score based on this and four related statements, has jumped about twenty-five percentage points since the late 1960s. *The Harris Survey*, September 8, 1986.
39. Campbell, op. cit., p. 218.

Conclusions

1. Details on the lack of consistent evidence for an altruistic personality trait or an altruistic personality type are reviewed in Dennis L. Krebs and Dale T. Miller, "Altruism and Aggression," in Gardner Lindzey and Elliot Aronson, eds., *Handbook of Social Psychology*, 3d ed., vol. 2 (New York: Random House, 1985), pp. 1–71, and especially pp. 29–34.
2. Eva Fogelman and Valerie Lewis Wiener, "The Few, the Brave, the Noble," *Psychology Today*, August 1985, p. 62.
3. Case investigator James Rethi, quoted in Denise Foley, "The Hero in All of Us," *Prevention*, August 1985, p. 79. Reprinted by permission of *Prevention*. Copyright 1985, Rodale Press, Inc. All rights reserved.
4. Phyllis McGinley, *Saint-Watching* (New York: Viking Press, 1969), pp. 6 and 17.
5. *New York Times*, March 5, 1985, p. C2. Copyright 1985 by The New York Times Company. Reprinted by permission.
6. For studies describing the transmission of moral values in general, see virtually any developmental psychology textbook. For evidence on the transmission of altruism in particular, see Ervin Staub et al., eds., *Development and Maintenance of Prosocial Behavior: International Perspectives on Positive Morality* (New York: Plenum, 1984).
7. For example, Virginia A. Hodgkinson and Murray S. Weitzman, *The Charitable Behavior of Americans: A National Survey* (Washington, D.C.: Independent Sector, 1986), p. 27; also, *The Gallup Report*, February 1982, p. 24.
8. The point on lack of frequency data is noted by some of the leading researchers in

the field. See Christina Maslach and Susan E. Jackson, "Burnout in Organizational Settings," in Stuart Oskamp, ed., *Applied Social Psychology Annual*, vol. 5 (Beverly Hills, Calif.: Sage Publications, 1984), pp. 133–153, and especially p. 133.

9. See for example the summarization in Dixon Wecter, *The Hero in America* (Ann Arbor: University of Michigan Press, 1963), particularly pp. 482–487.

10. McGinley, op. cit., p. 19.

11. There were approximately 278,000 "social scientists and urban planners," and also 846,000 "social, recreation, and religious workers" employed in the United States in 1984. This figure excludes teachers and counselors but includes economists and psychologists as well as all clergy. *Employment and Earnings* [Bureau of Labor Statistics] 32, January 1985, p. 176.

12. Figures on volunteer hours and equivalent staff positions are from Independent Sector, *Americans Volunteer 1985* [Summary Report] (Washington, D.C.: Independent Sector, 1986), p. 19. The 5:1 ratio need not be taken too literally, but may help establish the point.

13. The argument here is keyed to the human services and the nonprofit sector in general. Note, however, that the desired qualities of the local (nonprofit) hero and the successful (profit-making) large company show a high degree of overlap, at least judging from such best-selling accounts as Thomas J. Peters and Robert H. Waterman, Jr., *In Search of Excellence: Lessons from America's Best-Run Companies* (New York: Warner Books, 1982). Peters and Waterman also stress the value of high excitement and passionate commitment to a cause. And remarking on the common qualities they isolate, "Most of these eight attributes are not startling. Some, if not most, are 'motherhoods'." (p. 16)

14. See the review in John A. Hattie, Christopher F. Sharpley, and H. Jane Rogers, "Comparative Effectiveness of Professional and Paraprofessional Helpers," *Psychological Bulletin* 95 (1984): 534–541.

15. Data on the willingness and desire (as vs. the practice) of citizens to engage in more community activity are scattered and intriguing, if not particularly consistent. On the one hand, (*a*) "sizable majorities still express a deep commitment to nonmaterial values"; (*b*) 89 percent would volunteer for some kind of neighborhood or community activity; (*c*) 87 percent feel that volunteering some time to community service is a "very important" or "somewhat important" obligation of citizenship; (*d*) 78 percent agree that "every person should volunteer some of his time to help those who are less well off"; (*e*) better than half are "very interested" in helping solve the top ten rated community problems; and (*f*) 49 percent believe that they should volunteer, but personally have not done so.

On the other hand, (*g*) 66 percent are very satisfied or extremely satisfied with their community as it is; (*h*) public service rates below truck driving as a career choice of American youth; (*i*) 78 percent of a different youth sample feels that choosing a low-paying field is a mistake, even if you like it (as vs. 37 percent in 1966); (*j*) volunteerism in the 18–24 age bracket dropped 11 percentage points from 1980 to 1985; and (*k*) when the general population is asked about its favorite evening pastime, sixteen different activities get 2 percent or more of the vote, but community or civic activities fail to make the list.

There's a reservoir of community activism to be tapped; it won't be especially easy to tap it.

Sources: (*a*) *The Harris Survey*, March 28, 1985; (*b*) Stewart Dill McBride, "Gallup Urban Poll—Residents View Their Cities," *Nation's Cities* 16 (November 1978), p. 41; (*c*) 1984 National Opinion Research Center survey, cited in *Public Opinion*, October-November 1985, p. 32; (*d*) Hodgkinson and Weitzman, op. cit., p. 46; (*e*) based on a 1985 survey by R. H. Bruskin Associates, released by American Values (211 E. 43rd Street, Suite 1400, New York, NY 10017); (*f*) Hodgkinson and Weitzman, op. cit., p. 53; (*g*) *The Gallup Report*, June-July, 1982, p. 140 (66 percent figure derived from combining scale values of 8, 9, and 10 on a 10-point satisfaction scale); (*h*) *USA Today* [newspaper] March 29, 1984, p. 11A; (*i*) Srully Blotnick, "Why Hippies Beget Yuppies," *Forbes*, February 24, 1986, p. 146; (*j*) Independent Sector, op. cit., p. 5; (*k*) *The Gallup Report*, May 1986, pp. 7–9.

16. Some of these ideas are compiled in Bill Berkowitz, *Community Dreams* (San Luis Obispo, Calif.: Impact Publishers, 1984).

17. Ralph Waldo Emerson, "Heroism," in Brooks Atkinson, ed., *The Complete Essays and Other Writings of Ralph Waldo Emerson* (New York: Random House, 1940), p. 253.

Interview Participants

Names and Addresses

Organizational addresses are given when one is available. Brief current information about each program may generally be obtained by writing the organization, enclosing a SASE.

Lupe Anguiano, National Women's Employment and Education, Inc., 965 Longwood Avenue, Room 317, Bronx, NY 10459.

Frank Bowes, Scanlan & Bowes, 1012 Massachusetts Avenue, Arlington, MA 02174.

Ellen Cassedy, c/o 9to5, National Association of Working Women, 614 Superior Avenue, NW, Cleveland, OH 44113.

Chick Colony, P. O. Box 51, Harrisville, NH 03450. Also: The Harrisville School, Harrisville, NH 03450.

Homer Fahrner, 2606½ J Street, Apartment D, Sacramento, CA 95816. (Senior Gleaners: 3185 Longview Drive, North Highlands CA 95660.)

Mimi Fariña, Bread & Roses, 78 Throckmorton Avenue, Mill Valley, CA 94941.

Fran Froehlich, Poor People's United Fund, 645 Boylston Street, Boston, MA 02116.

Lois Gibbs, Citizen's Clearinghouse for Hazardous Wastes, Inc., P. O. Box 926, Arlington, VA 22216.

Kathy Levin, Magic Me, Inc., 4000 North Charles Street, Suite 312, Baltimore, MD 21218.

Candy Lightner, P. O. Box 121425, Arlington, TX 76012. (Mothers Against Drunk Driving [MADD]: 669 Airport Freeway, Suite 310, Hurst, TX 76053.)

Wally Olson, c/o Santa Monica Municipal Bus Lines, 1660 7th Street, Santa Monica, CA 90401.

Lucy Poulin, H.O.M.E., Inc. [Homeworkers Organized for More Employment], P. O. Box 10, Orland, ME 04472.

Vincent Quayle, St. Ambrose Housing Aid Center, 321 East 25th Street, Baltimore, MD 21218.

Bill and Helene Sample, Sunshine Foundation, 4010 Levick Street, Philadelphia, PA 19135.

Ray Shonholtz, Community Board Program, Inc., 149 Ninth Street, San Francisco, CA 94103.

Curtis Sliwa, The Alliance of Guardian Angels, Inc., 982 East 89th Street, Brooklyn, NY 11236.

Marti Stevens, RFD 3, Box 8130, Skowhegan, ME 04976.

Haroldline Trower, 1223 South 21st Street, Philadelphia, PA 19146. (Point Breeze Federation, Inc.: 1248 South 21st Street, Philadelphia, PA 19146.)

Henry Ware, 1951 Sagewood Lane, Reston, VA 22091. (Useful Services Exchange: 2310 Colts Neck Road, Reston, VA 22091.)

Phyllis and David York, TOUGHLOVE, P. O. Box 1069, Doylestown, PA 18901.

For Additional Information

Sources on participants, when available, are given in the following order: (A) books by or about; (B) periodicals or newsletters published by the program, generally available by subscription; (C) selected articles by or about.

Lupe Anguiano
(A) Anguiano, Lupe. *Women's Employment and Education Model Program* [set of six training manuals]. Mystic, Conn.: Twenty-Third Publications (P. O. Box 180, Mystic, CT 06355), 1983.

(C) Baldwin, Deborah. "Women Helping Women." *Common Cause*, March-April 1983, p. 40.
Washington Post, June 8, 1983, p. B1 +.

Ellen Cassedy
(A) Cassedy, Ellen, and Nussbaum, Karen. *9 to 5: The Working Women's Guide to Office Survival*. New York: Penguin Books, 1983.
(B) *9to5 Newsletter*. Published by 9to5, 614 Superior Avenue, NW, Cleveland, OH 44113. Also sells resource guides and reports.
(C) *Boston Globe*, October 25, 1985, p. 16.
Boston Globe, November 16, 1985, p. 19.
Dale, Duane, and Mitiguy, Nancy. *Planning, for a Change: A Citizen's Guide to Creative Planning and Program Development*. Amherst, Mass.: Citizen Involvement Training Project, University of Massachusetts, 1978, pp. 36–37.

Chick Colony
(C) *Boston Globe*, August 27, 1985, p. 11 +.
Christian Science Monitor, September 2, 1982, p. 1 +.
"W.S." "Zuked Out in New Hampshire." *Organic Gardening*, January 1983, pp. 106–110.

Homer Fahrner
(C) Faber, Nancy. "Homer's Army Gives Half the Fruits of Its Labor to the Poor, and Business Is Picking Up." *People Weekly*, October 25, 1982, pp. 42–43.
San Francisco Chronicle, November 15, 1982, p. 21.
"Senior Gleaners Distribute Leftovers." *Aging*, July-August 1980, pp. 36–37.

Mimi Fariña
(A) Bread & Roses. *Bread & Roses Handbook*. Mill Valley, Calif: no date.
(B) *Bread & Roses Newsletter*. Published by Bread & Roses.
(C) *Boston Globe*, January 24, 1986, p. 36.
Brand, Stuart. "Bread & Roses—Not a Marginal Act." *CoEvolution Quarterly*, Summer 1978, pp. 70–79.
"Fariña, Mimi." [Biographical sketch in] Irwin Stambler and Grelun Landon, *The Encyclopedia of Folk, Country and Western Music*. 2d ed. New York: St. Martin's Press, 1983, pp. 231–232.
"With a Cause No One Can Dispute. Mimi Farina Stages a Folkie Reunion at Berkeley." *People Weekly*, October 22, 1979, pp. 49–50.

Fran Froehlich
(B) Newsletter, published occasionally by Poor People's United Fund.

Lois Gibbs
(A) Gibbs, Lois M. *Love Canal: My Story*. Albany, N.Y.: State University of New York Press, 1982.

Levine, Adeline G. *Love Canal: Science, Politics, and People.* Lexington, Mass.: Lexington Books, 1982.

(B) *Action Bulletin,* and also *Everyone's Backyard.* Both published by Citizen's Clearinghouse for Hazardous Wastes. Also sells resource guides and reports.

(C) Langton, Stuart. "An Interview with Lois Gibbs." *Citizen Participation,* July-August 1982, p. 3 +.

Magnuson, Ed. "A Problem that Cannot Be Buried." *Time,* October 14, 1985, pp. 76–84.

Weiss, Michael J. "Lois Gibbs, the Love Canal Heroine, Is Making Hazardous Wastes an Industry of Her Own." *People Weekly,* February 22, 1982, pp. 42–45.

Kathy Levin

(C) *Baltimore Sun,* January 12, 1983, p. C1 +.

Commercial Appeal (Memphis, Tenn.), November 30, 1982, p. C14.

Candy Lightner

(B) *MADD National Newsletter.* Published by Mothers Against Drunk Driving.

(C) Friedrich, Otto. "Seven Who Succeeded." *Time,* January 7, 1985, p. 41.

Leo, John. "One Less for the Road?" *Time,* May 20, 1985, pp. 76–78.

Sellinger, Margie Bonnett. "Already the Conscience of a Nation, Candy Lightner Prods Congress into Action against Drunk Drivers." *People Weekly,* July 9, 1984, pp. 102–105.

Wilhelm, Maria. "A Grieving, Angry Mother Charges that Drunk Drivers Are Getting Away with Murder." *People Weekly,* June 29, 1981, pp. 24–26.

Wally Olson

(C) Levering, Frank. "First Person: Wally Olson." *California Living,* September 5, 1982, p. 15.

Los Angeles Times, January 22, 1981 (Metro section), p. 1 +.

Lucy Poulin

(B) *This Time.* Newspaper published quarterly by H.O.M.E.

(C) Garson, Sandra. "Sister Lucy Poulin: Ministry for Survival in Rural Maine." *Ms.,* February 1981, p. 25.

Washington Consulting Group, Inc. "Homeworkers Organized for More Employment." In Washington Consulting Group, Inc., *Uplift: What People Themselves Can Do.* Salt Lake City: Olympus Publishing Co., 1974, pp. 140–145.

Willis, John. "At H.O.M.E. with Lucy Poulin." *Yankee,* December 1983, p. 78 +.

Wood, John B. "A Place that Runs on Kindness." *Boston Sunday Globe,* July 25, 1976, p. 7 +.

Vin Quayle

(C) Kurtz, David. "St. Ambrose Housing Aid Center." In National Commission on Neighborhoods, *People, Building Neighborhoods: Final Report to the President and the Congress of the United States.* Case Study Appendix, vol. 2. Washington, D.C.: U.S. Government Printing Office, 1979, pp. 1186–1213.

New York Times, December 1, 1985, p. 1+.

Stokes, Bruce. *Helping Ourselves: Local Solutions to Global Problems.* New York: W. W. Norton, 1981, p. 66.

Bill and Helene Sample

(B) *Sunshine Foundation News.* Newsletter published by the Sunshine Foundation.

(C) Blank, Joseph P. "The Cop Who Spreads Sunshine." *Reader's Digest,* September 1982, pp. 102–106.

Philadelphia Inquirer, June 26, 1983, p. 11B+.

Wansley, Joy, and Lubow, Arthur. "A Philadelphia Cop Brings Some Sunshine into the Lives of Sick and Dying Children." *People Weekly,* March 3, 1980, pp. 26–29.

Ray Shonholtz

(A) Lynch, Judith, ed. *The Community Conflict Resolution Training Manual.* San Francisco: Community Board Program, Inc., 1984.

(C) Abramson, David M. "Against the Wall; How One Neighborhood Made Conciliation Work." *New Age Journal,* March 1984, pp. 44–45.

Fogarino, Shirley. "The Community Board Program: Neighbors Helping Neighbors." *Community Jobs,* December 1981-January 1982, pp. 3–5.

Shonholtz, Raymond. "Neighborhood Justice Systems: Work, Structure, and Guiding Principles." *Mediation Quarterly,* 1984 (No. 5), pp. 3–30.

Note: Shonholtz has written a considerable number of other essays and papers, both published and unpublished. The Community Boards office may be contacted for details.

Curtis Sliwa

(A) Haskins, James. *The Guardian Angels.* Hillside, N.J.: Enslow Publishers (Box 777, Hillside, NJ 07205), 1983.

Sliwa, Curtis, and Schwartz, Murray. *Streetsmart: The Guardian Angel Guide to Safe Living.* Reading, Mass.: Addison-Wesley, 1982.

(C) *Los Angeles Times,* November 17, 1985 (Metro section), p. 1+.

Newsweek, March 23, 1981, pp. 48–49.

"Sliwa, Curtis." *Current Biography Yearbook,* 1983, pp. 365–368.

Time, January 18, 1982, p. 21.

Haroldline Trower

(C) *Christian Science Monitor,* July 22, 1983, p. 14.

Philadelphia Inquirer, June 19, 1983 (Sunday magazine), pp. 22–25.

Philadelphia Inquirer, June 19, 1984, p. 2-B.

Note: For further information about the Philadelphia Green program in general, contact the Pennsylvania Horticultural Society, 325 Walnut Street, Philadelphia, PA 19106.

Henry Ware

(A) Tobin, David, and Ware, Henry. *The Barter Network: Building Community through Organized Trade.* Arlington, Va.: VOLUNTEER (1111 N. 19th Street, Arlington VA 22209), 1983.

(B) *USE Newsletter*, Published by Useful Services Exchange of Reston, 2310 Colts Neck Road, Reston, VA 22091.

Phyllis and David York

(A) York, Phyllis; York, David; and Wachtel, Ted. *Toughlove.* New York: Bantam Books, 1983.

York, Phyllis; York, David; and Wachtel, Ted. *Toughlove Solutions.* New York: Bantam Books, 1985.

(B) *TOUGHLOVE Notes.* Newsletter published by *TOUGHLOVE*. Also sells manuals, tapes, and other resource material.

(C) Lee, Linda. "Toughlove." *Redbook*, July 1985, p. 92 +.

Leo, John. "Getting Tough with Teens." *Time*, June 8, 1981, p. 47.

Neuhaus, Cable. "David and Phyllis York Treat Problem Teenagers with a Stiff Dose of Toughlove." *People Weekly*, November 16, 1981, pp. 101–106.

Bibliography

This selected list includes books on community and public service; books on heroes and heroism; recent articles on social heroism; and other sources of "local heroes."

Books on Community and on Public Service

Barber, Benjamin. *Strong Democracy: Participatory Politics for a New Age*. Berkeley: University of California Press, 1984.

Bellah, Robert N.; Madsen, Richard; Sullivan, William M.; Swidler, Ann; and Tipton, Steven M. *Habits of the Heart: Individualism and Commitment in American Life*. Berkeley: University of California Press, 1985.

Bender, Thomas. *Community and Social Change in America*. New Brunswick, N.J.: Rutgers University Press, 1978.

Boyte, Harry. *Community Is Possible*. New York: Harper & Row, 1984.

Dass, Ram, and Gorman, Paul. *How Can I Help?: Stories and Reflections on Service*. New York: Alfred A. Knopf, 1985.

de Tocqueville, Alexis. *Democracy in America*. Edited and abridged by Richard D. Heffner. New York: New American Library, 1956.

Fisher, Robert. *Let the People Decide: Neighborhood Organizing in America*. Boston: G. K. Hall, Twayne Books, 1985.

Gardner, John W. *Self-Renewal: The Individual and the Innovative Society*. New York: Harper & Row, 1963.

Gaylin, Willard; Glasser, Ira; Marcus, Steven; and Rothman, David J. *Doing Good: The Limits of Benevolence*. New York: Pantheon, 1978.

Hodgkinson, Virginia A., and Weitzman, Murray S. *The Charitable Behavior of Americans: A National Survey*. Washington, D.C.: Independent Sector (1828 L Street, Washington, D. C. 20036), 1986.

Jacobs, Jane. *The Death and Life of Great American Cities*. New York: Vintage, 1961.

Manuel, Frank E., and Manuel, Fritzie P. *Utopian Thought in the Western World.* Cambridge, Mass.: Harvard University Press, Belknap Press, 1979.

Morgan, Arthur E. *The Small Community: Foundation of Democratic Life.* Yellow Springs, Ohio: Community Service, Inc. (P. O. Box 243, Yellow Springs, OH 45387), 1984.

O'Connell, Brian, ed. *America's Voluntary Spirit: A Book of Readings.* New York: The Foundation Center (888 7th Avenue, New York, NY 10019), 1983.

Sennett, Richard. *The Fall of Public Man.* New York: Alfred A. Knopf, 1977.

Stokes, Bruce. *Helping Ourselves: Local Solutions to Global Problems.* New York: W. W. Norton, 1981.

Books on Heroes and Heroism

Babbie, Earl. *You Can Make a Difference: The Heroic Potential within Us All.* New York: St. Martin's Press, 1985.

Browne, Ray B., and Fishwick, Marshall W., eds. *The Hero in Transition.* Bowling Green, Ohio: Bowling Green University Popular Press, 1983.

Campbell, Joseph. *The Hero with a Thousand Faces.* 2d ed. Princeton, N.J.: Princeton University Press, 1968.

Coffin, Tristam P., and Cohen, Hennig, eds. *The Parade of Heroes: Legendary Figures in American Lore.* Garden City, N.Y.: Doubleday, 1978.

Fishwick, Marshall. *The Hero, American Style.* New York: David McKay, 1969.

Gerzon, Mark. *A Choice of Heroes: The Changing Faces of American Manhood.* Boston: Houghton Mifflin, 1982.

Hook, Sidney. *The Hero in History: A Study in Limitation and Possibility.* Boston: Beacon Press, 1955.

Kuralt, Charles. *On the Road with Charles Kuralt.* New York: G. P. Putnam's Sons, 1985. [See especially Part 1, "Unlikely Heroes."]

McGinley, Phyllis. *Saint-Watching.* New York: Viking Press, 1969.

McGinniss, Joe. *Heroes.* New York: Viking Press, 1976.

Schickel, Richard. *Intimate Strangers: The Culture of Celebrity.* Garden City. N.Y.: Doubleday, 1985.

Wecter, Dixon. *The Hero in America.* Ann Arbor: University of Michigan Press, 1983.

Recent Articles on Social Heroism in General

Articles noted by an asterisk include listings of specific "local heroes."

*Bertsche, Robert A. [and fifteen others]. "Local Heroes." *New England Monthly,* September 1986, p. 43 +. [See also similar feature in September 1985 issue.]

*Cassidy, Anne. "21 Kids Who Have Made A Difference." *McCall's,* July 1986, pp. 44–51.

*"The Esquire 1985 Register" ["Presenting America's New Leadership Class"]. *Esquire,* December 1985 [Special issue. See also similar special issue in December 1984.]

Etzioni, Amitai. "Teen Idols." *Public Opinion*, Summer 1986, p. 42+.
Foley, Denise. "The Hero in All of Us." *Prevention*, August 1985, pp. 72–79.
Fortino, Denise. "Why Kids Need Heroes." *Parents*, November 1984, pp. 214–229.
*Franklin, Ruth K., ed. "Heroes for Hard Times." *Mother Jones*, July-August 1986, pp. 20–28.
*Friedrich, Otto. "Seven Who Succeeded." *Time*, January 7, 1985, pp. 40–45.
Goldman, Peter. "Rocky and Rambo." *Newsweek*, December 23, 1985, pp. 58–62.
*Goldman, Peter. "100 New American Heroes." *Newsweek*, Summer 1986, Collector's Edition [special issue], pp. 47–94.
*"Heroes among Us." *50 Plus*, July 1986, pp. 9–37. [See also similar feature in July 1985 issue.]
Hoagland, Edward. "Where Have All the Heroes Gone?" *New York Times Magazine*, March 10, 1974, p. 20+.
*"Local Heroes." *People Weekly*, December 22–29, 1986, pp. 132–139. [See also similar features in 1984 and 1985 year-end issues.]
McBee, Susanna. "Heroes Are Back: Young Americans Tell Why." *U.S. News & World Report*, April 22, 1985, pp. 44–48.
MacLean, Christine K. "Who's Your Hero?" *TeenAge*, November-December 1985, pp. 26–30.
*Remsberg, Bonnie. "Fifty American Heroines." *Ladies' Home Journal*, July 1984, p. 85+.
Stark, Elizabeth. "Mom and Dad: The Great American Heroes." *Psychology Today*, May 1986, pp. 12–13.
Walden, Daniel. "Where Have All Our Heroes Gone?" *USA Today*, January 1986, pp. 20–25.
Wycliff, Don. "Where Have All the Heroes Gone?" *New York Times*, July 31, 1985, p. C1+.

Other Specific Sources of "Local Heroes"

See also asterisked listings in the preceding section.

Citizens Committee for New York City, Inc. *Citizens Report*. Quarterly newsletter listing "New Yorkers for New York" once a year. Published by Citizens Committee for New York City, Inc., 3 West 29th Street, New York, NY 10001. (This is one example of hometown awards, also found in many other cities.)
The Giraffe Project. 45 West 45th Street, Suite 402, New York, NY 10036 (New York office). An organization which promotes and publicizes ordinary people who "stick their necks out."
Reader's Digest. Publishes ongoing articles on an irregular basis, called "Heroes for Today."
VOLUNTEER, and ACTION [cosponsors]. The President's Volunteer Action Awards. National volunteer service awards given yearly in ten categories. For details, contact VOLUNTEER, 1111 North 19th Street, Suite 500, Arlington, VA 22209.

Among other national organizations that have sponsored public service awards, including awards for distinguished local community service, are the American Institute for Public Service, Citizens Forum/ National Municipal League, Common Cause, NOW, Partners for Livable Places, United Way, and the Wonder Woman Foundation.

Acknowledgments

I BEGAN this project to learn more about community work than I'd known before. If I succeeded, it's because of the people in this book. In talking with them, I felt enriched, humbled, and privileged. And I'm indebted not only for our conversations—their stories—but also for their full cooperation and complete graciousness throughout.

I'm grateful, too, to friends, acquaintances, and distant colleagues who helped me track down leads or make interview arrangements—among others, Pat Auletta, Annette Demby, Ellie Fusaro, Sophie Grillo, Richard Hammerschlag, Wendy Hazard, Lisa Stephano, Cindy Thomashow, Kathy Wallace, and Fran White. Thanks also to those I spoke to whose accounts are not included here, as well as to many others who gave ideas and encouragement along the way.

Professors James Hoopes at Babson College and John J. Fox at Salem State College were especially helpful consultants on interviewing and on transcript editing technique. When the initial editing was done, I was fortunate to find the added support I needed. Lynne Peters was a paragon among typists. The folks at my local Kwik-Kopy shop should know their help will be remembered. And Margaret Zusky, Marsha Finley, and Mark Corsey at Lexington Books saw what I was after and then supplied substantive, invaluable, and unfailingly cheerful guidance every step of the way.

My greatest support, though, was and continues to be my family. It was my mother who initially encouraged me to write, and my wife and children who coped with a writer's life-style during the past several years. This book is dedicated to them.

About the Author

B ILL BERKOWITZ, a community psychologist, has been teaching about, writing about, and directing community service programs for the past fifteen years. After receiving his doctorate from Stanford University, he taught at Lafayette College and the University of Massachusetts at Boston. Subsequently, he designed and administered a broad range of community outreach programs, including a free adult education center, a shelter for battered women, and a mental health consultation and education division. He is an elected Town Meeting Member in his home community, where he is active in neighborhood and town affairs.

His previous books, *Community Impact* (1982) and *Community Dreams* (1984), deal respectively with techniques and ideas for community service. Currently, he edits the "Community Action" column in *The Community Psychologist*, and teaches in the community social psychology graduate program at the University of Lowell, in Massachusetts.